PELICAN BOOKS

British Institutions
ADVISORY EDITOR: J. H. PLUMB

THE UNIVERSITIES

Vivian H. H. Green was born at Wembley, Middlesex, in 1915. He was educated at Bradfield College, Berkshire, and Trinity Hall, Cambridge, where he took a First in History and was awarded the Lightfoot Scholarship in church history and the Thirlwall Prize. In 1937 he went as a Gladstone Research Student to St Deiniol's Library, Hawarden, before going to lecture on church history at St Augustine's College, Canterbury. He was ordained in 1939 and subsequently became senior history master and chaplain at Sherborne School, Dorset, in 1942. Vivian Green, a doctor of divinity of Cambridge and Oxford universities and a Fellow of the Royal Historical Society, has been a Fellow and Tutor in History at Lincoln College, Oxford, since 1951. He was Senior Tutor there from 1953 to 1962 and Chaplain from 1951 to 1969. His publications include: *Bishop Reginald Pecock* (1945), *The Hanoverians* (1948), *Renaissance and Reformation* (1951), *The Later Plantagenets* (1955), *Oxford Common Room* (1957), *The Young Mr Wesley* (1961), *The Swiss Alps* (1961), *Martin Luther and the Reformation* (1964), *John Wesley* (1964), and *Religion at Cambridge* (1964). He is unmarried and divides his time between his rooms in college and his house at Burford.

BRITISH INSTITUTIONS

THE UNIVERSITIES

V. H. H. GREEN

PENGUIN BOOKS

Penguin Books Ltd, Harmondsworth, Middlesex, England
Penguin Books Inc., 7110 Ambassador Road, Baltimore, Maryland 21207, U.S.A.
Penguin Books Australia Ltd, Ringwood, Victoria, Australia

—

First published 1969

—

Copyright © V.H.H. Green, 1969

—

Made and printed in Great Britain
by Hazell Watson & Viney Ltd
Aylesbury, Bucks
Set in Linotype Times

CONTENTS

THE universities were undoubtedly one of the most significant creations of the medieval world. Their graduates helped to shape its thought, to create a mode of intellectual discipline, to lay the foundation for a scientific culture, to interpret its laws and its customs and to administer its governments. The universities were themselves a haphazard but natural outcrop of twelfth-century society. Life was at that time more peaceful and prosperous than it had formerly been. The onslaught of the barbarian invasions was at an end. Incipient industrialism and expanding commerce enriched the towns. As a result of the Hildebrandine revival in the church there was a growing demand for an educated clergy; the church needed canon lawyers and theologians to define and to expound its teaching and to support its authority with intellectual arguments. There had been a growth in literacy among clergy and laymen which enabled them to make wider use of written documents and to take responsibility in the increasingly sophisticated pattern of governmental administration both in England and on the Continent. Side by side with this there was a genuine thirst for knowledge and an expansion of learning, stimulated by the cultivated intellectual life of Islamic Spain which drew visiting scholars from every European country, and by the revived interest in Europe in Roman law, all of which promoted the foundation of schools where reputed teachers held forth to small groups of scholars. Controversy, simple and naïve in form until the twelfth century, became more penetrating and intellectually distinguished. Disputation in itself became a delight; 'Nothing,' as Robert de Sorbonne was to comment later, 'is fully known until it has been chewed to shreds in argument.'

Monastic and cathedral schools were already in existence, but in the twelfth century the monasteries, many of them dominated by theological and philosophical conservativism, were no longer the centres of culture they had once been. In any case they could neither house nor effectively control a motley collection of young students without harm to their own disciplined way of life. Nor could they provide a large teaching staff; cathedral schools often based their reputation on the presence of one distinguished scholar rather than on a group of teachers. Paris, however, the paragon of the medieval university, evolved out of schools like these, which were especially active in northern France. Those who wanted to study and to teach gathered together in groups independent of the monastic and cathedral schools, and, living as often as not in a strange city, found it necessary to create an organization, a guild, a *universitas societas magistrorum discipulorumque,* to safeguard their position in the community, to defend their privileges and to order their own lives. It was in this way that universities came into existence and teaching became institutionalized. Bologna, which was to be the chief centre for legal and canonistic studies, was essentially a university controlled by the students, German, French and English, who first combined to form a *universitas* in the middle of the twelfth century. This period also saw the growth of Salerno, which enjoyed a high reputation, as Montpellier was to do later, as a centre of medical studies. Paris came into existence more or less at the same time, as a *universitas* formed by the teachers there; unlike Bologna but like Oxford and Cambridge, Paris was ruled by its masters rather than its students. It became the focal point of theological scholarship and of all the more important intellectual controversies of the Middle Ages.

The rapid growth of the medieval universities testified to the social and intellectual need which they were meeting. They brought into existence an entirely new class of educated men, academics and intellectuals, a race of scholars and teachers who effectively shaped the character of Western civilization. If in the first instance the universities trained a clerical caste which dominated the culture and government of western Europe, ultimately they helped also to instruct the laymen, lawyers and doctors in particular, who were to challenge ecclesiastical control. The impact which the universities made on the church itself gave a cachet to learning and in all probability

8

helped to mould dogmatic and moral theology in a legal form; the simple piety of the monk and preacher gave way to the cool calculation of the university-trained theologian and canonist. Both clerics, often more in name than in vocation, and laymen staffed the increasingly bureaucratic governments of the future national states, so forming the managerial class of the Middle Ages.

In this way the universities came to occupy a unique, a key, place in European society. On the one hand they were subordinate to the authority of the church and the state, and they were aligned with the established order. They expounded the faith and they refuted heresy; they were the intellectual support of popes, kings and princes. Yet simultaneously they represented one of the liberal forces in the medieval world. Within the framework of the scholastic disputation, they discussed intellectual problems with remarkable freedom. They were repeatedly in conflict with their temporal and ecclesiastical superiors; it was, for instance, largely from the university of Paris that ideas detrimental to the monarchical authority of the pope stemmed in the late fourteenth and early fifteenth centuries. Although scholars have yet to trace convincingly the lifeline between the medieval university and the modern world, it is fair to assert that the universities cradled – or after much initial reluctance and resistance made their own – modern philosophy, scientific discovery and technological development. Their history testifies to a continuous tension between robust intellectual conservatism and progressive radicalism, in which often the former appears at first to be victorious, only to give way in the end to more liberal aspirations. The universities have unquestionably been, from the Middle Ages to the twentieth century, major contributors to world culture and civilization; and in this story British universities played, and continue to play, a vital part.

PART ONE

CHAPTER ONE

The Origins of Oxford and Cambridge

FOR many years legend as unhistorical as it was picturesque enshrouded the origins of the universities of Oxford and Cambridge; 'moonshine,' as one writer frankly admitted, 'and like many erudite disputations, where men reason without data, or even understanding their own terms, not worth a straw'. How the universities came into being remains obscure. They seem to have been an accidental by-product of geography and history. Oxford, a nodal centre of communications, was the home of religious houses and frequently visited by the royal court, and foreign scholars, attracted to English shores by the prospect of royal or archiepiscopal patronage, were teaching there as early as the reign of King Stephen. The groups of young men who congregated around these and other distinguished teachers were the nucleus of the future schools. But many another English town already housed a school of repute and could just as easily have become the site of a university.

If we cannot now know exactly why Oxford was chosen, we do know that factors at work in the late twelfth and early thirteenth century made the foundation of a university in England inevitable. There was everywhere in Europe at this time a tremendous flowering of the intellect, an enthusiasm for the acquisition of knowledge and an unprecedented concern with logical inquiry into the nature of things; the zeal for scholarship which invaded every court and country spawned cathedral schools and generated eminent teachers at whose feet eager young men sat to imbibe the new learning. Greater prosperity and the increasing flow of wealth provided the endowments needed to foster religion and scholarship for the benefit of both church and state. Paris was the first and for a long time the foremost community of teachers and scholars to which the name of university was freely given. England, though in some respects isolated from the intellectual currents running so strongly through European life, could not escape the influence of the continent with which it was under its Angevin kings politically and spiritually conjoined.

The quarrel between King Henry II and Archbishop Thomas Becket, leading to a temporary ban on English scholars studying in France (for the French King had given the arrogant if dedicated Archbishop refuge from Henry's iron wrath), may have served to enlarge the small community of scholars living at Oxford. The cluster of teachers slowly increased in number, drew more and more students to listen to their lectures, and acquired a rudimentary organization as its size grew with its reputation. By the early years of the thirteenth century the university of Oxford was a recognizable institution, with a chancellor (the office has been filled in unbroken succession certainly since 1221), proctors, doctors and masters,* faculties and lectures; it was acquiring property, slowly winning benefactors, lending money from its university chests to poor students and awarding degrees.

There may well have been a similar group of scholars at the fenland town of Cambridge, perhaps connected with the rich abbeys of the neighbourhood, but the event which could have transformed a school if such existed into a university was a migration of students from Oxford in 1209. The reason was a quarrel between the students and the townfolk, the first of many such, caused, so it was alleged, by the execution of a scholar in revenge for the murder of a townswoman by another student. Although Cambridge attracted less attention than Oxford, at least until the fifteenth century, neither in its character nor in its curriculum did it differ much from the older foundation. It too had acquired a chancellor by 1226, developed an organization very similar to that of Oxford, and won benefactors. Oxford and Cambridge had become the chief centres of learning in England by the middle of the

*The title of doctor was for some time interchangeable with that of master or professor; later the title master or magister was used for members of the faculty of arts while that of doctor was used to distinguish members of the superior faculties such as divinity or law.

thirteenth century, supplying the country with its leading clerics and administrators – the two were virtually synonymous at this period – and creating a pool of scholarship and ideas which undoubtedly influenced the increasing number of literate laity, whether they actually studied at the university or not.

These two medieval universities were haphazard growths rather than planned foundations, benefiting from precedent, especially from that of the highly reputed university of Paris, and created by experience. To function with a minimum of friction, they required rules of some sort: the ultimate pattern of their constitutions was as complex and intricate as the constitutional machinery of the medieval church. In the end a compromise between the hierarchical organization and the relatively democratic republic of doctors and masters provided a framework flexible enough to allow for the future development of the universities, and forged a bond of community which made them into a genuine *studium generale*. Neither Oxford nor Cambridge have ever completely lost their medieval impress, though at recurrent crises their character has been reorientated by external pressures.

*

The medieval university was not initially a collegiate institution. The majority of students lived in one of the many private licensed halls run by a master of the university. It was, however, realized that it would be more convenient and comfortable for serious graduates to live in common in a college than in the hurly-burly of a hostel. Thus the history of Oxford and Cambridge was punctuated by the foundations of colleges which were ultimately to become coterminous with the university. University College, Oxford, accredited by misinformed legend with King Alfred as founder, probably came into existence as a result of a benefaction from William of Durham who died in 1249. In the 1260s John de Balliol and his wife Devorguilla agreed to support a number of students at Oxford. Between 1262 and 1264 Walter de Merton, Chancellor of England, made over his estate at Maldon in Surrey to a community of scholars which by 1270 had settled permanently at Oxford. At Cambridge Hugo de Balsham, Bishop of Ely, founded Peterhouse in 1284. These colleges were intended primarily for poor scholars who were already graduates; those who were in possession of a benefice or of a private income were normally debarred from becoming members of the foundation though they were welcome to take rooms and to share in the common life as paying guests. Although the number of colleges steadily increased, they housed only a small fraction of the university population and had as yet little influence in the moulding of university policy.

For the universities to prosper they had to win favour from the established order. At all stages of their history their studies have been more or less closely correlated to the national needs. If the modern university sees its task as supplying the country with civil servants, administrators and technologists, the medieval university existed to train churchmen, canonists, monks and friars, schoolmen and schoolmasters. Its scholarship, like that of the modern university, was not an indigenous growth but a by-product of its social setting. Yet if the medieval universities required government patronage, they also needed, as do their modern counterparts, sufficient autonomy to be free of municipal or other external pressures. They needed the power to order their own affairs freely. In their early stages they wanted the backing of the Crown, which was usually generously given, to support the authority of their own officials over their own often unruly students, and against the townspeople, with whom for centuries they were to be engaged in a running dog-fight, as well as to give them protection against undue interference by the local bishop. Document after document testifies to their relentless determination to win jurisdiction over their undergraduates and to prevent exploitation by the townsfolk, more especially in the matter of rents and prices for food.

The universities represented then the training schools for the established order, even if the number of laymen educated there was only a fraction of the whole. The population of medieval Oxford and Cambridge was a motley one; there were travelling scholars, intellectual dilettantes, academic hangers-on, 'beatnik' clerics, hard-bitten threadbare men fascinated by glimpses into the sophisticated world of medieval philosophy. There were the scions of noble families, hardly a conspicuous group but never negligible; rumour asserted that King Henry V had studied at Oxford and his brother Humphrey, Duke of Gloucester, a leader of fashion and devotee of learning, proved a notable benefactor. Nonetheless the average student was either in holy orders or intending to take them. The episcopal registers are full of dispensations for non-residence granted to beneficed clergymen so that they could follow a course of study at the universities. With what relief must Sir Walter Strolringer, the rector of Wootton Courtenay in Somerset, given leave of absence by his bishop to study at a university for three years in September 1448, or Sir Philip Puttenham, the rector of Newton St Loe, given similar leave to study at Oxford in 1462, have left their boorish peasant flock for the intellectual stimulus and lively, if sometimes violent, life of a university town. In addition to the secular clergy, there were a number of monks and friars, residing at the special houses which their orders had established in Oxford and Cambridge, lecturing and learning before they moved to other monasteries or friaries in England or on the Continent.

The universities were clerical brotherhoods but they were colourful, often unruly and rich in their assortment of personalities. They were neither uniform in appearance and dress nor harshly ascetic. In some respects they were less class conscious then than later. Obviously the number of those who could study at the university was to some extent circumscribed by financial considerations. The student had to pay fees for his lectures, to buy his food, to pay his heavy degree fees, to clothe himself for a number of years and to purchase books and writing paper. His expenses were proportionally smaller than at a later date but they were not negligible. Many an undergraduate ran into debt. Many a graduate, temporarily short of money, had to borrow from the university chest and leave his books as a guarantee of future repayment. But bishops were often generous to would-be scholars; lay patrons supported poor students.

In 1419 Thomas Langley, the Bishop of Durham, gave William Ingleby an annuity of 100s. 8d. to keep him at Oxford. The interest in learning diverted many a benefaction from a monastic house to the university, and for some scholarship was a handsome investment which repaid the earlier mortgage.

All in all, the medieval universities reflected an aspiration to intellectual achievement which conditioned contemporary scholarship and helped to mould the manner of thinking of cleric and layman alike. To a later generation the atmosphere and scholarship of early Oxford and Cambridge may seem remote and antipathetic, but the scholastic philosophy of the period, the finest flower of its intellect, was itself an integrated aspect of the existing social order. Its influence declined not merely vis-à-vis the newly fashioned humanism of the Renaissance scholars but because it became less and less suited to a society that was increasingly lay in character and shaped by a competitive commercialism.

*

For the first two centuries of their existence Oxford and Cambridge had been firmly in the intellectual mainstream, gradually replacing the intellectualized Augustinianism which had been the fodder of university teaching in the middle of the thirteenth century with the coherent Thomistic philosophy; then, as fashion demanded, moving with the fourteenth-century modernists in the direction of nominalism. The best minds of the medieval university continued to grapple with a basic problem, though they would not have phrased it in this way, that of reconciling the received truths of religion with intellectual integrity. The renaissance of the twelfth century, to which the universities owed their birth, had made the conservatives aware that intellectual achievement could offer a challenge to revealed faith. There was no possibility, given the social and intellectual circumstances of the period, that the religious concepts which sustained the life and learning of western Europe could be abandoned or even directly questioned; but at least they could be brought into harmony with progressive thinking. That the solutions which were offered were not ultimately accepted casts no reflection on the importance of what was attempted or indeed achieved.

In the late fourteenth century the comparative academic calm of Oxford scholasticism was disturbed by the teaching of John Wyclif, who was for a short time master of Balliol College and subsequently continued to lecture in the university, and by the appearance of Lollards among the dons who followed him. Wyclif's preaching, especially in his later years – he died in 1384 – with its stress on the literal interpretation and authority of the Scriptures and its repudiation of so much of the teaching of the contemporary church, its sacramental theology and its ecclesiastical hierarchy, made him and his followers appear to be the nucleus of a revolutionary movement. In fact although Wyclif seemed to be a progressive thinker, his original teaching stemmed from a philosophical conservatism, a reaction against the prevailing school of nominalist philosophy in favour of ideas which would have been more popular a century earlier. Paradoxically, philosophical conservatism cradled religious radicalism. For twenty years or so the Lollard movement sprouted at Oxford, finding some support among the seniors; but the university quickly repented of this flirtation with his ideas on discovering his supposed heterodoxy, though the danger to the orthodox appeared greater than it actually was. The prominence of Lollardy at Oxford may have contributed to the rise in the reputation of Cambridge, which in the fifteenth century came to challenge the predominant position that Oxford had held hitherto in the scholastic life of the nation.

Lollardy was, however, a solitary regression in the forward development of the universities. In general they were in the forefront of intellectual movements, centres of lively and exciting discussion. They often housed scholars of original temper, whether the eccentric friar Roger Bacon in the thirteenth century or the thoughtful group of scientists and mathematicians who resided at Merton College, Oxford, in the early years of the next century. By the middle of the fifteenth century individual scholars at both Oxford and Cambridge were beginning to be aware, though in a cautious and conservative spirit, of the classical revival that was taking place in Italy. They

19

brought back books and manuscripts to their libraries by the Cam and the Isis; they copied the ancient writings, improved their prose style and aped rather than adopted the fashions of their *avant-garde* contemporaries. The revived interest in Greek learning led to a fresh insight into the meaning and relevance of the New Testament, sowing the seeds of a new intellectual outlook, even though the Aristotelian tradition remained as strongly entrenched as ever. As the sixteenth century opened the universities no less than the church and state were on the verge of some revolutionary changes.

By 1500 Oxford and Cambridge, two and a half centuries old, had established an order and curriculum which were to remain substantially the same for years to come. But in other aspects of university life change was inescapable. Economic and social factors diversified the personnel of the universities, and led eventually to the establishment and dominance of the colleges. The universities were still ecclesiastical in character and still designed to meet the needs of the church, yet they became more lay in spirit than they had been before. The Protestant Reformation effected a revolution in their lives and brought them more closely under the control of the Crown. Although the universities of the sixteenth and seventeenth centuries were strongly rooted in their medieval past they were very different institutions.

CHAPTER TWO

Oxford and Cambridge in Transition,

1500–1650

SIGNIFICANT changes which were greatly to affect the history of the two universities and to condition the place which they played in the life of the nation took place in sixteenth-century England. This was in general a period of transition. While much that had been typical of medieval society lingered on, many elements fundamental to the medieval way of thinking were displaced. The Reformation, severing the links which had bound the English church to the Pope, at once enhanced the authority of the Crown and strengthened the position of the laity. The clerical order, depleted in number by the dissolution of the monasteries and friaries, played a declining part in civil administration and even over education exerted less influence than it had done in the medieval period. Education remained a clerical monopoly, but was more subject to lay control, and scholarship was no longer the exclusive preserve of divines. Laymen played a prominent part in the new learning, more especially in the promotion of scientific research. Moreover the growth in the number of schools meant a great increase in the number of educated laity, some of whom were eager to avail themselves of a university education but did not intend to seek holy orders. The monastic halls of the universities were swept away; nothing was left of the friars who had played so prominent a part in their scholastic life. The colleges of the later Tudor period were founded by rich and pious laymen. The chancellors of the universities were no longer curial bishops but able and interested statesmen like Burleigh and Leicester. As a clerical institution the medieval university had looked ultimately to the Pope, and indeed sought his immunity from episcopal interference; but the breach with Rome placed Oxford and Cambridge completely at the mercy of the Crown.

The cultural scene too was changing rapidly. Scholarship

was powerfully affected by the new currents of humanism flowing from Italy and centres of Renaissance learning; if the scholastic method, and Aristotelianism in particular, continued to dominate the university curriculum, some of the long-accepted textbooks of medieval theology and the complex apparatus of canon law were dropped. There were economic changes at work which tended to concentrate affluence among the gentry and rich merchants, from whose families an increasing number of undergraduates were to come. Inevitably their cultural values were different from those of their clerical predecessors. Economic factors too helped to foster the growth of the colleges which later became undergraduate societies. Finally, although the confused and confusing features of English life in this period betray a continuing pessimism, endemic in the spiritual atmosphere, yet equally there was evidence of a growing ebullience and optimism, lusty and full-bellied, a pride in achievement from which the universities were not immune, and which made an enduring impression on the late Elizabethan age.

> O wonder!
> How many good creatures are there here!
> How beauteous mankind is! O brave new world,
> That has such people in it.

In such conditions neither Oxford nor Cambridge could stand still. Even before the fifteenth century closed they had absorbed some of the more superficial aspects of humanist thought: Italic epistolography, Ciceronean style, a readiness to learn Greek and a deep appreciation of antiquity; though the freshness and crisp criticism of the humanist approach, typical of Colet, Linacre, Grocyn and More, for the most part escaped the late medieval don, who before he could embrace his new love, had to discard his old mistress, scholasticism. The atmosphere of early sixteenth-century Oxford and Cambridge was not unresponsive to the new ideas. At Cambridge a devout and cultured churchman, John Fisher, the future Bishop of Rochester who fell an unhappy victim to Henry VIII's tyrannical policy, encouraged Renaissance scholarship. The

22

climate of opinion was reflected in the foundation of new colleges and of readerships. Corpus Christi College, set up at Oxford in 1517 by Richard Foxe, Bishop of Winchester, was designed especially to cater for the new studies. At Corpus the professor of Latin, who was to lecture daily on the classics, was instructed 'manfully to root up and cast out barbarity from our garden, should it sprout at any time'. Wolsey intended that humanist studies should have their place side by side with traditional scholarship at his new Oxford foundation, Cardinal College.

The humanist Vives was at Oxford in 1523. Both universities had been visited by Erasmus, the scholar who more than any other epitomized the Renaissance world, though Cambridge, which he found a rather disagreeable place, responded more actively to his teaching than Oxford, whose gracious hospitality had so delighted him. The young Cantabrigians read his edition of the Greek New Testament, published in 1516, with avidity. Moreover news soon filtered through to Oxford and Cambridge of the seemingly revolutionary writings of the German monk, Martin Luther, disclosing a new insight into the truths of Scripture and making some contemptuous of the narrow academic groves in which they lived. Authority frowned, banned and burned the Lutheran tracts, searched somewhat inefficiently in college rooms for the ill-omened literature; but the young dons' talk at the White Horse tavern at Cambridge where they were accustomed to meet was secret, seditious and stimulating.

*

Nonetheless the universities played no immediately important part in the dramatic events which ushered the Reformation into England. Perhaps the lack of any heartfelt resistance to religious change owed something to the sympathy with which some members of the university, like Thomas Cranmer, then a young fellow of Jesus, viewed the policy of the Tudor king. But their acquiescence in what then occurred was doubtless more the result of long-established loyalty to the Crown upon whose goodwill the universities so much depended. The Crown took effective measures to ensure that the universities toed the line. In 1530 Archbishop Warham sharply reprimanded the authorities at Oxford when the university showed inadequate enthusiasm for the royal cause. The practice of visitation by royal officials, utilized by Thomas Cromwell, was to be followed on many later occasions in the sixteenth century to impose compliance with the royal wishes.

Once the break with Rome had been achieved, the universities – and in this respect Cambridge from the start outpaced a reluctant and conservative Oxford – made a substantial and important contribution to the process of reforming religion. The reformed Church needed bishops to administer it, clergy to look after its parishes and scholars to expound its theology. Willy-nilly both Oxford and Cambridge had to perform a task which no other institution could do, and this they did. Even a superficial survey shows the close relationship between the universities and the post-Reformation episcopate; Cranmer had been a fellow of Jesus College, Cambridge; Stephen Gardiner, the Bishop of Winchester, master of Trinity Hall, Cambridge; Ridley, master of Pembroke Hall, Cambridge; Hugh Latimer, fellow of Clare Hall, Cambridge; Matthew Parker, master of Corpus Christi, Cambridge; Grindal, fellow of Pembroke Hall, Cambridge; Whitgift, master of Trinity, Cambridge. A college fellowship became the initial rung on the ladder of preferment which ended with the bishop's throne. But equally the universities supplied the theological apologists for the new order; Tyndale, Jewel, Hooker and many less well known.

Cambridge did more than provide the men who carried the various policies of Henrician and Edwardian governments into operation. In the late 1520s and early 1530s it nurtured a group of more radical religious thinkers who wanted London, Canterbury and York to take Wittenberg, Strasbourg, Zürich and ultimately Geneva for their models. Conceived by Luther out of Erasmus, influenced by the other continental reformers, holding to the use of a vernacular scripture and believing the absolute necessity for a Christian of justification by faith, this Cambridge group represented the advance guard in England of

24

extreme reformism. They were the spiritual ancestors of the Puritans. They were soon dispersed – many of the earlier leaders were executed in deference to the authoritarian majesty and theological learning of Henry VIII – but their religious radicalism did not die quickly in the Cambridge halls.

The death of the old king in 1547 and the accession of his son, the Protestant Josiah, Edward VI, offered a wealth of opportunity for the ultra-reformers to propagate their views. Men speaking English with a foreign accent, if they spoke it at all, appeared at college high tables and lectured in Latin to enthusiastic students, Martin Bucer at Cambridge, Peter Martyr at Oxford. If they found the dons less enthusiastic for the reformed faith than they had hoped, their very presence epitomized a movement in thought that was spreading quickly in reformed intellectual circles. Vestments were hurriedly packed into chests and cupboards; images and crucifixes were torn down. The early death of Edward VI and the accession of his Roman Catholic sister Mary in 1553 was a severe blow to the hopes of the Cambridge radicals. Even before the Marian persecution got under way many a Cambridge don was riding to the coast, and soon adapting himself to a new life in the garrets of Strasbourg, Frankfurt, Geneva or Zürich. Of those who died at the stake later in the reign Cambridge supplied the majority of the victims. 'Cambridge,' Macaulay commented 'had the honour of educating those celebrated Protestant bishops whom Oxford had the honour of burning: and at Cambridge were formed the minds of all those statesmen to whom chiefly is to be attributed the secure establishment of the reformed religion in the north of Europe.'

The accession of Elizabeth brought an end to the constant fluctuation in religious matters that had created so much anxiety in the universities. The old faith did not completely disappear. Pockets of Romanists persisted at both universities long after the accession of Elizabeth. The recusant Cuthbert Mayne, who was executed in 1577, had been a chaplain at St John's, Oxford, in 1566. Two rectors of Lincoln College, Oxford, and some fellows and students, among the latter William Giffard, a future primate of France, were of the old persuasion, but ultimately they were obliged to take refuge in a foreign land. In spite of his arbitrary treatment of his fellows, the Catholic Dr Caius continued to preside over the college at Cambridge which he had enriched so generously. But in fact the old religion was fading fast, especially among the up and coming classes of society.

The universities were ceasing to be the closed clerical corporations which in the main they had been up to the eve of the Reformation. Religious change naturally helped to bring this about, but other influences were also at work. Most striking of these was the growing importance of the colleges. With few exceptions the private halls in which most of the students had previously lived disappeared, their tenements in many cases bought by or otherwise absorbed into the bigger collegiate foundations. The endowments of the private halls were not adequate to cope with the economic stresses of the early sixteenth century. The old colleges were becoming richer from endowments and the benefactions of churchmen and laity; with the disappearance of the monasteries and the chantries, colleges and schools were virtually the only vehicles for the dispensation of charity, until new forms of philanthropy were developed in the next century. Learning had become a viable investment for this world as for the next. New colleges were founded at Oxford and Cambridge, in some cases with the active patronage of the Crown; Henry VIII used Wolsey's foundation, Cardinal College, to create Christ Church, Oxford, and founded Trinity, Cambridge. Elizabeth, who genuinely loved learning and delighted in her visits to the universities, where she readily sat through portentous Latin plays and dull majestic speeches welling over with obscure classical allusions, with typical parsimony accepted Dr Price's endowment for Jesus College, Oxford, on condition that she should be regarded as its founder. All the post-Reformation colleges, St John's (1555), Trinity (1554–5), Wadham (1612) and Pembroke (1628) at Oxford, Magdalene (1542), Emmanuel (1584) and Sidney Sussex (1596) at Cambridge, owed their existence to lay rather than clerical generosity.

The way in which money flowed into the universities for the

foundation of fellowships and scholarships illuminates the social scene. The largest amount of money provided by charitable benefactions in sixteenth-century England was given for the relief of the poor, but education was high on the list, receiving in all between 1480 and 1660 some £833,493, or nearly 27 per cent of the total. Much of this went to the foundation of grammar schools, but the universities shared in the stream of revivifying wealth, in part through scholarships which were established at the grammar schools with the object of enabling ambitious and able pupils to enjoy the advantages of education at Oxford and Cambridge, in part through the augmentation of college fellowships, the stipends of which had been badly hit by the current inflation, and the institution of new ones, and in part by the foundation of new colleges. In its effects, these 'benefactions were binding the schools to the universities by an intricate and well-considered system of endowed scholarships ... with the result that an impressive and most complex fabric of educational opportunity was extended across the country'.*

Before the onset of the Reformation the most generous benefactors of the universities had been great churchmen, and in spite of their diminished wealth in the post-Reformation period they did not relax their zeal for higher education; indeed they sponsored it with far greater generosity than religion itself. There was a striking decline in benefactions of all kinds during the actual course of the Reformation, reflecting a feeling of uncertainty as to the future of such predominantly religious foundations as the universities as well as the political anxieties and fluctuation of power during the period. But once the universities emerged from the ordeal of trying to align their policies with the differing objects of Henrician, Edwardian and Marian governments, they soon began to receive rich benefactions.

There was, however, a distinct change in the social pattern behind these gifts. There was no diminution in the readiness of the clergy, dignitaries as well as parish priests, to donate

*W. K. Jordan, *Philanthropy in England 1480–1660*, Allen & Unwin, 1959, pp. 49–50. For a fuller discussion see pp. 279–97.

money to the societies in which so many of them had been educated; but there was a very pronounced increase in the generosity of the mercantile class, though the amount of their gifts in proportion to their collective wealth has been over-stressed. An even more impressive series of benefactions came from members of the professional classes, lawyers, officials and administrators, reaching its apogee in the first three decades of the seventeenth century. Both classes surpassed the members of the great nobility and higher gentry in their generosity to education. After 1630 there was some decline in their gifts, because the unpopular policies followed by Archbishop Laud made merchants of Puritan leanings disinclined to give money to the societies he was seeking to supervise nor, although there was some revival during the Commonwealth, did the benefactions ever again achieve the same momentum.

The motive force behind such donations may well have been similar to that which had in past ages persuaded men to endow churches and monasteries and foster good works, the desire to win fame in this world and spiritual rewards in the next; but beside this there were others reflecting the spirit of the late Elizabethan age. Some benefactors were undoubtedly inspired by the desire to give boys at the grammar school the opportunity to study at Oxford or Cambridge which they themselves had not enjoyed. Many of the benefactions represented a combination of Puritan theology and commercial acuteness. On the one hand there was the wish to provide England with well-trained Protestants, clergy and laity, who could refute Romanism and serve the cause of the elect. On the other hand there was the desire to provide boys of the middle and lower classes with the opportunity to follow a secular career, to make the best of and to do the best in the ephemeral world. Few scholarships had been provided in the medieval universities. The benefactors of the Tudor period and the early Jacobean age changed the picture drastically. The connexions they established between the schools and the universities had far-reaching effects on university personnel.

The colleges, once hostels for post-graduates, became teaching establishments for young men, and expanded in number

28

and in buildings. They were full and flourishing societies in the seventeenth century. The total of those who matriculated at Oxford in 1621, 784, was not to be reached again until 1883. A high proportion of those who studied at the universities still intended to take orders; whereas in 1580 less than a quarter of the clergy of Worcestershire were graduates, by 1620 more than half were and before the end of the reign of Charles I some 84 per cent. What had changed in college life was the students' age rather than their vocation. Colleges were full of young men whose natural inclinations were not necessarily spiritual. The seniors shook their heads at the intrusion into courts and quads of young men with more money than manners, dressy, long-haired, high-booted, garbed more suitably, as Archbishop Whitgift was informed in 1602, for a court than a university. An increasing number of sons of the gentry and aristocracy were educated at Oxford and Cambridge, many of whom had no intention of taking orders or indeed of getting a degree and some of whom never matriculated; the university was simply a natural finishing school. The children of the commercial and professional classes came in growing numbers. Moreover the married clergy, probably the most important social phenomenon resulting from the Reformation, sent their sons, an entirely new type of entrant who was for long to contribute much to the political and cultural life of the nation; between 1620 and 1629 they formed nearly 14 per cent of the entrants to Caius College, Cambridge. Thus in one way and another, although the majority of the dons were in orders and most of the under-graduates were intending ministers, the clerical atmosphere of the universities had been greatly diluted.

*

Nonetheless the universities' main interest was still centred in ecclesiastical matters. They were inescapably immersed in the religious affairs of Elizabethan and Jacobean England, contributing weighty arguments to the current controversies and helping to shape the embryonic Church of England. The death of Mary Tudor in 1558 had left the universities, like the church, very confused. They had to be coaxed by the new Archbishop,

Matthew Parker, and by William Cecil to accept the Elizabethan settlement of religion. If Oxford was more attached to the old ways than Cambridge, both universities experienced a religious transformation in the years immediately following Elizabeth's succession. As former fellows returned from exile and convinced Protestants were elected to college offices, the colleges adopted Protestantism, though some were slower and more sporadic in doing so than others.

At both Oxford and Cambridge a group of radical Protestants came into existence, looking to Zürich and Geneva for guidance. They quickly attracted an undergraduate following; some young men at Cambridge tonsured the horse belonging to the Master of Trinity while he was at service in St Mary's in the mistaken belief that he was opposed to the reformers. Archbishop Parker himself, conciliatory and moderate in temper, was intensely irritated by what seemed to him to be the disobedient and pedantic opposition of the Protestant extremists, under the patronage at Oxford of Sampson, the Dean of Christ Church, and Humphrey, the President of Magdalen. He was at his wits' end to know what to do, more especially as Elizabeth herself and Cecil did not want to authorize a tough policy towards the University malcontents. Furthermore Leicester, the Chancellor of Oxford, had definite Puritan leanings. The upshot, typically, was a compromise, inelegant but flexible. Only a minority of the nonconformists were out and out Protestants, critical of the expedient but to them unjustified compromise with truth. These radical exponents of reform, mostly dons at Cambridge rather than Oxford, finding their position untenable or in some cases having been expelled, left the university to become ministers to zealous but factious little English groups in Holland or to preach the word with fitting solemnity to the elect in country or city churches of a more extreme persuasion. Less radical but still recalcitrant fellows were drilled or persuaded to conform, at least outwardly, to the sartorial and liturgical requirements of the established order.

University Puritanism for the most part avoided extremes of intellectualism or of exuberant enthusiasm; it was a solid and vital force, perhaps the single most important ingredient in church life in the closing years of Elizabeth's reign, with implications that carried beyond religion itself. It was founded on the Scriptures, nurtured in Calvinist doctrine – even the anti-Puritan Whitgift found the Calvinist notion of predestination sage and scriptural – and it looked forward to the establishment of a presbyterian form of church government. One of its more forthright exponents forced to leave Cambridge was Thomas Cartwright, Lady Margaret professor of divinity until Whitgift managed to secure his deprivation; his lectures on the early chapters of the Acts of the Apostles, listened to with bated breath by his audience, were an exposé of the contemporary church. Others less notable and perhaps less penetrating in their criticism remained as heads and fellows of colleges; at Oxford Rainolds, President of Corpus Christi and Henry Airay, Provost of the Queen's College; at Cambridge the regius professor of divinity, his brother-in-law the spry and much-esteemed Laurence Chaderton who lived to be a centenarian and was Master of Emmanuel College, a Puritan establishment, founded by Sir Walter Mildmay, Samuel Ward, Master of Sidney Sussex, William Perkins of Christ's and John Preston, President of Queens'. They and many another composed a formidable and learned phalanx, devout, Calvinist in theology and ethics, who sought to direct the church along Puritan lines and to ensure that college fellowships were filled with men of like-minded views concerned with feeding their pupils the pure milk of the divine Word. In this they had some success, assuring the steady infusion of the Puritan ethic into English society.

Trinity College, Dublin, was another outpost of Elizabethan Protestantism, suffused by the powerful influence of Cambridge Puritanism in which its early dons, Travers, Henry Ussher and Fullerton, had been educated. Two of the Provosts, Walter Travers and Richard Alvey, were Cambridge dons of definite Puritan leanings. Alvey's successor, Temple, a former fellow of King's College and a lay Puritan who had been private secretary to Sir Philip Sidney (Sidney had in fact died in Temple's arms) was a vigorous critic of Aristotelianism and an exponent of Ramist logic.* The notion of making a university out of the buildings of the disendowed St Patrick's in Dublin had been aired as early as 1563, but the actual foundation of Trinity College was really made possible by the growth in the number of English settlers on estates forfeited from the native Irish chieftains and the consequent need to provide educational facilities for their children. The resurgence in Ireland of recusancy which was promoted by the training of young Irishmen at Jesuit colleges on the continent convinced the Protestants in Ireland that a university should be founded to combat papalism. 'A new policy,' the Jesuits informed the Pope, 'has been adopted, whereby England, devoted to heresy, may draw Ireland into the same snare, and bind it closer to itself. This is the building of a certain ample and splendid College beside Dublin, in which the Irish youth shall be taught heresy by English teachers.'

In fact the college for long drew most of its pupils from the Anglo-Irish colonists. 'As for any maintenance to be hoped for from the better sort of this kingdom,' the Provost of Trinity, Walter Travers, wrote of the Irish landowners in 1594, 'so small is their affection towards that work, by reason of their backwardness in religion, as they will not so much as send their children thither.' Convinced by the argument that the lack of college facilities at home sent the youth of Ireland to be educated abroad, 'whereby they have been infected with poperie and other ill qualities', Elizabeth had granted the college a charter of incorporation in 1591. Dublin provided a site in the decayed monastery of All Hallows. The Lord Deputy and council promoted a public subscription. By 1597 the college had a provost, three fellows, ten scholars (among them James Ussher, the future learned archbishop of Armagh) and two servants. It remained small but its financial position was improved by grants of land from the Crown, and a library was built up. Its ethos remained predominantly Puritan.

*

*The teaching of the contemporary Frenchman, Peter Ramus, rejected Aristotelian dialectic, and so repudiated the scholastic teaching that had for so long dominated the universities.

Calvinist theology dominated both universities in the closing years of the sixteenth century and continued in the ascendant at Dublin, partly because of the degree of independence which the Tudor Queen allowed her universities. But it did not go unchallenged. Richard Hooker, who had been a fellow of Corpus Christi, Oxford, gave a masterly exposition in the *Laws of Ecclesiastical Polity* of the fusion which contemporary Anglicanism had achieved, combining patristic tradition, Catholic teaching and scriptural truth into an amalgam that was to be the one enduring factor of the English church. In 1596 Calvinism was criticized outright in the Cambridge pulpit by Peter Baro, a scholar of foreign extraction who had himself been ordained by John Calvin. The Puritan divines of Cambridge were gravely perturbed and denounced the offending preacher to the Archbishop, John Whitgift. The archbishop hoped to satisfy the heads of houses, as the heads of the colleges were collectively called, by publishing a series of articles which were Calvinistic in tone; but this only antagonized the growing body of anti-Calvinist opinion at Oxford and Cambridge, the strength of which he must have underestimated. The Queen, ageing but still shrewd, did not care for the way in which Whitgift was conducting the matter; the caucus of critics, shortly to be strengthened by the animadversions of the Dutch theologian Arminius and his followers against the rigid Calvinist precisions, found strong supporters outside as well as within the universities.

The accession of King James I in 1603 helped the anti-Puritan camp, for while the king, alert to the subtleties of theology, was intellectually a Calvinist, his experience of critics, shortly to be strengthened by the animadversions of the presbytery, his deep belief in divine right, his preference for episcopacy and his political inclinations all made him favour the rising Arminian party. 'Think how all things tend to declination from Religion,' the Puritan don, Samuel Ward, confided to his diary in January 1599, 'and that there beginneth a general defection in England.' Six years later he noted sadly,

Remember on Wednesday, January 18th, was the day when the surplice was first urged by the Archbishop to be brought into

Emmanuel College. God grant that other worse things do not follow the so strict urging of this indifferent ceremony. Alas, we little expected that King James would have been the first permitter of it to be brought into our college, to make us a derision to so many that bear us no goodwill.

But it was an Oxford man and a future bishop, Richard Corbet, who summarized Emmanuel's reputation when he wrote of a royal visit to Cambridge:

> But the pure house of Emmanuel
> Would not be like proud Jezebel,
> Nor show herself before the King
> An hypocrite, or painted thing:
> But, that the ways might prove all fair,
> Conceiv'd a tedious mile of prayer.

James might favour Calvinist theology but Arminian politics were more to his liking. He agreed reluctantly to the suppression of *The Interpreter*, a law-book compiled by Dr Cowell, the Master of Trinity Hall, Cambridge, which by its extravagant stress on the royal prerogative had provoked the ire of Sir Edward Coke and others who were trying to increase the power of Parliament. Where Cowell's judgement erred, however, was not in his holding these opinions but in expressing them. In 1625 another Cambridge don, a fellow of King's, Richard Montague, put forward Arminian and royalist views in his *Appello Caesarem*; this time Parliament was so angered that in 1626 it declared him worthy of punishment and ordered his books to be burned.

Thus in the early years of the seventeenth century the balance of power and the climate of opinion at both universities slowly changed. Something of the glowing optimism and self-confidence typical of the Elizabethan age evaporated as Europe entered a period of economic recession, and England was faced with political and religious strife and some degree of national humiliation. Puritanism still held its ground at the universities, especially at Cambridge where Emmanuel and Sidney Sussex colleges in particular were centres of Puritan teaching. The undergraduates flocked to the Puritan preaching centres and crowded out the lectures at Holy Trinity, Cambridge, where Richard Sibbes, who was Master of Catharine Hall from 1626 to 1635, John Preston and Thomas Goodwin attracted large congregations. The Sunday lecture at Holy Trinity at 1 p.m. was declared out of bounds because the undergraduates ceased to attend St Mary's in order to hear Sibbes. It was furthermore said that at Trinity, Cambridge, in 'some tutors' chambers (who have three or four score pupils) the private prayers are longer and louder by far at night than they are at Chapel in the evening'.

The tide was, however, turning swiftly against the Protestant extremists. It was impossible to matriculate at Oxford or to graduate at Cambridge without subscribing to the Thirty-nine Articles. In 1603 a grace, as a decree of the Senate at Cambridge was called, ordered that anyone who opposed the doctrine or discipline of the Church should be suspended from his degrees. The flexible control which the Elizabethan government had exercised tightened into a more rigid supervision unwilling to tolerate political or religious heterodoxy. In 1604, partly as a result of the efforts of Sir Edward Coke, the universities acquired the right to send two representatives to Parliament. By this means they hoped to defend their privileges and interests against their critics, but the Crown seemed to regard members of Parliament for the universities as its spokesmen in the House of Commons. In 1622 the Privy Council ordered both universities to burn the works of the German theologian Pareus who had questioned the royal prerogative.

Some of the Puritan dons, feeling the growing insecurity of the times, left their preferments and went abroad. William Ames, who had preached a vigorous denunciation of the Christmas festivities in 1609, became a professor of theology at Franeker in Holland. Many emigrated to New England, where two former fellows of Emmanuel, John Cotton and Thomas Hooker, presided over the destinies of the youthful university founded by another Emmanuel man, John Harvard. After a disputed election in 1626 Cambridge accepted as its chancellor the royal favourite, the Duke of Buckingham. 'What will the parliament say to us?' said Joseph Mead of Christ's who had supported Buckingham's rival, Lord Berkshire. 'Did not our burgesses condemn the duke in their charge given up to the Lords? I pray God we hear well of it; but the actors are as bold as lions, and I half believe would fain suffer that they might be advanced.' When the Commons quashed Buckingham's appointment, Charles I reminded them that it was no concern of theirs since the universities were corporations which drew their powers by charter from the Crown.

In Oxford too the royalist power was in the ascendant over the Puritan. Laud, an ardent protagonist of Arminian teaching and the royal prerogative, began as President of St John's and later Bishop of London a career that led him to supreme authority as Chancellor of the university and, in 1633, to become Archbishop of Canterbury. The Laudian Statutes no less than the lovely Canterbury quad at St John's are memorials to his deep and sincere affection for Oxford and his practical interest and very real power in all aspects of the university's life.

'At Woodstocke,' Thomas Crosfield, a fellow of the Queen's College, wrote in his diary for 23 August 1631,

his Majesty sate with our Chancelour ye Bishop of London for ye space of 6 houres considering & consulting about some seditious or suspicious sermons preacht in Oxon ... in conclusion sentenced Dr Prideaux to loose his place as ye cheife encourager of younger factious men, but ye Lord Chamberlane interceded for him & soe the punishment was not executed; but ye proctours were sentenced to be put out of their places.

At Cambridge the shift of power gathered momentum, though even the loyalists grumbled when Laud claimed an archbishop's authority over that university as well. Lancelot Andrewes and his successor as Master of Pembroke, Samuel Harsnett, followed an Arminian line. George Herbert who became orator in 1617 was much under the influence of Nicholas Ferrar, a former fellow of Clare, who in 1625 bought the manor house at Little Gidding in order to found a religious community. Matthew Wren and John Cosin, the Masters of Peterhouse, were strong protagonists of Laudain policy and introduced Catholic ceremonial into the newly built chapel: its consecration was celebrated in a poem by Richard Crashaw, a fellow of the college.

Laud had also been Chancellor of Trinity College, Dublin, since 1633. He was determined to weaken this Puritan stronghold and to extend to Ireland the policy of the Lord Deputy Wentworth of creating an efficient central government that would acknowledge the prerogative rule of Charles I. To this end Wentworth procured in 1634 the appointment of a high churchman, Dr William Chappell, a former fellow of Christ's, Cambridge, and a tutor of Milton (whom he had once chastised) as provost of the college. Chappell insisted on the wearing of the surplice on Sundays and Holy Days and on the performance of daily services in the college chapel and he discontinued the Irish lecture which his predecessor had introduced in 1628 to attract support from the native Irish. Meanwhile Wentworth, who sent his eleven-year-old son to Trinity, sought to create a party among the senior fellows, but only succeeded in creating internal dissension. After the period of confusion that followed the fall of Wentworth and Laud and the outbreak of civil strife the college settled down happily under a Puritan Provost, Winter, a graduate of Emmanuel, and loyal to the Commonwealth.

*

These changes at Oxford and Cambridge had interesting and important repercussions. Outwardly the universities seemed to function as before, in some respects with heightened efficiency. They were full* and prosperous (though benefactions by London merchants who favoured the Puritan colleges diminished); they were still in moderately close touch with recent advances in thought and learning. It is arguable that the tighter control being exerted by the now dominant party in the church and state had a detrimental effect on scholarship, discouraging radical and original thinking. A crop of criticism, some of it from reasonable men, sprang up, denouncing Oxford and Cambridge. Some was exaggerated and blended with

*Only at the outbreak of the Civil War did their numbers decline; between 1610 and 1630 they were at their highest. The usual estimates based on the number of those who matriculated represent perhaps only three quarters of the total student population.

malice, but the mounting chorus of complaints could not be disregarded. The universities were not completely subservient to the ruling establishment, but by the outbreak of the Civil War they were so obviously preserves of ecclesiastical and political royalism that they could hardly survive the fall of both without radical alteration.

Thus the policy fostered by the Tudor sovereigns, tightened and formalized under their Stuart successors, had the effect of crystallizing the royal and Anglican monopoly of the universities. Although some fellows were still inclined to Puritanism and critical of Caroline government, the majority of dons and heads were loyal to the King. Laud's dictatorial policies had helped to convert an unemployed intelligentsia, the most dangerous of men, into bitter critics and political malcontents. Many forces combined – neo-Calvinists, Presbyterians, Puritans, Independents, merchants and ministers, schoolmasters, writers and politicians – to begin an attack on the chief armoury of Anglicanism. They charged the universities with subsidizing idleness, teaching an out-moded scholasticism, fostering popery and disregarding the scriptures. 'For humane learning mingled with divinity, or the Gospel of Christ understood according to Aristotle, hath begun, continued and perfected the mystery of iniquity in the outward church,' wrote William Dell of Caius. They urged greater discipline and more dedicated scholarship; they wanted more attention paid to mathematics and science. They called for austerity of behaviour, an end to that 'great licentiousness and profaneness' whereby 'parents sending their children far from them, young and hopeful, have for all their care and cost, after several years received them back again with their tongues and Arts, profane, wicked, abominable and incorrigible wretches', and they were one with Laud at least in their dislike of long hair, high boots and gaudy costume.

Some looked enviously at their considerable endowments demanding an abolition of the tithes which formed a part of college revenues, and would readily have submitted the universities to the fate that a century earlier had befallen the monasteries. Even the Master of Emmanuel, Richard Holdsworth, who had some claim to be regarded as a Puritan, in 1641 surveyed the future with gloom and apprehension:

We will take our seats by the waters of the Cam, and weep when we remember thee, O Sion! We will hang our harps on the willows, and now at length bid a long farewell to learning. Farewell, ye stately ceremonies and thronged assemblies! Farewell, ye contests of scholars and honourable disputations, bright purple and adorning gown, maces, insignia, genius, polite learning, studies, order, discipline, and ye venerable foundations of our ancestors: and thou too, Religion, which hast so long adorned our Church of England! Tis now the twelfth hour alike of the Muses and of the Graces.

His fears were not unjustified. Oxford soon became the royalist headquarters and an armed camp. Cambridge submitted dolefully to Parliamentary control; and the waspish busybody William Dowsing hurried round the college chapels to note what ought to be demolished in the interests of scriptural religion. Oxford and Cambridge had fallen victim to new masters who had scant time for Arminian theology and polite learning. They were less inclined to make the universities preserves of clergy and gentry, readier to open their gates and more concerned with serious studies of a modern character; but they were as eager as Laud had been to tie the universities to the reigning order in church and state and like all reformers they were impatient of past traditions and of vested rights.

CHAPTER THREE

Oxford and Cambridge in Decline,

1650–1800

THE régime imposed on the universities after the defeat of
the Royalists and the execution of Charles I in 1649 was even
more inflexible than the one it had displaced and was totally
out of sympathy with the Anglican dons who governed Oxford
and Cambridge. A period of decline seemed to be setting in.
The universities had been almost emptied of their inmates; at
Oxford, college rooms had been inhabited by courtiers and
soldiers who often failed to pay their rent. The personnel of
the senior members changed radically as those who refused to
accept the Solemn League and Covenant, which in 1643 bound
Parliament to establish the Presbyterian system of religion, or
to acknowledge the Engagement by which Charles I in 1647
agreed to accept Presbyterianism for three years, were deprived
of their positions and forced to leave. Many of them were men
of admitted distinction like Sanderson and Sheldon, and the
replacements imposed on the colleges by the London Committee, set up by Parliament to regulate and reform the universities, were often mediocre scholars. The universities became in
the words of the Oxford antiquary Anthony Wood little better
than 'nurseries of wickedness, the nests of mutton tuggers,
the dens of formal drones'. The contumacious heads were
forced to vacate their lodgings, and the wife of the Dean of
Christ Church was carried by the Cromwellian soldiers into
Tom Quad in her chair. Yet the gloomy prognostications which
must have filled every loyal heart at the universities at the beginning of the Commonwealth were not fulfilled. Even the
royalist writer Lord Clarendon was obliged to admit that the
'stupidity, negligence, malice and perverseness' of the government, far from having failed to 'extirpate all the learning, religion and loyalty that had flourished there', had in fact 'yielded

a harvest of extraordinary good and sound knowledge in all parts of learning'.

The Commonwealth was certainly ruthless in its religious policy. The Prayer Book was proscribed. In practically every college senior and junior members alike were subjected to a stiffer religious control, requiring attendance at services and regular sermons. It was urged that there should be frequent preaching in the college chapels 'upon consideration that the maine end of the University is to traine up men well in Divine as Humane learning, that they may be able (when the Providence of God shall call them) to publish the Gospell of Christ to the conversion and building up of soules to eternal life'. Government control was, however, stronger on paper than it was in practice, and even under these impositions Oxford and Cambridge still flourished. In spite of the many deprivations there was a central element of continuity and college life went on very much as before. The new masters showed common sense in their handling of the situation; if, as Anthony Wood complained, there was 'preaching and praying too much', yet a blind eye was turned to the Anglican worship continuing within a stone's throw of the lodgings of the Independent Dean of Christ Church. Those who governed the universities were no strangers to their traditions. The Oxford vice-chancellors, Dean Owen and John Conant, were reasonable, scholarly men genuinely concerned with the interests of religion and learning. It was a moderate Puritanism that had proved victorious and the days of Calvinist extremism were over. Though still stubbornly entrenched in some hearts its doctrines of absolute reprobation and election appeared to the rising generation of young churchmen as unattractive as the formularies of the Anglicans.

One of the most interesting of the university groups to grow to maturity in this environment of comparative religious toleration was that of the Cambridge Platonists. These were mainly young fellows of colleges, significantly enough associated with Puritan foundations like Emmanuel and Christ's, who were bitterly opposed to the dark doctrines of predestination and eternal perdition and yet were no more inclined to accept

Arminian theology. While not denying the power of mysticism, they wished to demonstrate the reasonableness and humanity of Christian teaching; they saw no notable antithesis between the demands of faith and reason. Their leading spokesman, Benjamin Whichcote, Provost of King's, crossed swords with the Puritan Master of St John's, Anthony Tuckney, and they all – Whichcote, Henry More, John Smith and Ralph Cudworth – joined battle in the intellectual life of the seventeenth century. The Commonwealth in fact encouraged research and original scholarship. The university exercises remained the same and the syllabus did not change significantly, but there was a revival of interest in science and mathematics, to some extent stimulated by Puritan thought. Cromwell's brother-in-law John Wilkins, the future Bishop of Chester, became Warden of Wadham. Cromwell's physician Goddard, best known for his medicinal drops, a university burgess and a founder of the Royal Society, was made Warden of Merton. The Cambridge mathematician Seth Ward, who was later bishop of Salisbury, became professor of astronomy at Oxford. At the same time the new régime upheld a stern moral code, perhaps more readily received by the sons of the middle and professional classes who were in all probability beginning to replace the aristocratic playboys of earlier days. This change in the social structure of the undergraduate population could well have encouraged a more sober atmosphere and diminished the student capacity for roystering, wenching, drinking and the pursuit of pleasure. The colleges had recovered quickly from the depredations into their finances caused by their need to subscribe more or less voluntarily to the royalist cause, more or less compulsorily to the Parliamentary, and by the decline in the number of students; they were once more full and prosperous. Even so, the signs of underlying dissatisfaction are not difficult to detect. Political insecurity and continued resentment of the moral inquisition and high-minded tyranny of the Puritan religious policy combined with genuine affection for past traditions to make men look back longingly at the past and greet the restoration of Charles II in 1660 with real pleasure.

*

The Restoration however had disastrous consequences for the universities, though at first they were not apparent. There were still abundant indications of flourishing scholarship – the work, for instance, of Fell and Mill at Oxford and of Richard Bentley at Cambridge – and, especially at Cambridge where the influence of the Platonists eventually gave way to the cool, rational theology of the Latitudinarians, further signs of a reaction to the still persisting Aristotelianism and a deep interest in science and mathematics illuminated by the prestige of men like Barrow and Newton.

But there were also signs that fossilization was setting in. The Restoration signified for the universities the victory of Anglican orthodoxy. It re-established the Anglican monopoly of Oxford and Cambridge, where fellows and heads who had been expelled by the Puritans were reinstated and their successors removed: the Act of Uniformity of 1662 made it virtually impossible for a Dissenter to be a member of the university. The dual loyalty to Church and Crown became the foundation of government and the measure of reputation. Political nonconformists like Daniel Scargill of Corpus Christi, Cambridge, suspected of harbouring the atheistic notions of Thomas Hobbes, and James Parkinson of Lincoln College, Oxford, a supporter of Shaftesbury and the party who wished to exclude the Catholic James, Duke of York, from succession to the English throne, were deprived of their fellowships, and at the government's request Christ Church expelled John Locke from his studentship in 1684. In 1683 a number of seditious works, among them Hobbes's *Leviathan*, were burned in the schools quadrangle at Oxford, after appropriate extracts had been read out by the regius professor of divinity to prove their dangerous nature, in the presence of a large assembly of dons and to the huzzas of the undergraduates.

Loyal as the university's seniors were to the doctrine of passive obedience to the Crown, they valued their devotion to the Church of England even more highly. They resisted fiercely James II's attempt to bring pressure to bear on college elections in favour of Roman Catholics; when in 1687 a new President of Magdalen was to be elected the fellows refused to accept either of the king's nominees, the drunken Papist, Anthony Farmer, or Samuel Parker, the Bishop of Oxford who was ineligible for election under the Statutes. The fellows were summoned to the dean's lodging at Christ Church. 'Ye have been,' the king told them, 'a stubborn, turbulent College. ... Is this your Church of England loyalty? Go home and show yourselves good members of the Church of England. ... Get you gone, know I am your King. I will be obeyed, and I command you to be gone. Go and admit the Bishop of Oxford, Principal, what do you call it, of the College?' The king's folly brought its own ruin. He was obliged to allow the restoration of the fellows whom he had expelled from Magdalen and when he fled the country in December 1688 the Protestant fellows of the colleges of Oxford and Cambridge breathed again. The accession of William III however proved another trial of conscience for the loyalist dons. Though they had resisted James's religious policy they had at least known him to be their rightful king; but as for William, they questioned his very claim to the throne. Many dons therefore refused to take the oath of allegiance as the law obliged them to do, whereupon an Act of Parliament deprived them of their offices. Dons from both Oxford and Cambridge were joined by four hundred churchmen and six bishops, headed by Archbishop Sancroft, who suffered the same fate and came to form the group known as the Non-Jurors. This crisis past, the universities once more settled down to their appointed task of training the young and of upholding orthodoxy in church and state.

*

The time was ripe for a policy of *quieta non movere*. It can hardly be doubted, though much of the accepted picture needs modification, that Oxford and Cambridge were about to enter the least distinguished era in their long history, and perhaps, outside the Church of England which they continued to supply with ministers, the nadir of their influence on the nation's life. The number of undergraduates fell sharply. Under the Anglican monopoly the older universities slumbered through the eighteenth century, while in the Scottish universities and the new Dissenters' academies intellectual life flourished. The clerical control over the colleges was detrimental both to their efficiency and scholarship. The majority of fellowships had become the preserve of the Anglican clergy and were regarded as a stepping stone to preferment rather than an opportunity for genuine study and research; this meant that fewer fellows resided in college and that the standards demanded of candidates for election to fellowships were very probably lowered. Tutorial duties once conscientiously carried out were now neglected, though not as badly as has since been supposed. 'We were lectured immediately after chapel,' wrote Gunning of his undergraduate days at Cambridge, 'and generally in a very hasty manner, as Parkinson not infrequently was equipped in boots and spurs, which his gown but ill concealed.' Many of the professors had ceased to lecture at all, since audience and stipend alike were impossibly small. At Oxford the syllabus was still dominated by an outmoded scholasticism but even at Cambridge, where Newtonian and Baconian thought had eventually triumphed, the degree course was arid and uninteresting. The Laudian statutes of Oxford and the Elizabethan statutes of Cambridge cried aloud for reform; but contemporaries shuddered at the very sound of the word.

The Church of England, understandably, had grown suspicious of change. It had witnessed the growing popularity of Deism and it feared for the faith. It was on the defensive and stood *super antiquas vias* believing with unrealistic complacency that the universities were still the homes of exemplary scholarship and true religion. There were careful tutors, some outstanding scholars, any number of cultured and widely-read men; but the scholarship of the older universities in the eighteenth century was desiccated, ponderous and pedantic. The ancient and complex system of examinations was grinding to a halt. 'We are obliged to misspend so much time here,' the future Bishop Butler wrote of Oxford in 1717, 'in attending frivolous lectures and unintelligible disputations, that I am quite tired out with such a disagreeable way of trifling.' While many a poor boy still came to the university and achieved distinction there, undergraduate life had become expensive and there were more noblemen and gentlemen commoners, more of the *bon ton* who flaunted their sartorial elegance and wasted their time in frivolous pleasures, than there had been in the previous century. The intellectual quality of the undergraduate population suffered especially after 1660 as the grammar schools stagnated and failed to award the scholarships to the universities with which benefactors of the late sixteenth and early seventeenth century had endowed them. The lesson was plain; while life in the senior common and combination rooms may well have been on occasions cultured and agreeable, as institutions Oxford and Cambridge were in some danger of petrifaction.

Political as well as social and religious factors were to blame. The accession of the Hanoverian George I in 1714 profoundly affected the future of Oxford, since it brought to an end the close alliance, interrupted only by James II's aberration, between the university and the Crown since the Restoration. Cambridge, on the other hand, equally undistinguished as a home of original scholarship, was attached to the new dynasty. The Oxford professor of poetry, Thomas Warton, commenting on the gift of Bishop Moore's library to Cambridge and the dispatch of a garrison to Oxford wittily epitomized the situation:

> The king observing, with judicious eyes,
> The state of both his universities,
> To one he sends a regiment: For why?
> That learned body wanted loyalty.
> To th'other books he gave, as well discerning
> How much that loyal body wanted learning.

It was Cambridge that received preferential treatment from the Hanoverian ministers. With the Duke of Newcastle first as its High Steward and then from 1748 to his death in 1768 as Chancellor it basked in royal patronage, at least until 1760 when on the accession of George III Newcastle lost favour. Its studies, suffused by the ideas of Bacon, Locke and Newton rather than of Aristotle, were in many respects more modern and interesting than those at Oxford, but it lacked genuinely creative scholarship and the stream of learning, if in the main channel of contemporary ideas, was still sluggish. The pall of the established church lay heavy on both universities, maintaining an essentially clerical personnel, excluding non-Anglicans from membership and reducing them to little more than breeding-grounds for the gentry and aristocracy.

Oxford's future was further darkened by the political situation which led to its long alienation from the government. Although the university was high Tory in feeling, it had made no initial display of hostility to George I; but it soon discovered that it had lost royal favour and was the target of criticism. 'King George,' Dr Haywood of St John's is reported to have said, 'had suspended his favours at present from ye University by some misrepresentations.' The misrepresentations were on a major scale. Both universities were the targets of Grub Street publicists, Deists, Dissenters and plain Whigs who did not mince their words and deliberately blackened the universities' reputation. Their intemperate sallies helped to create the picture of the eighteenth-century university which is still with us. Oxford was, as it has so often been, the focal point of attack. Its high church theology and its supposed Jacobitism, its reputed indolence and low morality aroused its critics to bitter vehemence.

Nicholas Amhurst, a young don of St John's who was expelled from his fellowship for alleged libertinism, in *Terrae Filius* (1721) painted a dark picture of the university; he asked whether the universities in

The present unregulated state . . . are not nurseries of pedantry instead of sound learning, of bigotry instead of sound religion; whether their statutes . . . are not generally perverted, or partially executed; whether the publick discipline is not wretchedly neglected; and the publick exercises confin'd to nonsensical jargon, and the mere burlesque of true knowledge

and providing a good deal of detailed if biased evidence he had no doubt that the answer was in the affirmative. In his play *The Humours of Oxford* (1730), a Whig cleric from Wadham depicted the dons as contemptible pedagogues or low-living

47

men of the world. 'Why,' says the Oxford scholar, Ape-Hall, described as a 'trifling ridiculous fob, affecting Dress and Lewdness', 'he is a Fellow of a College; that is to say a Rude, Hoggish, Proud, Pedantick, Gormandizing Drone – a drearing, dull Sot, that lives and rots, like a Frog in a Ditch, and goes to the Devil at last, he scarce knows why.' In the fourth act the don sang a song:

> What class in Life, tho' neer so great
> With a good Fellowship can compare?
> We still dream on at our old rate
> Without perplexing Care ...
>
> An easier Round of Life we keep
> We eat, we Drink, we Smoak, we sleep
> And then, then, then
> Rise and do the same again.

Why, asked John Toland, another of the critics, 'may not Oxford ... be reformed or purg'd by a Royal Visitation tomorrow, as Aberdeen was the other day, or as Oxford itself was at the Reformation?'

At one time it looked as if the Whig government might be persuaded to take radical measures to curb the universities' independence, and indeed it put forward proposals for a royal visitation which would have made the universities completely subservient to the Crown and so to the political party in power. Fortunately a division within the ministry brought these extreme measures to nothing. The ministry then fell back on two other methods, both of which proved of no advantage to the universities and of not much use to the government. First it virtually cut off hope of preferment from all but its protégés, with the net result that Oxford became a provincial backwater and a supporter of the independent Tory cause. Secondly, at the instance of Bishop Gibson, it created regius professorships of modern languages and history at both Oxford and Cambridge with the intention of training young men for its service, but this excellent scheme was never brought to fruition. More noticeably the ministry interfered in university affairs, seeking to build up a caucus of dons Whig in complexion and favourable to itself, but except in a few colleges which were already mainly Whig, such as Christ Church, Merton, Wadham, Exeter and Jesus, these manoeuvres and manipulations met with limited success. Their only result was to multiply the intrigue and jobbery already too symptomatic of senior common rooms. The accession of George III in 1760 and the subsequent election of Lord North as Chancellor of Oxford effected a reconciliation with the Crown, so that from that point both universities relied on the Crown for protection against their adversaries.

The consequences of all this were indeed disastrous, though the abundant evidence of scandal and intrigue has to be placed side by side with the quiet achievements of individual scholars and conscientious tutors. If the exercises for degrees had become outmoded formalities, there is conclusive proof – proved by the contents of college libraries – that undergraduates as well as dons engaged in extra-curricular study. The studious man had ample opportunity to read widely and fruitfully. He might well emerge from his university as cultivated and as well educated within contemporary terms as his successor two centuries later. The reading lists of John Wesley as an undergraduate at Christ Church and as a fellow of Lincoln include poetry, drama, history and science as well as classical and theological literature. Nor were all the dons the boorish clerics who appear in their critics' pages. If, for instance, we had a mere superficial acquaintance with Dr Richard Farmer, the Master of Emmanuel from 1775 to 1797, we might see in him the familiar eccentric and unclerical clubman. His bizarre personal appearance and behaviour gave rise to the saying that his three greatest loves were old port, old clothes and old books, just as there were three things which no one could persuade him to do, to get up in the morning, to go to bed at night and to settle his bills. But this canon of St Paul's, whose published works were so very peripheral, was a highly esteemed member of the Literary Club, the friend of Dr Johnson and the supporter of Pitt who offered him a bishopric, which he refused. The catalogue of his library, containing some 8,155 books and running to 379 pages, was a truer index to the real man. The eighteenth-century universities were neither as corrupt, as indolent nor as inefficient as they have been made out to be; but they had grown increasingly out of touch with the needs of their time.

A minority within the universities and many intelligent commentators without realized that this was so. 'A learned man! – a scholar! a man of erudition! Upon whom are these epithets of approbation bestowed?' Sydney Smith asked in the *Edinburgh Review* in 1810.

Are they given to men acquainted with the science of government? thoroughly masters of the geographical and commercial relations of Europe? to men who know the properties of bodies and their action upon each other? No; this is not learning; it is chemistry, or political economy – not learning. The distinguishing abstract term, the epithet of scholar, is reserved for him who writes on the Æolic reduplication and is familiar with Sylburgius his method of arranging defectives in $\dot\omega$ and $\mu\iota$ . . . . His object is not to reason, to imagine, or to invent; but to conjugate, decline and derive. . . . Would he ever dream that such men as Adam Smith and Lavoisier were equal in dignity or understanding to, or of the same utility as, Bentley and Heyne?

Adam Smith had himself condemned the older universities as the 'sanctuaries in which exploded systems and obsolete prejudices found shelter and protection'. The public exercises for the first and second degrees, commented John Napleton of Brasenose College in 1773, 'are in truth for the most part performed in so negligent a manner, that is equally impossible they should contribute to the advancement of learning, to the improvement or reputation of the candidate, or to the honour of the University'. 'Equally silly and obsolete . . . a set of childish and useless exercises', was the opinion of Vicesimus Knox, Headmaster of Tonbridge and a former fellow of St John's, Oxford. 'So futile and absurd,' he declared, 'as to deserve not only the severity of censure but the utmost poignancy of ridicule.' 'What do you think,' Lord Chesterfield had written to his son, 'of being a Greek Professor at one of our Universities? It is a very pretty sinecure, and requires very little knowledge (much less than I hope you have already) of that language.'

The situation at Cambridge was not very much better. One college, St John's, under the lead of its Master, William Powell, had introduced a system of annual examinations for all its members. John Jebb wished to extend the procedure to the whole university but all his attempts to get such a grace accepted or to bring about any reform of the examination system were frustrated by the inertia of contemporary opinion. Yet Cambridge with its mathematical bias was in some respects better placed than classical Oxford. Inevitably it was the older schools, with their essentially classical curriculum, who supplied Oxford with its undergraduates, while the demands of the Cambridge course were met most often by the newer grammar schools, especially those in northern England. Isaac Milner, Edmund Law, Archdeacon Blackburne, William Paley, Richard Watson, William Wilberforce and the poet William Wordsworth were all Cambridge luminaries hailing from the north.

The exclusiveness of Oxford and Cambridge was even more strongly attacked than the narrowness of the education they provided. The Dissenters, especially influential among the mercantile and professional classes, whose own academies compared so favourably with the universities at this time, criticized the obligation to subscribe to the Thirty-nine Articles which virtually debarred Nonconformists from admission to Oxford and prevented them from taking a degree at either university. Indeed an increasing number of liberal-minded university members among whom John Jebb was the most prominent, wished to modify if not to eliminate this requirement. Patronized by Edmund Law, the Master of Peterhouse, the group was especially strong at Jesus College, Cambridge, where it included Gilbert Wakefield, Robert Tyrwhitt, William Frend and Thomas Edwards. They petitioned against the subscription to the Thirty-nine Articles required of all candidates for degrees (and in 1772 a grace to abolish it was defeated in the Cambridge Senate by only eight votes), supported English parliamentary reform and the American rebels.

But the cause of university reform was too closely associated with the criticism of established order for it to make much headway. The Church of England feared for its monopoly and was alarmed by the spread of unbelief in fashionable circles. At the same time the rise of Methodism in the very midst of Oxford and the continued existence of a small body of Methodists and Evangelicals represented a threat of another kind. The last sermon that John Wesley preached before the university at St Mary's in 1744 had been a scathing denunciation of the university's deficiencies. Between the Scylla of unbelief and the Charybdis of enthusiasm, the university Anglicans made their cautious and conservative way. Six students were expelled from Oxford in 1768 for their so-called Methodism. The group agitating for abolition of religious tests was discredited in the eyes of many people when several dons in its midst, most spectacularly John Jebb who made his views known in 1775, began to propagate the doctrine of Unitarianism that denied the divinity of Christ. The rise of political Jacobinism, encouraged by the happenings in France, made the university Tories look to their defences and cemented the alliance with the established order in church and state.

The liberal, William Frend, an associate of Joseph Priestley, was expelled from his fellowship of Jesus College and banned from Cambridge for a pamphlet *Peace and Union recommended to the Associated Bodies of Republicans and Anti-Republicans* because it was alleged to have brought the church into disrepute. The vice-chancellor who presided over Frend's trial was the redoubtable Evangelical, Isaac Milner, the President of Queens', who was quick to see Jacobinism in the most harmless action and even feared that a meeting of the British and Foreign Bible Society might foster political disaffection since it had been called into being by the undergraduates rather than by the dons. At Oxford Thomas Beddoes, who had attracted some attention by his lectures on chemistry, was obliged to resign his position for his republican sympathies and settled at Clifton where he established a 'Pneumatic Institute'.

But beneath this frost of repression there were signs of returning life. Some of the Oxford colleges, notably Christ Church, Balliol and Oriel, were beginning to take their teaching in hand and the Hebdomadal Board itself had awakened to the need to provide an intellectual incentive for the more intelligent undergraduates. In 1800 a statute was introduced which provided for an examination for the degrees of Bachelor and Master of Arts and of Bachelor of Civil Law. When it was put into operation in 1802 only two candidates presented themselves for honours, but the seed from which the Oxford Honour Schools were to spring had been planted. The stagnation which settled on Oxford and Cambridge in the eighteenth century must not be allowed to hide from us the currents which continuously flowed under the surface. They were not yet strong enough to disturb the sluggish waters, but they soon gathered into a swift flowing stream as the universities entered their period of greatest change, the nineteenth century.

CHAPTER FOUR

Reaction and Reform at Oxford and Cambridge in the Nineteenth Century

No significant institution in Britain was untouched by reform during the nineteenth century. Each in its turn was obliged to adapt itself to new social needs and to a changing social structure. The ancient governing class still retained what historians must now see to have been a precarious hold over the country; but its supremacy was challenged by an expanding middle class made affluent by industry and trade. Commercial progress was stimulated by the new colonialism which had brought into existence a great dominion under British control scattered over the world. Industrialization proceeded apace to meet the demands, prompted by the initiative and impetus of British businessmen abroad, of the newly developed countries as well as of the expanding home market. English society became rapidly more urbanized; it no longer admitted the governing power of squire or parson though it still allowed them their traditional place in its hierarchy.

These developments created an urgent need for a highly educated class of administrators, and demanded a far more efficient governmental machine than that which had dealt with public business in such a leisurely fashion in the eighteenth century and was still contriving to do so in the reign of George IV. Whether utilitarianism was an acceptable political philosophy or not, there was no doubt that 'utility' had become a watchword. There was thus a growing impatience with inefficiency and indolence and a desire to bring out-of-date institutions more into line with modern needs. The reform and expansion of the Civil Service, replacing patronage by a competitive examination, the widening of the frontiers of the empire, the great increase in the number of schools, made necessary more Civil Servants, more colonial administrators and judges, more lawyers and schoolmasters. Where else could

54

they be trained, but at the universities? The middle classes were hammering at their gates.

Oxford and Cambridge were still primarily training schools for the clergy of the established church; 413 of the 1,239 undergraduates who matriculated at Trinity, Cambridge, between 1831 and 1840 were to be ordained, and twenty years later, of 1,388 who matriculated between 1853 and 1862, 496 took holy orders. But, as the number of undergraduates grew steadily, it was apparent that Oxford and Cambridge were taking far more students than even a missionary church could require; and the majority of them found their way into the learned professions and government service. Economic developments demanded a new type of skilled intelligence, that of the scientist and technologist, but this the older universities were slow to recognize. It was abundantly plain that the semi-clerical seminaries, which did not even teach theology very satisfactorily, and which were in the main the preserves of a privileged class of gentry and aristocracy, could not hope to hold their own in the bustling Victorian world without a drastic change of character. Furthermore an education at Oxford or Cambridge was so expensive that only men of means could afford to send their children there without the assistance of a scholarship. The clergy, Mackaye was made to say in Kingsley's *Alton Locke,*

[have] got the monopoly of education in England, and they get their bread by it at their public schools and universities, and of course it's their interest to keep up the price of their commodity, and let no man have a taste of it who can't pay down handsomely. And so these aristocrats of college dons go on rolling in riches and fellowships and scholarships that were bequeathed by the people's friends in old times just to educate poor scholars like you and me.

Before Oxford and Cambridge could supply the country with its politicians and colonial administrators, its lawyers and doctors, its schoolmasters and Civil Servants, they had to undergo a major face-lift. Cambridge was still governed by the Elizabethan statutes of 1570 which had been deliberately designed to make constitutional change difficult. Oxford was regulated by the Laudian statutes of 1636, which had merely recodified what was already in existence. They had doubtless been excellent in their time, but had become so fossilized as to be incapable of practical articulation. As a result university government had fallen into the hands of a select conservative-minded oligarchy, at Cambridge the Caput and at Oxford the Hebdomadal Board, dominated by the aristocracy of the university, the heads of the colleges. The machinery of university government, democratic on paper, was in practice cumbrous and ineffective. The university itself did very little for the undergraduate. It demanded from him fees for matriculation and for his degrees; he might fall foul of its disciplinary officials, the proctors. It appointed the professors, but, at the end of the century as at the beginning, they were mostly underpaid and inefficient. The courses on which they had to lecture had nothing to do with the curriculum for degrees so they were hardly to blame if no one came to listen to them. By the end of the century many professors treated their jobs as sinecures.

The colleges had long since taken over the main functions of the university, to educate as well as house the undergraduates. Little objection could be taken to this state of affairs if the colleges performed their functions effectively. But with fewer fellows living in college and the university exercises becoming an empty formality, instruction was left to one or two of the fellows who served as tutors and lecturers. While some of the tutors performed their tasks competently, college lectures had tended to become dreary and unoriginal introductions to their subject. 'It would scarcely be believed,' said George Pryme who went up to Trinity in 1799, 'how very little knowledge was required for a mere degree when I first knew Cambridge. Two books of Euclid's Geometry, simple and quadratic equations, and the early parts of Paley's Moral Philosophy were deemed amply sufficient.' John Calcott, an elderly fellow of Lincoln College, Oxford, a pupil recalled later, 'rang such learned changes on his three great questions – the nature of wild honey, the relative situation of Galilee and Judea, and the title of our Lord'. If an undergraduate wanted good teaching he had to go to a local coach who in return for relatively high fees put him through his paces. Only a few colleges had an entrance examination – Balliol had introduced one in the early years of the nineteenth century, and Trinity, Cambridge, had a relatively easy one. Indeed the very notion of such a requirement was angrily resented as an interference with the vested rights of the colleges. 'Mr Foster,' Frederick Faber told the aged President of Magdalen, Dr Routh,

has been taught Greek and Latin most laboriously by a clergyman. ... I understand a system has begun since I quitted Oxford of having a *real examination* at entrance and that young gentlemen are frequently subjected to the mortification of being rejected. Mr Foster senior does not choose to expose his son to this trouble. ... This young man ... wishes like his father to have the great advantage of residing in the University, though he never goes up for a degree.

Moreover the colleges had become co-optative oligarchies, often acting in violation of the statutes which dated from their foundation and which belonged to an age long since vanished. Many fellowships were tied to particular localities, and entailed a celibate life and the taking of holy orders. At Oxford only 22 out of 542 fellowships were open without restriction. Many colleges housed cultured, widely read men honestly interested in scholarship and conscientious in performing their duty; but both Oxford and Cambridge were weighed down by inertia. 'Lincoln,' Mark Pattison commented on his election to a fellowship there in 1839, 'had been let drop very low in the rank of colleges during the tutorship of Rose and Radford . . . Queen's and Magdalen, Jesus and St John's, were bad enough, but none of them could show such fossil specimens of the genus Fellow as our Kay senior, Thompson, Calcott, Meredith.' 'The Magdalen people,' J. A. Symonds wrote at a later date when elected to a fellowship,

are amusing. Their clerical society is of a toping sort. To drink sherry argues Radicalism with them, and they nickname each other jovially like boys. At night they often take their pipes comfortably together with beer & spirits & last evening I formed part of such a reunion – excellent for mirth & good humour but not remarkable for wits.

Even in the middle of the century a reverend fellow of St John's, Oxford, having heard the future Dean Stanley descant at some length on his tour of the Holy Land, explicably exclaimed, 'Jerusalem be damned, give us wine, women and horses.'

A majority of the colleges in fact were old-fashioned, comfortable clerical clubs, unsympathetic towards change, religious or political. They resisted it not merely because it might upset their leisurely existence but because it would overthrow the Anglican monopoly of education, opening the way to Dissenters and infidels. No wonder their ire rose when they read Sir William Hamilton's acid criticisms in the *Edinburgh Review*. 'The Academy of Oxford is therefore not one public University,' he asserted,

but merely a collection of private schools. ... The great interests of the nation, the church, and the professions [are] sacrificed to the paltry ends of a few contemptible corporations; and the privileges by the law accorded to the University of Oxford, as the authorized organ of national education, were by its perfidious governors furtively transformed to the unauthorized absurdities of their college discipline.

In 1837 Lord Radnor, in asking that a commission be appointed to inquire into university affairs, cited as evidence of their deplorable state the senior fellow of Merton who was a Lieutenant-General in His Majesty's service and a senior fellow of Brasenose, who had a stall in Hereford cathedral, held three livings in the same diocese which returned him £1,100, and possessed a cure of three thousand souls, while he was in fact resident in Paris. 'The truth is,' as Robert Southey put it, 'that the institutions of men grow old like themselves, and, like women, are always the last to perceive their own decay.'

*

The question was whether the universities could be left to carry out reform without outside intervention. The universities, Lord Melbourne declared in 1837, 'never reformed themselves; everyone knew that – everyone knew there was too much competition and jealousy, too many and varied motives, constantly in play, to prevent the desired effect'. Melbourne may well have been right, but it was not the opinion of the majority of university residents. Few dons can have believed in the implicit perfection of the universities as they knew them. The most that they could hope for was that the slow process of reform, of which the Oxford honours examination of 1802 was the first tangible proof, would be allowed to continue without much outside influence. The process gradually gathered momentum in the first half of the nineteenth century. Some of the colleges threw off their more parochial features. Under the magnificent Dean Cyril Jackson, whose influence stretched far into the polite world of fashion, politics and patronage, Christ Church became renowned for scholarship as well as for its aristocratic clientele; Canning, Peel, Hallam, Gaisford and Gladstone had all been there. The Tory Master of Balliol, John Parsons, strongly supported the proposed reform of the examination system, and gave the lead to the campaign to elect fellows for their academic worth. Oriel, under Provosts Eveleigh and Copleston, went even further, throwing open its fellowships for award by competitive examination and attracting to them the ablest men in Oxford: Pusey, Keble, Arnold, Hawkins, Newman, Hurrell Froude, Whately. The Cambridge colleges, over-shadowed by Trinity and St John's, proved less active in this direction, but Christ's, under its progressive Master, Dr Graham, sought permission to alter the statute so that fellows would be allowed to marry and non-Anglicans to hold fellowships; the Tory Visitor to the College, invoked by the more reactionary fellows, frustrated this move. 'A few motes,' D. A. Winstanley commented, 'had been removed, but most of the beams had been left.'*

While some changes took place inside the colleges, more were made in the university regulations. In the first place professors were now expected to lecture. The Tory Lord Liverpool invited Edward Nares to become the professor of history at Oxford in 1813: 'I have no difficulty now in offering you the Professorship of Modern History, upon the understanding that

*D. A. Winstanley, *Early Victorian Cambridge*, Cambridge University Press, 1960, p. 196.

you will read a course of lectures annually, or every alternate year...' A long tradition was broken when Herbert Marsh as Lady Margaret professor of divinity at Cambridge delivered a course of lectures which was well attended. But the efficiency of the professors was still hindered by the inadequacy of the stipends which the university could afford to pay them and by the failure to correlate what they taught with the examination system.

Methods of teaching and examining had however begun to change for the better. At Oxford the honours examinations in *literae humaniores* (or Greats as it came to be called) and in mathematics attracted an increasing number of the better students, even though most of them essayed no more than a pass degree. Its introduction brought some improvements in the tutorial system since colleges were more inclined to elect as fellows men who had performed well in the honour schools. Between 1807 and 1815 seventy-two of the men placed in the first class took fellowships. Yet it must be admitted that the curriculum in classics and mathematics was, as the able but unpopular Dr Tatham urged in a series of assaults on the examination at its first introduction, far too narrow, and still unduly dominated by Aristotelian philosophy. 'The old Moral Philosophy of Aristotle, Cicero or Epictetus, however admirable in their days, is at this day not worth a louse,' he commented in his blunt Yorkshire way.

How preposterously absurd it is, to send the youth of a Christian University, in the nineteenth century, to learn their Moral Philosophy from Aristotle, that uncircumcised and unbaptized Philistine of the schools. ... Why is Natural Philosophy, the Queen of all Theoretic Science ... *totally omitted*? Is it because it owes its vast extension and improvement to those illustrious moderns, a Bacon and a Newton, who were Cambridge men?

But no one paid any attention to the eccentric and deeply disliked Dr Tatham. 'After your four-years labour,' he said in a parting shot, 'on studying *Dialectica* is crowned with the desired success in ranking your names ... in the *First Class*, well may ye deserve to be pronounced *Egregii*, for, doubtless, ye will prove *Egregious Blockheads* unqualified to cope with Art or

Science, and unprepared for the Study of the learned Facul___.

If the continued emphasis on Aristotelianism and outmoded logic (illustrated by the fact that Dean Aldrich's text book which John Wesley had used was still a basic text over a century later) was the bane of Oxford education, Cambridge suffered from an over-emphasis on mathematics. At the start of the nineteenth century candidates for higher degrees and for a first degree in law or medicine, neither held in high repute, were merely obliged to perform certain exercises in disputation, called acts and opponencies. The principal examination, known as the Senate House Examination, touched lightly on moral philosophy but was almost entirely concerned with mathematics. 'After you have resided something more than three years, at the conclusion of the tenth term,' wrote J. M. Wright of Trinity who matriculated in 1815,

in the month of January, you're examined in the Senate House, for four successive days, in Mathematics and Metaphysics. All men of the same standing, amounting to two hundred or upwards, are divided into six classes, according to their merit, as ascertained at the private examinations of each college. Printed papers, containing each about twenty questions, are laid before each class, the solution of each question being previously determined upon by the examiners numerically. At the close of the examination these numbers are summed up for each examinee, and he who got most is called Senior Wrangler, then followed by about twenty all called Wranglers, arranged in the order of merit. Two other ranks of honours are there – Senior Optimes and Junior Optimes.

The dominance of mathematics long continued to do injustice to the candidate who was not mathematically inclined. In 1822 Dr Wordsworth, the Master of Trinity, managed to secure the introduction of a classical tripos, but demands for a similar examination in theology met with no success. Eventually the Senate agreed to the introduction in 1843 of a so-called voluntary examination in theology which most of the bishops came to demand as an essential preliminary for ordinands; 14 candidates took this examination in 1843, 83 in 1845 and 205 in 1851. Although something had been done to eliminate abuses, it was only too plain that the progress in educational reform at both universities was likely to be slow and painful.

For many reasons already outlined Oxford and Cambridge failed to make the changes demanded by the changing times. But to the sorry sequence of inertia and inefficiency must be added one factor which more than any other explains their resistance to reform; they were constantly bedevilled by religious controversy. At Cambridge, where the Evangelical revival greatly affected college life, the admission of Dissenters to the university constituted a burning issue. Unlike Oxford, the colleges were able to admit non-Anglicans and in special circumstances made use of this right; but no non-Anglican could proceed to a degree or hold office in the university. A group of liberal dons, which had much support in the country, especially from Dissenters, tried to bring an end to this state of affairs. The non-regent house of the Senate* managed in 1829 to pass a grace in favour of Roman Catholic Emancipation, but only because Macaulay had packed a stagecoach from London with non-resident liberals; the Senate however petitioned against the bill, as it was to do in subsequent years against the passing of the Reform Bill and various other reforms. Professor Pryme introduced a motion to abolish or at least to modify the religious tests, but the grace was vetoed in the Caput by Dr King, the Tory Vice-Chancellor. A similar motion to excuse candidates for medical degrees from subscription to the Thirty-Nine Articles was treated in the same way.

A group of liberal dons subsequently petitioned Parliament to pass legislation to abolish the tests except for degrees in divinity; and a Dissenting M.P., G. W. Wood, introduced an amendment permitting 'His Majesty's subjects generally the right of admission to the English Universities, and of equal eligibility to degrees therein', except for degrees in Divinity, which was carried by a large majority. Even his Cambridge supporters were alarmed by the wording of the bill which seemed to imperil the sacrosanct rights of the colleges and they persuaded Wood to modify its phrasing. The bill was however

*The regent house consisted of the teaching masters and residents, the non-regent mainly of non-residents.

rejected on its second reading in the House of Lords by over a hundred votes. Evangelicals and 'high and dry' clergy were equally opposed to the relaxation of the requirement. They believed that it was impossible for the 'internal system of collegiate discipline and the course of academical administration' to be effectively adjusted so 'as to comprehend persons of different religious opinions, without the neglect of religious ordinances, the compromise of religious consistency, or the destruction of religious peace'. The regius professor of divinity, Dr Turton, argued that if Dissenters were allowed to take degrees, the university might be in danger of becoming a Dissenting academy. Connop Thirlwall, then a tutor at Trinity, replied to Turton, refuting his arguments and criticizing compulsory attendance in chapel, thus making the Master of Trinity, Dr Wordsworth, so angry that he ordered Thirlwall to vacate his tutorship. The high feeling generated by this question deflected attention from the more important issues of academic reform. These were the more resolutely disregarded because of the apparent, and to the conservatives alarming, connexion between those who wanted to change academic practice and those who called for changes in the Anglican church.

Meanwhile Oxford, if anything more closely identified than Cambridge with the privileged position of the established church, was involved in even fiercer religious controversy over the new and growing Tractarian movement,* which came into the open when John Keble protested in a university sermon at the way in which the Whig government interfered with the Irish bishoprics in 1833. The movement was in theory indifferent, in practice inimical, to the cause of university reform. Its objectives were purely religious, but it was necessarily opposed to any move that could conceivably alter the Anglican character of the university. It was concerned that this should be the fruit of a genuine spirituality, not a mere formal observance. Neither the Tractarians nor their critics had much in common with the

*The *Tracts for the Times* were first published in 1833 and were designed to disseminate Church principles; hence the name Tractarian given to the movement which aimed to preserve Church and university from their enemies.

liberal reformers. The crisis came with the university's condemnation of Tract No. 90* and the subsequent admission of Newman into the Roman church; once again the pressing problems of an improved curriculum and a more efficient administration were forgotten in the bitterness of the struggle.

*

The moderate reforms achieved in the early decades of the century were not enough to quieten the growing dissatisfaction in the nation with the way the two old universities were managing their affairs. Some critics, like Sir William Hamilton, attacked university life on all fronts, its ineffective teaching, its neglect of real research, the leisure and indolence of its common rooms and its misuse of great endowments: 'it is from the State only, and the Crown in particular,' his article in the *Edinburgh Review* concluded, 'that we can reasonably hope for an academical reformation worthy of the name.' Lord Radnor's demand in 1837 for a royal commission of inquiry into the state of the universities caused a flurry; the fall of the Whigs in 1841 and the return of Peel for the moment shelved the question and the die-hards breathed again, though W. D. Christie, the Member for Weymouth, once more urged the setting up of a commission in April 1845. Lord John Russell's appointment as Prime Minister in 1846 again raised the issue, so that the Senate at Cambridge, in anticipation of a royal commission, appointed a syndicate to revise the statutes of the university. Meanwhile a liberal group, including the Unitarian M.P. James Heywood, a self-appointed *vigilante* against the older universities, petitioned Parliament, declaring that the universities had signally failed to advance learning and demanding a commission of inquiry. In 1847 Kay-Shuttleworth visited Oxford to get information with a view to future legislative action and in April 1850, Lord John Russell announced in the House of Commons that the government proposed to inquire into the state of the universities. A commission was set up; the die was cast.

*A tract in which J. H. Newman had tried to show that the teaching of the Thirty-nine Articles was not out of line with that of the Formularies of the Council of Trent.

What did the commission accomplish? In the early stages of their inquiry the commissioners met with hostility and obstruction. The Vice-Chancellor of Cambridge, the high Tory Dr Corrie of Jesus, proved completely uncooperative. 'After having ascertained from high legal authority that the University Commission is without the form of law,' he announced stiffly, 'and is moreover, regarded as unconstitutional, and of a kind that was never issued except in the worst times, I feel obliged by a sense of public duty to decline answering any of the questions which I had the honour to receive from you a short time ago.' The Vice-Chancellor of Oxford informed the commission that he doubted its legality. The Bishop of Bath and Wells and the Earl of Pembroke, both Visitors of colleges, and the Dean of Christ Church, failed to acknowledge the commissioners' letters. Bishop Phillpotts of Exeter, a notorious Tory, declared that the inquiry had 'absolutely no parallel since the fatal attempt of King James II to subject [the colleges] to his unhallowed control'. At Oxford only eight out of nineteen colleges were ready to cooperate. 'From the majority of the Colleges, as Societies,' the commissioners stated, 'we have received no assistance.'

To the Lady Margaret professor of divinity the appointment of the commission was 'an unconstitutional stretch of prerogative, fraught with immediate evil, and still more dangerous as a precedent'. There was a spate of pamphlets, serious and facetious, conservative and radical. The commissioners were attacked for intending to build up the university at the expense of the colleges which would become 'little more than temporary lodging houses, with no claims to ... love or sympathy'. The Warden of Merton, made anxious by the conversion of the Member for Oxford, W. E. Gladstone, to the cause of reform, sadly commented on Oxford's fate, that 'in the season of need and peril she finds in one of her servants the ablest supporter of the measures she disapproves'. Sewell of Exeter advised Lord John Russell to consult the 'Artful Dodger': 'I could tell you a good many tricks that you'd like to know, how to get hold of people's pocket-handkerchiefs, and make 'em believe you're their friend, and are going to help 'em, and then get their purses.' Meyrick of Trinity reiterated that it was 'right and desirable that University Education should in the main be in the hands of the clergy of the Church'. This was also the view of the Tractarian professor of Hebrew, E. B. Pusey, who in evidence of premonitory length discursed gloomily on the iniquities of the German professorial system, the evil influence of John Locke, the temptations afforded to undergraduates by lodging-houses and the prospect of infidelity which any breach in the monopoly of university education by the Church of England was bound to provoke. But the commissioners, able, conscientious men, toiled on, amassing facts and figures, collecting a veritable farrago of miscellaneous information which it proved extremely difficult to reduce to shape.

Their recommendations, though they did not wholly satisfy radical opinion, were far-reaching. They advised that the university governments should be remodelled to become more democratic in their procedure and less under the influence of the heads of houses; at Cambridge the Senate took over the powers of the Caput and at Oxford the Hebdomadal Council replaced the Hebdomadal Board. They urged the extension of the system of honour schools and triposes. They thought that more attention should be paid to the specialized schools of law and medicine; they were eager to encourage the study of mathematics and science and to raise their standing within the universities. They deprecated the existence of closed fellowships and the requirement that almost all fellows must be in or about to take holy orders of the Church of England. They were strongly in favour of extending the professorial capacity of the university, and they suggested that the colleges should help the university pay the professors' stipends. They were eager to ensure that more people availed themselves of a university education, and they recommended that distinctions between noblemen, gentlemen-commoners and commoners, which Pusey and others so hotly defended, should be eliminated. They wanted to reduce the expenses of a university education; they recommended the setting up of additional private halls and granting undergraduates permission to live 'in private lodgings, without connexion with a College or a Hall', a proposal that naturally raised a storm of protest. They had felt unable to grasp firmly the savage nettle of religious subscription, though they made it clear that they disapproved of the existing position.

The commission had no powers to compel the adoption of its recommendations, and it was apparent that they would be strongly criticized and extensively amended before they were embodied in legal form. Parliament however agreed to establish an executive commission to carry them out. The bill appointing the commission was guided through the Commons with unwearying energy by Gladstone, to whom was also delegated the direction of the University Reform Bill, introduced into the House of Commons on 17 March 1854. James Heywood at once introduced an amendment abolishing all religious tests, which Russell and Gladstone with some reluctance accepted. Eventually a compromise was agreed upon which abolished tests for matriculation and for the first degree. 'Neither in nor out of Oxford,' John Keble wrote gloomily on hearing the news, 'when once this change has taken place, will the old Oxford feeling be possible.' In the end, although the test of orthodoxy was no longer to be applied for matriculation and the bachelor's degree, it was still applicable to the mastership, for a vote in Convocation and for appointment to college fellowships. The bill received the royal assent on 7 August 1854, and a similar bill relating to Cambridge was passed in 1856.

The University Reform Bills were later thought to be too moderate, 'merely an enabling Act,' as Mark Pattison, the future Rector of Lincoln, described the Oxford bill, 'removing two of long standing, and giving very inadequate relief from two others'. The commissioners had not touched, he said later, the 'ark of our covenant', the endowments of the colleges. The religious tests had not been eliminated altogether; the Church of England, though with reduced powers, was still very much in control. The legislation in fact left much standing that was later to be swept away, but by avoiding extreme measures the commissioners succeeded in amending where a more ruthless hand might have destroyed the ancient traditions of Oxford and Cambridge. 'Their spirit,' as the high church *Guardian* phrased it, 'has been conservative and conciliatory ... they have laboured to reform, not to root up, to invigorate, not to revolutionize, the Oxford system.' This policy, though it may have disappointed the radicals, had very real results. The government of the universities had been made less oligarchical, more efficient and representative. The colleges were given a limited amount of time in which to bring their own statutes into line with the commissioners' recommendations; if they failed to do this they were liable to coercion. Lincoln, Corpus Christi and Exeter Colleges re-cast their statutes in their entirety. Other colleges modified their qualifications for fellowships, abolishing the regional restrictions and in some cases the obligation to take holy orders, and suspending some fellowships to provide funds for the new professorial chairs.

Much was done to foster scholarship and research, by revising the system of examinations and introducing new honour schools. In 1848 before the appointment of the commission, Cambridge had decided to institute a Moral Sciences and a Natural Sciences Tripos. The first of these was a portmanteau affair which embraced the study of moral philosophy, political economy, modern history, general jurisprudence and the laws of England; criticized by many dons as fostering a 'shabby superficiality of knowledge' it attracted comparatively little support. Only 66 candidates took the tripos in the first nine years of its existence and none at all in 1860; but in 1868 it gave birth to the Law and History tripos. At Oxford the Law, History and Natural Science Honour Schools had been established in 1853. All told, it looked as if the curricula of the older universities were being brought into line with modern needs.

Perhaps the most dramatic change was in the climate of the universities and colleges. Although vested interests were preserved they had experienced a sharp and salutary shock. Thomas Thornely, a young undergraduate at Trinity Hall in 1873, might in later life recall 'the large limbed, portly ecclesiastics of ample girth and imposing presence, whom one used to see sailing down King's Parade in swelling silks' and W. E. Heitland who went up to St John's, Cambridge, in 1867 could remember dons of the old type who still persisted in his early years as a fellow. But in fact the senior common and combination rooms witnessed the infiltration of an entirely new type of don, lay in interests and inclinations, much more concerned with scholarship and research and deeply interested in his subject; men like the philosopher T. H. Green or the classicist Henry Nettleship who were concerned with breaking new ground in their own fields of study. Few except the gloomily prescient Pusey were as yet aware of it, but the process of secularization had begun. The Oxford liberals enjoyed the fruits of victory: Mark Pattison after an ignominious defeat at the hands of his diehard opponents in 1851 was ten years later elected Rector of Lincoln; Benjamin Jowett was made Master of Balliol. Their appointment must have been particularly galling to the conservatives, for both Pattison and Jowett, along with Frederick Temple and other well-known Oxford dons, had contributed to *Essays and Reviews*, a series of essays that displayed shocking theological modernism and, in the teeth of conservative opposition, had been published in 1860. Other eminent liberals acceded to professorial chairs, A. P. Stanley to that of ecclesiastical history, Goldwin Smith to that of modern history, Conington to that of Latin, Max Müller to that of European languages. Above all the influence of John Stuart Mill and his philosophy suffused radical Oxford thinking.

*

But it was soon plain that for the liberal academics reform had not gone far enough. Although much had been accomplished by the reform acts, they – like the reform act of 1832 – were more important for what they implied than for what they actually did. They offered a demonstration of how to transform deeply conservative institutions without destroying them, how to respect tradition while adapting it to contemporary needs. But the forces of change had been set in motion and this precariously balanced compromise could not last long. The new legislation weakened and at the same time called in question the privileged position of the Church of England, but it did not do away with it. It compelled the universities to provide new professorships, lecture rooms, laboratories and libraries but did not take action to secure enough funds for them; the autonomy of the colleges and their financial affairs went unchallenged. Although the liberals, under pressure of a Tory reaction, found their forces at Oxford less strong than their optimism had led them to believe, and although their leaders were divided and as persons somewhat lacking in attraction, the force they represented was plainly in the ascendant; more changes were to come.

In the twenty or so years which elapsed before the second royal commission of 1872, liberal and secular thinking spread far and wide. The malcontents seized upon the problem of the religious tests. The Oxford bill, as we have seen, laid down that no oath or declaration of belief should be required at matriculation or for a degree of lesser standing than that of M.A., but office-holding and membership of Convocation, the final legislative body in the university consisting of all masters and doctors on hall or college books, were still confined to Anglicans. The Cambridge bill permitted all degrees, except those in divinity, to be taken without subscription; but only Anglicans could become members of the Senate or fellows of a college. Although enlightened churchmen like J. B. Lightfoot and W. E. Gladstone wholeheartedly supported measures for the abolition of religious tests, the tests represented to many dons the last bulwark against infidelity and immorality. Lord Robert Cecil, opposing a bill which had been introduced by Pleydell-Bouverie in 1863 to allow colleges to throw open their fellowships to non-Anglicans, asserted that the bill would not merely 'change the character of the universities as religious seminaries, but . . . destroy their influence and position altogether'. The Cambridge Senate passed a grace petitioning against the bill (which was refused a second reading) by 120 to 25 votes. Few years passed without some attempt to bring about parliamentary legislation on this matter. In 1869 a bill passed the Commons but was thrown out by the House of Lords. It could not, however, be delayed indefinitely, and in 1871 to a chorus of gloomy prognostications from elderly clerics the bill received the royal assent. 'It had taken eight years,' D. A. Winstanley wrote, 'of parliamentary warfare and public agitation to overthrow a system which was highly detrimental to the efficiency of the Universities, an affliction to tender consciences, and harmful to the reputation of the Church of England.'*

It now remained to 'liberalize' the educational system of the universities. It was not only the senior common and combination rooms that had experienced the impact of social change in the past two decades; it had had repercussions in the junior common rooms too. The undergraduates, though the majority had always been children of the gentry or richer middle classes, had been very variously prepared for university. Some were the well-taught products of private tuition, others the victims of the haphazard and primitive methods of the old public schools. A new phenomenon had, however, appeared which was to condition the social structure of the older universities until the end of the Second World War, the Victorian public school, representative of an expanding system of education designed to meet the needs of the affluent middle class. These schools fulfilled admirably the requirements which society placed upon them, to act as a training ground for colonial administrators and civil servants, for politicians and lawyers, but their products were not necessarily reading men. The acidulous Rector of Lincoln saw his hopes of a genuinely intellectual revolution foiled through the grafting on to university life of the ideas and values of the contemporary public school; those of Christianity influenced by a Platonic conception of the good life in which stress was laid on athletic achievement. Much as Pattison might deprecate the 'mastery which the athletic furor has established over all minds in this place', he was fighting a losing battle. It was the views of Jowett, the influential master of Balliol, that commanded respect; for him the function of the university was education rather than scholarship, education for life in the public-school understanding of the phrase. The chief duty of the tutorial fellows was to teach the undergraduates, only incidentally to undertake research.

Pattison's opposition to this point of view was made plain in his important and prophetic book, *Academical Organ-*

*D. A. Winstanley, *Later Victorian Cambridge*, Cambridge University Press, 1947, p. 89.

ization, published in 1868. 'Let Oxford become,' he wrote, 'as nothing but artificial legislation prevents it from becoming, the first school of science and learning in the world.' Insisting that neither the universities nor the colleges were private enterprises but national institutions, he recognized that state interference could only be kept at bay if both made the fullest use of their endowments. Pattison would have eliminated the pass man from the university altogether, for he did not think it the function of the university to provide a home for the 'foppish exquisite of the drawing-room, or the barbarized athlete of the arena'. He would have reduced even further the extent of clerical influence. He recommended that fellowships should be awarded for research which in the present state of affairs was being sacrificed to teaching. 'The fact that so few books of profound research emanate from the University of Oxford materially impairs its character as a seat of learning, and consequently its hold on the respect of the nation.' He was eager to ensure that poor men could avail themselves of the education that the university offered, and he was concerned to encourage the study of science. Indeed he went so far as to suggest that Merton and Corpus Christi should be combined to form a single college for the study of biology, chemistry and other branches of science.

Above all he urged that the university should aim at producing a 'professional class of learned and scientific men'. The chief function of the university, he repeated time and time again, was learning and research. 'We shall never place our University on a sure footing as long as we regard the undergraduate alone as the end and purpose of the institution.' But the cause which he was preaching was not a popular one in late nineteenth-century Oxford or Cambridge. The universities were to be geared to the needs of contemporary society, and administrators were more necessary than research workers. 'The separation between Jowett and myself,' Pattison wrote, 'consists in a difference upon the fundamental question of university politics – viz. Science and Learning v. School keeping.' It was Jowett whose word was to prevail.

But even Jowett's ideals could not be realized without further reform. In 1872 Gladstone's government established a new commission under the chairmanship of the Duke of Cleveland, this time with a brief to inquire into the revenues and properties of the two older universities. It was a comment on changing ideas that the legislation necessary to implement the commission's recommendations was introduced by a Tory ministry. Many new chairs and readerships were established, and the richer colleges called to contribute towards their upkeep. A common university fund was founded which was to be administered by a specially appointed delegacy. New regulations provided that professors should be appointed by boards of electors and established faculties of theology, law, arts and sciences. The colleges were given to the end of 1878 to make further changes in their statutes; as a result fellows were no longer required to be celibate or to take holy orders. These reforms were to determine the character of the universities and colleges until the royal commission of 1923.

*

By 1880 the pattern of modern Oxford and Cambridge had been set. They had become lively centres of educational activity and of genuine scholarship, supplying the nation with its clergy, its administrators, its schoolmasters and its professional men. In spite of their preoccupation with teaching, they had also established a world-wide reputation for scholarship. They had as yet few competitors, even among the newly founded universities, so that a professorial chair at Oxford or Cambridge represented, as it long continued to do, the crown of academic achievement. A fellowship at a college provided a comfortable and civilized environment in which a serious scholar could work without too many calls on his time or too great an intrusion of outside anxieties or administrative demands. Few fellows, though they were now free to do so, made any headlong rush into marriage.

The conservative rearguard at both universities watched the crumbling of the bulwarks with dismay; the publication of Charles Darwin's *Origin of Species* in 1859, the famous meeting of the British Association at Oxford and the appearance of

Essays and Reviews in 1860, and the failure of the attempt in 1863 to impeach Jowett for heresy, all accelerated the erosion of the established order. 'An indefinite extension of the professoriate,' Lord Francis Hervey gloomily observed in 1876, 'meant a number of luxurious residences, children in perambulators wheeled about in the Parks, picnics in Bagley Wood, carriages, champagne, and the abandonment of celibacy and culture.' But to abandon one was not necessarily to abandon the other; while the diehards sulked in their comfortable rooms, there were few signs of the disasters they had predicted. Their younger disciples came to terms with modern thought. In philosophy utilitarianism waned and idealism gained ground, providing an opportunity for a *rapprochement* with theology. Historical and legal studies were based more surely than they had been in the past on original sources; theological scholars adopted similar techniques. There was a growing if tardy realization of the importance of natural science. All the portents pointed away from the old theological view of knowledge as the exposition of a received body of information towards a genuine spirit of critical inquiry and a readiness to widen the field of man's understanding.

Once more full, flourishing and prosperous, though adversely affected by the agricultural depression of the eighties, the universities of Oxford and Cambridge seemed to have weathered the storm. They had lost the political and ecclesiastical status they had once enjoyed but they had gained immeasurably in scholarship and international reputation. They had been transformed out of all recognition from the old-fashioned and exclusive semi-clerical seminaries of the early 1800s into world-reputed centres of research and learning.

CHAPTER FIVE

The Scottish Universities

THE Scottish universities had a very different history, and followed a pattern more familiar on the continent than in England. Political and economic differences had from a common origin bred two distinct types of university, producing at Oxford and Cambridge a strong sense of community centred on a nucleus of inherited collegiate wealth and on the continent a more open and flexible structure which employed a rudimentary collegiate system but never allowed the colleges the controlling interest they had assumed in England. At some of the continental universities the students possessed powers which placed even their professors at a disadvantage, and exercised an effective influence on university government, represented vestigially even now by the Scottish system of allowing students to elect their rector. In general the students were allowed to live where they liked and their extra-curricular activities did not come within the scope of university discipline. As a result of this somewhat amorphous character there was very limited contact between the teaching body, which used the lecture as the main method of instruction, and the students. The frequent migration of teachers and students from one university to another led to a stimulating exchange of ideas but further weakened the sense of community.

The Scottish universities were close to the continental in their teaching and organization, though they did not display all the same characteristics and were differentiated from them, as from their English contemporaries, by special political and economic factors. In a country as poor as Scotland they could not hope to expand on a large scale, let alone build up colleges to compare with those that did so much to determine the character of Oxford and Cambridge. Although they enjoyed a certain degree of autonomy, they were more susceptible to external pressures, from the Crown, the Kirk and, at Edinburgh, the town council. Most undergraduates went to the university nearest to the area in which they lived; at first few were as well equipped as their English counterparts who benefited in the sixteenth and seventeenth centuries from the existence of richly endowed grammar schools. The life of the universities was often dislocated by internal dissension that wasted already meagre resources; ludicrously Aberdeen housed two institutions of university status, King's College and Marischal College, in bitter rivalry with each other.

In these unpromising conditions of political and religious strife and of the material poverty that prevailed until in the eighteenth century the opening up of the Atlantic trade made industrial development possible, it is remarkable that the universities survived at all, and astonishing that they should have continued to produce scholars of such quality that, at least in the eighteenth century, stimulated by comparatively progressive if not consistently excellent teaching, they cast Oxford and Cambridge into the shade. Early in their history the universities became an essential element in Scottish national life, representing a cultural tradition so deeply engrained that in Scotland's darkest days it was never wholly obscured. Their existence may be explained in terms of the church's need for learned ministers, especially after the abolition of episcopacy, but they were never merely recruiting grounds for the presbytery. They were cherished by national feeling and were regarded with pride as an expression of Scottish scholarship.

It may seem surprising that Scotland had no universities until the fifteenth century. The explanation is primarily a matter of politics. Medieval Scotland was sparsely populated and those who wished to avail themselves of a university education were, as elsewhere, mainly men intending to take or already in holy orders. Some went to Oxford and Cambridge. Robert Bruce's brother, Alexander, who became Dean of Glasgow, studied at Cambridge. When political conditions strained relations between England and Scotland, the young Scots travelled to foreign universities, to Orleans and especially to Paris, where there was a strong Scots colony; in 1326 the

Bishop of Moray set up a special fund to assist students from his diocese studying there.

Two events changed this situation. The first was the outbreak of the Great Schism in 1378. The election of rival popes, Urban VI and Clement VII, divided allegiance along national lines, England following Pope Urban, France and Scotland upholding the claims of Pope Clement. The Scots, already alienated from England by political hostilities, were deterred all the more from studying in English universities. They were soon to be discouraged from studying in France too. The political situation there was confused. The sporadic insanity of the king, Charles VI, and the concurrent rivalry of aristocratic groups, Burgundians, Orleanists and Armagnacs, made Paris a turbulent city. The authorities in church and state, influenced particularly by the cogent arguments of the rector of the university of Paris, Jean Gerson, were drifting towards an attitude of neutrality in regard to the claims of the two popes. The Scots, who had remained loyal to the Clementine pope, Benedict XIII, found this intolerable and forsook the French universities as well.

In May 1410 a group of Scottish masters, most of whom had originally graduated at Paris, began to teach at St Andrews and in 1412 acquired recognition from the bishop, Henry Wardlaw, who subsequently secured a charter for the establishment of a university there from Pope Benedict, then exercising a very much diminished sway over his faithful followers from a remote outpost in Peñiscola. The foundation of the first Scottish university was thus the outcome of ecclesiastical politics, but in its early years its growth was somewhat slow. The fifteenth century witnessed the birth of two other universities, one founded at Glasgow in 1451 by Bishop Turnbull and the other at Aberdeen in 1494 by Bishop William Elphinstone. These new foundations owed their existence to other forces at work in Scottish national life.

The cultural climate of Scotland in the fifteenth century was curiously and inexplicably rich, fostering native writers and poets who have not ceased to be read. It is difficult to account for this resurgence of culture in a country which was in so many ways still disordered, primitive and poor, but by comparison with other periods in Scotland's history this was a time of peace and even of security. The court, especially in the days of James IV, was a centre of patronage. There were fruitful contacts with the continent. The future pope, Pius II, visited Scotland on a diplomatic mission, observing on his journey that 'there is nothing the Scots like better to hear than abuse of the English'. For some time the continental universities continued to attract Scottish scholars, many of whom studied at the feet of the Italian stylists of the Renaissance and at the university of Cologne, and through them Renaissance thought and scholarship made its way north. John Major, who had studied at Cambridge and taught at Paris, in 1518 became the principal regent at Glasgow, leaving four years later for St Andrews where, after a further sojourn in Paris, he became provost of St Salvator's College. He had a well-deserved reputation as a political thinker and was one of the last great scholastic writers. Of almost equal distinction was Hector Boece, who had studied and taught at Paris and was associated with Bishop Elphinstone in founding the university at Aberdeen where he collected a group of scholars and learned teachers. Although he was so much engrossed in administrative work, Boece found time to write biography and history, publishing in 1527, six years after the publication of Major's *Latin History of Greater Britain*, a valuable history of Scotland. Even Erasmus wrote to Boece congratulating him upon the contribution which Scotland was making to the learned arts; and that great scholar was genuinely moved when he learned that Archbishop Stewart of St Andrews, under whose aegis St Leonard's College at St Andrews had come into existence, had died on the battlefield at Flodden.

The new universities naturally adopted the scholastic curriculum and the academic government typical of other late medieval universities. In organization they bore the impress of their continental antecedents, especially of Paris, though the statutes of St Andrews as revised by Bishop Kennedy owed something to those of Cologne University. When Pope Nicholas V approved the establishment of a *studium generale* at Glasgow he specifically bestowed on its members the privileges and exemptions enjoyed by members of Bologna university, a city of which he had been bishop, probably to stress that he was giving to the new foundation the best that he could bestow. The new constitution, however, was in general modelled on that of St Andrews. The constitution of Aberdeen was similar to that of St Andrews, but owed something to the pattern of Orleans where Bishop Elphinstone had studied civil law.

The universities were divided into 'nations', each under the presidency of a procurator; Fife, Angus, Lothian and Alban (i.e. the rest of Britain) at St Andrews, Clydesdale, Teviotdale, Albany and Rothesay at Glasgow, Mar, Buchan, Moray and Angus at Aberdeen. The effective head of the university was the rector, who was surrounded on state occasions with due ceremonial. He summoned the general congregations or *comitia* consisting of all who had matriculated in the university. He was chosen by a system of indirect election; at Glasgow each of the procurators of the four nations selected four 'intrants' who then nominated the rector. Although the rector's judicial and disciplinary powers were considerable, they were not absolute, for he was subordinate both to the chancellor, who for a long period was usually the bishop of the diocese, and to certain university officials, at Glasgow his four deputies and the procurators, at St Andrews an official known as the conservator. The teaching masters were organized in faculties presided over by a dean. The curriculum, differing little from that of other universities of the period, was scholastic in substance, sustained by lectures and examined by means of exercises, disputations and determinations. The age of admission was low. At Glasgow in 1535 a boy of thirteen was allowed to determine, that is to maintain a thesis in the scholastic disputations which completed the exercises for the B.A. degree. At St Andrews the faculty of arts insisted on a minimum age of fifteen for a determinant, thus suggesting that thirteen was the normal age of entry.

The founders appear to have hoped that their universities would develop along collegiate lines. Bishop Kennedy set up

St Salvator's at St Andrews in 1450, providing for its income by appropriating to it the teinds, or tithes, of four parishes in Fife: Cults, Kemback, Dunino and Kilmany. Possibly on the model of New College, Oxford, it was intended to maintain a provost, two teachers of theology, four masters of arts and six poor scholars, the numbers doubtless a deliberate play on the Saviour and the twelve apostles. In 1512 Prior Hepburn turned the hospital of St Leonard into a college of poor clerks. In 1537 Archbishop Beaton, made anxious by the speculative teaching which he associated with St Leonard's, founded another college at St Andrews, St Mary's. At Aberdeen the college of St Mary of the Nativity, usually known as King's College in honour of its patron, James IV, was founded in 1505.

*

After promising beginnings the early life of the universities was complicated by the confusions of political and religious strife. King James I, supported by the Bishop of Glasgow, after his return from imprisonment in England, followed an anti-papal policy and tried to remove the college recently founded at St Andrews to Perth where it would have been more securely under royal control. Even in the fifteenth century Scottish scholars who wished to deepen their scholarship and to secure papal patronage and preferment were tempted to study abroad and so failed to complete their courses at the native universities, to the loss of the latter. University expansion was hamstrung by lack of revenues and was often the battleground of rival factions. At St Andrews the enmity between the Pedagogy* and St Salvator's reached such a height in 1470 that men from the college attacked their opponents with bows and arrows. Closely tied to the church and their archiepiscopal chancellors (St Andrews became an

---

*The *Paedogogium* or Pedagogy was the name given to the house attached to the Faculty of Arts where lectures were given and residence was provided. It was situated on a tenement given by Bishop Wardlaw in 1430 (R. G. Cant, *The University of St Andrews*, Edinburgh, 1946, pp. 14–15).

archbishopric in 1465, Glasgow in 1483) the universities were inevitably disorientated by the changes that followed the victory of Protestantism, though some of their more learned scholars had already been attracted by the new religious ideas.

The Protestant reformers had no intention of destroying the universities, but they wished to ensure that they became seminaries suitable for the godly ministry and centres of scriptural faith and learning. Although they detested Aristotelianism, they contemplated few changes in the curriculum itself. Their plans, formulated in the First Book of Discipline published in January 1561, envisaged a national system of education under the general supervision of the Kirk, to be carried out by three colleges at St Andrews, one for arts and medicine, one for theology and one for moral philosophy and two in Glasgow and Aberdeen. This scheme was never put into operation, for political affairs continued confused and inflammable. The universities in fact could do little more than hold their own, preserve their property from confiscation and keep an eye open for any benefits that might come their way. Glasgow acquired a small endowment from Queen Mary which had been formerly in the possession of the Blackfriars. In 1563 the Scottish Parliament appointed a commission, which included the scholarly reformer George Buchanan, to visit St Andrews and to propose improvements, but these seem never to have been implemented. Eleven years later the Regent Morton went to St Andrews to remedy defects in its government, but it was not until 1579 that a new constitution, the *nova erectio*, was promulgated.

By this time the more or less complete predominance of the Kirk and the need to ensure a supply of ministers trained on Genevan lines conditioned the immediate future of Scottish higher education. The new constitution of St Andrews, which reinforced the close connexion between the reformed church and the universities, made provision for additional theological professorships, among them a chair of Hebrew. It was probably drawn up by Andrew Melville, a scholar of great distinction who had been professor of humanity at the Genevan academy; certainly it represented his views. An able administrator and an inflexible controversialist, Melville came to St Andrews in 1580 after providing a new constitution for the university at Glasgow.

The reform of St Andrews and Glasgow seems to have stimulated the town councillors of Edinburgh to initiate an undertaking long under discussion but never as yet set in motion, the establishment of a 'college of theology' to provide 'useful members to serve the Kirk of God and the commonwealth'. With the approval of James VI, the town council decided in 1582 to utilize the estates and resources granted to it by Queen Mary from the despoiled church to found a college. The first students were admitted in 1583. Some additional endowments were acquired, among them the residue of a bequest made by Robert Reid, the Bishop of Orkney, who had died in 1558 leaving 8,000 marks for an institution providing courses in canon and civil law, a condition which the college for long failed to fulfil. Ten years later, on 2 April 1593, George Keith, fifth Earl Marischal, founded a college with faculties and the right to grant degrees at Aberdeen.

Although the foundation of these colleges, for they do not yet fully deserve the name of universities, reasserted the dominance of the Kirk and in some sense the insularity of Scottish higher education, the late sixteenth century had brought a refreshing breath of air into university scholarship. Andrew Melville had studied under Peter Ramus, the leading critic of the Aristotelian method, and subsequently transplanted the new methods of teaching to Scotland. The Aristotelian pundits of St Leonard's were 'owirhurled' by Melville's determined policy. Under his stimulus the universities leaped into new life. He offered chairs to the English Puritans Thomas Cartwright and Walter Travers. 'No place in Europe,' his nephew James commented, 'comparable to Glasgow for guid letters, during these yeirs, for a plentiful and guid chepe mercat of all kynd of langages, artes and sciences.'

The universities, however, were not to be allowed uninterrupted growth. They were dogged by the bitter ecclesiastical controversies which caused such havoc in Scottish life until 1690. The Crown took an interest in the universities both from a sincere desire to encourage learning and from an awareness of the need to create the nucleus of a party loyal to itself and devoted to episcopacy. Charles I demonstrated his devotion by confirming the university of Glasgow in the possession of its ecclesiastical revenues and subscribing £200 towards college building, though ironically enough it was left to Oliver Cromwell to carry out the royal promise in 1654. The universities were the nursery not merely of the future ministers of the Scottish church but of the sons of lairds and lords who would one day be prominent in Scottish national life. 'Has my Lord, your father, sent you heir,' a principal of Glasgow remarked severely to a son of Lord Herries, 'to spend your tyme with debauchit persones of the town?' University affairs were the affairs of the country, and to control them was vital to the control of Scotland itself.

Opposing the court and the bishops there stood the Kirk and the presbytery. The career of Andrew Melville dramatized the issues involved. He was an adamant opponent of the episcopal system, concerned to establish the presbyteral form of church government and critical of the royal headship of the church; it was he who in 1596 had plucked James VI by the sleeve and called him 'God's silly vassal'. In 1585 he made a carefully prepared attack on the king's powers in church affairs and had to flee suddenly to England, where he made contact with the Puritan dons at Oxford and Cambridge. Eventually he made his peace with the king, but this did not prevent James, after the General Assembly, meeting at Perth in 1597, had witnessed a successful attempt to increase royal authority over the church, from visiting St Andrews and depriving Melville of the rectorship. Melville continued, however, as principal of St Mary's and in 1599 was made dean of the faculty of theology. James esteemed Melville's erudition and may possibly have been flattered by the Latin ode which Melville wrote to commemorate his accession to the English throne, but he could not tolerate for ever defiance over ecclesiastical matters from a long-winded, learned and pugnacious man who had been known to clutch at the archbishop's rochet and exclaimed 'Romish rags'. Deprived of his principalship, he was held in custody, characteristically covering the walls of the room in which he was confined with Latin verses written with his shoe buckle, before he was given permission to go into exile in France. But his ideas were not so easily banished; his antagonism to the bishops and to the royal supremacy in the church and his vigorous affirmation that Presbyterianism was the only scripturally acceptable form of church government typified a point of view clung to by many in the Scottish universities.

*

The early seventeenth century was a period of uneasy peace, stirred by underlying tensions. King James's policy did not lack wisdom. He was eager to conciliate the moderates who held, possibly correctly, that only cooperation with the Crown could provide the stable government necessary for the cultivation of true religion and scholarship. Aberdeen prospered under the wise governance of Bishop Patrick Forbes. At St Andrews Archbishop Gladstanes set up a new commission of visitation in 1607 (which included the future primate George Abbot among its members) and seems to have envisaged remodelling the university along the lines of Oxford and Cambridge, but after he died in 1615 its life was largely uneventful and undistinguished. But swift currents of dissatisfaction were flowing under the surface. At Edinburgh one of the regents, James Reid, provoked by a local minister's assertion that philosophy was the 'dish-clout of Divinity' declared in reply that 'Aristippus said he would rather be a Christian philosopher than an unphilosophical divine'; he was denounced to the town council and obliged to resign, though compensated with an honorarium. At St Andrews Archbishop Laud, who had come to Scotland for the coronation of Charles I in 1633, tried to reinstitute university services in the ruinous church of St Salvator's. These were, however, matters of trivial moment, soon eclipsed by the thunder of real war.

The Bishops' Wars (1639–40), so called because they were

caused by Scottish dislike of the English prayer book and episcopacy, ended with a momentous victory for the presbytery which was bound to leave its mark on the universities. Except at Edinburgh, where the town council was the ultimate authority, the universities had been subject to episcopal control. At St Andrews there was at first some opposition to the National Covenant (1638) which pledged the Scots to insist that the English withdraw the hated prayer book, but the dons soon came to terms with their Presbyterian rulers. At Edinburgh the appointment in 1640 of Alexander Henderson, 'minister of the Great Kirk of Edinburgh', as rector of the university opened a period of progress. The universities all gained financially as a result of revenues granted to them from the four Scottish bishoprics which had been dissolved. The General Assembly had no wish to diminish the usefulness of the universities, but felt some changes were called for; when it met at St Andrews in 1641 it instituted a commission of visitation.

The commissioners' work lasted seven years, their final report seeking to standardize the curriculum for all universities, though preserving scholasticism as its dominant feature. The Kirk naturally sought to reinforce its control. 'Pondering how important the right constitution of the College of Divinity may be for the whole Kirk of Scotland' the commissioners decided to place the appointment of the divinity professors at St Andrews in the hands of the General Assembly. Everywhere minute attention was paid to the students' spiritual welfare. At St Andrews they were to be catechized each Wednesday; on Sunday mornings the regents were required to expound the 'controversies of religion' before the college went to worship at the parish kirk. At Glasgow as elsewhere the celebration of saints' days had ceased and the students were no longer obliged to attend church except on Sundays, but the masters, besides reading the scriptures to their classes, were to inquire 'what conscience each scholler makes of secret devotion, each morning'.

The Restoration almost inevitably ushered in a period of despondency, since it meant not merely the loss of revenue, as the estates taken from the forfeited bishoprics were restored to them, but a return to episcopal governance and a renewed attempt to consolidate royal control. Yet it was during this time that Glasgow enjoyed for five years the services of the future historian and bishop, Gilbert Burnet, as professor of divinity. At St Andrews the chair of mathematics was held by James Gregory, the friend of Newton and a ripe scholar. Edinburgh saw the beginnings of the medical school, sponsored by the enthusiasm for botany of Sir Robert Sibbold and his associates; in 1685 the town council appointed three members of the College of Physicians (which had secured a patent from the Duke of York four years earlier), Sibbold among them, to be professors of medicine in the 'University in this city', one of the first occasions on which the college had been officially so described.

*

The fall of James II and the accession of William III in 1689 reversed the policy initiated by the Restoration, once again the bishops gave way to the Kirk. The policy of conciliation which was to lead to the Act of Union in 1707, though not unopposed, was in full swing, and the universities benefited from it. The Scottish gentry and nobility still preferred to send their sons to complete their education at a native university and it was through the universities that the Crown hoped to forward the essential task of wooing the governing classes from their attachment to the Jacobite dynasty. It seemed equally important to have in the church a well-informed and well-disposed ministry.

The Crown therefore revived its policy of patronage. William III granted £300 a year to each of the four societies from the revenues of the former bishoprics. In 1693 he approved the appointment of an additional professor of theology and the award of bursaries in divinity. A regius chair of ecclesiastical history was established at Edinburgh in 1702; Queen Anne modified the grants which William III had made to the universities but founded a chair of law at Edinburgh, at long last fulfilling Bishop Reid's request. At Glasgow, already the recipient of some useful benefactions, among them the money left by John Snell in 1677 to enable students from Glasgow to study at Oxford, eight new chairs were founded and the university's teaching capacity thus greatly enlarged. The chair of mathematics was held by George Sinclair, known as the author of the doubtless compelling *Satan's Invisible World Discovered* and of treatises on mathematics, hydro-statics and astronomy, a man who had in 1670 been largely responsible for bringing the water supply to Edinburgh and who utilized the system of measuring the height of hills by noting, with the aid of mercury, the changes in atmospheric pressure. Grants to Glasgow from the Crown, always eager to foster loyalty among its alumni, proved a mutually profitable investment. When the Jacobite threat loomed with frightening nearness in 1715 the faculty bravely agreed to supply a company of foot-soldiers, so winning for themselves, as Townshend put it, a 'just title to his Majesties favour when the concerns of the Faculty shall require it'. A year later George I allotted £100 for the establishment of a chair of ecclesiastical history and £70 for the augmentation of professorial stipends.

In this burgeoning of university life St Andrews continued the only withered branch. Although it too enjoyed the royal bounty, its colleges, never very generously endowed, suffered from the reversion of the parish tithes to their original purpose without compensation, and the buildings went to rack and ruin. The fundamental reasons for the decay of St Andrews were political. Although the Convention Parliament of 1690, which had offered William and Mary the Crown of Scotland and asked for the abolition of the 'great and intolerable griev-ance' of episcopacy, had purged the university of senior mem-bers suspected of favouring the exiled Stuart king, James II, the university was still associated in the mind of the English government with disaffection. Indeed its reputation was such that in 1697 its chancellor, the future Duke of Atholl, sug-gested that it should be removed to Aberdeen. In 1718 a com-mittee of visitation arrived to restore loyalty and true learning. By 1745 it had learned that it was more desirable to conform, and offered its chancellorship to the Duke of Cumberland, later the ill-reputed victor of Culloden. But the town of St Andrews, no longer the ecclesiastical capital of Scotland, had ceased to prosper; it compared unfavourably with Glasgow, now enriched by the American trade and by the new pattern of finance and industry. It was thought expedient to unite the three colleges into a single entity, though only St Salvator's and St Leonard's were amalgamated, the buildings of the latter being sold for an absurdly small sum and its church left to fall into ruin. 'Had the university been destroyed two centuries ago,' Dr Johnson commented during a visit to St Andrews in 1773,

we should not have regretted it, but to see it pining in decay and struggling for life fills the mind with mournful images and ineffectual wishes. . . . It is surely not without just reproach that a nation, of which the commerce is hourly extending, and the wealth increasing, denies any participation of its prosperity to its literary societies; and, while its merchants or its nobles are raising palaces, suffers its universities to moulder into dust.

The charge was in fact less than just, for although St Andrews could boast no more than one hundred and fifty students, Aberdeen had three hundred, Edinburgh six hundred and Glasgow four hundred. While these universities were not free from the abuses seemingly endemic in the ecclesiastical and intellectual life of eighteenth-century Britain, such as nepotism, patronage, factiousness and neglect of duty, as centres of learning and intellectual activity they could claim to be superior to Oxford and Cambridge. At Glasgow, for which a commission appointed in 1727 had issued a new body of statutes, the eighteenth century was a period of many-sided achievement, and this in spite of the oligarchical control exerted by an intensely quarrelsome faculty solicitous of its rights, and of the influence, now declining, of the Kirk, with its closely meshed interests of kinship and patronage. The autobiography of 'Jupiter' Carlyle revealed a society in which there was a good deal of social intercourse between senior and junior members of the university who met together to discuss literature and recent books. He mentions a performance of Addison's *Cato* in which the heroine's part was taken by the principal's pretty young daughter, Molly Campbell. The Literary Society of Glasgow, founded in 1752, numbered lairds, merchants and professional men among its members as well as professors. The presence of distinguished scholars, some of whom achieved a European reputation, must have stimulated intellectual life. In a university where the study of logic was still dominant, it is hardly surprising to find a galaxy of well-known names. Francis Hutcheson, who lectured in English (rather than the usual Latin), a liberal in outlook, the correspondent of David Hume, was the author of influential works in moral philosophy. His pupil Adam Smith, after a period as Snell exhibitioner at Oxford, went as a lecturer to Edinburgh, returning to Glasgow as professor in 1751. He resigned his chair in 1764, but his acquaintance with Glasgow businessmen and his study of logic and moral philosophy stood him in good stead when he came to write *The Wealth of Nations*. Probably the most distinguished of the other professors was John Millar, a brilliant lecturer and teacher who held the chair of law, two of whose pupils became professors at Moscow.

The progress made in mathematical and scientific studies was the more impressive when contrasted with the state of affairs at the English universities. The professor of mathematics, Robert Simson, was reputed for his rediscovery of the 'Grecian Geometry'. Robert Dick, professor of natural philosophy from 1751 to 1757, was the patron and helper of James Watt, whom he appointed to clean and repair some astronomical instruments recently bequeathed to the university. Watt resided in the university as 'mathematical instrument maker' from 1757 to 1763 and continued to act in that capacity until 1773. It was at the suggestion of a student, John Robison, later lecturer in chemistry, that Watt turned his attention to the application of steam to the propulsion of wheeled vehicles and so set to work in 1763 on a model of the Newcomen engine. The university subscribed £200 towards the execution of Watt's plan for a canal to bring coal more cheaply from Monkland to Glasgow. After he moved south Watt still kept in contact with the university and in 1806 was given the degree of doctor of laws. In chemistry Dutch influence, especially the work of Boerhaave, whose *Elementa Chemiae* was translated in 1727, fostered a more systematic study of the subject. Joseph Black, who held chairs of medicine and chemistry at Glasgow and Edinburgh, made some important discoveries, among them the phenomenon of the latent heat of steam.

At Edinburgh the development of the medical school was the most significant event. The college of surgeons, which had received a new charter in 1694, was enabled by the town council's grant of unowned corpses to open an anatomical theatre, but conditions long remained primitive, even after a professorship of anatomy had been created in 1705 for Robert Elliott. In 1720 Alexander Monro, who had studied at London and Paris and at Leyden under Boerhaave, was appointed professor of anatomy and this inaugurated a new era, for he established a proper anatomical school (wisely sited in the college buildings after an Edinburgh mob, roused by rumours of body-snatching, had launched an attack on the surgeons' hall) and soon attracted an increasing number of students, especially after the establishment of the Royal Infirmary in 1738 which facilitated clinical studies. The foundation of chairs of medicine was in part a result of the enlightened policy of the town council, much influenced by George Drummond, the provost from 1715 to 1766. In other respects Edinburgh showed less initiative than Glasgow, though the cultured society which flourished there, of which the *Edinburgh Review* was the quintessence, testified to the continuing intellectual life of the Scottish capital.

It is not easy to explain the exuberance of Scottish culture at this time.* It must surely reflect the excellence of the parish and high schools, fostered by legislation in 1646 and 1696, which were controlled by the Kirk but were paid for by a compulsory assessment levied on landlord and tenant, and served to create a society that was literate, mobile, and, if spiritually authoritarian, socially democratic. Perhaps it was

---

* cf. the views of H. R. Trevor-Roper, 'The Scottish Enlightenment', in *Studies in Voltaire and the Eighteenth Century*, ed. T. Besterman, lviii, 1635–58, Geneva, 1967.

partly a sequel to the growing wealth of Scottish society, the comparative prosperity of Glasgow as a result of the Atlantic trade (though the loss of the American colonies caused a severe if temporary economic depression there) and the vitality of urban life sustained by an interchange between academic and mercantile society not to be found at Oxford or Cambridge. Perhaps the fact that the Kirk exerted less effective control than it had once done is not unrelated. In theory the powers of the Kirk were still considerable; an act designed to exclude Episcopalians and Jacobites from the universities had been passed in 1690, obliging all professors to make a declaration before the Presbytery that they accepted the confession of faith and the formularies of the Church of Scotland. In practice a requirement that could have given the Kirk a stranglehold on the universities was only a formality, easily evaded or complied with. The Kirk naturally controlled the appointments to the theological professorships, but in eighteenth-century Scotland theology was a comparatively unimportant subject. 'The professor's Theology,' commented 'Jupiter' Carlyle, 'was dull and Dutch and prolix.'

By and large the climate of the Scottish universities in the eighteenth century was secular and liberal. The prevailing tone was set by the moral philosophers, among whom David Hume was the most influential figure, and was represented by the sympathy shown in its early stages for the French Revolution. At Glasgow three academics cheered the fall of the Bastille: the lawyer John Millar presided over a dinner to celebrate the event, the philosopher Thomas Reid, who succeeded Adam Smith, subscribed to a fund to aid the revolutionaries, and John Anderson presented the French with his shock-absorbing gun-carriage and balloons for carrying messages. St Andrews awarded a medical degree to the future revolutionary Jean-Paul Marat, a strange enough choice but not so bizarre as it might seem, since these degrees, at least at St Andrews, were no more than a formality. Only in medicine were degrees taken at all; the curriculum had at long last shaken itself free of scholasticism and its rituals, and students in other disciplines no longer bothered to graduate. The serious student who might come from any class of Scottish society,* was therefore free to follow courses of an interesting modern character, and in this he was helped by the teaching system. The Scottish professor was more likely to be a specialist than the tutor who was responsible for teaching all subjects at Oxford and Cambridge. These conditions provided fertile ground for the ideas of Bacon, Newton and Locke, and for the influence of the Dutch universities, especially of Leyden and Utrecht, so that the eighteenth century saw the Scottish universities, excepting St Andrews, become more adventurous and dynamic while their counterparts in England were suffocating under the weight of tradition.

*

The picture, however, was not entirely rosy. St Andrews was moribund, and elsewhere there were many signs of neglect and factiousness. At Glasgow the faculty formed an academic oligarchy, manipulating its privileges in the spirit of a narrow and self-regarding corporation. At Edinburgh the relations between the town council who held the ultimate authority over the university, and the Senatus Academicus, relations which had been friendly for most of the eighteenth century, deteriorated rapidly after 1815. In 1810 the town council had passed an act regulating the matriculation fee and making it compulsory for all students, but the Senate thought that the town Council exceeded its powers when in 1815 it interfered with the distribution of the matriculation fund without consulting the university authorities. The Senate protested and in 1824 made a claim not easily supportable in law, that they possessed an 'exclusive right both to originate and carry into execution' all arrangements for graduation. A bitter struggle then broke out over the medical curriculum and the appointment of a

* Between 1740 and 1839 13 per cent of the students at Glasgow came from families of the nobility and landed gentry (by comparison with 35 per cent at Cambridge between 1752 and 1849), and 11 per cent from industry and commerce (at Cambridge 8 per cent). Whereas there were virtually no working-class children at Cambridge, at Glasgow a third came from labouring families.

professor of midwifery which ended with the town council's decision to impose a visitation on the university. The Senate then petitioned Robert Peel, the Home Secretary, to appoint an extraordinary commission. The upshot was the appointment in 1826 of a royal commission to visit all the Scottish universities. The appointment was the immediate outcome of an internal squabble, but it was widely recognized that the changing conditions of Scottish life and the need of the universities to adapt to them made some reforms imperative.

In fact the commission had a very much delayed reaction. It performed its task with commendable skill and compiled daunting volumes of evidence, but when its report was presented in 1831, it was shelved. This seems uncharacteristic of the reforming Whig government then in office, but doubtless it had more important legislation on its plate. The universities took advantage of the breathing space to initiate reforms themselves. Edinburgh, which had conjured up the commission, turned out to be its unhappiest beneficiary. In a series of expensive and prolonged lawsuits arising out of the strife between the Town Council and the Senate which, commented Lord Justice Clerk, 'exceeded in bulk every case that [he] ever saw', the town council's cause was upheld against that of the university whose standing in law, Lord Glenlee decided in 1829, was 'that of a minor corporation subordinate to the corporation of the City and Town Council'. The senate which in 1833 had appointed the redoubtable Sir William Hamilton as its secretary did not readily accept the decision, and petitioned Lord Melbourne to sever their relationship with the town council which had treated the university 'with indelicacy, not unmixed with contempt'. The councillors replied that the university showed 'a quibbling contentious spirit'.

The crisis which faced the Church of Scotland in 1843, splitting it into two groups, the Established Church and the schismatic Free Protesting Church, was a momentous event for Scottish university history. It did not add to academic harmony when the Edinburgh councillors, most of whom had become members of the Free Church, agreed to allow the seceding congregation of Greyfriars Kirk to use the chemistry lecture room for worship, an action which the Senate not improperly described as a 'glaring appropriation of University property to purposes utterly unacademical'. On the other hand the disruption did emancipate the lay professors from the religious test, at a time when some people were seeking to revive it, and fostered the spirit of reform in matters other than ecclesiastical.

These had in fact been receiving some attention. Edinburgh was not so bogged down in controversy that all academic progress had come to a halt. A number of new chairs were created, several of them in medical studies, and in 1833 English became the medium for all university examinations. St Andrews meanwhile was slowly putting its house in order. Stricter regulations governed the conferring of medical degrees and teaching. As in other universities an attempt was made to re-impose a curriculum and to insist that students proceeded to graduation. The buildings, many of which were in a state of great disrepair, were set to order; Robert Reid, the King's architect for Scotland, was commissioned to prepare plans for their reconstruction, which was carried out in 1829–30. Thomas Chalmers, an ardent Evangelical and social reformer, who returned to St Andrews as professor of moral philosophy in 1823, brought a strong moral impact to bear upon university affairs. He left to become professor of divinity at Edinburgh and, after 1843, principal of the New College of the Free Church in the same city. He disapproved of obligatory attendance at the college kirk and he criticized what seemed to him to be the irregular behaviour of the professorial body, in particular the practice of the so-called Candlemas dividend by which the professors divided the surplus revenues of each year among themselves. At Glasgow and the two colleges at Aberdeen further attempts at reform were made.

The Universities Act of 1858 was not therefore very much of a surprise, though the universities we know today are the outcome of the changes it set in motion. The bill was introduced on 22 April 1858 by Mr Inglis, later Lord Justice General of Scotland, in a speech declaring that the 'Scotch universities had lost sight of their proper objects; and their educational establishments had descended below the requirements of the age'. The substance of the bill was the recommendations of the Royal Commission of 1826. In one particular only was there a change, in part arising from the religious crisis of 1843. The commissioners had recommended in their report that a religious test should be imposed on all professors, but the tests had been repealed in 1853. Except for principals and professors of theology, members of the senate were only required to state that they would not put forward views 'opposed to the divine authority of the Holy Scriptures or the Westminster Confession of Faith'. In 1859 principals were no longer required to take this oath.

A new group of commissioners set up under the act of 1858 had some 126 meetings before the end of 1862. In their hands the constitutions of the universities were remodelled. The chancellorship continued as an office of dignity. The rectorship was soon reduced to the same level by a decision that merely confirmed changes already made. It seems probable that medieval university students had cooperated with the masters in electing the rector, but this privilege had quickly and properly become the prerogative of the seniors and the office itself became the perquisite of the principals of colleges and divinity professors. At Glasgow a commission of inquiry had restored the right of election to the students in 1727; similar moves had been made at St Andrews * and Aberdeen. At Edinburgh where the rectorship was long held by the lord provost of the city there was not this precedent. The commission of 1858 however conferred on all matriculated students the right to elect a rector, thus effectively making a mockery of the election (though it is interesting to recall that among the first rectors elected were John Stuart Mill† and W. E. Gladstone) and reducing the office itself to a meaningless formality. The principal continued to be the executive head of the university. The commissioners created for each university a court

* At St Andrews junior students were excluded from 1475 to 1625 and from 1642 to 1826, but thereafter voted regularly.

† See A. J. Mill, 'The First Ornamental Rector at St Andrews University', in *Scottish Historical Review*, 43, pp. 131–44.

in which non-academics were in the majority and endowed it with many if not most of the powers until now exercised by the senate, except in matters that were the specific concern of the faculty. They also established a General Council, consisting of graduates and those who had been matriculated students for four sessions, which was empowered to elect the chancellor of the university.

The changes initiated by the Act of 1858 opened a period of expansion and advance in Scottish higher education, though it was slow to begin. St Andrews was in many ways still academically inert. In 1876 it had only 130 students (compared with 677 at Aberdeen where Marischal and King's Colleges had been fused together in 1860, 1,773 at Glasgow and 2,351 at Edinburgh) and although it had a distinguished principal in the church historian and philosopher John Tulloch the likelihood of its closure was again discussed. In 1874, to the dismay of many at St Andrews, the foundation of a university college at Dundee was proposed. It was delayed by a depression in the jute trade, a major source of Dundee's wealth, but was finally made possible in 1881 by the generosity of the Baxter family. As an affiliated college it proved to be a source of strength. Under Principal Donaldson the history of St Andrews took a turn for the better. Relations between staff and students, made difficult in Tulloch's time by the disorder caused by college 'rags', improved. The Universities (Scotland) Act of 1889 which widened the membership of the university court reiterated the court's right to appoint and confirm professors: an ordinance of 1891 eliminated the private patronage which governed three chairs: the chair of humanity had been in the gift of the Duke of Portland, civil history, of the Marquis of Ailsa, chemistry, of the Earl of Leven and Melville. The degrees of bachelor and doctor of science were instituted in 1876 and a joint medical school was set up at Dundee in 1898. The tide had turned, and St Andrews' reputation mounted steadily.

Glasgow university, set at the heart of a noble but hardly beautiful city, showered through the years with industrial grime, could never have the same appeal; but it had become a vigorous institution. Some of its professors were men of European reputation, such as the classical scholar, R. C. Jebb, Edward Caird, the philosopher who was later master of Balliol, and William Thomson, later Lord Kelvin, who had actually entered the university at the early age of ten and at twenty-two, already a fellow of Peterhouse, Cambridge, became in 1846 professor of natural philosophy, a chair that he held for fifty-three years. In Kelvin's lifetime the university was revolutionized. Kelvin himself established the first laboratory in experimental philosophy in 1855. The degree of bachelor of science was instituted in 1872, though there was to be no faculty of science for a further twenty years. The technological side was strengthened when in 1912 the Royal Technical College became affiliated to the university. By 1900 Glasgow had some thirty-one professorial chairs; thirty-six more were to be added in the next half century. The university had been obliged in 1870 to leave its old buildings, enriched by centuries of past history (though dismissed by John Wesley in 1753 as no larger nor at all handsomer than those of Lincoln College, Oxford), since they had become an island in an industrialized region often shrouded in sulphurous gloom. The college was sold to the City of Glasgow Union Railway for £100,000 and the university moved to its more spacious site on Gilmorehill.

Thus by the 1870s the Scottish universities were again making steady advances in all fields of learning, and the chronicle of their achievement in the next ninety years did not differ very much from that of the universities south of the border.

CHAPTER SIX

The Rise of the Modern Universities

THE monopolistic control which Oxford and Cambridge exerted over higher education, though not uncriticized, long remained practically unchallenged. At critical moments in their history their status had seemed to be in danger. In spite of Henry VIII's known esteem for learning, some of the dons, aware of the considerable capital endowment tied up in the colleges, must have watched the dissolution of the monasteries and the subsequent confiscation of the property belonging to the chantries with concern. Similar fears were expressed with greater justification at the time of the Commonwealth, not merely because the universities' property was in danger of being confiscated but because of the talk of establishing new universities, purer in religion, more forward-looking and freed from the stifling influence of scholastic learning. Already in the reign of Edward VI Sir Thomas Gresham, the founder of the Royal Exchange, had bequeathed his home in Bishopsgate as a centre for a future college. In 1612 Gresham College was described by Sir George Buck as the university of London, but it was on too restricted a scale to merit the title. Nonetheless it counted among its professors in the first half of the seventeenth century men of outstanding capacity. 'The fame of it,' wrote an early eighteenth-century Gresham professor, 'went over the whole world.... There's hardly any part of useful knowledge that has not received great accessions from thence; and some of the most considerable discoveries in philosophy, physics, anatomy, in all the parts of mathematics, in geometry, in astronomy, in navigation, came forth of Gresham College.' But the college had never been a serious rival of the older universities.

In 1643 the Westminster Assembly of Divines which had been called to give Parliament advice on the further reformation of religion supported a motion for founding a university in London. Two years previously the people of Manchester had asked for a university since 'many ripe and hopeful wits [were] being utterly lost for want of education'. The Puritan Master of Caius College, William Dell, thought that it would be

> more advantagious to the good of all the people, to have Universities or Colledges, one at least in every great town or city in the nation, as in London, York, Bristow, Exceter, Norwich and the like; and for the State to allow to these Colledges an honest and competent maintenance, for some godly and learned men to teach the Tongues and Arts, under a due reformation.

But the only scheme that came within reach of fulfilment was a plan for establishing a university for the north at Durham. The college which had Cromwell's approval was to be paid for out of appropriated chapter lands; a provost, Philip Hunton of Wadham (whose book on monarchy was among those burned by the university of Oxford in 1683), and some fellows and schoolmasters, among them a few Oxford dons, were appointed but the Restoration brought all these plans to nought. After the Hanoverian succession the older universities seemed to be in danger of losing their independence, and the idea of creating new ones sank out of sight.

The Dissenters had founded several academies in the eighteenth century, some of which were very lively establishments, providing courses which compared favourably with the instruction given at Oxford and Cambridge. Leading industrialists in Manchester, Liverpool and Birmingham gave the money which in 1757 brought into being the Warrington Academy, intended to educate ministers who should be 'free to follow the dictates of their own judgement, in their enquiries after truth, without any undue bias imposed on their understandings' and to give laymen who intended to go into teaching or commerce 'some knowledge ... in the more useful branches of literature, and to lead them to an early acquaintance with, and just concern for the true principles of religion and liberty, of which principles they must, in future life, be the supporters'. Joseph Priestley, who was tutor in language and literature and lecturer in history at the Warrington Academy, had himself been educated at the Dissenting academy at Daventry. For some thirty years Warrington fulfilled its role, and its traditions were carried on by its successors, the Manchester Academy (the lineal ancestor of the Unitarian college of that name at Oxford) and the short-lived Hackney Academy where the chemist John Dalton was for six years professor of mathematics and experimental philosophy. By the early nineteenth century, however, these academies were deteriorating into sectarian theological seminaries.

The influence of the Dissenters did not stop short at the foundation of their own academies. They participated in the voluntary literary and philosophical societies which in the latter years of the eighteenth century were promoting an interest in science and its application to industry. The Royal Institution in London and other societies in Manchester, Birmingham, Leeds and Newcastle included among their members Dissenting ministers as yet debarred from the universities, doctors, technicians and businessmen, who were often concerned as well with political reform and liberal theology, and who, in spite of their middle-class character, criticized the established order. The nurseries of this order were Oxford and Cambridge; to the growing chorus of critics of the older universities, among whom the Nonconformists were particularly vociferous, the societies added their voice, and by their activities in other fields did much to create the climate in which the new universities came to be founded.

But it is doubtful if Dissenting opinion on its own could have done this if social changes had not created a new demand for education. Two principal features of the early nineteenth century were the rapid growth of the population and the greater affluence of the managerial class (if the expression is permissible) created by the profits of capitalistic industrialization. The expansion of the industrial cities of the north encouraged, though not immediately, a growing sense of civic pride. Wealth provided the means for new endowments. Apart from London and Durham, the new universities owed their existence to civic initiative and the generosity of rich manufacturers, often Nonconformist in their religious affiliations, who were disinclined to contribute to the traditional, and alien, centres of learning. Josiah Mason, who sold cakes on the Kidderminster streets as a child and left school at eighteen, and through his energy and initiative accumulated a fortune from the manufacture of steel pins and electro-plate, became the virtual founder of Birmingham university. But although individual contributions to the new universities were often substantial, they were insufficient for future expansion. All the new universities in the nineteenth century were crippled by lack of funds, so that research was difficult, teaching sometimes inadequate and the provision of civilized amenities impossible. The phrase 'redbrick', though not truly applicable to either London or Durham, conveys something of the utilitarian character of the new foundations, a sombre contrast to the mellow bricks of the Cambridge colleges and the crumbling stone of Oxford.

The new universities were not, however, in the first instance the produce of a benefactor's whim or of municipal or county pride. They came into existence to meet a genuine demand which Oxford and Cambridge could not or would not supply. They were not intended to rival but to supplement the older institutions. Oxford and Cambridge were essentially finishing schools for the children of the governing classes, for the clergy and the higher administrators; very few sons of the working or of the lower middle classes found their way there, even as sizars or servitors.* They retained a strongly Anglican bias, even after the abolition of the religious tests in 1871. The best of their studies were humanistic rather than scientific. Their teaching was not so much bad as increasingly out of step with the intellectual developments of the times. 'It seems,' Joseph Priestley had written in 1764, 'to be a defect in our present system of public education that a proper course of studies is not provided for gentlemen who are designed to fill the principal stations of *active life*, distinct from those which are adapted to the *learned professions*.' It was a long time

---

* Sizars were poor scholars of Cambridge and Trinity College, Dublin, who received an allowance from the college and performed some of the duties later discharged by college servants.

before Oxford and Cambridge were adequately equipped to offer, for example, training in law and medicine.

The demand for better educational facilities was felt at all levels. When Joseph Lancaster opened his elementary school at Southwark in 1798 he initiated the Lancastrian scheme of undenominational education, so praised by the philosophic radicals, which spread rapidly through the country. As an antidote to this secularist education the National Society for the Education of the Poor according to the Principles of the Church of England was founded in 1811, under the management of Andrew Bell. More schoolmasters were needed, more doctors to care for a rapidly growing population increasingly concerned about health and hygiene. The most urgent demand, already making itself felt by 1800, was for men adequately trained in the theory and application of science. Skilled technicians and scientists were essential for British industry if Britain was to keep its place in competitive world markets. This fact was highlighted by the Great Exhibition of 1851, and reiterated thereafter by many intelligent observers. It was slowly realized that specialized industry required specialized training; later in the century the civic universities developed courses in mining, brewing, dyeing and textiles, and the more complex techniques of their several local industries; at the beginning of the twentieth century Reading turned its attention to specialized courses in agriculture. There was even a small but insistent demand that the full facilities of a university should be offered to women, since more and more of them were being educated. Although the blue-stocking seemed, as to some she still does, an occasionally incongruous and awesome representative of her sex, the newer universities were somewhat readier to take her to their bosom, if this uncongenial term may be allowed, than Oxford and Cambridge, which remained until later in the century exclusively masculine societies.

The conditions that led to the industrial revolution of the nineteenth century created both the demand for and the means of supplying new centres of university education, and the story of their development should have been one of excitement and adventure. There were other precedents from which to learn. The example of the Scottish universities and of the university of Virginia, set up by Thomas Jefferson in 1819 and partly staffed by English professors who soon afterwards took chairs at the new university of London, cannot have gone unnoticed. The efficiency and progressive character of the German universities, notably Berlin, founded in 1809, and Bonn, founded in 1818, had many admirers among contemporary educationalists. Matthew Arnold and others familiar with the pattern of continental education compared the German professorial system with the English, to the disadvantage of the latter, and were concerned at the small number of British students who attended university, a much smaller proportion of the population than sought admission to university in America or on the continent. How many young men there must have been in Britain wanting a university education but without hope of getting to Oxford or Cambridge!

In spite of propitious circumstances it was a long time before the new universities were solidly established. Their history, though occasionally redeemed by major advances in learning and impressive achievements of scholarship, was scarred by intrigue and controversy, dogged by lack of financial resources and circumscribed by scarcity of students who were sufficiently intelligent and adequately prepared for university education. It was this low level of intelligence rather than any lack of proficient teachers that prevented many colleges from offering courses of more than matriculation standard, in spite of ambitious plans to award their own degrees. A college could only do this once it had been raised by royal charter to university status; until then its students had to take the external degrees of London university. Comparatively few availed themselves of this privilege. Most students were irregular in their attendance, many of them going to evening rather than day classes, and for a long time the new colleges offered only meagre academic and social facilities. Their growth was blighted by the short-sighted meanness so characteristic of second-rate academics and municipal politicians.

*

The university of London was first in the field. Its actual
foundation represented less an urgent need than a protest on
the part of Dissenters (who since 1812 had been thinking of
establishing a Dissenting university), and of secularists and
radicals, at the continuing dominance of Oxford and Cambridge, and even at Toryism itself. The idea germinated
during a visit which Thomas Campbell made to Germany in
1820, but was not made public until 1825. 'The plan which I
suggest,' Campbell wrote in *The Times* of 9 February 1825,
'is a great London University. Not a place for lecturing to
people of both sexes (except as an appendage to the establishment), but of effectively and multifariously teaching, examining, exercising, and rewarding with honours in the liberal arts
and sciences, the youth of our middling rich people, between
the age of 15 or 16 and 20.' A council representing all
the interested parties was formed, but the project soon ran
into difficulties.

The council proposed to raise a capital of not less than
£100,000, but though the shares (which promised a return of
6 per cent, a complete illusion since the stock never gave a
dividend) were taken up it was not easy to get the money. The
plan was bitterly attacked for religious reasons. The curriculum had been intended originally to include theological
instruction, but it was found that there was so much disagreement as to what should be taught that it was more discreet not
to teach it at all. The sponsors, so the Council of the college
declared, 'were thus compelled by necessity to leave this great
primary object of education, which they deem too important
for compromise, to the direction and superintendence of the
natural guardians of the pupils'.* This to its critics seemed to
open the way to Dissent and infidelity. 'This must be opposed
and rejected,' Sir Robert Peel wrote to the Dean of Christ
Church, with reference to the bill that Henry Brougham
proposed to bring forward in the House of Commons to give a
charter of incorporation to the London college. 'Was there any
public discussion on a London University? on the impolicy of

*Quoted in H. H. Bellot, *University College, London, 1826–1926*,
University of London Press, 1929, p. 56.

forming a university, a place of education for adults in the metropolis? on the effect of excluding religion from the public education of youth?' If the older universities opposed the new university because they feared its anti-religious tendencies and were jealous of its wish to grant degrees, the existing medical schools were suspicious of its attempt to poach in their terrain. The university was 'a humbug joint-stock subscription school for Cockney boys, without the power of granting degrees or affording honours or distinctions, got up in the bubble season'.* R. H. Barham satirized the project in *Stinkomalle Triumphans* and T. E. Hook in *The Cockney College*.

In spite of the criticism of vested interests and its own precarious financial position, the 'radical infidel College' became a reality. With some £33,675 in the kitty, in February 1827, it was decided to go ahead with building on some eight acres of waste land in Gower Street. Recalling that the university was intended not merely to provide higher education for those who were unable to enter Oxford and Cambridge but also to give its students the opportunity to study subjects outside the curricula of the older institutions, the council appointed a number of young men to professorships in a wide range of subjects. 'The London University,' Emily Eden wrote, 'has opened with most unexpected success. They have nearly two hundred and fifty students entered already, and several of the Professors have distinguished themselves much in their introductory lectures, and there have been crowds sent away who were anxious to hear them.' 'All the accounts I have,' Brougham, perhaps not an impartial witness, wrote to Earl Grey, 'agree in this, that the delight of all who have been admitted was perfect; 700 or 800 were allowed to attend the opening lectures (including the students). The first two (medical) lectures, have had the greatest success!' The prospect was unduly and unnaturally rosy.

The critics of the new university had not been idle. They had found a protagonist in the scholarly and energetic rector of Lambeth, George d'Oyly, who in an open letter to Robert Peel

John Bull, vii, 7 May 1827.

agreed that a new university was necessary to cope with the needs of an increased population, especially a growing wealthy middle class, and to meet the spread of the 'strong spirit of intellectual improvement', but urged that the university of London was inadequate by reason of its failure to provide spiritual and moral instruction. A new college was proposed, and a meeting subsequently held on 21 June 1828 at the Freemasons Hall, attended by three archbishops and seven bishops, and presided over by the Duke of Wellington. At the meeting, the Duke declared that the new college should

enable that youth to perform their duties to their Sovereign and to their country in their various stations of life; and above all to give them knowledge of God (*cheers*) – a knowledge of the principles, precepts, and examples on which all his doctrines are founded (*loud cheers*) – a knowledge which shall teach them to be satisfied with their lot in this life, and give them hope in the mercies of God for the future one (*continued cheering*).

Funds were to be raised partly by donations and partly by subscriptions in the form of £100 shares which were to carry a promised dividend of 4 per cent. A list published shortly after the meeting showed that £30,794 had been collected from 242 people, of whom 88 were clergymen. A site was at first fixed on in the region of the newly opened Zoological Gardens; but there was an outburst of protests from the residents. 'A college in the park would be much worse than the menagerie of wild beasts, unless the latter also were allowed to roam at pleasure.' Eventually a site to the east of Somerset House in the Strand was accepted on a beneficial lease from the Crown.

King's College, London, was launched therefore with enthusiasm. 'The finishing blow,' as *John Bull* put it, 'has been given to the stye of infidelity building at the end of Gower Street.' But the college soon found itself in as grave difficulties as University College and over the same issues, religious policy and financial resources. Peel's acceptance of Roman Catholic Emancipation split the high Tory phalanx and gravely affected the financial support promised to the college; Lord Winchilsea, for instance, withdrew his promised donation because he was unconvinced that the teaching would be 'truly religious, scriptural and permanently Protestant'. The college opened its doors on 1 October 1831, but financial stringency made it difficult to secure an adequate staff and to recruit students. All students were obliged to attend the prescribed course of religious instruction, but the obligation was remitted for those who were able to attend lectures but were not regular members of the college. Thus although the principal and the professors had to be members of the Church of England (save for the teachers of oriental literature and modern languages), the system of entry was almost as free as that to University College.

King's College was granted its charter of incorporation in 1829. St David's College, Lampeter, founded by Bishop Burgess in 1822 to educate ministers for the church in Wales, also acquired a charter in the same year. This would seem to have strengthened University College's case for incorporation, especially as the Whigs had been recently returned to power. 'The Duke,' Newman wrote from Oxford, 'has begun his campaign by advising us strenuously to resist the London University granting degrees in arts and divinity.' The case for incorporation was argued before the Privy Council in 1834. Sir Charles Wetherell put forward Oxford's objections, arguing that the King could not legally incorporate a university in England which did not conform with the doctrines, discipline and teaching of the Church of England. The medical profession was opposed for different reasons. 'We advise the Joint-Stock Company in Gower Street,' the *London Medical Gazette* stated, 'either to give up their aspirations after exclusive privileges, and just to manufacture degrees on their own bottom, or let them at length be shamed into modesty, and take their place with other great schools.' Ultimately the charter of incorporation was granted in 1836 to a 'University of London' at which University College and King's College were able to present their candidates for degrees.

Durham University had been brought into being through very mixed motives. The chapter of Durham Cathedral seemed to many to be so scandalously wealthy that a majority of the canons became convinced that they could only prevent the

107

diversion of their resources by the ecclesiastical reformers through sponsoring the foundation of a college. 'It appears to me morally certain,' Prebendary Durell wrote in July 1831 to Archdeacon Thorp, who was so long to preside as warden of the new university,

that as soon as the Reform Bill is disposed of, an attack will be made on deans and chapters, and as certain that Durham will be the first object. It has occurred to us that it will be prudent if possible to ward off the blow, and that no plan is so likely to take as making the public partakers of our income by annexing an establishment of enlarged education to our college.

The chapter was divided as to what should be its function and character, but ultimately the more progressive group, with the support of Bishop Van Mildert, and of his successor Bishop Maltby, managed to ensure that it should not be too narrowly theological or exclusively concerned with training the clergy. A draft scheme was drawn up by Thorp and received parliamentary approval in 1832. A set of statutes was formulated two years later, appointments were made, students admitted, and degrees awarded. To some its origins seemed too ominously ecclesiastical, though Keble, anxious at the crisis through which his own university was passing, cherished the hope that 'if Oxford should fail in its maintenance of the faith, Durham would still witness to the divine truth of the Catholic tradition.' The Whig government, however, wishing Durham to admit Dissenters to membership and degrees, delayed the grant of the charter of its incorporation until June 1837.

The many favourable omens that attended the founding of these new institutions soon seemed to disperse. There was only a trickle of entrants. That 'failing body, the University of Durham' had 31 men reading arts, 30 theology and 21 engineering in 1840. Ten years later 73 men were reading arts and 41 theology but no one offered engineering. By 1860 the total was 51 in all, 30 arts men, 20 theologians and one engineer. In February 1862, the number of students had sunk to the new low of 46; in 1861 only 19 degrees and licences were conferred. The situation at the London colleges was better but not encouraging. At King's, after a period of moderate prosperity, the number of students fell sharply from 1853 to 1868, in arts from 106 to 66, in medicine from 199 to 130, in theology from 78 to 41. At University College the founders hoped for 2,000 students, a number which was not to be reached for eighty years. In 1829–30 630 men enrolled; thereafter there was a decline. It may be that there were fewer intelligent men than the founders had supposed who wished to avail themselves of a university education; but it was more likely that many who would have wished to do so could not afford even the comparatively small fees which attendance at a university demanded. Apart from the public schools and a few independent and grammar schools, the English educational system was not geared to the preparation of pupils for a university course, nor for the most part were employers, or even parents, eager to promote the higher education of working-class boys.

Yet the main reason for this unhappy story is to be found in internal rather than external factors. The colleges' endowments were wholly inadequate and the fees did not allow them to do more than meet their day to day expenses. Their professors were miserably paid and their lecture rooms and laboratories poorly equipped. At first most of the professors at University College were guaranteed £300 a year for three years, but this subvention could not continue. Thereafter the professors were obliged to depend on their fees, two thirds of which went to the professor and one third to the university. Some professors made as much as £500 or £700 a year, while others were inadequately recompensed; the professor of English received £30, his colleague in philosophy £21 and in German £11 10s. The fees of John Austin, the distinguished jurist who occupied the chair of jurisprudence, amounted to £120 in 1829–30 and fell to £32 in 1832–3. 'The expenditure has been lavish,' his wife commented,

the plans are ill-digested, and vibrating, like all things in which the Whigs have a hand, between the desire of being popular and the fear of being unfashionable, so as of course to satisfy neither class whom they seek to conciliate by cowardly half-measures. The Council are not united, and the professors as a body are openly at war with the council.

'I understand,' said the witty Sydney Smith, 'they have already seized on the air pump, the exhausted receiver, and galvanic batteries, and that the bailiffs have been seen chasing the Professor of Modern History round the quadrangle.'

But it was no laughing matter. Inadequate financial resources militated against the employment of a first-class staff; the better men tended to move away and some of those who were left, who at Oxford or Cambridge could have been discreetly hidden, could at a new university effectively ruin a department. It was said of Richard Potter, the professor of natural philosophy from 1841 to 1865, that 'he was worn out; he had lost his memory and not a few of his wits'. His colleague, John Hoppus, the professor of philosophy from 1830 to 1866, effectively killed any interest in the subject. 'After his first or his second lecture he seldom had a pupil, because, burying his face in his manuscript, he mumbled so that only an acute ear could catch much of what he said, and those who caught something called it rot.' The professor of zoology, R. E. Grant, 'had been known in the absence of students, to address the boy who dusted the bottles'. These were doubtless exceptions but the scene was a grey one, made the worse by the bitter and acrimonious quarrels which split the faculties, and to which the medical department was particularly liable. The gradual abolition of religious tests and the reform of the older universities had weakened the new universities' position; the improvement in the medical schools and the reform of legal education initiated by the Law Society in 1833 in part explain the lack of students and teachers which faced the new foundations with a crisis in the middle years of the century. 'The college,' Crabb Robinson wrote of University College in 1852, 'is far from having yet answered the great purposes originally announced.'

Nonetheless it is possible to detect signs of progress. The curriculum at University College had been broadened to include English language, philology and literature. A faculty of science with the power to grant degrees had been set up in 1860. Two years earlier the system of affiliated colleges was abolished and the examinations were thrown open to all without the requirement of any certificate of studentship. As a result many more candidates presented themselves for the degree examination of the university, 450 in 1858, 1,450 in 1870. Some felt that there was a real danger that the college might deteriorate simply into an 'examining machine'. King's, too, though financially in deep waters – it had sold its silver spoons and replaced them by electro-plate – having rid itself of its principal, the verbose Dr Jelf, reorganized the curriculum, improved its technical education and revolutionized its medical school and hospital through the installation in 1877 of Joseph Lister as professor of surgery and the development of antiseptic surgery. Durham, reaping the results of a royal commission which had been set up to inquire into its problems in 1862, went ahead steadily if not very conspicuously; its numbers increased from 41 in 1861 to 119 in 1891. It was strengthened by the inclusion of the Newcastle School of Medicine and Surgery, founded in 1834, into the university as the faculty of medicine. Yet its prestige was still so low that the Chancellor of the Exchequer, Robert Lowe, could think of no better reason for raising Owens College, Manchester, to university status than that it would swallow up the effete university of Durham. Owens College, opened in 1851, was the first of a new type of university. The country was in the throes of an expanding industrial revolution; new markets were opening in Europe and overseas for its manufactured goods. But a series of trade fluctuations revealed the risk of contraction and depression and brought home the need to ensure Britain's continued lead. The new technological age required a continuous process of self-examination and a measure of insight into economics and mechanics as well as inventive skill if the markets for British goods were to be retained and expanded. The older universities were beginning to wake to the need for training scientists, though they were, in Arnold's opinion, characterized by an 'indisposition and incapacity for science'. The newer universities were already placing much emphasis on the subject, but even so could not provide adequate facilities for the teeming millions of the industrial north and the Midlands; it was up to them to create their own.

In 1852 the North of England Institute of Mining was set up, to provide technical and scientific instruction that would promote the safety and efficiency of the mines. Its plans were discussed but not followed up at Durham. A college of physical science was opened at Newcastle in October 1871, with the express purpose of giving instruction in science as applied to English mining, agriculture and manufactures. In 1880 the leading mineowners agreed to endow it with a chair of mining, the first of its kind, and in the same year established another at Birmingham. Six years later the foundation stone of a new college was laid at Newcastle by Sir William Armstrong, whose name it was to bear. In 1860 John Scott Russell proposed the establishment of a technical university to consist of fifteen local colleges, each specializing in the industries of their particular region. By the end of the century many new colleges had been set up, to meet the immediate needs of the economy, allied even to a specific trade, but in response also to a larger vision.

The university of Manchester originated in the bracing commercial and industrial milieu of a prospering city, though an environment in which such literary and academic families as the Gaskells and Martineaus flourished had also a strong cultural side. 'In all directions,' H. L. Jones told the Manchester Statistical Society in 1836,

the circle of Manchester is full of life and intelligence; manufactures of every kind occupy the inhabitants of the towns; the movement of money is immense; commercial activity is carried to an extraordinary pitch; mechanical ingenuity receives there daily new developments; the minds of men are in a state of electric communication of ideas.

The commercial aristocracy of Manchester in the mid-nineteenth century was self-made, liberal and Nonconformist with a strong sense of moral and communal obligation. It was profoundly suspicious of ecclesiasticism – as late as 1911 a proposal to hold an annual university service in the cathedral was frustrated by sectarian feeling – but it was neither secular nor anti-religious; many of the early promoters and dons of the college were men of deep religious convictions. John Owens, the man through whose generosity the college came to be founded, had his own brand of religious principle; a Nonconformist by origin, he ceased attending chapel after he had found the privacy of his pew invaded and henceforth attended an Anglican church. Starting life as a cotton spinner, he had made a fortune selling cloth to America and the East, and in 1846 he bequeathed £96,654 11s. 6d. to found a college that should be non-sectarian. He regarded higher education as the best panacea for the evils of society, as well as a sound business investment, for the college was to provide Manchester and its neighbourhood with 'such departments of knowledge as are most generally subservient to the purpose of commercial life'.

Private benefactions were the salient factor in the establishment of several other colleges. In 1850 H. R. Hartley bequeathed a large sum to the corporation of Southampton (though as a result of litigation less than half the original amount eventually reached them), initiating what was after long decades to become the university of Southampton. Josiah Mason subsidized the college which for long bore his name at Birmingham, laying the foundation stone on his eightieth birthday, 23 February 1875; the college was opened by the scientist Thomas Huxley in 1880. Similarly Sheffield owed much to the generosity of a local steelmaster, Mark Firth.

The university of Wales was simply a product of local feeling, though the small support that it long received from municipal bodies showed how limited was its appeal to most Welshmen. In 1853 B. T. Williams had written a pamphlet on 'The Desirableness of a University for Wales' but ten years elapsed before anything of a practical nature was attempted. The creation of a federal university around the nucleus of St David's, Lampeter, which had acquired a limited right to give degrees in 1852, was suggested but religious division made the scheme impossible. In 1867 some of the chief promoters, among whom the autocratic, rhetorical and overwhelmingly enthusiastic Hugh Owen was the leading spirit, bought the Castle Hotel, Aberystwyth, for £10,000 (the hotel had been built originally by a speculator who gambled on the increase in the tourist traffic as a result of the opening of the Cambrian railway but he went bankrupt). Although only a quarter of the purchase money had been paid, the college opened with 26 students in 1872. Its opening coincided with an agricultural depression, so that its growth was slow and status impoverished: for many years its very survival hung in the balance. By 1880 there were still only 57 students, and of the 313 who had been at Aberystwyth to that date the majority had come from Cardiganshire. The university college for South Wales and Monmouthshire founded at Cardiff in 1883 and another for North Wales which was established the following year in the former Penrhyn Arms at Bangor weakened rather than strengthened the effort to create a Welsh university. The government, persuaded by a recommendation of the committee which it had set up in 1880 under the chairmanship of Lord Aberdare to inquire into higher education in Wales and Monmouth, made a grant, the first of its kind, to the nascent university, diverting, however, the entire £4,000 from Aberystwyth to Bangor. The increase in the number of colleges meant simply a multiplication of inferior educational establishments; in 1890 Bangor had some 117 students, Aberystwyth less than 130 and Cardiff some 150. Even the grant of a university charter in 1893 did little to restore faith in the project. Two decades were to elapse before the university of Wales contributed very much to the academic life of Britain.

Leeds owed its existence neither to an individual philanthropist nor to civic patriotism but rather to the development of the medical school which had been established in 1831. As early as 1826 the idea of a university for the town had been mooted by John Marshall, the M.P. for the county, a pioneer in flax spinning and the president of the Leeds Philosophical and Literary Society. He urged that there should be 'no religious test or theological professorships', nor in fact was a faculty of theology established until 1934–5. Competition from the Continent threatened, profits were falling and the local manufacturers were ready to support the setting up of a college for higher education. 'Without education,' as Thomas Nussey, a Leeds merchant phrased it in 1867, 'we cannot expect to have skilled workmen of the highest class.' When therefore the Yorkshire College of Science was founded in 1874 (though it did not acquire the name until four years later), beginning life in a disused bankruptcy court, it was designed to give instruction 'in such sciences and arts as are applicable or ancillary to the manufacturing, mining, engineering and agricultural industries' of the county and its three professorships were in experimental physics, geology and mining, and chemistry. In 1884 the medical school was included in the college. It was, however, soon apparent that some members of the college council thought that the college ought to provide a liberal training in arts. Their critics argued that this function was already being fulfilled by the Cambridge extension lectures, and it was the support which these evoked which enabled Sir Edward Baines, the proprietor of the *Leeds Mercury*, to put forward proposals for founding chairs in classics and literature. Even so the inadequacy of its teaching prevented its admission to the federal Victoria University, which had been set up more or less under the presidency of Owens College in 1880 and it was not admitted until 1887.

The Cambridge extension lectures were largely the brainchild of James Stuart, an enlightened Cambridge don who in 1866 put forward the idea of bringing to those whose circumstances made it impossible for them to go to Oxford and Cambridge some of the benefits of their teaching, through the medium of public lectures. From 1867 he was lecturing, usually on astronomy, to crowded audiences of working-class men and women in the industrial towns of the north and midlands. The demand was so great that Cambridge established a special syndicate to operate the work, with Stuart as its secretary. Besides contributing to the enlargement of the Yorkshire College the lectures were a seminal force in the establishment of colleges at Bristol, Sheffield, Nottingham and Reading. Bristol was further inspired by Jowett of Balliol, both his own college and New College contributing some £300 for five years towards its cost. The college was established in 1876 and was fortunate to enjoy the services of two outstanding principals, the economist Alfred Marshall and the chemist William Ramsay.

At Sheffield the extension lectures, excepting those on logic, attracted so much support that the local Member of Parliament, A. J. Mundella, expressed the hope that 'instead of being a branch of the University here [they] would really have a Sheffield University' and the local steelmaster Mark Firth (Sir Charles Firth, of the same family, began as a lecturer in the college his distinguished career as a historian) generously agreed to foster such a foundation, purchasing a site and financing a building which was opened in 1879. While the trust deed forbade the demand of any religious test and described the object of the college as the promotion of the 'moral, social and intellectual elevation of the masses', Firth himself wanted the college to 'extend the range of instruction whenever the technical resources for this shall be available, so as to include a system of technical education for the due qualification of the artisans of the town', and to prepare students for matriculation at 'one of our national universities'. For a long time its existence was precarious; it was carried through its dark days by the dogged determination of its principal and first vice-chancellor, W. M. Hicks, a mathematician who had been a fellow of St John's, Cambridge. Negotiations for admission to membership of Victoria University opened in 1895 but were brought to a curt and even rude conclusion in 1898 when admission was refused on the grounds that its facilities were inadequate, its premises poor, its finances unbalanced and its pupils of mediocre quality. It would have been difficult to rebut any of these charges but there was hardly a university outside of Oxford and Cambridge of which this was not true at some time in the nineteenth century.

Nottingham, another child of the extension movement, also failed to fulfil its early promise. The extension lectures aroused such interest that a number of public-spirited citizens urged the building of a permanent college which could house the lectures, and provide a library and a chemical laboratory. The town council welcomed the idea and the college was opened in 1881. In this case the instruction was to be primarily in 'those branches of knowledge which are capable of practical application in the various industrial pursuits' of the region, and was of an elementary nature. The college was connected with London university, which admitted its students to external degrees, though only six first degrees were taken there before 1890. The day students, most of whom were women, were outnumbered, as at Bristol and elsewhere, by the evening students, who became even more numerous as the technology of the local industries developed. Classes in lace and hosiery were opened in 1882 with the financial assistance of the Drapers' Company. With the advent of the Technical Instruction Act of 1889, local authorities were given the right to levy a penny rate to promote technical education. The Nottingham corporation which had showed an interest in and a readiness to support its youthful college unusual at the time agreed to sponsor a technical school which was to be associated with the university college.

Yet all was far from well. The teaching staff resented the domination of the council's committee of management, and the corporation's power was not much weakened by the new constitution of 1903. The townspeople were mainly indifferent or even hostile to what was locally dubbed 'the great white elephant of Shakespeare Street': the college, it was urged, had 'failed to establish itself in local consciousness as one of the emblems of civic pride'. Stranded between indifference and interference, unblessed as yet by any substantial benefactions, the college was not given much encouragement even by the local industries it was supposed to benefit, for they were mostly in the hands of comparatively small masters, many of whom had little time for higher education. To D. H. Lawrence, who was a student at the teachers' training department between 1906 and 1908 but hardly an impartial witness, the college was no more than 'a little slovenly laboratory for the factory'. Errors in the returns of the number of students made to the Board of Education led in 1911 to the resignation of the principal, J. E. Symes, a somewhat rigid radical idealist whose relations with the corporation had been far from smooth. The Board of Education reported that the standard of work was no better, possibly worse, than that of the average secondary school or technical college. The natural science department gave the impression of 'dirty corners and confined spaces'. The report questioned Nottingham's claim to be a university college, administering a salutary shock which started an improvement in standards as well as a broadening of the framework of government.

*

This mixed parentage of means and motive inevitably brought forth a very varied offspring, and the new centres of learning displayed a widely differing range of achievement. Some were quick to acquire teachers and departments of great reputation, others were less fortunate. The only constant factor was the generally poor calibre of the students. Owens College, Manchester, in spite of early difficulties, was one of those that soon became famous as a centre for advanced learning. This was largely the result of the work of two men, H. E. Roscoe, who was professor of chemistry from 1857 to 1886, and A. W. Ward, the principal from 1889 to 1897. Both were much influenced by the pattern of research they had seen in contemporary German universities and sought to encourage within the college a spirit of genuine intellectual inquiry, which, as Roscoe phrased it, ought to be the 'vitalizing spirit of academic corporations'. As one of those who initiated experimental scientific work Roscoe brought Schorlemmer over from Germany in 1874 to fill the first British chair of organic chemistry. The milieu at Manchester was never purely scientific; the presence of Charles Hallé, the German who sponsored art and music, testifies adequately to the rising reputation of the city and college as a cultural centre. In 1870 the status of the college was further consolidated. Until then it had been governed by trustees, able, liberal-minded men, often from Dissenting families, but a Parliamentary Act in that year created a constitution comprising a president, court, council and senate. The college was finally awarded the accolade of full university status. 'I have always thought,' Lyon Playfair commented in 1876,

that Owens College ought to develop into a 'teaching University'. England contains no teaching University like the Scotch and German Universities ... Oxford and Cambridge have exalted the preparatory pedagogium, or Arts Faculty, to be the end instead of the beginning of the Universities, and thus have cut themselves off

from the professions ... Durham ... is too ecclesiastical to succeed. Manchester can become a teaching University for England
with the specific object of liberalizing professions and industrial
occupations ...

So Owens became the first constituent college of the new
federal Victoria University in 1880.

The university college at Liverpool afforded a shining example of the opportunity that the new universities could provide for brilliant young men on the threshold of a distinguished
career. From humble beginnings in a disused lunatic asylum,
the college progressed so far that it was admitted as a constituent member of Victoria University in 1884. It numbered
among its dons the English scholars, A. C. Bradley and Walter
Raleigh, Oliver Lodge, who held the chair of physics from 1881
until 1900 when he was appointed first principal of the university of Birmingham, Ronald Ross who was professor of tropical medicine and C. S. Sherrington who occupied the chair of
physiology. Augustus John taught for a time in the School of
Architecture and Applied Arts which had been established in
1894.

In fact it was Liverpool's proud boast, Ramsay Muir said
in 1901, that it was the first British university 'to treat architecture as on a level with other professions by devising a university curriculum for it; one of the first to attempt high
commercial education; the first to bring modern science
systematically to bear upon the plagues which hinder trade
in tropical regions'; it was also the first to appoint a professor
of veterinary medicine.

Birmingham, which received its charter of incorporation in
1900 – the enthusiastic support of Joseph Chamberlain was
largely responsible for this – was especially interested in developing skilled techniques, such as the biochemistry of fer-
mentation and allied topics relevant to the needs of the
brewing industry. Chamberlain brought Sir Oliver Lodge from
Liverpool to be its Principal. 'He collected half a million,'
Lodge said later, 'and when I remonstrated that buildings did
not constitute a university, that personnel was the greatest
thing to aim at, he said "No, spend the money now, give

people something to see, and I will get the other half million without much delay." ' An endowment of £50,000 from Sir James Chance provided a chair in engineering. The professor of mining, R. A. Redmayne, was responsible for the construction of a model coalmine used for instruction and underground surveying. The economic historian, W. J. Ashley, influenced by German and American treatment of the subject, sponsored the institution of a degree in commerce. At Leeds the department of mining specialized in the study of rescue apparatus for use amid noxious gases. Bristol, which obtained a charter of incorporation in 1909, had a number of specialized institutions, among them the Agricultural and Horticultural Research Station at Long Ashton, set up by the National Fruit and Cider Institute in 1903. Reading early made a special feature of agricultural studies.

Given the external and internal difficulties with which the civic universities were confronted, it is the more remarkable that they achieved so much. In spite of some mediocre staff and students, there had been developments of real importance. The admission of women, for instance, opened a new era in British education. Queen's College, London, had been founded in 1848, and Bedford College was established by Mrs Elizabeth Reid in 1849, but the movement for the higher education of women, meeting with a good deal of scorn and patient obstruction, hung fire. Elizabeth Garrett's decision to become a trained doctor brought about the formation of a committee in 1862 to secure the admission of women to the university examinations. In the 1860s women were allowed to attend some university lectures. Under the auspices of the London Ladies Educational Association university lectures for women only were arranged. Classes met and separated at the half-hours, when it was thought that the men might be otherwise engaged, and the women were admitted by a side door to avoid the risk of being seen crossing the front quadrangle. In 1878 the university agreed to permit women to take its degrees, though they were not fully admitted to the faculty of medicine until 1917, and in 1913 London was the first university to appoint a woman to a chair. The question of admitting women to Durham was raised in 1881 but the resolution was so hedged with restrictions that the advocates of women's education were dissatisfied; 'We asked for bread,' said Mrs Aldis, 'and they have given us a stone.' The actual admission of women students was postponed until 1895, and they were not fully admitted as members of Convocation until 1914. At Manchester women were admitted as students in 1883, though under strict regulations which were only gradually removed. Institutions for the higher education of women had been opened at Oxford and Cambridge well before the end of the century; but it was some time before they acquired parity of esteem with the men's colleges.

The question of admitting women was not the only bone of contention. London in particular was the scene of continuous discord, which came to a head with a plan for making University College and King's College into a teaching university as the Albert University of London, leaving London university as a purely examining institution. The project had the backing of the Inns of Court, the Law Society and the Royal College of Physicians and Surgeons. The government appointed a commission under Lord Selborne in May 1888 to investigate the plan; the commission, characterized as its critics said by 'incompatible futilities', opposed the notion of a second university for London, though it recommended the broadening of the existing teaching faculties. Unfortunately the Senate and Convocation were so much at odds that it seemed impossible to do this. Subsequently the government appointed in 1892 a new commission under the chairmanship of Lord Cowper which reported in 1894 in favour of the existing university, recommending that there should be two sets of examinations, one internal and one external. The proposed bill which was to implement these recommendations, drafted by Haldane in cooperation with Sidney Webb, at first failed to find support – it was cast out by the House of Lords, partly by the opposition of the bishops – but on the third occasion Haldane himself made such an impassioned speech that it was agreed to set up yet another commission under Haldane's friend, Lord Davey. This eventually formulated new statutes for London university which received the sanction of Parliament.

The complicated and tedious affairs of London were repeated on a smaller scale in the north where the constituent colleges of the Victoria University found it increasingly difficult to keep in step with each other. Inter-regional jealousies were supplemented by administrative and financial problems, and aggravated by disagreements on matters of policy. Leeds and Liverpool quarrelled bitterly in 1890 over a proposal to establish a chair in theology. Moreover each of the university colleges was beginning to hanker after full university status. In 1901 Ramsay Muir published a powerful plea for raising Liverpool to full status, founding his arguments on the important and original contributions which the college had made to education, and the corporation of Liverpool, resenting the dominant position of Manchester, levied a penny rate to maintain the proposed university. Leeds, the weakest of the trio, opposed the break-up, but in 1903 both Manchester and Liverpool secured their incorporation as fully fledged separate universities, thus leaving Leeds as the sole surviving partner in the Victoria University. Sheffield, a disgruntled and unsuccessful applicant for membership at an earlier date, opposed Leeds's claim to be entitled the Yorkshire University, and itself applied for full status, which it received in 1904. These teething pains were made worse by the constant financial problems created by inadequate resources, which the first subsidies from the Treasury alleviated but did not solve.

*

The new universities were, however, cautious in their experimentation. They did not strike out along very original lines. They borrowed the system of education which their professors had known at Oxford and Cambridge, sponsoring humane studies in departments which were often weak and lifeless. They had come into existence in a haphazard way in response to certain social needs which they did something to meet. Neither their founders nor their professors were perhaps very clear as to what should be the function or purpose of a university. 'To place a university in the middle of a great industrial and manufacturing population,' Joseph Chamberlain declared, 'is to do something to leaven the whole mass with higher aims and higher intellectual ambitions than would otherwise be possible to people engaged entirely in trading and commercial pursuits,' but it is to be feared that the language was more rhetorically compelling than historically accurate.

This is not to belittle what was achieved; yet, without the financial resources at the disposal of Oxford and Cambridge, let alone their traditions, the new universities inevitably took second place to the older foundations. Too often the colleges were ill-housed in industrial cities in poor areas; they had the misfortune to be shaped by Victorian aesthetics. It was euphemistically said of the buildings at Leeds that 'there was more Etruscan fortitude than Roman beauty in their general design'. Their social life was restricted, for although some halls of residence were opened, they were for the most part non-residential. (Even in 1952 half of the students at Sheffield either lived in the city or within a radius of thirty miles. On the other hand Reading was a pioneer in the provision of halls of residence; by 1913 there were five halls accommodating 278 out of 290 students.) Since many of their students came from lower middle-class and working-class homes, their environment and tastes remained in part proletarian and their social usage was often unavoidably philistine. In a sense difficult to define the new universities communicated knowledge rather than culture. Yet they had overcome immense difficulties, providing opportunities for men and women who would otherwise have never had the benefit of a university education. They represented a great and dynamic breakthrough in higher education, fracturing the centuries of dominance by Oxford and Cambridge and in so doing stimulating the latter to improve their own systems.

CHAPTER SEVEN

The Twentieth-Century Revolution

IF the nineteenth century was the seed time of the modern university, the twentieth century saw the seed come to harvest. The whole story in fact was not unlike the parable of the sower; the harvest was often full and remarkable but it was also irregular and uneven in pattern. In an effort to avoid the faults that had seemed all too characteristic of the older universities in the past, modern universities responded to contemporary social needs without thinking very deeply or creatively about their ultimate function in society. They essayed learning but fled from commitment. For both the new foundations and the old it was perhaps difficult to establish a balance between stability and progress, and inevitably in the tension between the two there was a degree of self-questioning, illustrated, for instance, by the setting up of the Franks Commission at Oxford in 1964. So much had been changed by then that it was impossible for any ivory tower to survive without having had its foundations sapped. But it was an open question whether some of the buildings which replaced the ivory towers were not, to extend the metaphor, pre-fabricated.

By the early twentieth century the developments which had been put in train by the university reform acts had done much to bring Oxford and Cambridge, as far as their administrative efficiency and curricula went, more into line with the times; but they left over many traditional modes of thought and behaviour which still aroused criticism. The last half-century has seen the steady disappearance of most of these, so that the two older universities are in many respects as 'modern' as the more recently founded institutions, disagreeable as it is to their critics to admit that this is so. In 1900 both Oxford and Cambridge were still privileged strongholds of the Church of England, but the process of secularization begun many years before accelerated especially after the end of the First World

War, as chapel attendance ceased to be compulsory and as religious belief itself was more insistently questioned by seniors and juniors alike. While religious instruction and worship continued to be available, the specifically religious character and Anglican tone of the universities had vanished more or less completely.

It was more to the point that Oxford and Cambridge still remained in 1900 the principal finishing schools of the upper and middle classes, recruiting most of their undergraduates from the independent public schools. Compton Mackenzie recalls that when he was an undergraduate at Magdalen in 1901 about half the 160 undergraduates came from Eton and a quarter of the remainder were Wykehamists, Harrovians and Carthusians. The college was perhaps even at that time exceptional in the exclusiveness of its clientele, but the aristocratic playboy and the indolent passman were still much in evidence at Oxford and Cambridge before 1914. The Master of Magdalene, Cambridge, indicated that a quarter of those who had matriculated in 1909 had failed to take a degree; of these 'a very large number consisted of men who came up to have a good time, and did not care to read or work hard'. Students of this sort became rare after 1918 but did not disappear entirely until the Second World War. Even in more recent times some colleges have drawn more exclusively from the older public schools than desert alone might seem to justify; though it is fair to guard against the snobbish inversion which takes it for granted that intelligent boys from the as yet independent schools should be excluded in favour of drearier candidates from humbler surroundings.

A major revolution had however been brought about in the social texture of the older universities by the institution in 1920 of state scholarships and county awards. At first a slow trickle, then a steady stream, of boys entered the colleges from lower middle and working-class homes and grammar schools. It has, however, often been said that even in the 1950s and 1960s Oxford and Cambridge have drawn their non-public-school boys from the larger grammar schools, and that the number of men from a working-class background is still small, especially by comparison with those in other universities. A fifth of the undergraduates at the university of London in 1955 were of working-class origin; 18 per cent had been to boarding schools and 58 per cent to L.E.A. secondary schools. In all other universities except Oxford and Cambridge 70 per cent came from L.E.A. schools, 10 per cent from boarding schools and 30 per cent from working-class homes.* In 1961–2 39 per cent of the undergraduates at Oxford and 25 per cent of those at Cambridge came from schools maintained by local authorities; in 1965–6 40 per cent at Oxford came from maintained schools and 41 per cent from independent schools (by comparison with 19 per cent and 62 per cent respectively in 1938–9). By the 1960s Oxford and Cambridge were beginning to siphon talent from all types of school.† A central clearing house for admissions, the Universities' Central Council on Admissions, was established in 1961 to cope with the excessively complex problem of multiple applications and with the object of coordinating the entrance requirements of the different universities. Oxford and Cambridge became members of this body in 1965. The virtual disappearance of the playboy and the dilettante may have deprived the universities of colour and of grace, which their undergraduate societies (and even, it must be confessed, some of their senior common rooms) seem sometimes to lack, but it was plainly no longer expedient, and even possibly unjust, that Oxford and Cambridge should be the preserves of the former governing classes. In fair exchange they became the breeding ground of the future managers of Britain's politics and industry.

Oxford and Cambridge made two further concessions to the twentieth century in the tardy recognition that they at last gave to women's degrees, and in the increasing emphasis which they

* There has in fact been no major increase in the working-class share of entry to the universities since the Education Act of 1944; it remains 25–26 per cent.

† In 1967 there were 3,689 applications for the entrance examination to Oxford, of whom 1,817, or 49 per cent, got places. The proportion of those admitted from maintained schools has risen steadily; 1938–9, 19 per cent; 1958–9, 30 per cent; 1964–5, 34 per cent. During the past three years (1965–8) it has averaged 41 per cent.

placed on scientific studies. Most of the women's colleges at Oxford and Cambridge were founded in the last three decades of the nineteenth century. Girton College, founded originally at Hitchin in 1869, moved to its present site at Cambridge in 1873 and Newnham, which owed much to the support of the liberal-minded Henry Sidgwick, was more or less established when Miss Clough was appointed Mistress in 1871. Of the Oxford colleges Lady Margaret Hall had been founded in 1878 and Somerville, named after the scientific writer Mary Somerville, in 1879. St Hugh's was founded by Miss Wordsworth, the first Principal of Lady Margaret Hall, in 1886 and St Hilda's, the ground for which had been purchased by Miss Beale, the Principal of Cheltenham Ladies' College, opened as a training college for women teachers in 1893.

Both Oxford and Cambridge, for so long exclusively masculine and mainly celibate societies, were understandably reluctant to assimilate women into their corporate life. They allowed women to attend university lectures, at first with a chaperone – though there were a few lecturers who both deplored and forbade their presence – and to sit the university examinations at which many girls performed with credit. But they would not admit them to degrees or give their dons the same status as their male colleagues. Furthermore the women's colleges were, as they long continued to be, far worse off financially than the men's societies.

In an attempt to resolve the controversial problem a syndicate at Cambridge recommended in 1897 that women should be given the titles of their degrees without becoming actual members of the university. This was an entirely paradoxical solution which would have created, as one of its critics suggested, 'a large unenfranchised class, a species of Uitlander'. The natural home for such a society, the legal historian, F. W. Maitland, commented wittily, would be the waiting room at Bletchley station: 'You wait there; but you do not wait there always. You change for Oxford and Cambridge.' But the proposal was voted down by 1,707 votes to 661. Its rejection was greeted with even more fervour by the undergraduates than it was by their seniors. The Cambridge Union condemned the syndicate's recommendations by 1,083 votes to 138 and over two thousand young men petitioned the vice-chancellor against the granting of degrees to women which 'would prove injurious to the position and efficiency of this University'.

The situation at Oxford was very similar. Here, however, the authorities, in response to a direct request by the chancellor, Lord Curzon, sponsored the setting up of a Delegacy of Women Students and admitted the women's colleges, together with the Society of Oxford Home Students, from which St Anne's was eventually to burgeon, as recognized societies. The immense social changes precipitated by the First World War meant that neither Oxford nor Cambridge could for ever delay full recognition, yet opinion was still very divided as to the best solution to the problem. The syndicate which the Council of the Senate had set up at Cambridge presented no uniform view: half of its members recommended that women should become full members of the university, the others revived the notion of a separate women's university. As both these suggestions proved unacceptable, it was proposed simply to give the women the title of their degrees, a motion that was passed by 1,011 votes to 369. Even this change aroused resentment among the die-hards, so much so that a senior member led a gang of undergraduates to damage the bronze gates which had been put up at Newnham in memory of the first Principal. Meanwhile at Oxford women had been given the right to matriculate as members of the university and to become full members of it; they were permitted to take all degrees, except curiously enough those in theology. The Second World War and its aftermath destroyed the last vestiges of inequality. In 1947 Girton and Newnham were accorded a status similar to that of the men's colleges; women were admitted to actual degrees and full membership of the university. At Oxford the women's colleges received full parity of status in the 1960s so that it is now possible for a woman to hold the office of vice-chancellor.

The other major concession to the twentieth century was the slow but steady acceptance of natural science as one of the principal objects of study and research. It was indeed the older universities' realization that they could not finance out of their own resources the expansion needed for the development of scientific studies which persuaded them, reluctant as they were, to accept grants from the Treasury. The First World War had underlined the necessity for subsidizing scientific research. A memorandum put forward by the Board of Education stressed the failure of the universities to provide an adequate supply of scientific workers, with the result that in 1915 the government set up a Department of Scientific and Industrial Research, which was constituted a committee of the Privy Council. Surviving the wars it was to be the main grant-in-aid for scientific research for the next half century.

The increase in the number of research workers in all fields was a phenomenon of the first decades of the century. When a conference of representatives of Commonwealth universities met in London in July, 1912, it was suggested that British universities should institute the degree of doctor of philosophy for post-graduate research work. This was strongly supported by the Foreign Office as many colonial and foreign students preferred to do their research work in America or Germany, where they could earn a doctor's degree, rather than in England, where they could only achieve a bachelor's degree. In 1917 Manchester, Liverpool, Leeds, Sheffield and Birmingham agreed to adopt a common course of action and were joined by all the universities except Cambridge which preferred to keep to the M.Litt. and M.Sc., though it soon came into line. It must be doubted whether the introduction of the degree materially diverted many foreigners and colonials to undertake research in Britain; but there was a steady, though not as yet a spectacular, increase in the number of graduate students at the universities.

*

There was no doubt that Oxford and Cambridge retained their pre-eminence among the British universities, even if the complacency of earlier years had given way by 1960 to a good deal of self-criticism and even a hint of introspective anxiety. The newer universities had long laboured under immense disadvantages. The money at their disposal, though steadily mounting as a result of state aid, was insufficient to finance expansion.

The advice given by the local businessmen and administrators, who dominated their courts and councils, did not always work in their true interests. 'Municipal rivalries, personal ambitions and rhetorical phrases,' the historian A. J. Grant commented at Leeds in 1902, 'have destroyed a most promising experiment in university education.'

The real defect of the newer universities was to be found neither in their scholarship nor in their constitutions. It still lay in the comparatively poor quality of their student intake, except possibly in those fields in which they specialized, such as agriculture at Reading, or in which they had an outstanding reputation, as for instance the school of medieval history under Tout and Tait at Manchester, or that of dentistry at Sheffield or the medical school at Edinburgh. The poor quality of the average student was largely the result of social factors, more especially the character of British education before 1939 which, by and large, encouraged boys and girls to leave school at an early age. There was comparatively little incentive for a boy to go to a university unless he was thinking of becoming a schoolmaster; business and industry, the two main takers of the later period, absorbed only a few graduates before 1945. Nor were the scholarships and awards adequate enough to maintain the impoverished student, even if he continued to live at his own home near the university. The very regional character of these universities, the extent to which they relied for their entry on the local grammar schools, their somewhat drab social pattern, ultimately diminished their intellectual capacity. It was not until the revolutionary changes in British education after the Second World War, in practice enabling the majority of those who were capable of getting anything out of a university education to go there with a county or state grant, that the picture was altered in a very material fashion.

There were, however, important developments in all the universities in the first half of the twentieth century. Most obviously this was a period of continued expansion. The growth of the university of London raised the problem of how to administer effectively such a conglomeration of different institutions. The Davey Commission had recognized 24 constituent colleges; between 1902 and 1925 eleven more were added. Yet there was no physical centre to this wide empire. In 1920 the university was offered $11\frac{1}{2}$ acres in Bloomsbury by the government on condition that King's College would also move there; but King's was disinclined to leave its old locale in the Strand, and the land was sold back to the vendor. In 1927 the university, assisted by a grant from the Rockefeller trustees, finally purchased the site on which the university buildings were to rise. It was not, however, easy to bring the federation of colleges into a harmonious relationship. In particular the Imperial College of Science, which combined the former Royal College of Science, the Royal School of Mines and the Central Technical College, and which had been given a charter in 1907, was reluctant to surrender its own wish to become a separate university. Eventually new statutes were drawn up for London, and came into operation on 21 March 1929. These provided for the setting up of a University Court for the whole university, which would distribute the grants which it received from the University Grants Committee and the London County Council to the constituent institutions.

Elsewhere the pattern which had been already established was followed; though geographical factors obliged universities more and more to develop their new buildings on the peripheries of the great cities. Birmingham commenced the development of its Edgbaston estate as early as 1900 though the buildings in Mason Street were not vacated entirely until after 1950. Exeter, another creation of the University Extension movement, founded in 1901, was in part able to leave its confined quarters in Gandy Street and move to the beautiful Streatham estate, which had been acquired in 1922. Nottingham, benefiting from the generosity of Sir Jesse Boot, later Lord Trent, had buildings spreadeagled across a fine campus. Leeds embarked on an ambitious plan for rehousing the university in 1924 and received a generous donation from Sir Edward Bretherton. The notion of founding a university college at Leicester, originally associated with a possible war memorial, was first aired in 1917–18 and won generous local support. The college was established in October 1921 in the old lunatic asylum with Dr Rattray, a Unitarian minister of liberal views, as the acting principal, three assistants to teach Botany, Geography and French and nine students. A university college had been set up at Hull in 1926 and was endowed with a quarter of a million pounds by T. R. Ferens. A new constitution was devised for the university of Durham and came into being in 1937; as a result the Newcastle School of Medicine and Armstrong College were merged into King's College, Newcastle, which was recognized as a constituent college of the university of Durham.

These developments were important but not spectacular. They represented in one view the continued 'planless expansion' of higher education. It was perhaps inevitable that in many respects the new universities should appear rather angular and untidy replicas of Oxford and Cambridge. Their first professors had been necessarily drawn from the older universities, and tended therefore to make their own departments something of a carbon copy. Their faculties were sometimes small and parochial, especially in those subjects like classics, for which they often had only a few undergraduates. This was a serious drawback as the universities failed to create the integrated courses which would have proved most useful to their students. In similar fashion the early wardens of the residential halls and hostels may have tried to make their societies too reminiscent of Oxford and Cambridge quadrangles; but high tables, grace and sherry were not the civilizing influences which it was hoped that they would be, and in some respects undergraduate life was apt to be crude and unsophisticated. There was also a danger that the continued expansion of the universities would lead to a lowering of standards: the number of university teachers, excepting Oxford and Cambridge, rose from 1,478 in 1910 to 3,819 in 1938–9, 7,682 in 1949–50, 11,483 in 1959–60, and, inclusive of Oxford and Cambridge, reached over 25,000 in 1965–6,* and while over three quarters of the

* Full-time academic staff at Oxford in 1922 numbered 357, in 164–5, 1,127. See A. H. Halsey and M. Trow, 'University Teaching: the structure of a profession', *Anarchy and Culture*, ed. D. Martin, Routledge & Kegan Paul, 1969, pp. 37–50.

dons at Oxford and Cambridge held first class degrees, this was only true of just over half the staff at the other universities.

The First World War was the decisive end of a period in the history of Oxford and Cambridge as indeed in so much else. It had soon emptied the universities of all their students save those unfit for military service; the numbers of men at Cambridge at the start of the academic year in 1913, 1914 and 1915 were 3,263, 1,658 and 825; by Easter 1916, they had fallen to 575. Moreover the war acted as a social catalyst, challenging many established ideas and injecting the young soldiers who returned to the universities with a questioning and critical mood. Although they were on occasions unwilling to buckle to the traditional etiquette and disciplines, especially of the older universities, by and large they settled down happily to the new life. Once the war generation had graduated, some at a comparatively elderly age, the stage might have seemed set fair for steady expansion and consolidation.

And in a sense these were the key-words of the inter-war years at the British universities. Except for Leicester and Hull, no new university colleges were founded, but there was considerable building, especially of scientific laboratories. The clue to this expansion was the rapid rate at which government subsidies to universities began to increase, though the depression of the 1930s may have slowed it down. Individual donors also provided princely benefactions, Lord Nuffield at Oxford, Sir Edward Bretherton at Leeds, and Herbert Austin at Cambridge. There were constitutional changes at Oxford and Cambridge arising out of the report, published in 1923, of the royal commission which the government had set up in 1919 under the chairmanship of H. H. Asquith, and of the subsequent statutory commission presided over by Lord Ullswater. Many new professorial posts were created, there were significant changes in the honour school examinations and new courses were established, most notably that of philosophy, politics and economics (modern greats) initiated at Oxford in 1920. Thus the universities expressed their continuing anxiety to prepare their students for the modern world, as well as to improve the facilities for scientific research.

It is not very easy to describe the mood of the universities in the inter-war years. The student population of the 1930s was certainly in many respects disturbed and anxious, made so by the self-evident mediocrity of many contemporary politicians, by the forbidding threat of mass unemployment and the challenge to a liberal philosophy of life offered by the violent actions of the rising dictatorships. The mood appeared in some respects schizophrenic in its outward manifestations, leading on the one hand to ardent support of the League of Nations, disarmament and pacifism, and on the other to combat in the International Brigade in the Spanish Civil War. The outlook seemed pessimistic. The university authorities sometimes gave the impression of an uncritical complacency, sponsoring progressive developments without very much concern with basic essentials; though to their credit must surely be placed the welcome given to the growing number of foreign scholars exiled from their own countries by the intolerant malevolence of their rulers.

The Second World War shattered the steady development of university life though the universities were not to be as empty as they had been in 1914–18; many of their senior members were usefully employed in government service. With the return of peace they had to cope with a back-log of demands for places, and they were soon full to overflowing. The Ministry of Labour and National Service laid down that ninety per cent of places in 1946 were to be filled by ex-service applicants. It was soon apparent that there was a revolutionary change in the economic and social climate of the country which was no longer content that so small a proportion of its sixth-formers should enjoy the benefits of a university education. The effects of the Education Acts of 1944 and 1945, the provision of secondary school education for all who wanted it, the raising of the school leaving age, the improved facilities at grammar schools, the escalation of county and state grants so that by 1969 there was hardly a university student who was not in receipt of a grant, the immense increase in the amount of money distributed by the University Grants Committee, the greater readiness of industry and business to employ graduates and the more widespread belief among sixth-formers that a university course was a natural sequel to school, resulted in a tremendous expansion in the number of potential university entrants and in the foundation of new universities. Cambridge had 5,374 undergraduates in 1938–9, 5,865 in 1946–7 and 7,016 in 1954–6. Whereas there had been 20,000 full-time students in British universities in 1900–1, there were 50,000 by 1938–9 and this figure had risen to 82,000 in 1954–5 and 118,000 in 1962–3. The older university colleges were raised to full status; Nottingham, Southampton and Hull by 1948, 1952 and 1954, Leicester in 1957 and Exeter in 1955; Newcastle parting from Durham achieved university status in 1963. Dundee, which became separated from St Andrews, achieved full status in 1967.

Committee reports and speeches by educationalists, industrialists and politicians reiterated the need for more graduates. The Association of Scientific Workers in 1944 demanded an immediate expansion of existing universities and the raising of the existing university colleges to full status. The Association of University Teachers asked for a fifty per cent increase in the student population, radical changes in the constitutional structure of the universities and improved salaries for university lecturers. A committee set up under the chairmanship of Sir Alan Barlow in 1945 reported that the existing 55,000 scientists should be increased to 90,000 by 1955. Other committees examined the needs of education (McNair report), agriculture (Loveday report), medicine (Goodenough report), oriental languages (Scarborough report), and social studies (Clapham report). There was an impressive growth in the number of research workers; in 1938–9 there had been 389 at Cambridge, in 1947–8, 578 and in 1954–5, 1,028. 'The truth is,' the Vice-Chancellor of London declared in 1946, 'that all the professions are pressing us, as universities, to take on a greater part, if not the whole of the requisite professional or technical training for their own professional subjects.'

The edifice of reports dealing with the problems of higher education was crowned by the Robbins commission. A committee under the chairmanship of Lord Robbins had been set up to 'review the pattern of full-time education' in February 1961, representing an informative and massive report in October 1963. It recommended a coordinated policy for higher education on the ground that, unless higher education was speedily reformed, there was little hope of 'this densely populated island maintaining an adequate position in the fiercely competitive world of the future'. The committee envisaged a rise in the number of post-graduates from 9,500 in 1961–2 to 32,000 by 1980–1 and a consequential increase in the number of university students, so that by 1980–1 some 346,000 out of a total of 558,000 places should have been provided in universities. This could only be achieved by a further impressive expansion of the facilities offered by universities and technical colleges. The simple faith which the committee showed in the potential intellectual capacity of British youth and the likely remedial impact of higher education on British economy was touching rather than persuasive. Many of their recommendations were, however, valuable and helped to shape the future of the universities.

*

The lessons of Oxford and Cambridge and of the other universities were not forgotten when after the Second World War a spate of new universities were projected and founded: Keele (North Staffordshire), Sussex (Brighton), Kent (Canterbury), Essex (Wivenhoe Park, Colchester), East Anglia (Norwich), York, Warwick, Lancaster and Stirling. The university colleges of the past era had had to instruct their students according to a syllabus over which they had no real control since they were simply fulfilling the requirements of the university whose external degrees their students were taking. They lacked capital for necessary developments and were partly dependent on private generosity for expansion. The new universities were in every way much more advantageously placed. Where the earlier foundations had been haphazard the new universities were carefully sited and conscientiously planned in all particulars; the government provided the capital and the recurrent costs. Furthermore a determined and deliberate effort was made to avoid some of the defects which had characterized the older universities. They were definitely not intended to be replicas of Oxford and Cambridge. Their founders – the University Grants Committee, and the committee which it established to plan the new institution – were aware that a new university must have its own character and identity, not because they disapproved of the older pattern but because they did not want more second or third-rate imitations. The modern universities were to stand on their own feet, equal to but different from the old universities. Hence the stress that was laid by the planners of the university of Essex on separate apartments or flats for students with a common living room and a small kitchen: 'A university,' the vice-chancellor of Essex commented, 'should ... provide an experience of living as well as the opportunity for learning. Without this, education is dehumanized, the student himself defrauded.' The new system was to some extent a recognition of a current trend, a reaction from living in community and an emphasis on a privacy of existence as far as possible outside the direct interference of college or university.

The determination to break away from the conventional pattern has appeared most conspicuously in the build-up of departments and the nature of the degree course. In the belief that no single university is competent to develop advanced studies in every faculty, the modern universities have made a self-denying ordinance to specialize in certain fields to the exclusion of others. The tendency has been to create large strong departments divided into specialized schools. They have abandoned the conviction that it is necessary to promote studies in all the older disciplines; at most of them no law is taught, and theology and classics only at Canterbury.* On the other hand they have all made provision for the modish study of sociology. A cultural background for specialized studies is provided by integrated courses. Keele instituted a foundation year that combined arts and science studies. Sussex, York (though here a student can follow a single honours course), East Anglia and others sought to marry depth with breadth. The schematic curriculum is often interesting and inviting; at Warwick the

*Lancaster University has a chair of religious studies.

historian may expect a term either in Florence or in the United States.

The planners were particularly aware of the gulf between the scientist whose interest was confined to his own subject, and sometimes to a small section of that, and the arts man who retained an underlying contempt for science, often the continuum of a division which had come into being in the upper forms of school. 'All undergraduates,' Asa Briggs wrote of Sussex University, 'would be expected not to study a multitude of unrelated subjects side by side or one after the other, but continuously to relate their specialized study to impinging and overlapping studies.' To break down rigid specialization the academic courses at Sussex have been organized in schools of studies, to free the students from the restrictions often imposed by a faculty or departmental system; multi-subject honour courses are offered, history, language and philosophy (on which much stress is placed) being studied in close association with each other under the cover of English, European, American, Asian or African studies. Some attempt has been made to study science in its social context. On paper at least this seems to be an advance on the Keele requirement that all scientists should study one arts subject and vice versa. 'The weekly lecture on the modern European mind,' David Daiches wrote some two years after the university had opened in 1961,

the audience of undergraduates and faculty packed on the steps of an inadequate lecture-theatre in the unfinished Physics building, the excited struggle in argument to the refectory afterwards for lunch, and the reverberations in unexpected places all the week, are the most remarkable evidence of intellectual vitality that the university can yet show.

There is no question that the planners have planned skilfully and well; but it remains to be seen whether the planned syllabus, given the natural level of the intelligence of the majority of university students, may not prove too ambitious and over-elaborate.

The more recently founded universities have had their critics. They have urged that it would have been more sensible to have founded the modern universities in large urban aggregations, an idea in part rejected on the grounds of cost, rather than to have placed them arbitrarily in parkland in the vicinity of towns that are little more than centres of large markets such as Norwich, Canterbury or Colchester. The choice of the site of some of the new universities appears rather the result of regional pressures than long-term considerations. The creation of a university town such as is envisaged at Wivenhoe Park or has to some extent occurred already at Keele must make social cohesion difficult outside the academic community; there is a danger that the university may exist in a semi-polarized social and cultural isolation. Others have declared that it would have been both cheaper and more efficient to have greatly expanded the existing universities which already possess the very expensive facilities, libraries and laboratories, that the modern universities have had to start from scratch; nor have such critics been rebuffed by the argument that there is an optimum number of students beyond which a university cannot be a socially coherent unit. Finally it has been observed that whereas the universities of the earlier period were organic if haphazard growths, the newer universities are samples of a planned economy; but some have doubted whether the premises upon which the planning was founded may not prove fallacious. They question whether in fact there are out of the expanding total population as many men and women as for instance the Robbins Report has suggested who are capable of benefiting from a university education,* or whether the country's need of graduates is as great as it has been made out to be by progressive educationalists. It is not even clear as yet how the modern universities are going to develop, whether, for in-

---

*The Robbins committee recommended more than 40 per cent increase in four years, from 139,000 places in 1963–4 to 197,000 in 1967–8; in fact in 1968 the universities offered nearly 220,000 places. Between 1962–3 and 1967–8 the number of students engaged in full-time higher education increased from 217,000 to 376,000. It is anticipated that this number may reach 750,000 by 1982; but there is already some evidence of unemployment, or of unsuitable employment, among highly qualified arts graduates. See Richard Layard and John King, 'Expansion since Robbins', *Anarchy and Culture*, ed. D. Martin, op. cit., pp. 13–36.

stance, the apparent fashionableness of Sussex would quickly fade (as Keele's seems to have done), or whether economic stress might not ultimately pare some of the elaborate and expensive planning. It would be a pity if the modern universities, the expression of a buoyant optimism and a faith in the future that was not very typical of British life in the 1960s, do not in time become the essential and valuable contribution to higher education that their planners hoped that they would be. They have at least considerable attraction and much merit.

The forerunner of the 'whitebrick' universities was that of North Staffordshire, sited at Keele, the former Victorian mansion of the Sneyd family, three miles from Stoke-on-Trent. The idea germinated in 1946 but the first plans were rejected by the University Grants Committee. Established successfully in 1949–50, Keele was the brainchild of two remarkable men, both ailing septuagenarians, A. D. Lindsay (Lord Lindsay of Birker), the Master of Balliol, and a Socialist cleric and alderman, the Rev. Thomas Horwood, vicar of Etruria. Although Lindsay, whom Horwood persuaded to accept the principalship, did not live long enough to see much of what he had planted bear fruit and in spite of the fact that for much of the time he was an ill man who did not find it easy to see eye to eye with his colleagues, the university was an expression of his basic attitude to education. He had no wish to found a university simply along the lines of the existing foundations. He insisted that it should be residential and he was concerned that it should be fully co-educational. Much influenced by the Manchester school and through it by German university theorists, he put a high value on research, but he subordinated the research-worker and the specialist to the good teacher. He believed that the modern university's essential function was to provide for careers in the post-war world and, shades of Jowett, he wanted to foster the all-round man whose education embraced an understanding of science as well as of humane studies. The most striking feature of the curriculum was the compulsory foundation course. Arts and Social Science students were obliged to take a subsidiary course in a natural science or mathematical subject and students of science had to offer a subsidiary subject in an Arts or Social Science course.

Keele, as it were, set the pattern, though it was not slavishly copied; a conspicuous variety of differing modes and operations arose among its followers. Sussex, the first of these, for which Hardy Amies designed the ceremonial robes of honorific doctors, was soon in the course of construction at Brighton, and it admitted its first students in 1961. The university of Essex sprang from a recommendation of the County Council in 1959 and came into being two years later, admitting its first students in 1964. York (1963) was founded on the collegiate pattern of the older universities. It was designed to have eight colleges, of approximately 300 students, half of whom would be resident, the remainder living in lodgings or student flats. The colleges were not to be autonomous nor would they control admission, but they were to be centres of teaching on a tutorial pattern. East Anglia (1963), Kent (1965), Warwick (1965) and Lancaster (1964) all have their special characteristics. Nor must it be forgotten that various technological colleges have been raised to university status. In addition to the technological universities at Edinburgh, Strathclyde* and Heriot-Watt,† another Scottish university was founded at Stirling in 1967. A second university projected for Northern Ireland at Coleraine to reinforce Queen's University, Belfast, founded in 1845, admitted its first student in 1968.

The expansion of the universities is contemporary history, history that is not easily recorded or analysed. There are many who believe sincerely that in a truly democratic society there should be equal opportunity for all children, and that a university education should be provided for all those who wish to avail themselves of it. There are others who find in education the idealism for making a better world which they no longer find in religious belief. But basically university expansion

*Originated in 1796 under the will of John Anderson, professor of natural philosophy at Glasgow; it was affiliated to the university of Glasgow in 1913.

†It started life as a school of arts in 1822, turned to scientific and practical studies and was affiliated to the university of Edinburgh in 1933.

since the end of the Second World War has been rooted more realistically in the compelling necessities of history. After 1945 Britain found herself in a competitive world, often outclassed by the great powers, Russia and the United States, and in an economic position that was only precariously solvent. Commercial expansion and scientific advance were the prerequisites and the essential complements to economic solvency and political reputation. The universities have become an investment in which a great deal of money is being poured. It remains to be seen whether the universities pay the dividends which the politicians desire. Fortunately it is impossible for the historian to identify properly, certainly not to prejudge, the effects of a movement which is still in being and has yet to reach its maximum impetus and full fruition.

ORIGINS AND STRUCTURE OF CIVIC UNIVERSITIES

	Precursor	Opened	University charter granted	Medical School Started or to start	Medical School Incorporated in university or precursor	Full-time Student Population 1967/8 Total	Under-grad %	Post-grad %	Science-based* %	Non-science based* %	Resources 1967/8 Library† (,000 volumes)	Recurrent grant £m.
OLDER												
Birmingham	Mason Coll.	1880	1900	1841	1892	6401	77	23	62·9	37·1	725	5·4
Bristol	University Coll.	1876	1909	1833	1893	5612	84	16	54·2	45·8	340	3·7
Leeds	Yorks. Coll. of Science	1874	1904	1831	1884	7946	84	16	59·5	40·5	700	5·5
Liverpool	University Coll.	1881	1903	1844	1884	6299	83	17	68·9	31·1	580	4·6
Manchester‡	Owens Coll.	1851	1880	1825	1872	7437	83·5	16·5	51·1	48·9	765	5·5
Newcastle	Physical Sci. Coll., later Armstrong Coll.	1871	1871 (Durham); 1963 (N'castle)	1833	1852 (Durham); 1963 (N'castle)	5420	86	14	68·5	31·5	400	4·1
Sheffield	Firth Coll.	1879	1905	1828	1897	5301	86	14	67·5	32·5	370	4·0
Belfast	Coll. of Q.U.I.	1845	1908	1878	1845	5473	90·5	9·5	55·1	44·9	400	2·7
YOUNGER												
Exeter	Technical and Extension Coll.; University Coll.	1894; 1922	1955	—	—	2970	85	15	32·9	67·1	205	1·5
Hull	University Coll.	1928	1954	—	—	3516	89	11	41·3	58·7	290	1·9
Leicester	University Coll.	1927	1957	—	—	2874	82·5	17·5	42·2	57·8	250	1·6
Nottingham	University Coll.	1881	1948	1970	1970	4526	79	21	60·9	39·1	330	2·8
Reading	University Coll.	1892	1926	—	—	4258	86	14	45·8	54·2	320	2·5
Southampton	Hartley Inst.; University Coll.	1862; 1902	1952	1971§	1971	3852	81	19	53·3	46·7	300	2·6

Notes: * Figures in these columns assume 1964-5 pattern maintained.
† Approximate figures.
§ Probable but not certain date.
‡ Excludes University of Manchester Institute of Science and Technology.

SOURCE: *Financial Times*, 11 March 1968

PART TWO

CHAPTER EIGHT

Administration and Government

S O M E knowledge of the history of the way in which the universities have been administered is an essential prerequisite to understanding their present function in society. When the medieval university came into being, its obvious overlord was the bishop of the diocese in which it was located; Oxford lay in the care of the Bishop of Lincoln, Cambridge of the Bishop of Ely. It was not very long before the national, and the international, reputation of these growing communities of scholars brought on to the scene both royal authority and ultimate papal supervision. Furthermore from its very start the university enjoyed its privileges as a result of backing from the Crown; in return it had to admit the Crown's intervention, even when its own interests were not necessarily being served. Papal authority, more remote and less easy to put into operation, was more tenuous; but it was invoked by the universities against the local bishop and even against the Archbishop of Canterbury, who by the end of the fourteenth century regarded the universities as within the sphere of his own metropolitan visitation. To the end of the Middle Ages it was to the papal court that university scholars looked for preferment and patronage.*

There was, however, another side to the story. The university was, as its very name implies, a corporation or community of scholars, many of them young intelligent men of critical minds, sturdily independent in character, who were less likely than some other contemporary groups to be subservient to authority. It is worthwhile recalling that while medieval society was authoritarian by nature and firmly convinced that the hierarchical principle was founded on divine law, medieval men and women were solicitously concerned with a just acceptance of

---

*See E. F. Jacob, 'English University Clerks in the Later Middle Ages', in *Essays in the Conciliar Epoch*, 3rd edn, Manchester University Press, 1963, pp. 207–39.

their rights. From the very start the scholars of the universities were therefore aware of the need to protect their privileges and to regulate their own affairs. Apart from the chancellor, who was originally the bishop's official, they had no natural head. The university was a republic of free men who were entitled to have their say in the conduct of their own business. It was perhaps no accident that the universities came into existence at the same time as the concept of representation, which led to the genesis of parliamentary assemblies such as the English Parliament, the French States General and the Spanish Cortes. If in the last analysis the government of the university was something of a compromise which admitted the ultimate right of external authorities, such as the bishop, the pope and the king – the final legatee of this system was to be the Crown or its agents – yet the scholars shared freely in regulating their own affairs and were accorded a substantial degree of autonomy. The older universities thus secured a measure of freedom which they never lost, even if they have occasionally abused it, and attained a degree of administrative initiative and a spirit of independence which most non-British universities have lacked. It was to prove their most precious heritage, and it still remains their principal protection against undue domination by the state and contemporary pressure groups.

The administration of Oxford and Cambridge was modelled on that of the university at Paris, and was set up to meet certain needs and to solve certain problems which inevitably arose from the continuing existence of a large floating population of scholars and students in a medieval township. There had to be a guiding hand to deal with the disciplinary problems typical of a violent age, to undertake negotiations with the authorities in town and church, to fix regulations, to administer jurisdiction and to deal with all the hundred and one problems that were bound to arise in establishing exercises for degrees, in awarding them and in financing the business of the university.

It seems very likely that it was mutual interest that drew the scholars together into faculties or departments, of which there were five: theology, canon and civil law, medicine and arts. The faculty of arts, though technically inferior to the others,

148

was very soon the most important. The masters who made up
the senior members of Oxford and Cambridge were divided into
two groups. The masters actually employed in lecturing and
teaching, who after graduation had been given the *licentia
docendi* (the licence to teach), were known as the regent masters.
They were supplemented by non-regent masters, graduates who
presided over residential halls or were engaged in university
work other than teaching. From the very start it was clear that
the masters and the faculties needed representatives invested
with executive powers to negotiate with outside bodies. Probably it was in this way that the first essentially university
officials, the proctors, came into existence. Elected by the
faculty of arts they quickly came to represent the whole body of
scholars. In 1248, for instance, they were to be found at Wood-
stock arguing on behalf of Oxford University against the Jews
and the townspeople in the presence of King Henry III.

As the principal executive officers of the university the proctors acquired very considerable powers.* They supervised lectures, disputations and other exercises for the degree. They
controlled the sale of foodstuffs, to prevent the exploitation of
undergraduates by the townsfolk and other unscrupulous merchants, and were empowered to bring before the chancellor's
court monopolists and forestallers, who would buy a scarce
commodity, force up its price and sell it at a profit. They were
in some sense responsible for the finances of the university,
having charge of the university treasury or chest and of the
caution money deposited as security for the performance of
the degree exercises. They were endowed with authority to
punish offenders who contravened university regulations, to
suspend residents (or gremials as they were technically described) from the power of voting and to prevent non-residents
from taking degrees. They had a virtual right of veto (which
the faculty of regent masters in arts may have possessed originally) as well as the power to take independent action supposing
the chancellor failed in his duty to the regent masters. Their

*For a good brief review of the proctors' functions see W. A. Pantin
in the *Annual Report to the Delegates of Privileges, 1967–8*, Supplement
no. 3 to the *Oxford University Gazette*, vol. XCIX, March 1969, pp. 1–9.

disciplinary power, with which proctorial authority is usually connected, was, as it still is, only a small and even a subordinate part of their duties.

Although the proctors were the most active university officers, the chancellor took precedence of them. It would, however, be inaccurate to suggest that the chancellor was in his own person the head of the university; his authority was conjoint with that of the proctors. Originally he had been an episcopal official, but he soon became primarily the chief official of the university. He was never, as were the proctors, the mouthpiece of the masters; he was the bridge between the university and the church, the bishop, the pope and the king. His executive powers were considerable, being both an extension of the episcopal authority with which he had originally been invested and of privileges which he had been given by the king. As early as 1251 the chancellor of Oxford was empowered to punish clerks for all crimes except those of the most serious nature such as murder and manslaughter. In 1260 he was granted authority over the Jews, a powerful community in Oxford who were involved in disputes with the scholars over the rates of interest which they levied for loans. In 1279 Archbishop Pecham decreed that a sentence of excommunication by the chancellor was valid throughout the southern province. His judicial powers exercised through the court over which he or his deputy presided included the right of imprisonment, expulsion, suspension and loss of privilege and the imposition of fines. Eventually he came to have very considerable powers over the town as well as the university, the cause of continuous and prolonged resentment.

The chancellor, who had either to be a doctor of divinity or a doctor of canon law, was elected by the regent masters and confirmed in his authority (at Oxford) by the Bishop of Lincoln, who could also recall his commission. At first he was a resident don – Robert Grosseteste was the first chancellor of Oxford (1221) of whom we know, Hugh de Hotton, of Cambridge (1226) – but by the end of the fifteenth century at both universities the office of chancellor was beginning to be filled by a diocesan bishop. It was, however, ridiculous to suppose that a busy bishop, devoted as he might be to the interests of the university, could exercise a more than cursory supervision. As a result the chancellor's duties were gradually taken over by a deputy, whom he appointed, known as his commissary or vice-chancellor. Although the chancellor's powers were so substantial he was never an autocrat. It was possible to appeal from the chancellor's ruling to the body of regent masters, known collectively at Oxford as Congregation, and from Congregation to Convocation, an even wider body consisting of the regent and non-regent masters.

For the masters represented the determinative corporations in the universities, which, like other medieval guilds, were hierarchical in organization, but had many features of republican and democratic societies. The Congregation of regent masters at Oxford was the pivot of the university organization, possessing an initiative and a position which the individual faculties lacked. It seeems probable that there were three bodies or meetings which dealt with university business at Oxford in the Middle Ages; the rather sparsely documented Black Congregation which consisted of the regent masters in arts, the Congregatio Minor or Congregation which comprised the regent masters from all the faculties and was the effective executive meeting of the university, and the Congregatio Magna or Convocation, consisting of both the regent and the non-regent masters, that is, the teaching and administrative personnel of the university.

Congregatio Magna or Convocation, normally meeting in St Mary's Church, alone had the power to make permanent statutes; it was the final court of appeal and the supreme governing body of the university. A late fifteenth-century document gives an account of the way in which a statute was made in the medieval university. First of all the proctors brought the proposed statute before the Black Congregation for initial discussion. Then the following day Convocation was summoned so that the non-regent masters, informed of the contents of the proposed statute, could elect 'scrutators'. The statute was then discussed at length by Congregation in St Mary's. Before the vote was taken the different faculties had an opportunity to consider the matter individually; the theologians gathered in the Congregation house, the lawyers went to the chapel of St Anne, the physicians to the chapel of St Thomas, the proctors and the regent masters to the chapel of the Virgin Mary, while the non-regents presided over by their scrutators remained in the choir. In this instance the proceedings lasted five days.

As the Scottish and continental universities were divided into 'nations', so the English medieval universities were separated roughly into northerners and southerners, the dividing line being represented not by the river Trent as was once thought but more probably by the river Nene.* The presence of many young men drawn from all parts of the kingdom, often passionate in their opinions and sometimes given to violence, was a frequent cause of indiscipline. Divisions between northerners and southerners seem to have been one of the most obvious causes of dispute. The university accordingly followed the custom of appointing its own officers, some thirty-four in all including the proctors, according to the same regional distinction. Only the officers of the chancellor – the chaplains, bedel and registrar – seem to have been excluded from this system. As a result colleges which already had strong regional associations became even more closely identified with the northerners or southerners.

This administrative pattern established at Oxford was paralleled by developments at Cambridge. Here too the head of the university was the chancellor assisted by the proctors, whose functions were very similar to those of their Oxford contemporaries; likewise the chancellor was more often represented by a resident deputy, the vice-chancellor. The graduate masters were similarly divided into regents and non-regents each constituting one house at the Senate. Under the general supervision of the chancellor and proctors a variety of officials performed the tasks necessary to a growing organization: bedels† of

* See A. B. Emden's essay 'Northerners and Southerners in the Organization of the University to 1509' in *Oxford Studies presented to Daniel Callus*, ed. R. W. Southern, Oxford, Clarendon Press, 1964, pp. 1–30.

† The beadle (the archaic form 'bedel' is still in use in Oxford) was a functionary who preceded the rector or chancellor in processions (the only duty he still performs), took the votes in Congregation, read out its statutes and decrees, announced lectures and so forth.

theology, canon law and arts, scrutators who counted the votes
in the non-regent house, taxors who were responsible for tax-
ing the private halls and carried out some of the functions
(such as presiding over the assizes of bread and beer,* and of
weights and measures) which were performed at Oxford by the
clerk of the market, a registrar or university scribe and
librarian.

The medieval undergraduate would have been more aware
of the university machine than his sixteenth-century successor,
for it was the university which taught and examined him,
awarded him a degree and gave him, if he was so qualified, the
right to teach. It did not, however, house or feed him: this
was left to the principals of private halls.† An Oxford ordinance
of 1420 laid down that all scholars and their servants had on
their arrival to take an oath that they would obey the statutes,
accept the government of a principal and not live in a private
house. The principals were to swear that they would only admit students of good character who would regularly pay their
dues and obey the statutes. The private halls were residential
hostels which had to be licensed by the university, and the
principal had naturally to obey its rules and regulations. He
was free to administer his hall as he thought suitable, imposing
such additional rules as he held to be needful for his students.
The connexion between the university and his hall was, however, a tenuous one and did not demand the loyalty that the
colleges later came to do.

In the medieval university, as it has already been pointed
out, the colleges played only a minimal part, and their connexion was not much closer than that of the private halls.
Their administrative structure, however, disclosed their potential significance. The colleges were small bodies of graduates –
some included poor scholars – living in common. They were
endowed with more or less property, according to the genero-

---

* In most medieval towns the assizes regulated the weight of bread
according to the price of wheat and the price of ale according to the
price of wheat, barley and oats.

† See W. A. Pantin, 'The Halls and Schools of Oxford' in *Oxford
Studies presented to Daniel Callus*, op. cit., pp. 31–100.

sity of their founder and later benefactors. The college statutes provided for a head, known by various titles, and a number of fellows or scholars; in certain colleges, provision was made for poor scholars maintained out of the foundation (for instance at Clare College, Cambridge, and Exeter College, Oxford), and ultimately for fee-paying undergraduates; Magdalen College, Oxford, appears to have been the first to have made statutory provision for them. The number of fellows was regulated by the extent of the endowments.

In most colleges the master was elected by the fellows. He was the effective business manager of the house, but was generally assisted by a number of officials selected from among the fellows, deans, bursars, or treasurers, as well as by chaplains, bible-clerks, manciples, butlers, cooks and barbers. In general the fellows had to be in orders – though this was not the case at Trinity Hall, Cambridge, where the stress was on civil and canon law – and vacant fellowships were filled by the master and fellows by election. In many respects a college was a university in miniature, dining, worshipping and possessing property in common. Matters of dispute were referred to the Visitor of the college, usually a diocesan bishop, who had the final say in interpreting the statutes. In other ways, though by and large they were less well-endowed, colleges were like monastic houses, requiring similar bursarial supervision. Such provision as there was for lecturing and teaching was limited. It was the transformation of colleges into undergraduate societies which changed their character and brought the government and administration of the universities under their control.

This was, as we have seen, the major revolution of the sixteenth century. The process by which the colleges obtained control over the university may be obscure, but it resulted from the disappearance of most of the private halls and from the fact that the university's officials were drawn from the colleges. Furthermore membership of Congregation and Convocation came to be limited to fellows and members of colleges. At Cambridge the power of government was gradually collecting in the hands of the Caput, a body which consisted of the vice-chancellor and some five persons usually chosen from among the heads of colleges. The approval of this oligarchical body was necessary before graces were placed before the Senate, which increasingly found itself at their mercy and its power much prescribed. These administrative changes, foreshadowed in earlier statutes, were crystallized in the Elizabethan statutes of 1570 which were imposed in spite of protests from the regent masters who believed, rightly, that they were losing a considerable part of their power and influence.

At Oxford an almost identical trend created the Hebdomadal Board, consisting of the heads of colleges, and led to the recodification of the statutes carried out under the direction of Archbishop Laud in 1636. These statutes provided a thorough and detailed account of how the university should work. Congregation was defined as comprising the vice-chancellor, the proctors, the resident doctors, professors, public lecturers and regent masters; its functions were to discuss the resolutions of the Hebdomadal Board, to admit to degrees, to grant graces and on occasion dispensations. Convocation, consisting of regent and non-regent masters and doctors, was empowered to accept or reject motions relating to statutes and other matters brought forward by the Hebdomadal Board after they had been submitted to Congregation. As at Cambridge the medieval pattern of administration might seem unaltered, but real power had glided smoothly from the masters and doctors of the university to a select group of the heads of houses: both universities had become co-optative oligarchies, open to the many defects inevitably bred by exclusive and unchallenged power.

There was relatively little change in the government of the older universities between the end of the sixteenth century and the middle of the nineteenth. Not until 1854 were there any changes made in Congregation or Convocation. The administration became static and the cumbrous and outmoded governmental machinery became further and further separated from the real needs of the universities. The constitutional structure was superficially democratic, but with the direction of their affairs in the hands of an oligarchy, all proposals for changing or reforming the administration were more or less automatically blocked at the outset.

The modern administration of Oxford and Cambridge, though set in a frame that is medieval, is virtually a creation of the royal commissions. The university reformers of 1854 were determined to break the oligarchical control which had so far stifled change. At Oxford they replaced the Hebdomadal Board by the Hebdomadal Council so that the views of the senior and teaching members of the university might be represented. In addition to its *ex-officio* members, the chancellor (naturally an absentee), the vice-chancellor and the proctors, it was henceforth to consist of six heads of houses, six professors and six members of Convocation, each of these groups being elected by members of Congregation. In 1913–14 its composition was further changed in favour of the masters; the heads of houses were reduced in number from six to three and the members of Convocation were increased from six to nine. The Hebdomadal Council functioned as the university cabinet, responsible for making major decisions and initiating all significant legislation but answerable to Congregation and Convocation.

The reformers also remodelled Congregation, which from 1854 consisted of all members of Convocation resident in Oxford. (In 1913–14 it was limited further to all members of Convocation who were engaged in teaching or administration in Oxford.) Its proceedings were to be conducted in English rather than Latin – the predominance of the classics was already on the wane – though it was not until 1965 that the university agreed that its statutes should all be in English. Congregation was given the authority to receive, reject and propose amendments to the statutes which were submitted to it by the Hebdomadal Council. The commission of 1923 confirmed that a statute or decree submitted to Congregation automatically became law if it passed without a division or was given a two-thirds majority. For some time it was impossible for Congregation to initiate legislation, but in 1958 it was agreed that six members of Congregation could initiate a debate on a resolution. If the resolution was carried and had at least 40 votes in its favour, the Hebdomadal Council was obliged to introduce legislation in accordance with it. Side by side with the remodelled Congregation there survived the Ancient House of Congregation, the former meeting of the regent masters, but its powers had become purely formal, being confined in the main to the conferring of degrees, and the Franks Report of 1966 suggested reasonably enough that they should be transferred to Congregation itself.

Convocation was not changed by the Act of 1854. It continued to consist of all the masters of the university, resident and non-resident, and apart from electing the chancellor it had the not inconsiderable power of voting on decisions which had not secured the two-thirds majority in Congregation. (The Franks Report suggested it should be divested of all powers save the election of the chancellor.)* Since it included past members of the university, a high proportion of whom were at one time country clergymen, it was more likely than were the resident members of Congregation to take a conservative and reactionary line, as it did in the controversial debates over the proposals to abolish compulsory Greek and to give degrees to women.

The university reform acts had similar effects upon the administration of Cambridge. A syndicate suggested in 1852 that the powers of the Caput should be materially reduced; its authority in the future was to be restricted to the granting of degrees. All other graces or motions were to be the province of a Council of the Senate, representing major interests in the university, which was henceforth to be its chief administrative body, comparable to Oxford's Hebdomadal Council. The promoters of the Cambridge University Reform Bill of 1855 adopted this proposal which was, however, criticized by the university liberals as still permitting the vice-chancellor and the heads of houses too much authority. In response to this criticism, the framers of the Act of 1856 made sure that the

---

* A university decree of 1967 to this effect was challenged in 1969 in the House of Commons but a motion to annul the decree was defeated by 88 votes to 46.

vice-chancellor relinquished his right to veto legislation and they made provision for the Council to be elected by all the resident members of the Senate. The Caput and also a number of anomalous officials such as the taxors and the scrutators ceased to exist. The Act of 1877 did not significantly modify the constitution of the university; but the commission of 1923, bringing new statutes into operation, affected some important changes. What legislative power the Caput had allowed the Senate* was entrusted entirely to the Regent House, the old house of resident masters now remodelled and reinforced with new powers; it consisted of all members of the teaching and administrative staff of the university and colleges who were M.A.s, and it was they who elected the Council of the Senate. The Senate itself, consisting of all holders of the M.A. or higher degrees, became similar to Convocation at Oxford, its privileges being confined to the right to vote on certain formal occasions.

In spite of some significant modifications the constitutions of Oxford and Cambridge were still in 1969 very much as the statutory commissioners had left them in 1923. There as yet remained a reservoir of governmental power that was rarely utilized: at Oxford, the university still had authority to deprive any member of his or her degrees or to bring a professor to account before the visitatorial board. The chancellor's court was still in being, though amenable to the common law and not often convened. Since 1919, however, and more particularly since 1945, university business both at Oxford and Cambridge has increased enormously. Although the colleges, whose own administrations had been modified by the various commissions, remained powerful, the universities' authority was reasserted. The commission of 1877 had set in train the organization of the university teachers into faculties and boards, and as a result of the commission of 1923 the faculties were reconstituted. On Lord Curzon's suggestion a Board of Finance had been

---

*The Senate, it will be recalled, consisted of two houses, of regents and non-regents. Every M.A. who kept his name on the books of a college or hall was a regent for five years after the award of this degree, whether he was resident or not, after which he became a non-regent.

established at Oxford in 1912 to review the accounts of the universities and colleges and to advise the Hebdomadal Council on financial matters.

These were the first stages of an accelerating process. The growth in the number of university professors, readers and lecturers, and the consequential development of departmental organizations, especially in the sciences, provided a centre for loyalty and a system of administration that could rival the dominance of the colleges. The intensive building programme, the need to maintain constant contact with the University Grants Committee, the beginnings of a university rather than a college entrance examination, the continuous reappraisal of the final honour schools and triposes, the inflated expenditure, and the maintenance of relations with other universities, have all fostered the progressive expansion of the administrative machinery of the older universities, and the creation of a centralized secretariat.

These trends have led to much self-questioning. The problems confronting the ancient universities, Oxford's chancellor Lord Curzon commented in 1909, had 'assumed new shapes with the immense extension of the boundaries of human knowledge, the vastly increased demand for higher education, the wider conception of the duties of a modern university, and the emergence in the body politic of social strata that had previously lain lifeless and obscure'. The expansion has led some to question whether the present system by which heads of houses hold the vice-chancellorship in rotation (with the option of refusal), usually for two years, is in the best interest of the modern university; though there are powerful arguments against having a permanent administrative head. Changes of statute and much needed reforms have been frustrated rather than helped, according to the critics, by the cumbrous semi-democratic procedure of Congregation and Convocation and of the Regent House and Senate. They allege, and to this belief the number of lectures and demonstrators at both Oxford and Cambridge who do not hold fellowships gives some credence, that the interests of the university have been subordinated too much to those of the colleges; though in 1965 Congregation decided that in future all academic posts entitled the holder to a college fellowship,* a recommendation that had been made at Cambridge by the Bridges Committee, but had not been fully implemented. At Oxford the Franks Report suggested that election to college fellowships should be made jointly by the college and the university, though experience had shown that the influence which the faculties have secured over elections to fellowships at Cambridge has sometimes worked in a manifestly unjust way.

At Oxford the Franks Report made significant recommendations for modifying the university's governmental structure in the interests of greater administrative efficiency. 'We have no doubt,' the commission declared, 'that Oxford's machinery of government needs radical revision.' The report advised that the vice-chancellor should no longer be chosen only from among the heads of the colleges but selected from among the members of Congregation and appointed by a special nominating committee, a recommendation soon implemented by legislation. The powers of the Hebdomadal Council were to be greatly strengthened, making it the effective spokesman for the university and the moulder of its policy, to some extent at the cost of the democratic body of masters, Congregation. Thus the 1958 rule that allowed six members of Congregation to initiate debate on a resolution was to be replaced by a clause stipulating that twenty members would be needed to move such a resolution. Provided it had 75 votes in its favour, it could reject a measure submitted by Council, though Congregation had no mandatory authority over Council. The Report suggested other changes in the administrative machinery involving the appointment of administrative officers and a reconstruction of the General Board of Faculties responsible for the academic policy of the university. It also sought to reduce the

---

*The problem was solved in part by the creation of new graduate societies, Linacre (1962), St Cross (1965) and Wolfson (1965); but it was not easy for the other colleges to absorb the lecturers who had not been elected to fellowships at these new societies without upsetting the balance of their common life. Neither at Oxford nor at Cambridge had a wholly satisfactory solution been found by 1969.

much-criticized autonomy of the colleges,* while making plain the worthwhile character of a collegiate university. It recommended that a Council of the colleges should be set up with authority to bind the colleges by a majority decision, and to act as a liaison between the colleges and the University; though the workings of the conference of colleges which was instituted to prepare the way for this new body did not augur particularly well for the future.

Much of the report, though reasonable in tone and far from revolutionary, insufficiently so for some progressive critics, was in line with modern trends. It fostered the creation of a bureaucratic academic and administrative oligarchy, limited the individual preferences of colleges in the interests of now fashionable equality and uniformity, and showed perhaps too much deference towards the critics of the older universities, moved, as they have sometimes been, by envy, malice and misunderstanding. In its very concern with administrative efficiency some have scented the perils implicit in an over-bureaucratic administration, suspecting, possibly with justice, that there are those, especially outside the older universities, who would readily sacrifice grace and scholarship to an ephemeral efficiency. Yet it cannot be doubted that many of the recommendations of the Franks commission, when carried into effect, will remove some anomalies, promote administrative efficiency and by blending the independent traditions of the colleges with the needs of the university further establish Oxford's claim to take its place among universities of international reputation. A university, it needs to be stressed, cannot be run like a modern business. All in all, in spite of modern developments, Oxford and Cambridge have preserved the governmental forms of a past age, while adapting themselves to the needs of the present and bearing in mind their responsibility for the future.

*

*The outspoken views of Professor Darlington described the colleges as 'corrupt and self-perpetuating oligarchies inimical to original thought'. The report itself refers somewhat petulantly to the colleges 'infected by parochialism. They have put their right to dissent too high among their privileges.'

The way in which the constitutions of the newer universities have taken shape emphasizes the advantage of the older system. Few of the more recent foundations have been free from disputes caused by the divorce that existed at an early stage between government and administration on the one hand, teaching and research on the other. On the whole the teaching staff of the modern universities have had only a peripheral say in their administration. The element of self-government, the most precious feature of Oxford and Cambridge, has never been effectually integrated into their constitutions.

Durham alone preserved, if as an anachronism, the governmental form of the older universities, mainly because the statutes of 1834 were drafted by a former dean of Christ Church, Dr Smith, who had found his previous charge too magnificent and relaxed with conspicuous ease into a canon's stall. The affairs of the university were to be managed by a warden, a senate, which dealt with the ordinary business of the university, and a house of convocation which could confirm or reject what the senate submitted to it, though like that at Oxford it could neither amend nor initiate legislation. The royal commission of 1862 reconstituted the senate and reinterpreted the authority of the warden, the extent of whose powers may have accounted for some of the difficulties which confronted the university in its early years.

The constitution of London university gave rise to problems from the start and to involved and bitter controversy for many years. At its foundation final authority had been vested in the shareholders or proprietors; with the object of preventing an unscrupulous use of the vote by stock-jobbers the council of the college took some care in the allocation of shares. Executive authority resided in a council of twenty-four, who were elected by the shareholders. The council was empowered to appoint and dismiss all employees including the professors, though the latter had the right to appeal to a general meeting of their peers. The professors had no say in the governance of the university; a warden appointed by the council held the real power. In this explosive situation conflict was inevitable, as the first warden, Leonard Horner, acted in an autocratic fashion while the council's policy was both arbitrary and indecisive. The professors were treated with such indignity that several resigned; but their protest had its effect and led to a reconstitution of the university's government. The office of warden was abolished, a considerable financial saving as Horner had been drawing £1,000 a year; he was replaced by a secretary with a salary of £200, and a Senate was established. The status of the academic was thus enhanced and he was now in a position to bargain with the executive council of the college.

Grave dissatisfaction continued in spite of these reforms. The government of London university does seem to have been ill-advised and arbitrary. In 1858 the constitution was again reformed, but dissension between the Senate and Convocation, that is between the government and the teaching body, continued to affect its life. It was not until the new statutes of 1929 that London began to enjoy a measure of harmony in its government. Ultimately it became a federation of some thirty-four colleges, each of which possessed its own governing body and a fair measure of self-government. Each college had, however, to look to the university for its finances, its senior appointments and its examinations. Finance was controlled by a court that included members of the Senate and the London County Council, and in other matters the final authority was the Senate, which comprised college principals, members elected by the faculties, some representatives of Convocation and some co-opted members.

In most modern universities the government is vested ultimately in the university court, a large assembly (in 1964 129 at Manchester and Sussex, 605 at Sheffield), a majority of whom are not members of the teaching staff of the university but local members of parliament, church leaders, municipal dignitaries, and so forth. In practice the powers of the court have become purely formal, and it rarely meets more than once a year to review the financial account. With few exceptions, most notably Newcastle, the academic membership of the court is almost entirely confined to professors and heads of departments. The executive governing body is the council, very much smaller in size and responsible under the general supervision of the court for finance and external relations. It has the final authority in making academic appointments. It consists of representatives of the academic staff, again chiefly professors, nominees of local authorities and members appointed by the court; normally three quarters of the council are non-academic. The principal academic body is the senate, consisting of professors and representative members of staff, which moulds academic policy and is responsible for teaching, examinations and discipline. Academic work is naturally organized by faculties and boards. Bodies known as Convocation and Congregation, similar in composition to those of the ancient universities, exist, but their functions are purely formal. It is arguable that non-academic participation in the government of the university may have contributed skilled knowledge and experience unlikely to be possessed by the dons, but lay membership of court and council in most of the newer universities has been too preponderant. More to the point, since much of what is done in court and council is of a formal character, it can be maintained that the predominance of the professoriate * in the senate has placed far too much authority in the hands of the established order and has, with detrimental effects, prevented younger men and women from having any significant say in the government of the university or in moulding academic policy. The vice-chancellors, at London the principal, are the permanent heads of the university executive, usually appointed by the council or court after consultation with the senate. The rigidity of the governmental machinery of the new universities, even their much-boasted efficiency, must compare unfavourably with the degree of self-government and comparative liberty enjoyed by the average don at Oxford or Cambridge. A limited attempt has already been made in some colleges, notably at King's, Cambridge, to make provision for student participation in government. Students sit on many university committees. In April 1969, the Senate of Manchester university agreed to permit six students to attend its meetings when it discussed such matters as the curricula, examinations and teaching, and it set up a

* The proportion of scholars of professorial rank fell from 31·4 per cent in 1910 to 11·5 per cent in 1964.

committee consisting of equal numbers of staff and students to discuss matters of a similar character. Although extreme radical demands for student control over university government are unlikely to be satisfied, it seems probable that both in administration and discipline there will be a far greater degree of co-operation between junior and senior members than there has been in the past.

Lay interference in the universities has thus markedly declined since 1945, while scholars' control over their own affairs has increased. Simultaneously the scope of administration has been greatly widened, tending even in the comparatively small British universities to promote over-bureaucratization and impersonal relations; overweighty internal administration must inevitably provide a serious threat to academic self-government. While therefore the administrative organs of the modern universities have been geared to the supposed requirements of twentieth-century Britain, there remains more than a suspicion, from which neither Oxford nor Cambridge is immune, that administration in the 1960s is tending to become an end in itself rather than a means to an end.

'The peculiar merit of Oxford and Cambridge,' J. R. Lucas, a fellow of Merton, Oxford, who had previously held a fellowship at Cambridge, told the Franks Commission in 1965,

for a man of my age [35] or younger is that we are members of self-governing corporations rather than employees of an academic business. The fact that one has an effective voice in the running of University and College makes a very great difference both to the conduct of affairs and to one's own feeling about them ... academic considerations do not have to give way to administrative convenience.

Some universities have begun to integrate their academic staff more effectively into the government of the university by giving them representation on council and by introducing more representatives of the non-professors. At York seven out of the twenty-six members of the Council are academics and a General Academic Board of forty members elected from all members of the staff on which only a fifth need be professors is designed to collaborate with the Professorial Board itself.

CHAPTER NINE

The Economic Aspects of
the Universities

IT is rare to find in any description of the colleges or the universities a serious consideration of their economic and financial history. Yet this is fundamental to our understanding of the part they have played in English society; one can gain an insight into the development of that society simply by analysing the sequence of benefactors upon whom the universities have for so long depended. Within the universities economic pressures have often determined social structure: it is plain for instance that in Tudor times the colleges predominated because they were more richly endowed than the private halls and therefore better equipped to withstand the strain of rising prices. More recently state subsidization of the universities has again changed their character.

The medieval university was a more centralized community than its post-Reformation counterpart, though its growth had been haphazard and it had as yet no elaborate organization. It is difficult, if not impossible, to speak very exactly of the finances of the medieval university, but it seems that its basic costs were relatively small. The income that provided fellows' stipends and defrayed the necessary expenses incurred by its officials (inflated sometimes by the costly litigation so beloved by medieval men) probably came from students' fees and from various fines levied for misconduct. These expenses may also have claimed some of the revenue from the earliest and richest source of income, the benefactions which the university began to collect soon after its foundation from wealthy churchmen, devout nobles and their wives. These benefactions went a long way towards financing the new buildings that steady expansion required: the building programme claimed more and more of the growing revenues and often outstripped even the most generous gifts.

In the early years of Oxford its finances were simply organized. Its annual income in the middle of the thirteenth century is reckoned to have been fifty-two shillings, possibly the equivalent of £250 to £300 in modern terms. Bishop Grosseteste gave instructions that this money, together with any future benefactions, was to be housed in a chest kept at St Frideswide's and placed in charge of a canon of the monastery and of two persons appointed by the university. Although the university was hardly a wealthy institution, it was already aware of its responsibility to its students, graduates and undergraduates alike. The chancellor was empowered to make loans to poor scholars who did not hold a benefice worth more than ten marks. Provision was also made for the university's accounts to be presented each year to specially appointed auditors.

The earliest benefaction given to Oxford appears to have been a bequest of eight marks a year from the estate of Alan Basset which was made in 1243. The money, disbursed by Bicester Priory, was meant to pay for the maintenance of two scholars who were to be selected by his heirs. Six years later the university received a much more munificent gift, three hundred and ten marks, from the executors of William of Durham. Part of this money was to be placed in a chest for loans to poor scholars and the rest was to be invested in the purchase of tenements to support twelve masters who were to study theology, so creating a community which seems to have been the genesis of University College. Many similar gifts were made in the ensuing years, not only to subsidize the university's activities but often to come to the assistance of graduates and undergraduates by lending them money. The money was ordinarily deposited in chests, known often by the name of the benefactor, which were placed in the charge of the masters of the university. When a loan was made, a book was usually left as a 'caution' for the amount, a revealing insight into the comparative value of medieval books. If the loan was not repaid within the allotted time, the book was sold and the amount of the loan was replaced in the chest. If the book fetched more than the original loan, the surplus went to the owner. There were similar

167

chests in existence at Cambridge, among them the Holy Trinity chest, endowed with one hundred pounds by Bishop Bateman of Norwich, the founder of Trinity Hall. The chest was in the custody of three masters, one of whom had to be a member of Trinity Hall. Fellows of the college could borrow as much as four pounds, a bachelor thirty shillings and a scholar or a bedel twenty shillings.

Naturally enough the income and the expenses of students varied greatly. In the fourteenth century the annual expenses of a student at a hall kept by John Arundel, the future bishop of Chichester, were put at fifty shillings. Undergraduates had to pay for living in a private hall, for room rents and for 'battells', as the charges for food and drink were traditionally called at Oxford. There were payments to regent masters for attendance at lectures, fees to the university for disputations and determinations and for graduation. Graduation to a higher doctorate usually called for an expensive feast at the cost of the graduand. Breaches of discipline and misbehaviour could lead to the levying of fines by the various authorities. Inevitably there were expenses arising from the purchase of clothes, especially if the student aimed to be a young blood, an aspiration on which his elders surely frowned, and possibly from travelling, though most students doubtless walked home and the notion of going on vacation was foreign to the Middle Ages. The richer, and those more zealous for learning, bought manuscripts and books, both very expensive items. Although it is impossible to generalize, it appears likely that the standard of living at medieval Oxford and Cambridge was relatively austere. By and large the sons of rich men were only a fraction of the total student population; the majority of the students were either clerics or intending clerics, pledged if not to a life of holy poverty, at least to one that did not specialize in luxurious extravagance.

The wealth of the colleges multiplied as benefactions streamed in. Originally the gifts were in cash, but before long lands and manors, rectories and advowsons were passing into their hands. A college, intended to be a continuing corporation holding lands in mortmain, was thus endowed with capital from which it could house and maintain those who were fortunate enough to be of its foundation. Coffers filled as rents and fees from the new students flocking to the universities mounted year by year. But not every college had an equal share of this growing wealth. At one end of the scale there were rich colleges like New College, Oxford, and King's College, Cambridge. William of Wykeham, Bishop of Winchester, gave to New College manors, advowsons and rectories which brought in an annual income of £600, although the college was so much in debt by the 1430s that Bishop Beckington of Bath and Wells persuaded King Henry VI to grant it the confiscated property of the alien priories worth a further £75 a year. The annual income of King's College as a result of Henry VI's benefactions amounted to £1,000, but it was halved by the Yorkist resumption of Henry's estates in 1464. By the 1480s its income was in the neighbourhood of £750 and by 1546, for it had recovered some of its lost estates at the end of the fifteenth century, it was estimated to be £1,010 12s. 11½d. Two other fifteenth-century Oxford colleges were generously endowed: Archbishop Chichele expended £4,302 3s. 6½d. on manors, estates and advowsons as well as on books for the library and chapel of All Souls, while the receipts of Magdalen College, which had been founded by Bishop Waynflete of Winchester in 1448, amounted in 1487–8 to £700, in 1504 to £1,128 and in 1552 to over £2,000; its manor and estates were scattered throughout southern England.

The relative magnificence of these princely foundations was, however, far from typical. Many of the medieval colleges, though not exactly impoverished, often had difficulty in making both ends meet and in fulfilling the building plans of their founders. Hugo de Balsham, Bishop of Ely, the founder of Peterhouse, left it with insufficient endowments. His successor as bishop, Simon de Montacute, in giving the college its statutes in 1344 apologized for the paltry stipend of the Master, and a century after de Balsham's death the gross income of the foundation was only £91 a year, of which £40 came from the founder's rectory of Thriplow which he had appropriated to the college. Richard Fleming, Bishop of Lincoln, founded

Lincoln College in 1427 but left it inadequately endowed when he died four years later, bequeathing to the early rectors the job of scrounging benefactions from Fleming's friends like John Forrest, the Dean of Wells, and from the executors administering the charitable benefactions of great men like Bishop Beaufort and Bishop Beckington. The income of Exeter College, Oxford, which had been founded by Bishop Stapledon in 1314, amounted in 1477–8 to £64 6s. 11d. In 1535–6 it was assessed at £83 2s. of which £55 still came from Stapledon's original benefactions, notably the tithes of the rectory of Gwinear in Cornwall and of Long Wittenham in Berkshire. Oriel's accounts for 1451–2 show a total income of £184 9s.; of this £44 8s. came from the manor of Wadley, £32 from the city bailiffs for Bartlemas, £27 18s. 1d. from rents, £17 4s. 4d. from titles, among them that of the university church, St Mary's, which was in the college's gift. The rest came from room rents (the comparatively insignificant sum of 12s. 8d.), mortuaries and legacies and the churches of Coleby and Aberford, together with a handsome balance in hand of £35 8s. 6d. The income of Jesus College, Cambridge, which Bishop Alcock of Ely had founded in 1496 on the dissolved monastery of St Radegund's, amounted to £70 6s. in 1497–8.

These differences must have been reflected in the amenities, stipends and privileges enjoyed by the head and fellows of the colleges. The provost of King's College, Cambridge, for instance, had his own house and household, a stable of ten horses maintained by the college and a stipend of £100 a year. The Warden of New College had £40 a year as well as an entertainment allowance, six horses, and a separate housing establishment. The President of Magdalen College, Oxford, enjoyed £20 a year, two servants and a groom, an entertainment allowance and travelling expenses, and plate and household goods. But in 1344 the Master of Peterhouse had to be content with £2 a year as 'all that the present resources of the house can afford'. The President of Queens' College, Cambridge, was to be paid £3 6s. 8d. a year plus 2s. a week when he was in residence. The Master of Jesus College, Cambridge, received £6 13s. 4d. The stipends and allowances paid to fellows perhaps varied less, since it was in many colleges a condition of their tenure that they did not hold preferment or have an income beyond a stated sum; in such circumstances they had to resign their fellowship. This obligation accounts for the contemporary practice of letting out rooms to graduates, *commensales*, among them men of distinction like John Wyclif and Thomas Gascoigne, who could enjoy the amenities of college life without being bound by the conditions attached to receiving allowances or stipend; the rentals which they paid added in a small way to college revenues.

The sixteenth century saw an important change in the financial position of the universities and colleges. In fact the available figures suggest that few of the colleges were very wealthy; at Cambridge, King's had an annual income of £1,000 and St John's of over £500, but only three other colleges, Christ's, King's Hall and Queens', were worth more than £200 a year. At Oxford only five colleges had an income of over £200 and three, Balliol, Exeter and University, had under £100. The annual expenditure of the colleges was greater than the normal annual income, but the deficit was ordinarily covered by fines for leases, gifts and other incidental receipts. Although the universities continued to acquire benefactions, like all institutions with relatively stable incomes they were adversely affected by rising prices, especially after 1530. Extra costs, such as litigation arising out of disputes with the town and the annual tax for the assizes of bread and ale, placed the universities in financial difficulties which they took emergency measures to meet; at Cambridge in 1540–41 even the university candelabra were put in pawn.

These problems, however, were neither serious nor longlasting. In 1576 Parliament passed an important act, usually entitled Sir Thomas Smith's Act, which provided that in all leases that were henceforth granted by a college, the lessee would pay one third of his rent in corn or malt; corn was to be valued at 6s. 8d. a quarter or less and malt at 5s. a quarter or less, or in default of this at the current market price. This measure was an effective counter to the effects of inflation.

College finances also felt the impact of the changes taking place in the sixteenth century which were gradually turning the colleges into undergraduate institutions. As more students came to the universities, and from wealthier families, fees and room rents increased, though it is doubtful if at any time they amounted to more than a small proportion of total revenue. More importantly the rapidly growing numbers of undergraduates, and of servants to look after them, compelled the colleges to expand and to build. St John's, Cambridge, was one college which was attracting large numbers of men; it had 152 members in 1545, 287 in 1565, and 373 in 1672. The new buildings required were financed by various benefactors: Mary, Countess of Shrewsbury, paid for much of the second court and John Williams, the Bishop of Lincoln, who was to build the chapel of Lincoln College at Oxford, also contributed.

By the early seventeenth century university and college finance had become stabilized in a pattern that did not alter much until the middle of the nineteenth century. Naturally college revenues were affected by external pressures, political and economic – they took a little time to recover from the effects of the Great Rebellion – but the general outlines did not greatly change. Bearing in mind the differences that existed between the richer and the poorer institutions, a simplified picture shows a number of property-owning societies, rentiers in fact, administered by a co-optative body of clerical dons. The property was scattered throughout the length and breadth of England, but it was in the main agricultural, consisting of manors and farms. Colleges did, however, also acquire urban tenements, mainly in Oxford and Cambridge itself, but in some instances valuable London property. In the eighteenth century colleges were slowly beginning to broaden their field of investment. In 1749 St John's, Cambridge, began to invest in securities, though for many years such investment was regarded as a temporary measure to put a balance to good use.

Many colleges had been founded originally on appropriated churches; the foundation of Lincoln College, Oxford, was made possible by Bishop Fleming's decision to annex three Oxford churches, one of which he pulled down, and the subsequent appropriation to the college, by Bishop Rotherham, of Combe Longa in Oxfordshire and Twyford in Buckinghamshire. Clare Hall, Cambridge, was in part founded on the livings of Great Gransden in Huntingdon, Duxford St John in Cambridgeshire and Wrawby in Lincolnshire. A fair part of college revenue came from tithes, which was one of the reasons for Puritan criticism in the early seventeenth century. The advowsons, for long a piece of real property, which the colleges had collected in the late Middle Ages were substantially increased in number, so as to offer preferment and the chance of marriage to celibate clerical dons. In the first half of the eighteenth century colleges were particularly concerned with the purchase of advowsons for this reason; at Cambridge Clare Hall acquired twelve advowsons between 1719 and 1736, and St John's twenty between 1692 and 1736.

An important item of college finance was the purchase and sale of plate. It was natural for fellows to give plate, and conventional for fellow-commoners to do so on the termination of their residence; but there was much silver often of secondary quality which represented a short-term investment. In time of financial stringency it could be, and frequently was, sold. The demands of the Civil War wrought havoc with college silver, or the more valuable and beautiful part of it, but much plate was melted down in the ordinary course of business.

The college accounts, which most colleges have preserved, are of an unchanging pattern. The bursar, usually a fellow of the college often appointed to the office for a year, recorded revenue, expenditure and profit – and occasionally deficit. The annual audit day was an important occasion for the heads and fellows since on its outcome would depend their own stipends for the year. The estates which the bursar administered, albeit indirectly, carried burdens and responsibilities as well as fees and profits of one kind and another. Some of these were already by the sixteenth century of antiquarian interest. Manorial courts were still held on the estates where the college had manorial jurisdiction, ostensibly for the exaction of quit-rents and the enforcement of suits of court and other obsolescent acts of homage, but actually for the benefit of the steward, who reaped a rich harvest of fees even when the receipts of the college as lord of the manor were relatively small. Colleges holding estates naturally had to pay quit-rents themselves, though ironically the charges incurred in the payment of these customary dues often exceeded that of the dues themselves. Where the college had manorial rights, it long continued to enjoy age-old feudal privileges, such as the heriot, exacted by custom from certain copyhold lands on the death of the holder or the sale of the property, being anciently the best animal or chattel of the holder but by the sixteenth century a money payment. The college could also demand relief or the payment of double quit-rent by a freehold in every year in which any change took place in the ownership of the land; and penalty or mulct imposed for some infringement of the rights of the manor.

Timber rights were another valuable asset. Timber growing on land let to farms was the property of the landlord, not of the tenant, but timber growing on copyhold land belonged to the manor, not to the copyhold owner. Falls of wood on college estates were often resorted to in order to extricate the college from debts incurred by bad management. The profits of other falls of wood were added to the stipends of the head and fellows for the year in which they occurred. There was no thought of capitalizing revenue of this sort so as to strengthen the financial position of the college or to add to its usefulness as a place of education.

Given the importance of their agricultural holdings it is not surprising that colleges with even comparatively small estates displayed an interest in this major source of income and arranged for their head, the bursar and one or more of their fellows to visit their properties regularly, though the occasion seems often to have been an excuse for junketing rather than a serious economic inquisition. In 1613, so runs an entry in a Lincoln college account book, 'breakfast and supper in our journie to Petsoe, 9s. 6d; given to the servants at two severall times in our inne, 14d.; given to the pore, 2s. 5d; horsemeat, the first night, 2s. 6d.; supper, and drink in the morning as we returned, 9s.' In 1673 there was a visit to the college's Kentish estates; 'for boating it to and from Southwark', the entry in the accounts reads,

when we took places in the Canterbury coach, 1s; spent at the inne when we lodged in Southwark, 6s 2d; coach-hire into Southwark that night, 2s; coach-hire for Mr Rector, myself [the Bursar], Mr Radcliffe and Ellis, £2 8s; to the coachman, 1s; our dinner at Rochester, 5s 6d; bread and beer in the rode, 6d; for burnt brandy when we came to Canterbury, 8d; the charges to Mr Radcliffe going to Whitstable, 3s; coach hire to Sandwich, £1; our dinner there, 3s; the Canterbury bills for diet, lodging, and for horses to Whitstable, £3 18 2d; coach hire back again to London, £2 8s; to the coachman and postillion, 1s 6d; our dinner at Rochester, 6s 8d; bread and beer in the rode, 1s; coach hire to our lodgings in London, 1s; spent at the inne where Mr Rector lay when he came up to London, 2s 6d; Mr Rector's coach hire to and from London £1; to our man Ellis, 15s.

The payments paid at the renewal of leases aroused a special interest. It was usual to grant a lease for a number of years at a small yearly rent (usually called the 'reserved' rent) on condition that the lessee paid down a substantial 'fine' at the time of obtaining the lease. This fine was treated as part of the ordinary income of the year in which it was paid, and was divided among the head and fellows, so that in a year in which a considerable lease was granted the money value of a fellowship was much increased. The rents, which were normally paid half-yearly, were paid directly by the tenant (an occasion usually marked by some sort of entertainment for the tenant), collected by a representative of the college or simply transmitted by a carrier. Like other landowners, the college had occasionally to deal with unsatisfactory tenants by the summary process of distraint.

It is almost impossible to determine accurately a fellow's stipend between the late sixteenth and early nineteenth centuries, so great was the divergence between colleges and customs; but it is possible to indicate some of the multifarious items which might figure in it. Naturally fellows had their rooms rent-free; later in the eighteenth century when they were often non-resident, they were entitled to the rent of the room from the undergraduate or graduate to whom it had been leased. A resident fellow might also earn fees from giving tuition or from holding one or other of the college offices such as bursar, tutor or dean. At Lincoln College, Oxford, a fellow was entitled to gaudy and obit money; these were small payments in lieu of the money originally allocated to provide better food in hall on certain days, commemorating either religious festivals or the anniversary of the death of past benefactors on which a mass was celebrated until the Reformation brought this custom to a close. A fellow was given an allowance of 2s. a quarter for the laundress, 1s. for the barber and variable amounts in place of the vinegar, brawn and oysters to which he had been once entitled, and also received poundage, a percentage charged on certain items of each person's expenditure in the buttery and kitchen. In 1518 Edmund Audley, Bishop of Salisbury, formerly a fellow, gave the college a large sum of money to provide the Rector and fellows yearly with clothes of a uniform cloth and cut, as was done in some of the older and wealthier foundations. With this money the college bought an estate at Petsoe in the north-east corner of Buckinghamshire. The profits were divided among the fellows '*pro robis*'. At first the cloth was bought at London by a fellow expressly sent for the purpose, but after a few years the money ceased to be spent in this way and was used simply to augment the fellows' income.

The fellows of Lincoln were entitled to 'commons', the amounts allowed by the statutes to provide the common table for the Rector and fellows; indeed this was, according to the statutes, the basic income. But by Elizabeth's reign the economic conditions had so changed that the statutory provisions for a fellowship had become hopelessly inadequate. An entire redrafting of the statutes was needed, but this was out of the question, nor was it to take place until 1856. In default of revision the college had recourse to expedients which could evade the statute: one was to supply the fellows' table each week at a rate far in excess of the old allowances, and to pay for the difference out of the ordinary income of the college. These examples from one college indicate how a fellow was paid in most colleges before the universities were reformed.

The details of annual expenditure which the college accounts record are often curiously inadequate to convey a picture of the whole. They tell us little or nothing, for instance, of what was spent on food or drink because this was in the cook's domain. It seems very likely that the cook, who was a salaried member of the college, probably made a good thing out of cooking for undergraduates, and that there was often extravagance, waste and over-charging. But the accounts detail the stipends of college officials and servants like the maniple, the butler, the cook and the porter who were not fellows. They contain curious minutiae, such as the amount paid for a new broom or for the purchase of new pots and pans, what was paid for wine used at the communion service or for washing a surplice, what was given by way of charity to a beggar or to a man who swept the snow away or what was spent on the purchase of shrubs for the garden. Repairs to buildings, and new buildings, constitute a major item. Although the pattern of entries in the accounts appears conventional and even archaic it is possible to detect social change at work, the introduction and abandonment of custom, the end of the need to have fresh rushes for covering the floor of the hall or chapel and the commutation of dues in kind into money payments.

Undergraduate expenditure was even more varied; to the differences between colleges were added differences in individual taste. Surviving bills show what was spent on clothes, drink and books. A man had to pay rent for his room, that varied with its location and size, and for his battells. At his entry into his college rooms he paid a sum, usually a third of the assumed value, for the furnishings. A terminal fee was paid to his tutor. By the early nineteenth century, if he was keen to make a good showing in his examinations, he would have had to resort to a private coach; in the 1840s such a tutor cost £14 a term if the man went to him every day, £7 if he went on alternate days. The residents in college had to pay for the heating and lighting of their own room as well as what was expended on the common fuel and candles, and contribute towards the salaries of the maniple and the cook. The cost of a university course even for a normal fee-paying undergraduate rose steadily, and in the more fashionable colleges rose rapidly with the social status of the men who were in residence. On the other hand, at every period in the university's history, there were to be found thrifty students who found it difficult to make both ends meet, such as were, for instance, the brothers John and Charles Wesley.

The charges were never uniform but varied with the status of the undergraduate. Noblemen, gentlemen-commoners, scholars, exhibitioners, commoners, sizars or servitors – each gradation indicated by wearing of a particular gown – had its own fees, and the higher the rank the steeper the charge. At one college a gentleman- or fellow-commoner* had to pay £2 10s. at his admission (divided in varying proportions between the college, the bursar, the manciple, the Bible-clerk, the cook, the porter and the scrape-trencher) whereas a commoner only paid £1 0s. 6d., and his tuition fees were correspondingly higher. An economical fellow-commoner, a former member of Trinity College wrote in 1849, needed £500 a year, but £800 was not an immoderate sum.

The first university reform acts of 1854 and 1856 did not interfere directly with the financial affairs of Oxford or Cambridge, but did affect them indirectly, for the amount of building and additional lecturers they demanded could not be subsidized without an increase in funds. While the colleges remained rich, were indeed getting richer, the finances of the universities were stretched to breaking point. The commissioners who had been appointed in the 1870s to inquire into the universities were especially concerned with their financial set-up. They did their work thoroughly, calling for full statements of college accounts which they subjected to intensive scrutiny and analysis. The conservatives grumbled but ultimately complied. 'Great difficulty,' the secretary to the commissioners informed Washbourne West, the arch-Tory Bursar of Lincoln, 'has been found in extracting from them the results

---

* A student who by reason of his wealth and social position might be given some of the privileges of a fellow, notably membership of the senior common room.

corresponding with those supplied by other colleges', which was hardly surprising as part of the accounts were still in 1871 transcribed in Latin. The investigation, declared Perowne, the Master of Corpus, Cambridge, was a crying scandal: it 'transgressed the limit which ought to separate matters of a private nature from those which may be the legitimate object of official investigation'. But for the first time a curious public was able to descry the great discrepancies that existed between the richer and poorer colleges of the ancient universities. It was reckoned that the annual cost of a university education was between £40, for a sizar,* and £80, though the senior tutor of Pembroke, Cambridge, made a higher estimate of £137 and at Trinity, Cambridge, the annual expenses of a pensioner* were put between £150 and £200 a year.

The commissioners examined the universities' pressing needs for new buildings, laboratories and additional stipends. They found that their resources were clearly insufficient to meet them and they concluded that the only satisfactory solution to the problem was to impose a university tax on the colleges. At Cambridge this was fixed originally at £1,000 per college, which was to rise after 1894 to a minimum total levy of £25,000, but after some criticism by the Council of the Senate, the college quotas were transformed into percentage payments, resulting in a maximum total levy of £30,000 in 1896. The chancellor was empowered on the recommendations of the financial board to reduce the amount of college contributions. Similar results were achieved at Oxford where a Common University Fund was established.†

It was unfortunate that the commissioners had made their estimates when college incomes were at their highest – King's College, Cambridge, had an estimated annual revenue of £30,000 in 1871 – and before the onset of the agricultural depression of the 1880s. This hit every college. College bursars

* Students who received an allowance or grant from their college.

† The total income of Oxford university, the royal commission estimated in 1870–71, was £48,589, that of the colleges £397,015. By 1963 university income amounted to £6 million and that of the colleges, excluding board and lodging fees, £2,500,000.

were confronted with growing arrears of rent and falling incomes. 'Our pecuniary troubles through defaulting tenants,' it was noted in one college, 'are becoming very serious.' 'I hope,' wrote a Yorkshire farmer to his college bursar, 'you will show me as much mercy as you can. ... In this county every farmer seems poor and cannot pay.' 'Poor Dodge,' wrote one from Buckinghamshire, 'is sold up and gone! Lesters leave at Mich! Wootons have left! Sep. Harper leaves Poundon at Mich. ... It is true I fear that half of the farmers in the county are as bad as ruined.' In 1880 the farmers came to a tenants' dinner 'to dine but not to pay'. 'I can tell you,' the Rector of Lincoln wrote in 1882, 'that my receipts as Head are little more than half what they were ten years ago.' Whereas at King's College, Cambridge, between 1875 and 1877 a fellow could expect a dividend of £280 a year, before 1914 it was never higher than £130 and went as low as £80. At Christ's, Cambridge, the revenues of which had been recently much improved by the discovery of coprolite on college land (giving as much as £21,500 in twenty years), fellowships had been worth £300 a year in 1873, but the new statutes of 1882 fixed an upper limit of £250. At St John's, Cambridge, there was much the same story; dividends fell from £300 in 1872-8 to £80 in 1894. This naturally affected building and other plans and to some extent limited the improvements which might have been made between 1882 and 1914.

Although the universities continued to be short of resources to meet their rapidly expanding needs, there was a pronounced upward trend in college finances after 1918, and even more so after 1945. This was due to a number of things, among them better and more skilled management. King's College, Cambridge, owed an immense debt to the inspired direction of its finances by its bursar, the distinguished economist, J. M. Keynes. The agricultural depression had demonstrated the imprudence of basing college finances on a single industry. Some attempt had already been made to spread the load, by investing in railway stock and in government securities, and to find new sources of revenue. The Universities and Colleges Estates Act of 1858 gave the colleges the right to grant building leases and opened the way to important development. After the First World War the colleges adopted a much more flexible economic policy. They were ready to sell their less productive farms, even those that had been in the possession of the college for centuries, and to buy land of high quality. Land sold for development brought in new money: Merton College, Oxford, already a wealthy institution, was further enriched by large sums paid in return for development rights. Land assets were exchanged for much more widely spread investments in commercial and industrial properties, and substantial investment in securities proved very profitable.

This process however benefited only those colleges which had been generously endowed in the past, without making an appreciable difference to the few men's colleges and all the women's colleges who were not so fortunate. It has now become apparent that at Oxford at least the colleges may again have to accept some redistribution of income, and the Franks Commission recommended in 1966 a new and fairer system of college contributions based on total gross endowment income.

The new universities of the nineteenth century were from the start haunted by inadequate resources. Professors were underpaid, laboratories ill-equipped and amenities often deplorable. If they were to survive, it was essential that they should receive aid from the state, which had already recognized, if on a somewhat parsimonious scale, its responsibility to assist primary education. As early as 1852 Owens College, Manchester, asked for financial help, but nothing was done for another thirty years. It was in 1881 that the Aberdare Committee urged that University College, Aberystwyth, should receive £4,000 a year from government funds to help provide the impoverished principality of Wales with an effective system of higher education. The grant was given in the end to the university college established at Bangor in 1884 and another to the college founded at Cardiff in 1883: but this government action did create an important precedent.

Naturally the English colleges felt that they had as good a case. A Treasury grant was proposed and in the ensuing debate Sir Lyon Playfair argued cogently that the experience of commercial nations throughout the world is that the competition of industries is a competition of intellect. The difference between the policy of this and other countries is that, while in other countries the State recognizes the fruits of education and acts upon their perception of them, we leave the first steps to the efforts of intelligent men in various localities.

The government finally agreed in 1889 to allocate £15,000 to the university colleges. The grant was distributed by a committee, the ancestor of the University Grants Committee, that neutral and independent body which acts as the intermediary between the Treasury and the universities. The first Treasury grant was, perhaps, more symbolic than useful; by 1900 the total was still only £25,000. Eleven university colleges, increased to fourteen by 1904, were given grants ranging from £500 to £1,800. Small as the sums were, they may have saved some colleges from extinction; the total income of Firth College, Sheffield, for instance, was £2,200 and the Treasury grant of £1,200 made all the difference. But in some of the larger universities where new schemes, especially in science and technological subjects such as engineering, made impossible demands on the budget, the state grant soon disappeared. The £1,400 a year allocated to Leeds from 1880 was at once swallowed up by the deficit. The income of Birmingham was augmented by an endowment fund created in the 1900s through the enthusiastic advocacy of Joseph Chamberlain, but Bristol virtually survived for years only through the generosity of the Wills family. Oxford and Cambridge were as yet excluded from the grant.

Progressive educationalists were convinced that if the universities were to compete in any real sense with their continental counterparts and if they were to be very much more than poor relations of Oxford and Cambridge they required much more generous assistance from the state. 'Nothing,' said Sidney Webb, 'would be more widely popular at the present time, certainly nothing is more calculated to promote National Efficiency, than a large policy of Government aid to the highest technical colleges and universities,' and he estimated that they really needed something like £500,000. It is doubtful whether this action would have been as popular as Webb supposed, but in March 1904 the grant rose to £54,000 and a committee on which R. B. Haldane was the leading light was set up to consider the necessity of 'stimulating private benevolence in the locality of the university' (much was still expected of private enterprise in the early 1900s) and to concentrate financial assistance on those institutions which provided 'education of a University standard in large centres of the population'. The committee also recommended the establishment of a permanent advisory body to distribute the grants and to carry out the quinquennial visitations.

Though large achievements were still expected of private benevolence the ever-present need to foster industrial efficiency in the face of advancing foreign competition, a need that had prompted private benefactors to found some of the universities of the nineteenth century, was now outstripping even the most lavish private investment. Only the state could provide enough funds to finance research into the problems created by a growing population and limited natural resources of which the informed and thoughtful were beginning to be aware. The economists joined the educationalists in demanding state subsidies for education; the twin deities of intellectual interest and economic necessity presided over this stage of the universities' history as over so many others. Acts of Parliament in 1909–10 placed nearly £3 million at the disposal of the nation for the development of agriculture, rural industries and fisheries, and these made a precedent for grants to university departments engaged in forwarding the same ends. Already in 1890 the President of the Board of Agriculture had asked Cambridge to examine the possibility of promoting education in agriculture, and as a result a department of agriculture came into being, a university farm was set up at Impington and diplomas in agriculture and forestry became available; both the departments of agriculture and forestry were supported from funds supplied by the County Councils and the government. In 1911 the Development Commission sponsored a plan for setting up institutions to foster specialized research which would be of assistance to agricultural development. The first institutes were established at Cambridge for plant-breeding, at Rothamsted for plant nutrition, at Edinburgh for animal breeding, at Cambridge and Aberdeen for animal nutrition and at Oxford for agricultural economics. Comparatively little was done, however, before the war imposed a virtual closure on the universities.

The experience of the First World War brought home to the authorities the nation's need of scientific research and the comparative failure of the universities to satisfy it. In 1915 as a result of a report made by a committee presided over by Sir William M'Cormick, then the chairman of the advisory committee on grants to the universities, the Department of Scientific and Industrial Research was set up. Sir William presided over both committees until his death in 1929, but the Grants Committee was transferred from the supervision of the Board of Education and was brought once more under control of the Treasury, a deliberate action taken by H. A. L. Fisher, then president of the Board of Education, to prevent possible partisan dictatorship by a minister. The terms of reference of the University Grants Committee created in 1919 were to 'inquire into the financial needs of University education in the United Kingdom and to advise the Government as to the application of any grants that may be made by Parliament towards meeting them'.

With the return of peace the universities were confronted with greater demands on their funds than ever before. The state had an obvious duty to subsidize those ex-service men who wished to study at the universities, and to this end the Board of Education made some 26,000 awards. Furthermore in 1919 Parliament voted £1 million to the universities of which two thirds was allocated for general expenditure and a third for non-recurrent grants for capital expansion. But expansion was useless without students; and students could not avail themselves of a university education without grants. The scholarships and exhibitions offered by the colleges of Oxford and Cambridge were insufficient to meet the need. In 1920 two hundred awards were made; but they were suspended two years later at the time of the Geddes Economy Commisssion. At first such awards simply allowed a few abler boys to come to the university and made little difference to the social structure. But the number of awards increased steadily: 360 in 1936, 750 in 1947, 900 in 1950, 1,500 in 1952 and 2,000 in 1954. In the 1950s the local authorities, until their job was taken over by the state, made more than 10,000 awards, though these varied widely in value and availability.

It was plain that even the older universities could not hope to finance expansion, especially in science, out of their existing funds. The adverse effects of the agricultural depression of the late nineteenth century were not the only sign that college incomes were declining as demands on the university rose. 'The dilemma,' Professor Roach has sagely remarked,* 'was a cruel one; if the full contributions were exacted, the Colleges would be gravely harmed; if the contributions were materially reduced, the already insufficient resources of the University would be dangerously diminished.' The champions of college interests pointed out that the external income of the colleges was some thirty per cent lower than it had been in 1871; income from tithes alone had fallen by £15,000. At Cambridge it was proposed to suspend college contributions from 1890, but the scheme was abandoned. The older universities, like the new, were desperately short of money and could think of no expedients for raising it. The outbreak of the First World War only aggravated the problem, for the college incomes at Cambridge which were subject to university contribution actually fell by some £30,000 between 1914 and 1917. 'Large increases in annual and capital expenditure must be expected,' the vice-chancellor said in 1917, 'if the University is to meet the claims that may be made upon it as a place of teaching and research.'

When the war ended Oxford and Cambridge had really no alternative except to creep within the umbrella of state assistance. At Cambridge it was estimated that £23,000 a year was required for stipends, £30,000 a year for new posts and development of new departments and £750,000 for capital expenditure. The President of the Board of Education, H. A. L. Fisher, reminded Oxford and Cambridge that no grant would

* *Victoria History of Cambridge*, iii, *The City and University of Cambridge*, Oxford University Press, 1959, p. 270.

be forthcoming unless the colleges and universities agreed to a 'comprehensive inquiry' into their existing resources and 'the use which is now being made of them'. This was a disagreeable prospect for the more conservative minded, but, as J. J. Thomson, the eminent physicist who had been in 1918 appointed Master of Trinity, remarked cogently enough:

What is the alternative? . . . I dislike, and I suppose everyone here dislikes, the idea of receiving government money . . . I am convinced that the only alternative is to lose the efficiency of the University, and much as I dislike the receipt of money from the Government I dislike still more the idea of an inefficient University.*

The royal commission which was subsequently set up agreed that the work of the universities was badly hampered by lack of funds and suggested that the system by which colleges contributed to the university in proportion to their wealth, already in force at Oxford, should be adopted at Cambridge and that an annual grant of £100,000 should be made to both ancient universities together with £10,000 for the women's colleges.

The royal commission made a complete examination of university and college finance. It found that the total money available to the university and colleges at Oxford and Cambridge in 1920 amounted respectively to £824,710 and £719,554. It recommended an increase in existing stipends and the provision of an adequate retiring pension. The commissioners recognized that the cost of a university education at Oxford and Cambridge was bound to be high; but they thought that the cost of living could conceivably be lowered by more efficient catering in the colleges. For political reasons the commissioners' suggestions were not immediately implemented, but the statutory commission set up in 1924 was empowered to make concrete recommendations.

Increasingly generous aid from the state did not supplant private benefactions. The public grants for the quinquennium 1931–6 amounted to £1,830,000, but private gifts were still greater. Between 1929 and 1935 nearly £5 million was donated to universities. Immediately after the end of the First

* *Cambridge University Reporter*, 1918–19, p. 755.

World War the City livery companies had been generous in their gifts: the Glaziers Company contributed to the new department of glass technology at Sheffield University and the Clothworkers supported the department of textiles and colour dyeing at Leeds. The British oil companies gave £210,000 to Cambridge which was largely spent in an expansion of the chemistry laboratory. Other benefactions made possible the building of an institute of parasitology, a low temperature research station and an institute of biochemistry. The Rockefeller Foundation endowed both Oxford and Cambridge; the International Education Board which J. D. Rockefeller founded offered Cambridge £700,000, part of which went towards building the new university library. Among other benefactors, the trustees of Sir William Dunn gave £100,000 in 1922 towards the Sir William Dunn School of Pathology, and the motor manufacturer, William Morris, later Lord Nuffield, contributed large sums of money towards the study of medicine, as well as founding the college which perpetuates his name. After the Second World War a French millionaire, Antonin Besse, gave money to found a college at Oxford, known as St Antony's, which has specialized in the study of modern history and politics, and more recently Sir Isaac Wolfson's benefaction made possible the consolidation of a new graduate college at Oxford.

The economic history of the universities since the Second World War hardly requires description. Although there have been on occasions complaints of inadequate support, successive governments have been liberal in the amount of money they have granted to higher education. In 1945 the Chancellor of the Exchequer, Sir John Anderson, agreed to a grant of £4,149,000, and a further £1 million to cover the cost of improvements in medical education recommended by the Goodenough committee. In 1947 Hugh Dalton raised the grant to £9 million and subsequently it jumped to £20 million in 1952–3, £34 million in 1957–8, £69 million in 1964–5 and £81 million in 1966–7. Non-recurrent grants between 1945 and 1957 amounted to £230 million; between 1958 and 1967 they totalled £330 million and in 1968 £237 million. 'It is,' Sir

Stafford Cripps commented in 1948, 'on the advances that we make in scientific knowledge and on the energy, directive capacity and courage of the young graduates that the economic future of the country will largely depend.' Yet in an inflationary period, given the high cost of scientific equipment and new buildings, expansion was often delayed by inadequate resources. The University Grants Committee from 1953 to 1964, under the able chairmanship of Sir Keith Murray, later Lord Murray of Newhaven, responded diplomatically to the competing demands of the older and newer universities. It has been subject to occasional criticism because of its immunity from the normal process of government audit, but in general it has acted with commendable wisdom. In theory it is only a committee to advise the Treasury, subject to the general guidance of the Chancellor of the Exchequer, but the large sum of money which it dispenses and the part it plays in the formulation of policy makes it at least temporarily a department of state. Although the sum of money at their disposal always seems less than the universities require,* at no period have the universities and colleges in fact been so prosperous. The only faint uneasiness that may cross the mind arises from the relative loss of freedom† which financial dependence on the state must entail, no genuine danger in an age of benevolently disposed governments, but not perhaps a threat which should be entirely forgotten.

* Yet some criticism must be voiced of the unwillingness of the U.G.C. to finance plans for much-needed residential accommodation at the new universities, which have therefore been forced in the first instance to rely for this purpose on public subscription.

† Most universities protested strongly at the government's decision in 1967 to raise the fees of overseas students, but without effect. As a result Oxford (by 43 votes to 27 in Congregation), Cambridge (by 244 votes to 213 in the Regent House), Bradford and the Queen's University, Belfast, refused to comply with the government's request with adverse financial effects to themselves.

CHAPTER TEN

Learning, Study and Research

THERE has never been a period in the history of the universities when they have not housed scholars of world renown, though an exhaustive list of their names, familiar as they might be to scholars in their own subjects, would not convey much to the ordinary reader. We must take it for granted that from Roger Bacon and Duns Scotus, Wyclif and Erasmus, Jewell and Hooker, Sanderson and Pococke, Whichcote, Bentley and Porson, Locke and Newton to Maine and Pollock, Rutherford and Thomson, T. H. Green and J. B. Lightfoot, Acton, Firth and Powicke, there has never been a time in university history, new or old, when learning has not been illuminated by deep and original thought. 'Cambridge,' the poet A. E. Housman, who was professor of Latin, observed on a festive occasion, 'has seen many strange things. It has seen Wordsworth drunk, and Porson sober. Here stand I, a better man than Wordsworth, and a better poet than Porson, betwixt and between.'

It is by and large with the learning of the ordinary student rather than with the scholarship of the renowned that we are here concerned. What was studied at the universities during the different periods of their history? Education is a mirror of social change and contemporary culture; the university curricula must reflect the intellectual and social predispositions of the age. It would be folly to expect that very much attention should be paid to scientific or deductive thought in the Middle Ages, and more than surprising if it did not play an ever increasing part in the syllabus of the modern university. Yet it is equally important to bear in mind that the content of the curriculum or what was provided in lectures never at any time represented the whole intellectual interest of the serious student. In the Middle Ages there were scholars who interested themselves in scientific and mathematical concepts; in the late sixteenth and early seventeenth centuries there were men who read widely in the literature and histories of their own day and age though these were not prescribed texts. 'I was admitted,' wrote John Evelyn who went up to Balliol in 1637, 'into the daucing and vaulting Schole, of which late activity one Stokes, the Master, set forth a *pretty book* which was publish'd with many witty elogies before it.' 'I began,' he wrote two years later, 'to look on the rudiments of musick, in which I afterwards ariv'd at some formal knowledge, though to small perfection of hand, because I was so frequently diverted by inclinations to newer trifles.' 'In short, this morning's lounge,' Richard Graves wrote in his memoir of his contemporary, the poet William Shenstone who matriculated at Pembroke, Oxford, in 1732, 'which seemed mutually agreeable, was succeeded by frequent repetitions of them; and, at length, by our meetings likewise, almost every evening, at each other's chambers the whole summer; where we read plays and poetry, Spectators or Tatlers, and other works of easy digestion, and sipped Florence wine.' Although the poet William Wordsworth ceased to study for a degree at Cambridge, his sister Dorothy noted in 1791 that he was still reading literature in English, Italian, Spanish, French, Greek and Latin. No student of university learning can omit the importance of extra-curricular reading. Nonetheless the character and content of the degree course obviously counted for much both in shaping the mind and directing intellectual endeavour.

*

The medieval degree course took a long time to complete and was of a very complex structure. There were five faculties in the medieval university: arts, medicine, civil law, canon law and theology. The faculty of arts was the biggest and the most influential, since it was not possible to begin studying in one of the other faculties without first graduating in arts. This regulation had caused long and bitter disputes between the secular masters and the friars who wanted to proceed to a degree in theology without the initial studies in arts, which they took to be against the spirit of their orders. For the arts course was not, as is so often thought, theological in content. The majority of those who took it were destined for a career in the church and their study was placed necessarily in a distinctive and indeed definitive theological framework, but the course in arts was really rooted in the traditional syllabus of Roman times, the trivium, comprising grammar, rhetoric and logic, and the quadrivium of arithmetic, music, geometry and astronomy. The lecture and the disputation formed the chief method of instruction, and every student of the faculty of arts was obliged to place his name on the roll of a regent master who supervised his studies. After four years spent in attending lectures and disputations and in reading the prescribed texts, the undergraduate could supplicate for the degree of Bachelor of Arts and become, as the contemporary phrase put it, a candidate for determination. There was no written examination, though it is possible that those who had to testify to the candidates' fitness for the degree may have subjected him to some sort of intellectual test.

After graduation, the bachelor was free to follow a course of study and disputation, mainly in philosophy, lasting three years until his inception or admission to the mastership. The exercises leading to the master's degree took the form of a series of debates or disputations on set themes which were designed to test his knowledge and his intelligence. If his supplication was approved, the bachelor was presented by a regent master and took the oath in the presence of the chancellor, the proctors and the regent masters of his faculty. He was then given licence by the chancellor to lecture, to engage in disputations and to take part in all the functions belonging to a master in the faculty of arts. He still had to lecture and to take part in debates for at least two years, after which he could then remain a regent master 'at will', drawing fees from those he was engaged in teaching. If he ceased to lecture he became a non-regent master.

Many masters, and later the statutes of colleges imposed such an obligation on most of their fellows, proceeded after their regency to a higher degree in one of the superior faculties, medicine, law or theology. The medical course required six years' further study; the reading prescribed, Galen, Hippocrates, Isaac's *Liber Februm* and Nicholas' *Antidotarium*, demonstrates the traditional and conservative character of the course, which naturally involved no experimental work. The course of study for a higher degree in civil or canon law was almost as long. The exercises in the faculty of theology were longer, as the candidate for the B.D. had to spend some seven or eight years in the study of the Bible and on Peter Lombard's *Book of the Sentences*, and to preach on various occasions before the university. Once a bachelor and after two further years of study he became eligible for the doctorate of theology or divinity.

Such was the general form and content of the medieval syllabus at both Oxford and Cambridge. It was in many respects a formidable and prolonged intellectual exercise and there must have been many who never came near to completing it. The comparative scarcity of books entailed much learning by rote, obliging the student to place great dependence on the lecture as the exposition of a text to which he may not himself have had access, but the medieval capacity for memorization, which the very slowness of reading a contemporary manuscript fostered, was considerable. The medieval scholar tended to rely on his authorities and to argue from them rather than to develop a critical spirit of inquiry. The disputation and the debate must have however formed an excellent training in logical argument.

Nonetheless it has to be admitted that this medieval syllabus had certain inherent defects. It has been said that it forbade speculation, so bringing about an encystment of the intellect which stifled initiative and experiment. It is true that experimentation was in general foreign, if not as entirely alien as is currently supposed, to the medieval mind, but speculation was a necessary ingredient in the scholastic disputation. If the scholastic method did not in fact foster a critical or sceptical attitude to theology, this was because religious fideism was an essential element in the cultural climate, not because the medieval church deliberately shut its mind to innovations, though it was concerned that the boundaries of speculation should be fairly tightly drawn. Perhaps the chief defect of the medieval university course was its academic rigidity as much as its intellectual conservatism. The rise of the nominalist school of scholastic philosophers at Oxford in the fourteenth century might seem to demonstrate that scholasticism was not necessarily conservative at all, for nominalism was fundamentally radical, harbouring though not germinating a latent scepticism. But scholasticism demanded a set of rules, a mastery of form and pattern in argument in which there was a danger of the spirit being stifled by the letter of the law. Content could be easily sacrificed to the frame of argument in which it was presented, the subtlety of the demonstration, the cogency of the final syllogism. Suspecting initiative and doubting enterprise, conservative in approach even when the thinking was potentially radical, relying on traditional authorities, the university schoolman shied away from novelty. As a result his studies inevitably tended to become narrow and stereotyped.

*

What difference did the religious and intellectual changes of the sixteenth century make to university studies? At first sight Aristotelianism remained dominant and continued to condition the university degree course, at least at Oxford, for another two hundred and fifty years. 'I shall never be persuaded,' commented Sir Walter Ralegh, representing what progressive thinkers believed, 'that God hath shut up all light of learning within the lanthorn of Aristotle's brains.' But if radicals like Bacon held that the dominance of Aristotelianism at the universities was the 'most effective hindrance to natural philosophy and invention', Aristotle remained still the 'philosopher' of the post-Reformation and post-Renaissance university, so much so that at Oxford in 1586 questions 'disagreeing with the ancient and true philosophy' were not even allowed to be discussed. The authorities prescribed by the Elizabethan statutes for reading at Oxford, Virgil, Horace, Cicero, Aristotle, Plato, Porphyry, Boethius, Euclid, Orontius and Joannes de Sacrobosco, were very much the same as those read by the medieval schoolmen. The Edwardian statutes for Cambridge reaffirmed the supremacy of Aristotle, Plato and Pliny in philosophy, of Hippocrates and Galen in medicine, the *Elenchi* of Aristotle, the *Topica* of Cicero, Quintilian and Hermogenes in dialectic, and of Melas, Strabo, Pliny, Ptolemy and Euclid (to which two more recent writers, Tunstall and Cardan, were then added).

Both the content of the undergraduate degree course and the methods of teaching an examination remained predominantly scholastic and logical. 'In your answering,' James Duport, a Cambridge tutor, remarked in the 1630s, 'reject not lightly the authority of Aristotle if his owne words will permitt of a favorable and sure interpretation.' The Edwardian statutes laid down that the Cambridge undergraduate was to study arithmetic, geometry, astronomy and cosmography in his first year, dialectics in his second, metaphysics and physics and ethics in his third and fourth years. This was modified in 1559, and the changes were subsequently confirmed in 1571; henceforth he was to devote his first year to rhetoric, his second and third years to dialectics and his final year to philosophy (i.e. metaphysics, physics and ethics). It is not known how rigidly this syllabus was adhered to.

The course in logic, though founded on the works of Aristotle, involved for most undergraduates a consideration of the relevant text books: Keckermann's *Systema Systematum*, Burgersdicius's *Institutionum Logicarum Libri Duo*, Heerebord's *Annotamenta* and Eustachius of St Paul's *Summa Philosophiae Quadripartita*. The study of logic which was intended to enable the student to find out what was true necessarily involved a training in logical argument. Indeed in its precise Euclidean structure late sixteenth- and early seventeenth-century thought and writing was profoundly affected by these logical studies. The student of logic had to learn to 'oppose' a proposition (that is, to give the contrary and contradictory statements), to 'aequapolate' (to give the possible equivalent formulation) and to 'convert' (to give the correct juxtapositions of subject and predicate). He was not only expected to develop an argument according to the correct procedure, and there were nineteen legitimate methods, but also to recognize the fallacies implicit in the forty-five illegitimate forms.

Of the other subjects of the so-called arts course rhetoric was in the main directed to the acquisition of a good Latin style and its use in argument and exposition. Richard Holdsworth,* formerly a tutor at St John's College, Cambridge, advised students in the 1640s to 'spend every afternoon or at least two in a week making Latin exercises in a plain style, for reading without practice will never make you a Latinist'. In his exercises Alexander Bolde, who became a fellow of Pembroke, Cambridge, in 1610, discussed such subjects as whether the knowledge of virtue and the ignorance of vice were equally profitable or whether Julius Caesar was justly put to death. The last of the arts subjects, ethics, the determination of moral objects, for long bulked large in medieval and Renaissance study, and in it the student made use of the writings of both Protestant and Roman Catholic theologians.

The sciences, metaphysics, physics, mathematics and cosmography, were too subordinate to traditional concepts to be called scientific studies in any meaningful sense. 'The realm of knowledge,' Mr Costello has written,†

was divided into four provinces (each province concerned with some phase of being): metaphysics (being in general), physics (being as qualified), mathematics (being as quantified), and cosmography (the being of the geographical world). The very neatness of such an arrangement concealed an intransigence, and seemed to excuse Cambridge dons, and too many other scholastic masters, from any obligation to rethink the old curriculum in terms of the busy findings of the new mathematics and the New Sciences.

Metaphysical argument was founded on reason without reference to revelation. The student had to deal with such questions as whether God knows the contingent future antecedently or

* The attribution of the *Directions for a Student* (printed in H. F. Fletcher's *The Intellectual Development of John Milton*, Illinois University Press, ii, 1961, pp. 623–4) to Holdsworth's authorship has been challenged (Christopher Hill, *Intellectual Origins of the English Revolution*, Oxford, Clarendon Press, 1965, pp. 307–8).

† W. J. Costello, *The Scholastic Curriculum at Early 17th Century Cambridge*, Harvard University Press, 1958, p. 148.

knows the future action of a man which will come to pass only if a condition is fulfilled. Physics or Natural Philosophy, which was supposedly the study of changeable being in terms of matter, form, time, place and extension, and which included both human psychology and the study of sensible phenomena, was dogged by traditionalism. Scientific observation surrendered to accepted metaphysical conventions and in the process generated what can only be called a load of scholastic rubbish. 'Because woman,' so went one argument,

is of a moister and more frigid temperament than man, she grows more quickly and has more excrescences such as hair. ... Hence also we understand why woman has a sharper and subtler voice than man, why she is more timid, generally more flighty, and withal more graceful, because of the coldness and moistness of her temperament.

Neither mathematics nor cosmography developed very far within the context of the traditional syllabus.

There was a threefold method of instruction and examination; the lecture, the disputation and the declamation. It was modified to some extent by the development of the tutorial system, and the utility of the lecture diminished somewhat as a result of the greater prevalence of the printed book, but remained an essential part of the course. Private lectures took place in colleges and public lectures in the schools. At Cambridge lectures in theology, civil law, medicine and mathematics were given four times a week, usually between 7 and 8 a.m. Dr Cowell, the master of Trinity Hall, Cambridge, who died in 1611, bequeathed money for a college lecture in logic, which was to be held at least four times a week during term and for two hours from six to eight in the morning. The first hour 'I will to be bestowed in the examining the former days lecture, & in instructing the auditors, how to make use of logique by objecting & answering one the other.' The second hour was to be given up to a new lecture, 'in such deliberate manner, that the auditors may take it by yr penn from his mouth'.

Disputations, private in college, public in the schools, formed a very necessary part of the course and were normally provided for in the college statutes. At Trinity, Cambridge, disputations were held three times a week after morning chapel, on Monday, Wednesday and Friday, in philosophy or theology. The university required every student to appear four times in the schools during his four years as an undergraduate, twice as answerer or defendant, and twice as an objector. These statutory appearances, which were called quadragesimals, were made in Lent.

From Ash-Wednesday, unto the said Thursday, all the Commencers (except some few whom the father shall think fit to dispense with) are to come to the Schools upon every Monday, Tuesday, Wednesday, Thursday & Friday, at one of the clock in the afternoon, and to bring thither with them everyone a Sophister [a bachelor].

The exercises lasted from 1 to 5 p.m. though 'every day at 3 of the clock all the Bachelors and Sophisters may goe out till 4, & refresh & recreate themselves'. The disputations at the time of commencement often drew much attention, they were surrounded with a great deal of ceremonial and could establish the reputation of a successful respondent. The subject of the theses under dispute varied – a Mr Boyes in Elizabeth's reign debated whether the threat of punishment was a sufficient deterrent of crime – but the method of argument had become stylized and syllogistic. 'Dispute,' James Duport, elected a fellow of Trinity College, Cambridge, in 1627, advised, 'always Syllogistically at *least* Enthemematically and as much as you can Categorically.'

The declamation, which could take place in a college as well as in the schools, was a set speech designed to prove the candidate's proficiency as a rhetorician and a stylist and to display his classical knowledge. 'When you write Latine,' a candidate was sensibly advised, 'let your stile be clear & perspicuous, smooth, & plaine, & full, not darke and cloudy, curt, crabbed, & ragged, and let your stile be nervous, & vivid, & masculine, not inert, flat and languid.' Further exercises were required for the mastership and for the higher degrees, of which that in divinity was the most sought after. The official course of study of the sixteenth and seventeenth centuries in time degenerated into a farce; the lectures became stale formalities and students used arguments and illustrations drawn from well-thumbed commonplace books. But insufficient tribute has been paid to the intellectual demands of the scholastic discipline. It was subject to defects, but at its best it may have been as adequate a test of human intelligence as the much praised courses of the twentieth century.

While university studies were predominantly scholastic, scholasticism itself had not been unaffected by contemporary pressures. The most important of these in the sixteenth century was humanism. At first humanist influence was slight and was assimilated within the scholastic teaching; revived interest in classical learning was expressed through improved epistolography and various rather jejune attempts to present scholastic ideas in a more modern style of writing. But it also led patrons genuinely stimulated by the new learning to purchase classical texts. Scholars like Robert Fleming, the Dean of Lincoln, and John Free studied in Italy during the fifteenth century and brought back manuscripts which they presented to university and college libraries. English students gradually began to imbibe something of the spirit of the Italian revival. Greek scholars, often penurious and obsequious, earned an honest penny through teaching the Greek language newly fashionable in academic circles. Indeed the attention paid to Greek was the distinctive feature of Renaissance humanism in England. The new learning represented by scholars such as Colet and More, Grocyn and Linacre, above all Erasmus, caused a very important shift of interest which was bound to affect university scholarship.

It did not immediately affect the syllabus, since the universities were at first mainly concerned to improve facilities for training the clergy, but as religion gradually relinquished its monopoly, education began to feel the humanist influence. 'The main innovation of humanist writers on education,' Dr Simon has observed,

was that they laid emphasis on 'the formation of character and not on the acquisition of knowledge', that they saw the great figures of Greece and Rome not as paragons of learning but as 'paragons of human excellence'. This was fundamentally a lay approach corresponding to the social changes of the age. ... The emphasis laid on rhetoric at the expense of concentration on logic was particularly significant in this context; while logic was the particular sphere of the philosopher, rhetoric was proper to the popularizer, the link whereby learning was communicated to men at large.

The Edwardian statutes at Cambridge added Homer, Demosthenes, Isocrates, and Euripides to the scholastic authorities. At Oxford Bishop Foxe of Winchester in founding Corpus Christi College in 1516–17 provided especially for public lecturers in Latin, Greek and divinity; the Greek lecturer was expected to comment on set Greek authors or to teach Greek grammar. The lecturer in divinity was explicitly advised to rely on the patristic writings rather than on commentaries of the medieval schoolmen, for studies in divinity, if in no other subject, had been much affected by cultural change. In spite of opposition from the so-called Trojan party, the sponsors of Greek learning gained ground. Thomas Cromwell's Visitors, the notorious Richard Layton and his colleague, John London, the Warden of New College, Oxford, in 1536 urged the provision of public lectures in Greek at New College, All Souls and Magdalen. When Henry VIII established Christ Church a decade later, he established five regius professorships, of divinity, Hebrew, Greek, civil law and medicine.

Cambridge, at first slower to respond, soon rivalled, indeed outshone, Oxford as a centre of the new learning, very probably as a result of the interest of John Fisher, Master of Michaelhouse, who became confessor to Lady Margaret Beaufort, mother of the king, Henry VII, and herself a notable friend to scholarship at both Oxford and Cambridge. She had already founded lectureships in divinity at both universities; but doubtless as a result of Fisher's influence Cambridge ultimately secured the greater share of her benefactions. Although he was not himself a scholar of the first rank, Fisher, as able as he was genuinely pious, patronized the early Cambridge humanists, and it was probably through his intervention that Erasmus was persuaded to visit Cambridge and then to live for two years at Queens' College, teaching and complaining acidly about the less pleasing features of Cambridge life, among which he counted some of his colleagues. Although Erasmus did not greatly care for Cambridge, he found disciples and made friends there, and it was during this sojourn that he prepared his monumental work, the edition of the Greek New Testament, which was published in 1516, two years after his departure. The contagious enthusiasm of John Cheke, the first holder of the regius professorship of Greek founded by Henry VIII, did much to establish Greek studies. 'Sophocles and Euripides are now more familiar than Plautus was when you were here,' Ascham told a Cambridge friend in 1542 or 1543,

Herodotus, Thucydides and Xenophon are more widely quoted and read than Livy then was; Demosthenes is as familiar as Cicero once was; there are more copies of Isocrates in the students' hands than there were of Terence. Nor do we despise the Latin writers. ... This zeal for literature has been kindled and sustained by the labours and example of Cheke. He has read in public lectures free of charge the whole of Homer and the whole of Sophocles twice, all Euripides and almost all Herodotus.

It was through Erasmus and many lesser known members of the universities that the new learning became associated with the beginnings of Protestant theology in England. Cambridge found it easier to accept the religious changes initiated by the government of Henry VIII since opinion there had been affected by what was happening in Luther's Germany and by the diffusion of humanist thought. The faculty of canon law disappeared, together with the degree and the prescribed course of study. Some of the scholastic authorities, such as Lombard's *Sentences*, once an integral part of the divinity course, were eliminated and replaced by commentaries founded on the original Greek and influenced by the teaching of the reformed Church. 'It is scarcely thirty years ago,' Erasmus wrote as early as 1516,

when all that was taught in the University of Cambridge, was Alexander, the Little Logicals (as they call them), and those old exercises out of Aristotle, and *quaestiones* taken from Duns Scotus. As time went on, polite learning was introduced; to this was added knowledge of mathematics; a new, or at least a regenerated, Aristotle sprang up; then came an acquaintance with Greek, and with a host of new authors whose very names had before been unknown, even to their profoundest doctors. And how, I would ask, has this affected your university? Why, it has flourished to such a degree that it can now compete with the chief universities of the age, and can boast of men in comparison with whom theologians of the old school seem only the ghosts of theologians.

The authority of the schoolmen had been thus sedulously undermined at Oxford as well. 'We have set Duns Scotus in Bocardo [the Oxford prison],' an Oxford wit observed gleefully, 'and have utterly banished him Oxford forever, with all his blind glosses, and is now made a common servant to every man, fast nailed upon posts in all common houses of easement.' At the end of the sixteenth century progressive thinkers were beginning to absorb the ideas of the French scholar, Peter Ramus, a trenchant opponent of Aristotelianism. Erasmus could, however, hardly have foreseen the onset of Calvinist teaching upon which from the middle of the sixteenth century lectures and determinations for degrees in theology were founded. Since most of the fellows took such degrees, there was in fact a very much more emphatic change in the intellectual climate of both Oxford and Cambridge than a superficial survey of the syllabus might suggest.

*

As important as the shifts of intellectual fashion were the alterations in the teaching system itself, especially the widespread introduction of the tutorial system. Although there had been some teaching in colleges before the end of the fifteenth century, most undergraduates were instructed through the medium of the lecture. The changes in the character of the colleges, the growing number of laymen who matriculated, the early age at which many of them entered the colleges, precipitated a new and important factor in supervision, the college tutor. Of forty-seven fellows at St John's, Cambridge, in 1565, forty-two had pupils: three had fifteen or more, twenty had five or more, but most had three or four. The tutors were responsible for their work and conduct, and advised their pupils about the administration of their finances. Normally they had rooms on the same staircase in the college buildings or nearby.

In many cases a close relationship developed which endured into later life. When Symonds d'Ewes was a fellow-commoner at St John's, Cambridge, his tutor Richard Holdsworth went home with him after he had ended his residence, 'not only to perform the last loving office to me, but to receive some arrearages due to him upon his bills'. The Puritan John Preston was described by Fuller as the 'greatest pupil-monger in England in man's memory, having sixteen fellow-commoners (most heirs to fair estates) admitted in one year at Queens' College'. Samuel Ward, then a fellow of Emmanuel, wrote sadly in his diary on 14 November 1599 'about 4 o'clock befor day, ytt pleased God to take away my puple Luck'. Joseph Mead of Christ's lectured to his pupils' daily and tried to provide for their personal interests by setting them each a special task. They went to see him in the evening to report progress and he sought to answer any queries that they had. 'And then, having by prayer commended them and their studies to God's protection and blessing, he dismissed them to their lodgings.'

When Robert Norgate was Master of Corpus he indicated that the tutors were to provide in college three lectures, on Aristotle at six in the morning, on Greek at 12 noon and at 3 p.m. a rhetoric lecture 'of some part of Tully'. (It is incidentally of some interest to observe that rhetoric had begun to displace grammar.) On Wednesdays and Fridays 'one of the fellows in his order handleth some place of the scripture, whereof he taketh occasion to entreat of some commonplace of doctrine . . . .' On other days lectures were followed by exercises or discussions. In 1628 Thomas Crosfield, a fellow of Queen's College, Oxford, sketched in verse a typical day in his life. It began with prayers and a Latin sermon:

> I'th'morning pray'd & heard a Latin sermon
> Wch was composed and preached by Mr Forman.

After a business visit to the town he attended to his pupils:

And to my pupils read Enunciations
Modificate, & went to disputations.
These done we din'd, & after did resort
To bowle i'th garden & to have some sport.
Then after this we heard ye disputations
About the Vulgar and English translations.

The day ended with further reading:

In general, thou has bene studious
When prayers and ye lectures both were done.

There must have been some careless and indolent tutors but a surprising amount of evidence testifies to the care with which many performed their duty in the late sixteenth and early seventeenth centuries. The conscientious tutor must have greatly influenced his pupil in his reading and studies generally. The evidence for the impact which the Puritan dons of Christ's, Emmanuel and Sidney Sussex had on their pupils is unquestionable. Richard Holdsworth suggested that his pupils should devote the morning to logic and philosophy and the afternoon to humane letters. His recommended reading list catered deliberately for those who came to the university 'not with the intention to make scholarship their profession, but only to get such learning as may serve for delight and ornament, and such as the want whereof would speak a defect in breeding rather than scholarship'. It included works 'on natural philosophy, modern history, classical history, and literature in translation, post-classical Latin literature, modern languages, practical morality and divinity, manners and courtesy, and heraldry'. The attribution to Holdsworth of the so-called *Directions to Students* has been questioned, and its value as evidence has been criticized; but it can hardly be doubted that a college tutor could persuade his pupil to read widely outside the syllabus, nor that many students, like John Wesley in the early eighteenth century, followed this advice.

Under the Commonwealth the universities were condemned for their continued adherence to scholastic learning, 'monkish sophistry' as John Milton called it, and there was a welcome injection of mathematical and scientific inquiry at this period.

Even when, with the Restoration, the universities took up again the well-worn curricula of the past, the new and fascinating ideas that had been generated within their borders were not completely stifled. If Oxford remained wedded to the past, at Cambridge the reaction against Calvinism associated with the Cambridge Platonists, who put an over-confident trust of divine powers of human reason to direct men to the truths of divine revelation, gave way to the cooler rationalism of the so-called Latitudinarians. The writings of John Locke, rejected at Oxford, found a warmer reception at Cambridge where Baconian logic began to gain a following and Sir Isaac Newton initiated a mathematical tradition that was never discarded.

*

Although Cambridge had come to terms more effectively with new developments in learning than Oxford, both universities were at their lowest ebb in the eighteenth century. Lectures, when they were given, and tutorials, as the young Gibbon commented, were unexciting, formal and dull; the well-thumbed textbooks provided no real stimulus to genuine learning. The universities still housed scholars of considerable eminence, like the Hebraist Kennicott, and well-read cultivated men; and there was ample opportunity for a serious man to study widely on his own. But by and large the exercises for degrees at Oxford had degenerated into meaningless formalities.

The Cambridge system worked more efficiently, but the standard seems to have been as low. The exercises and disputations may still have afforded an excellent discipline in dialectic; the divinity disputations, still required for degrees in theology, could draw a crowd if the respondent had a reputation, as Isaac Milner had in 1786. The other exercises were, however, gradually overshadowed by the Senate House Examination. This was at first intended to supplement the disputations, but in the end it became the main test of a candidate's abilities, especially as the proceedings were conducted in English. Lists of successful candidates were first published in 1747; five years later the candidates were divided into wranglers, senior and junior optimes. In 1763 it was agreed that the position of the senior and second wranglers should be determined by means of an examination rather than by disputation. By 1779 the examination lasted four days, including a set of papers on 'natural religion, moral philosophy and Locke's essay'.

The Cambridge syllabus, less scholastic than Oxford's, was primarily a mathematical test. John Jebb, who argued strongly for improved university examinations, outlined the studies that were expected of an able undergraduate in 1772:

the first six books of Euclid, plane trigonometry, the first rule of algebra, mechanics, hydrostatics, apparent astronomy, and optics; the 11th and 12th books of Euclid, conic sections, spherical trigonometry, the higher parts of algebra, Newton's *Principia*; problems on extractions of roots, solution of algebraical equations, and book-work of fluxions; Locke's *Essay*, Butler's *Analogy*, Clarke's *Attributes*.

The syllabus had changed little when John Wright went up to Trinity in 1815. In his first term he went daily at 9 a.m. to the mathematical lecture by Mr Brown, who told his pupils to prepare propositions of Euclid, and at 10 to the Greek lecture by Mr Monk. Monk, Bentley's biographer and later Bishop of Gloucester, told his class to construe any part of the opening of the *Seven Against Thebes*, to give the geography of the scenes and the history of the *dramatis personae*. In his third term Wright studied the *Eighth Muse* of Herodotus and plane trigonometry. In his second year he went to lectures on the seventh book of Thucydides and in mathematics on statics and dynamics, noting that the lectures were 'more thinly attended than ever, although there yet remained a good sprinkling of the Reading Men'. Later in his second year he read Locke and Dugald Stewart in metaphysics, Paley's *Moral Philosophy* and *Evidences of Christianity* and St Luke in Greek, and in mathematics, the second, third and fourth parts of Wood's Algebra and Spherical Trigonometry. He notes the rush to the library to secure the books that the undergraduates wanted for their study;

The libraries were now again ransacked of their copies of Campbell on the Gospels, Beausobre on the New Testament (most excellent books these), Watt's Scripture History, Valpy's New Testament. . . . Garnier's Algebra and Analyse Algebrique, together with Lacroix's Algebra, and some others, and Cresswell's Spherics must be purchased.

In the third term of his final year he applied his mind to conic sections, popular and plane astronomy and Newton's *Principia*: 'With astronomy I was both delighted and astonished.' The annual examination at Trinity at the end of this year included papers on Thucydides, Livy, Newton, Locke, *Hecuba*, St Luke's Gospel, mechanics, conics, spherical trigonometry, astronomy and moral philosophy.

Even when the teaching was conscientious, however, scholarship was neither original nor profound. The professors had come to have a scant regard for their duties and in the eighteenth century all but a few treated their positions as sinecures. The reasons for this were not far to seek. At Oxford the regius professors of divinity, civil law, medicine, Hebrew and Greek still received the stipend of £40 which had been fixed in 1546, though the regius professor of divinity had acquired a canonry of Christ Church and the rectory of Ewelme, and the regius professor of civil law a lay prebend at Salisbury. The professorship of moral philosophy carried a stipend of £100 but from 1673 to 1829 was held *ex officio* by the senior proctor. The professor of experimental philosophy enjoyed £30 a year until the Prince Regent raised it to £100.

By comparison the regius professor of history with a stipend of £371 was well-paid. The experience of Edward Nares who held this office from 1813 to 1841, contriving to acquire the rectory of Biddenden in Kent and to perform his professorial duties by sporadic visits to the university, underlines some of the difficulties of being a professor in unreformed Oxford.

I had come fully prepared to read twenty lectures on modern history, twelve on political economy, and to preach three sermons at St Mary's. . . . The first thing I heard was that I was likely to have no audience at all, because the Dean of Christ Church was to preach at the opening of a new church in the parish of St Ebbe. . . . On Tuesday . . . my lectures on history were to commence. In the preceding year I had a class of more than 120. This year the number was reduced to seven, and three of these had attended the previous course.

On another occasion there was 'not a single person in the school but myself'. In 1835 'I found only six names entered to attend my lectures, but I was resolved to proceed.' When he entered his lecture room, however, it was already occupied by the professor of moral philosophy. Ultimately the Registrar let Nares have his office where 'I read my first and most important lecture to the only two auditors at leisure to attend me'. 'The undergraduates,' he noted, 'were too much occupied in preparing for their public examinations to attend any of the professors.' A Cambridge graduate of the 1820s, on the other hand, noted that

> The King's Professor of Civil Law delivers his [lectures] at Trinity Hall in three successive terms. The Plumian Professor gives lectures, experimentally explaining the theories of Mechanics. . . . In Modern History, you may hear also, most excellent disquisitions, Professor Smyth having, for these twenty years past, devoted nearly the whole of his time to that. Woodward's Professor of Geology, at present time indefatigable Mr Sedgwick, gives a very instructive course of lectures.

Such activity was something of an innovation, for William Lax, the Lowndean professor of astronomy at Cambridge from 1795 to 1837, had never delivered a single lecture nor had Francis Barnes, the Knightsbridge professor of moral philosophy from 1813 to 1838.

The divinity professors alone seemed to have been assured of an audience, as many bishops demanded a certificate of attendance at their lectures from their candidates for ordination. By and large the lectures seem to have been edifying rather than stimulating. The regius professor at Oxford, John Randolph, delivered lectures in a monotone by candlelight to soporific undergraduates, though things were changed under his successor, Charles Lloyd. At Cambridge the Norrisian professor simply read out passages from Pearson's book on the Creed; 'and there being so much irreverence and disorderly conduct,' wrote one of his listeners, 'that for the life of me I could not get through the course. ... Many times have I seen them [the 'gay-men'] in their extreme desire to escape the bore, as they called it, of being detained an hour, creep out on all-fours, the Professor being a man of such small altitude, that the wags became eclipsed by the table.'

*

In the early years of the nineteenth century a serious examination system was introduced at the older universities. The Oxford syllabus was conservative: grammar, rhetoric, logic, moral philosophy and the elements of mathematics and physics. The examination, instituted in 1800, was at first oral, but written work was required after 1807. By 1842 there were five days of examination. From 1830 candidates were likely to be examined in Greek and Roman history, poetry and moral and political science 'in so far as they may be drawn from writers of antiquity'.

The honour schools of *literae humaniores*, established as separate examinations in 1807, had been a major breakthrough. It laid the foundation for the seemingly impregnable reputation of the Greats course, a combination of philosophy and of ancient history. Indeed the pre-eminence of Oxford and Cambridge in classical scholarship, sustained at an earlier date by Bentley and Porson, was never seriously challenged, though their standards had fallen low by the beginning of the nineteenth century. 'Four years are spent,' an Oxford man said, 'in preparing about fourteen books only for examination. . . . These are made textbooks, read, re-read, digested, worked, got up, until they become part and parcel of the mind.' The teaching was often perfunctory and uninspired, and of a lower standard than that of the classical forms of the better public schools. At Cambridge, where the tripos was introduced in 1824, until 1857, the would-be classicist had to satisfy the examiners in mathematics. 'The interests of learning,' Frederick Temple bluntly told the royal commission in 1850, 'are intrusted to those who have neither talents nor inclination for the subject.' The situation was improved by the example of men like Benjamin Jowett, who became tutor of Balliol in 1842 and professor of Greek at Oxford in 1855, and by the appearance of profound scholars acquainted with the intricacies of German textual criticism, such as Ingram Bywater and Henry Nettleship at Oxford and Henry Jackson and R. C. Jebb at Cambridge. Although Jowett was far from being a meticulous scholar, he revived interest in Plato and by relating Greek studies to the modern world invested the subject with a liveliness which it had lacked in the hands even of good classicists like Gaisford and Monk. In such circumstances the 'verbal criticism and philological research' of Cambridge and the 'abstract speculation' and historical studies of Oxford opened a new era in the study of the classics.

The reorganization of the honour schools which Oxford and Cambridge had initiated just before the establishment of the royal commission of the 1850s, possibly to forestall criticism of the narrowness of the curriculum, and which was carried further in the years immediately ensuing, widened the range of studies in which undergraduates could take their degrees and in which colleges were sooner or later to appoint lecturers and fellows. It is impossible to follow the fortunes of every individual school but even a glance at some of them illuminates the general trend.

Since the ending of the Second World War the schools of modern history at Oxford and Cambridge have attracted a larger proportion of the undergraduates than any others. Yet the study of history was for long an academic backwater. The regius professorships had been founded in 1724, probably at the suggestion of Bishop Gibson of London, in part to supply the government service with properly trained young men and in part to attach the universities to the Hanoverian régime. While the professors were at first conscientious the government soon lost interest in the project. There were probably not enough vacancies in the diplomatic and civil service to meet the demand and for the posts that were vacant candidates were much more likely to be chosen by patronage than by merit. The professorship became a sinecure, though it was held occasionally by men of distinction; Thomas Gray at Cambridge and Joseph Spence at Oxford were men of literary eminence, and Henry Beeke of Oxford was an economist upon whose services the government placed some reliance. Yet even when the professor was obliged to lecture, as Edward Nares had already discovered, his lectures were treated as of no importance.

In 1853 Oxford and in 1868 Cambridge set up the joint schools of law and history. The marriage was soon ended by divorce: at Oxford in 1872 and at Cambridge in 1873 the history school was established independently. 'I can but fear the worst,' the diehard Tory Dean Burgon wrote in 1849,

a majority of fourteen in Convocation voted in favour of the establishment of a fourth school – namely Modern History. We did indeed by a large majority reject the details of this novelty, but the principle has been admitted – yielded to pressure from without – and I can but think it is a most dangerous step. ... We all flatter ourselves that we are in the most conservative trim, but rightly or wrongly we have fallen into the weakness of yielding to the spirit of the age.

Twenty-one years later when J. B. Lightfoot told the vice-chancellor of Cambridge that he wished to found a scholar-ship for the study of church history, he declared that he had

long felt that the study of history does not receive proper encouragement in this University, and at the present time, when the just demands of natural science are so eagerly urged, there is a great danger that an instrument of education, which I venture to consider even more important, may be forgotten.

His fears proved groundless. The schools of modern history at both universities, winning lustre by the work of J. R. Green, E. A. Freeman and Bishop Stubbs at Oxford and by that of Sir John Seeley, Lord Acton, Mandell Creighton and F. W. Maitland at Cambridge, to name but a few luminaries, soon attracted some of the ablest undergraduates.

In the course of a few decades the study of history itself underwent a revolutionary change. It ceased to be a pastime for the amateur of cultivated interests and literary aspirations and became an exacting profession, demanding a highly skilled technique and the capacity to use and interpret original sources, though it must be confessed that as history became more scientific it tended to become more unreadable. The new approach, which owed something to the work of J. B. Bury at Cambridge, was in the main associated with the school of history at Manchester under the direction of Tout and Tait, and later of Sir Lewis Namier. Tout wished to raise history from amateur to professional status, to follow techniques similar to those which the British exponents of the physical sciences used in their work. The school soon won an international reputation and fertilized the teaching of many other universities; Sir Maurice Powicke, one of the most distinguished of Oxford's medievalists, had been a professor at Manchester. The tradition of literate history was expertly maintained by G. M. Trevelyan at Cambridge, later Master of Trinity College. At both universities large faculties had been created to cope with the heavy teaching demands; and the study of history, at one time concentrated on England and Europe, widened to embrace the whole world.

*

During the closing years of the nineteenth and the opening of the twentieth centuries there was a revolution not merely in the subjects but in the method of study. Whereas in the past reliance had been placed on authority and exact scholarship, greater attention was now given to intelligent understanding and to creative and original thought. Universities were to be, as a writer has put it recently, a 'forum where the resources of trained intelligence are applied as keenly to men's ultimate convictions as to the atom or the cell'. Native conservatism often found it difficult to accept new syllabuses; but everywhere new courses were being devised.

The story of the modern languages school at Oxford illustrates some of the difficulties confronting the reformer. The regius professors of history instituted by the Crown in 1724 had been made responsible for appointing teachers of modern languages, a function which they continued to perform after their own posts had become sinecures. This system lingered on well into the nineteenth century; the Italian lecturer whom

Thomas Gray appointed at Cambridge in 1768 was teaching Wordsworth the elements of Italian twenty years later. When the German lecturer at Oxford, Bramsen, died in 1845, the professor did not replace him but continued to employ the Italian teacher Cardi until his resignation in 1850; thereupon he added the joint salary of the two teachers of £42 per annum to his own professorial stipend. Meanwhile the architect Sir Robert Taylor who died in 1788 bequeathed a large sum (ultimately settled after his son's death in 1834 at £65,900) for teaching European languages at Oxford. From this the Taylorian Institution was built, to the designs of Charles Cockerell; but the study of languages still flagged in spite of the stimulus given to philological scholarship by the appointment of Max Müller as professor in 1854. In fact the university had not enough money to finance the teaching, even after the modern language honour school was set up in 1904, nor were colleges ready to allocate fellowships in the subject (indeed in the 1920s, apart from the professors, there were only two fellowships). The greater part of the teaching was therefore done by paid hacks. Even in 1919 the stipends of the twelve persons employed in teaching languages, including the two professors, averaged only £282 a year.

The growth and development of the English school at Cambridge reflected rather different problems. Since 1878, when the Senate sanctioned the setting up of a board for the study of modern and medieval languages, English had simply been one subject taught under the aegis of the board. The teaching concentrated on linguistics and philology, but the accident that the leading philologists, Braunholtz and Breul, were Germans gave the reformers the opportunity during the First World War to establish the English tripos, which they did in 1917. The old guard led by the disappointed and embittered A. J. Wyatt and supported by three stalwart females fought strongly against the new proposals but in vain. Sir Arthur Quiller-Couch, the professor (a chair of English had been created in memory of Edward VII by the benefaction of Harmsworth in 1910), was amiably persuaded to support the new venture, but the real lead was taken by Sir William Ridgway, a patriotic Tory as well as an active university politician, and by H. M. Chadwick, the professor of Anglo-Saxon (until he withdrew in 1926 to the fastness of the faculty of archaeology and anthropology), assisted by a number of younger dons, I. A. Richards, M.D. Forbes and E. M. W. Tillyard.

Unlike the Oxford faculty of English – an honour school had been established there in 1897 – the English school at Cambridge was mainly concerned with the study of English literature in its historical and social setting, and with fostering a scholarly and scientific but not an arid literary criticism. In spite of his professional study Chadwick was violently opposed to making Anglo-Saxon, which he regarded with contempt as literature – he had been known to dismiss the *Pearl* as 'bloody nonsense' – an essential part of the school. Among its early products were the future poet and critic, William Empson, who subsequently became professor of English at Sheffield, and F. R. Leavis, who was to be in the 1930s the school's *enfant terrible*. Leavis's somewhat dogmatic but penetrating judgements, often phrased in strangely ponderous prose, reached a wider public through the medium of the magazine *Scrutiny* and challenged the criteria of criticism then in vogue at Cambridge. For Leavis literary criticism was necessarily a 'discipline of intelligence and sensibility'.

The essential discipline of an English school is the literary critical; it is a true discipline, only in an English school if anywhere will it be fostered, and it is irreplaceable. It trains, in a way no other discipline can, intelligence and sensibility together, cultivating a sensitiveness and precision of response and a delicate integrity of intelligence – intelligence that integrates as well as analyses and must have pertinacity and staying power as well as delicacy.

Leavis's Parthian shots created depression and dismay at Cambridge, to some extent dividing and even embittering the faculty; but his high standards had immense influence over the course of English studies in nearly every British university, even though Oxford, still cherishing its philological courses, remained for long relatively immune to change.

The more recently founded universities could only devise syllabuses and award their own degrees once they had been granted a royal charter, and until then their undergraduates took the external degrees of London University. For some time the instruction provided was more suited to the needs of a school than of a university; nor were the degrees awarded comparable to those given by the older institutions. Durham, an undistinguished society closely connected with the cathedral chapter and mainly concerned with the training of ordinands, modelled its syllabuses on those of Oxford, but the general level of performance was inevitably lower than that of its mentor. The system of instruction at University College, London, and at Manchester, owed much to the models afforded by the Scottish universities. Originally a course was instituted to include Latin and Greek in the first year; after this the student was theoretically entitled to specialize in philosophy or science. In fact the early students simply enrolled for the lecture courses in which they were interested. This changed in 1836 when London was given the right to award its own degrees. A student had at first to follow a course at one of the recognized colleges, but after 1858 anyone could enter for a degree, a move which had the effect of making the university into a vast examining machine, though initially the number of candidates was limited. In the early days of the university the London degree was a general one, candidates being obliged to show that they had an adequate command of four of the following subjects: mathematics and natural philosophy; chemistry; animal physiology; vegetable physiology and structural botany; classics; logic and moral philosophy. Until the reorganization of London university in 1898–9, King's College had its own courses and comparatively few of its students presented themselves for a London degree.

Many of the other university colleges were necessarily closely associated with London since until they achieved full status their curriculum was moulded by the requirements of the London degree. Some of the colleges had arrangements with Oxford and Cambridge by which their students were exempt from a first year at the older universities if they had followed successfully a degree course at their provincial college. Most of their students, however, took the London degree. Some university colleges, as the Yorkshire College, Leeds, had originated as colleges of science and had added arts departments as they sought to extend the range of the education they provided. At its foundation Firth College, Sheffield, advertised day and evening classes in mathematics, classics, ancient history, modern history, chemistry, physics, mechanics, and the theory of music, adding some modern languages and biology shortly afterwards. In the first year the standard approximated to that of the requirements for London matriculation. It was hoped that in their second year the students would be able to take the London Intermediate Examination and ultimately present themselves for the London degree, but very few of them got that far. At the end of each session college examinations were held on which a certificate, classified according to merit, was awarded, enabling a student who had regularly attended to become an associate of the college.

The trustees of Owens College, Manchester were much influenced by the Scottish universities which 'have in no respect been framed or modified with reference to the means, or pursuits, or habits of the aristocracy; their system is that of a general plan of education by which persons of all ranks may be equally benefited'.* With this in mind they drew up a general course which involved classical languages and literature, mathematics and natural philosophy and, after some discussion, mental and moral philosophy on the grounds, as Dr Vaughan of the Lancashire Independent College put it, that 'one of the great wants of modern Europe is that the masculine good sense of Englishmen should be brought to bear on those subtle speculations and weighty moral questions which are now elaborated elsewhere ... to ends so much more mischievous than usual'. English language and literature were added because grammar was highly regarded as teaching the 'accuracy of language which is essential to the accuracy of reasoning'. Natural history and some modern languages were included as secondary subjects. Finally they made some provision for students 'not intending to go through the regular

* Quoted in H. B. Charlton, *Portrait of a University, 1851–1951*, Manchester University Press, 1951, p. 28.

course' to attend classes in subjects that were likely to be professionally useful to them as 'engineers, machinists and other pursuits in practical science'. In fact comparatively few of the first students followed a regular course of study, apart from those wishing to work for the external degrees of London.

All this was changed when the Victoria University was established in 1880, and degree courses were instituted. The numbers attending evening classes dwindled while there was an increase in the number of students attending full time with a view to a degree. Between 1882 and 1903 121 Manchester students, including 40 women, were awarded honours degrees in Arts and 364, including 15 women, honours degrees in science. Leeds, like its academic colleagues in the Victoria University, from the start distinguished between an ordinary and honours course; in 1950, however, the pass degree was abolished (except in technological subjects) and degrees were henceforth awarded with honours either in General Studies or in Special Studies (for arts and pure science). As soon as Sheffield was made a university in 1905 it made provision for degrees in arts, science, medicine, engineering and metallurgy. It proposed that degrees in the two latter subjects should be awarded either after a full three years' course or a full one year course followed by attendance at evening classes for four years. Although Liverpool awarded degrees on evening classes, the proposal did not meet with the approval of the other universities who feared that the possibility of graduating on evening-class work might prejudice the standard of scientific and technological degrees. Sheffield agreed therefore to operate the system only for degrees in metallurgy, though Manchester awarded degrees in commerce and administration in part on work done in evening classes. The new universities did not find it easy at first to establish an adequate academic standard and often appointed examiners from the older universities to assist them in this task.

A major revolution in university study occurred with the growth, especially after the ending of the First World War, of graduate study and research. The reputation of individual departments drew more and more research students from every quarter of the globe: by 1961–2 the number of full-time post-graduate students in British universities amounted to 19,400. Of these 4,500 were studying education (the growth of the education departments mostly pioneered by the newer universities is itself a not unimportant aspect of university history), and 11,300 were doing research, usually for an advanced degree. The total compares unfavourably with similar statistics for the United States, more especially as it includes some 5,400 students from overseas; but it shows nonetheless the advance that had been made since the introduction of research degrees some half-century earlier.

As in the Middle Ages men came deliberately to work under the supervision of a master. This was especially the case with scientific faculties, but was also true of the humanities. It is well demonstrated by the growing reputation of the Oxford school of Philosophy which under such exponents as the late J. L. Austin, A. J. Ayer and G. A. Ryle attracted an increasing number of graduate students. Drawing its nutriment from the teaching of the Cambridge professors like G. E. Moore and the eccentric Ludwig Wittgenstein and reacting against the once dominant idealism of Bosanquet and Bradley, Oxford philosophy passed through a series of phases, an arid logical positivism merging with mathematical analysis and semantic studies. In some respects philosophy seems now to be engaged in an academic take-over bid. At Oxford it interpenetrates a number of honour schools, including those of Greats, P.P.E. (Philosophy, Politics and Economics) and the recently-established P.P.P. (Philosophy, Psychology and Physiology); it bulks large in the curriculum of Sussex and other newly founded universities. Oxford has set up an examination for post-graduates, known as the B.Phil., which can be taken in a wide range of subjects but which has proved immediately popular among would-be philosophers.

Research rather than scholarship – if we may differentiate between two closely allied activities – may appear to be the major industry of the modern university. Yet it is useful to recall a comment made in the Robbins report that there are many persons of first class ability, particularly in the humanities, who have never engaged in research in the narrow sense or felt any urge to publish, but whose breadth of culture, ripeness of judgment and wide-ranging intellectual curiosity are priceless assets in a department or college.

Learning, scholarship and research have undergone many changes and variations in eight hundred years of university history. At all times they have tended to reflect, and have been closely allied with, the moral, social and religious ethos of the age, but there have always been those scholars who have stood for independence of thought and creative endeavour. The historian may well find it difficult to trace any pattern in the very diversified field of university learning in recent decades. To some it has appeared of a somewhat pedestrian and unadventurous character, dominated by the accumulation of superfluous theses and by the multiplication of specialized articles on ever more recondite topics, suggesting perhaps an onset of the petrifaction to which scholasticism succumbed in the later period of its history. In a brilliant but abrasive and one-sided essay,* Perry Anderson suggests that British culture, itself stagnant, has been chiefly fertilized by expatriate refugees (F. R. Leavis in literary criticism and J. M. Keynes in economics alone excepted), by Ludwig Wittgenstein in philosophy, Bronislaw Malinowski in anthropology, Lewis Namier in history, Karl Popper in social theory, Isaiah Berlin in political theory, Ernst Gombrich in aesthetics, H. J. Eysenck in psychology and Melanie Klein in psychoanalysis; and that their work and teaching were allergic to radical change as they cherished the stability and traditions of the country which they had made their home. He argues that Britain has been by-passed in many notable fields, especially in psychology and sociology, by continental and American scholars, and, like other radicals, he deplores the lack of any revolutionary or Marxist tradition of any dimension in British culture, which he characterizes as 'reactionary and mystifying'. Apart from the selective nature of the evidence upon which the author founds his thesis, and his

* 'The Components of the National Culture' in *Student Power*, ed. A. Cockburn and R. Blackburn, Penguin Books, 1969, pp. 214–84.

failure to recognize those British scholars who have earned a world-wide reputation in science and arts, there may be a tithe of truth in his assumption that modern British scholarship, by comparison with that of the last half of the Victorian era, has tended to be unadventurous and averse to experimentation. It is possible that learning has become too professionalized, more of a task and less of a delight, too swamped by the concept of teaching and research as a job to be done rather than as a vocation to be followed. There are too few who would agree with the seventeenth-century Lord Halifax that 'the struggle for knowledge hath a pleasure in it like that of wrestling with a fine woman'.

Yet this creeping tendency to be cautious and conventional, ominous as it may be, has not yet extinguished the desire which drives the majority of university teachers to explore the terrain of knowledge and to find out new truths, not to subordinate learning to a particular philosophy of existence or politics, but to push intrepidly into the unknown. The supposition that a revolutionary situation might release a flow of creative scholarship is largely unsupported by history; on the contrary, all societies which seek to dictate the particular line along which academic thought must move have proved ultimately stultifying to genuine scholarship. However closely associated with the established order, British universities have never purposely contrived, as has happened in some twentieth-century universities elsewhere, to subordinate the search for knowledge to the dogma of a political party, a racial programme or an intolerant philosophy. To their credit, even in their darkest hours, they have remained unswervingly loyal to what they have conceived to be the pursuit of truth.

CHAPTER ELEVEN

The Universities and Science

IT is a truism to say that the twentieth century is pre-eminently the age of science, but nevertheless a relevant one, since the assimilation of science in all its multifarious branches into the university curriculum did more than anything else to change the balance of subjects studied and to affect the nature of the university community itself. The intrusion of science was inevitable, though the universities were more reluctant than eager to deal in new forms of learning. For a time at least it has fractured the common cultural heritage; if intelligent men are able to paper over the cracks and to bridge the gulf between science and non-science, yet the majority, and this is especially true of undergraduates, tend to live in two different worlds. In the social as well as in the intellectual environment there was – and is – a visible cleavage between the scientist and the non-scientist, which creates tensions, doubtless temporary, but certainly real.

The dominance of science had significant sequels. The need to build laboratories and equip them with extraordinarily expensive apparatus, and to find a sponsor for research projects, forced the universities into ever greater dependence upon the state, a state which by reason of its economic and industrial needs had a vested interest in promoting scientific progress. At Oxford and Cambridge the multiplication of lecturers, demonstrators and research workers whom it was impracticable for colleges to absorb into their own senior common rooms created problems which at one time threatened a collision between the colleges and the scientific departments. A *modus vivendi* had to be found; but in the transitional stage the tensions between arts and science were further strained by the technological revolution.

The revolution was, however, an intellectual as much as technological one. The explosive impact of the scientific method necessarily affected the treatment and interpretation of the older studies. Sooner or later the unity of knowledge had to be recovered and the balance between science and arts restored; the antithesis between the two worlds of thought could only be a temporary phenomenon, and it was clear that the universities would have an essential and vital part to play in the integration of all forms of culture.

The massive development of science in the twentieth century might seem to suggest that the universities had largely disregarded science in the past. British universities by comparison with some of their continental counterparts, such as Leyden and Padua in the seventeenth century, were certainly slow to pay attention to developments in scientific subjects. Their essentially clerical character and their inherent conservatism of outlook, their vested interest in a centuries-old scholasticism, worked against the appreciation of science or scientific thinking. Oxford and Cambridge were principally engaged in training clergy for the ministry of the Church of England and in guiding the sons of the gentry and aristocracy along the path of polite learning; for neither of these two objects was scientific knowledge essential. They continued to supply as best they could what the country needed at the time. It was only when the divorce between the country's needs and what the older universities were still supplying became apparent that the latter, somewhat reluctantly, began to foster the new disciplines. The newer universities from the start were more amenable and set themselves to carry out the task the older universities were apparently neglecting. It may seem therefore that the connexion between the universities and scientific development dates more or less from the mid nineteenth century. For many years it was not a true marriage, occasionally an irregular relationship, more often a mere dalliance; but such attachments may play a significant part in shaping the lives of those concerned. In any case the union has now been legalized and, if we may carry the metaphor further, has since the middle of the last century borne numerous offspring.

*

Actually scientific studies at university could claim a long lineage. Medieval scholarship, concerned with the study of metaphysics, logic and philosophy, was only inferentially and sporadically interested in practical and empirical problems, and in any case academic science in the Middle Ages was more or less completely separated from technology; but it would be misleading to suppose that medieval scholars at Oxford and Cambridge were entirely unaware of the problems posed by science. Robert Grosseteste, the first chancellor of Oxford, fused his scientific views into a philosophico-physical theology, but his experimental interest in physics and optics was genuine and scholarly.* It was probably his work that inspired the Franciscan friar, Roger Bacon, himself an Oxford man and the greatest experimentalist of the thirteenth century. Although Bacon achieved less than was claimed for him by later writers, his approach was an innovation in being empirical and deductive. He was very much the odd man out among his scholastic colleagues though in the late thirteenth and fourteenth centuries a really remarkable group of scientifically minded men, members of the youthful Merton College, were concerned with abstract mathematical problems as well as more practical scientific questions.

If academic science within the universities did not amount to much in the medieval period, there seems to have been an awakening of interest in the late sixteenth and early seventeenth centuries, a harbinger to the scientific renaissance of the Commonwealth and Restoration. The extent, even the existence, of this resurgence of interest has been a matter of dispute. The older universities kept by and large to the scholastic curriculum, and were not exceptionally responsive to the scientific discoveries of the age, since their reverence for the criteria of the scholastic philosophers made them reluctant to accept conclusions based on experimental evidence. Medical studies in particular languished as a result of the reliance placed on authorities who were already discredited by continental medical scholarship. William Harvey, like many others, after gradu-

* See A. C. Crombie, *Robert Grosseteste and the Origins of Experimental Science, 1100–1700*, Oxford, Clarendon Press, 1953.

ating in medicine at Cambridge moved to Padua to pursue his researches into the circulation of blood, since Cambridge could offer no adequate facilities for medical research. 'Going on Wednesday,' wrote Joseph Mead who became a fellow of Christ's College, Cambridge, in 1613,

from Jesus College pensionary with Dr Ward to this College through the closes and gardens and espying a garden door open I entered and saw there a hideous sight of the skull and all other bones of a man with ligaments and tendons hanging and drying in the sun by strings upon trees &c. I asked what it meant. They told me it was the pedlar they anatomized this Lent and that when his bones were dry they were to set together again as they did naturally and so reserved in a chest or coffin for their use who desired such an inspection. It was the garden of one Seale a surgeon and a chief in the dissection. . .

Nevertheless the older universities may have made, on the theoretical level if not the practical, more of a contribution than has sometimes been allowed. 'By recognizing the existence of new theories and ideas,' Professor Curtis has written,*

and by pondering them and using them for the instruction of pupils, many masters and tutors won acceptance for some of the most important innovations. Furthermore this activity within the universities did more than merely reflect the process of change. Oxford and Cambridge were in a significant way nurseries of the new philosophy rather than intellectual backwaters into which contemporary currents of thought swept a stray eddy or two. They created an educated public which could appreciate and encourage scientific pursuits. They provided much of the basic training for the new philosophers themselves and gave some of the most important of them leisure to pursue their work. Finally, notwithstanding the spirit of Aristotelian orthodoxy which pervaded their statutes, university men challenged traditional authorities and did much to clear the way for new philosophical and metaphysical systems.

But while Professor Curtis reminds us of the intellectual liveliness of Oxford and Cambridge, he may have made exaggerated claims for their responsiveness to Renaissance science. 'I had

* M. H. Curtis, *Oxford and Cambridge in Transition, 1558–1642*, Oxford, Clarendon Press, 1959, p. 231.

none to direct me,' John Wallis wrote of his time at Emmanuel College, which he entered in 1632,

what books to read, or what to seek, or in what method to proceed. For mathematics (at that time, with us) was scarce looked upon as academical studies, but rather mechanical; as the business of traders, merchants, seamen, carpenters, surveyors of lands, or the like. ... And amongst more than two hundred students (at that time) in our college, I do not know of any two (perhaps not any) who had more of mathematics than I. ... For the study of mathematics was at that time more cultivated in London than in the universities.

Wallis, writing as an octogenarian, might be accused of exaggerating the state of affairs at Cambridge, were it not for corroborative evidence. In 1587 William Harrison had commented that 'Arithmetic ... geometry and astronomy ... are now smally regarded in either university.' William Gascoigne told the mathematician William Oughtred who matriculated at Cambridge in 1592 and taught himself mathematics in his spare time that when he left Oxford in 1640 he did not know what a proposition in geometry meant. 'Where,' said Hall, a stern critic of the ancient universities, 'have we anything to do with mechanic chemistry? ... Where is there an examination and consecution of experiments? ... Where have we constant reading from either quick or dead anatomies, or any ocular demonstration of herbs?'

Beside these partisan statements, of doubtful reliability, what other evidence is there that scientific interests were cultivated at Oxford and Cambridge in the closing years of the sixteenth century? They were perhaps no more than the spare-time interest of a minority, but they must have made a greater impact on the general climate of thought than the contemporary critics of the universities realized or admitted. Many of the leaders in scientific learning of the time had been educated at Oxford and Cambridge, some held fellowships there and others returned there later on in life to take up appointments. Even in Edwardian Cambridge, Sir Thomas Smith won distinction as a mathematician; he was later to make a study of astronomy, navigation, astrology, alchemy, medicine and economics. He had the works of Copernicus and Ramus in his library, and founded two readerships in mathematics at Queens' College, though motivated as much by *pietas* as by a conviction that the universities should be paying more attention to scientific studies. Nathaniel Torporley, formerly of Christ Church, was sometime secretary to the famous French mathematician Viète. John Thorborowe, later Bishop of Worcester, was reputed a 'lover of natural and experimental philosophy, a great encourager of Thomas Bushell [a mining engineer who had once been a page to Francis Bacon] in his searches after mines and minerals'. Thomas Harriot who graduated at St Mary Hall in 1580 subsequently became mathematical tutor to Sir Walter Ralegh and was sent by him to act as surveyor on Sir Richard Grenville's expedition to Virginia in 1585. Harriot's posthumous *Artes Analyticae Praxis ad Equationes Algebraicas resolvendas* shows that more than any other English scholar he was responsible for the formulation of modern algebraic principles. As an astronomer he made use of the telescope to observe the orbits of the planets, and is said to have anticipated the discovery that they are elliptical. From one hundred and ninety-nine observations of sun spots from 8 December 1610 to 18 January 1613, he deduced the sun's axial rotation, and on 17 September 1607 he noted from Ilfracombe that he had seen Halley's Comet.

It must be pointed out that Harriot's most important work, like that of other prominent mathematicians and scientists of the age, was done after he had left the university; this was the case with John Dee, William Gilbert, Edward Wright, William Oughtred, John Wallis, and many others. Wright, formerly a fellow of Caius, revolutionized the science of cartography by explaining the method of constructing maps based upon Mercator's projection. Nathaniel Carpenter, a fellow of Exeter, an eminent geographer, left Oxford to become chaplain to Archbishop Ussher in Ireland. 'Alas!' Bishop Williams of Lincoln told the mathematician, John Pell,

what a sad case it is that in this great and opulent kingdom there is no public encouragement for the excelling in any profession but that of the law and divinity. Were I in place as once I was, I would never give over praying and pressing his Majesty till a noble stock and fund might be raised for so fundamental, universally useful and eminent [a] science as mathematics.

But it would be unwise to argue that because men such as these left Oxford and Cambridge for London and elsewhere the atmosphere of these universities was antipathetic to scientific and mathematical studies. When Richard Hakluyt the younger arrived at Oxford (where he was to give lectures on geography and navigation and to publish in 1582 his first book, the *Divers Voyages touching the Discovery of America*), he entered into a company of men of like interests. Sir Henry Savile was lecturing on astronomy. The Lady Margaret professor of divinity, Edward Cradock, was a reputed alchemist and a friend of John Dee who stayed with him at Christ Church in the autumn of 1581. Another friend of Dee was the long-lived Thomas Allen, who resigned his fellowship at Trinity in 1570 to retire to Gloucester Hall – the halls were possibly more favourably disposed to scientific learning and Puritan religion than the colleges – where he continued to study and to teach until he died in his nineties in 1632. Richard Madox of All Souls, who was a proctor in 1582, left a record of his dining engagements, which shows us men of common interests meeting in a social context and dining together.

Henry Gellibrand who went up to Trinity in 1615 was persuaded by hearing one of Sir Henry Savile's lectures to devote his life to mathematical studies, the fruit of which was his *Trigonometria Britannica*. He constructed a dial for the college and later as a result of his studies in magnetism discovered the secular variation of the declination of the magnetic needle. Gellibrand, subsequently a professor of astronomy at Gresham College, like many of the early mathematicians and scientists, had Puritan leanings and provoked Laud's wrath by countenancing an almanack for 1631 drawn up by his servant, William Beale, 'in which the popish saints were superseded by those in Foxe's *Book of Martyrs*'. When William Harvey visited another Trinity experimentalist, George Bathurst, he found in his college room 'a sitting hen and a nest of eggs' and later with Bathurst 'daily opened an incubating egg to discern the progress and way of generation'. The frieze of the modern Upper Reading Room at the Bodleian Library, contemporary with its seventeenth-century foundation, included, among the pre-Protestant martyrs like Wyclif and Hus, Copernicus, Tycho Brahe, Paracelsus, Vesalius, Mercator and Ortelius.

Further evidence that the new scientific ideas were becoming more than a minority interest is furnished by the new provisions made for teaching in these fields, hitherto very meagre and unofficial. In 1619 Sir Henry Savile founded chairs in geometry and astronomy, the former of which brought the eminent geometrician Henry Briggs back to Oxford, and Sir William Sedley set up a chair in natural philosophy. Richard Tomlins of Westminster established a lectureship in anatomy in 1622 because 'down to the present day, in neither of the universities of this kingdom ... hath there been any anatomy lecture founded or instituted'. At Cambridge anti-Aristotelian notions and new scientific ideas were at least for a time widely diffused, especially in the more Puritan colleges, St John's, Emmanuel, Christ's and Sidney Sussex. Fulke of St John's, later Elizabethan Master of Pembroke, was a critic of astrology and a student of astronomy and optics. John Dee, also of St John's, was one of the original fellows of Trinity College, Cambridge. William Oughtred, who composed his *Early Method of Geometrical Diallying* while an undergraduate, an ample proof of his assertion that he was self-taught, William Buckley and Laurence Rooke, one of the founders of the Royal Society, came from King's. Four of the first six Savilian professors at Oxford were Cambridge graduates. The Puritan Samuel Ward counted 'my pride in doing things in geometry' a sin, an indirect testimony to his interest in scientific studies which other entries in his diary confirm.

*

It seems very likely that there was a decline in scientific studies as in much else after 1612; this would account to some extent for the charge of neglect levelled at Oxford and Cambridge by their Puritan critics. There is little doubt that the Commonwealth government opened the gates wide for renewed attention to scientific developments. Seth Ward, who lectured in mathematics at Cambridge in 1654, replying to Hobbes's attack on the universities, declared that many scholars knew as much about mathematics as did Hobbes himself. 'Arithmetic and geometry,' he affirmed in his *Vindiciae Academiarum*, 'are sincerely and profoundly taught, analytical algebra, the solution and application of equations, containing the whole mystery of both those sciences, being faithfully expounded in the Schools by the professor of geometry, and in many several colleges by particular tutors.' In 1657 Walter Charleton wrote that 'Our late wars and schisms having almost wholly discouraged men from the study of theology, and brought the civil law into contempt, the major part of young scholars in our universities addict themselves to physic.' John Wilkins, a former graduate of Magdalen Hall, had been made Warden of Wadham, a college which became a focal point for some of the scholars who were to help found the Royal Society in 1662. In a university where Aristotle's writ was still law, Wilkins attacked the subservient attitude taken by scholars towards his authority. He was equally familiar with scientific ideas, as his discussion of the notions of Bacon, Kepler and Galileo in his *Discovery of World in the Moone* (1638) demonstrates, and adept in inventing mechanical ingenuities, as in his *Mathematical Magick*.

The inter-connexion between Puritanism and scientific interests has been often stressed and analysed. Puritanism was naturally inimical to the dominant Aristotelian scholasticism and drawn to the anti-Aristotelian ideas of Peter Ramus;* most of the leading Puritan dons of late sixteenth- and early seventeenth-century Cambridge, among them William Perkins and Laurence Chaderton, and John Rainolds at Oxford, were Ramists. Moreover the Puritan concern with religious experi-

---

*In his *Dialectica* Ramus 'emphasized the process of making arguments and not the formal abstract rules for marshalling them in the course of a dialectical exercise'. It has however been argued convincingly that there was a closer connexion between Aristotelian philosophy and experimental scientific thought, especially on the Continent, than scholars will readily admit.

THE UNIVERSITIES AND SCIENCE

ence, as the necessary confirmation of genuine faith, had parallels with the scientific method. In a limited sense Puritanism could be called the religion of experiment. It labelled as superstition the belief in wonder-working miracles and it was critical of the miraculous outside the evidence of Scripture. The distinction between natural and supernatural knowledge made by its theologians fostered the independence of the former.

The very connexion between Puritanism and the scientific approach must have done something to further suspicions of science in the minds of the orthodox and conservative. This would account for the diminution in scientific studies at Oxford and Cambridge after the Restoration. 'Plebeians and mechanics,' said the Bishop of Oxford, whom James II tried to force on the unwilling fellows of Magdalen as their President, 'have philosophized themselves into principles of impiety, and read their lectures of atheism in the streets and highways'. Natural philosophy, declared Thomas Hobbes, regarded by so many of his critics as himself a purveyor of atheistic notions, 'is removed from Oxford and Cambridge to Gresham College in London, and to be learned out of their Gazettes'.

In fact, in spite of all that what was going on at Oxford and Cambridge, London, and Gresham College in particular, was the chief centre for the dissemination of the new scientific knowledge. 'In the eighty years before 1640,' Christopher Hill has stated,*

England, from being a backward country in science, became one of the most advanced. English astronomers were making telescopic observations of the heavens long before Galileo's discoveries were announced; they at once tested and confirmed them, and suggested their possible relation to other problems of physical astronomy. . . . This intellectual revolution, in its initial stages, was virtually ignored by the official intelligentsia. The science of Elizabeth's reign was the work of merchants and craftsmen, not of dons; carried on in London, not in Oxford and Cambridge.

*C. Hill, *Intellectual Origins of the English Revolution*, Oxford, Clarendon Press, 1965. His views have been criticized. See 'Science, Religion and Society in the Sixteenth and Seventeenth Centuries', *Past and Present*, 28, 1964, pp. 81–101; 29, 1964, pp. 88–97; 31, 1965, pp. 97–126; 32, 1965, pp. 110–112.

The main centre of this activity was Gresham College. Its interests were not confined to science but most of its professors were active in promoting scientific studies in mid-seventeenth-century London. But it should not be forgotten that its professors were dons from Oxford and Cambridge, some of whom continued to hold fellowships, and that the college owed much to the older universities from which it stemmed. It was designed by its founder, the merchant and financier Sir Thomas Gresham, as a teaching institution staffed by seven professors who were to deliver courses of lectures, in English for the citizens, in Latin for foreigners. These lectures were not, as were most university lectures, commentaries on a set text but were practical and utilitarian in character; the professor of astronomy, for instance, was to illustrate the use of nautical instruments and the principles of navigation for the benefit of mariners. Although it is doubtful whether the Gresham professors resided in the college, it became a centre for advanced scientific teaching and provided scientists with a place for discussion and meetings which they had hitherto lacked.

The professors included men of first-rate quality: Henry Briggs, a member of William Gilbert's circle, who published books on arithmetic, geometry and trigonometry, publicized and developed Napier's invention of logarithms, taught long division by modern methods and popularized the use of decimals; Edmund Gunter who followed up Briggs's work on logarithms and with Wells and Pett devised a more exact method for calculating a ship's tonnage; Henry Gellibrand, who wrote on navigation; and Richard Holdsworth, who held a Gresham chair of divinity between a fellowship at St John's and the mastership of Emmanuel. 'I must congratulate the City,' said Christopher Wren in his inaugural lecture in 1657 as professor of astronomy at Gresham College, 'that I find in it so general a relish of mathematics and the *libera philosophia*, in such a measure as is hardly to be found in the academies themselves.' It is hardly surprising that in 1648 the creation of a university for London was suggested.

*

After the Restoration the paths of Oxford and Cambridge diverged, the older university holding more strictly to orthodox theology and Aristotelian learning while Cambridge, politically as well as ecclesiastically more liberal, favoured Baconian logic and Newtonian mathematics. At Oxford, in spite of its early association with the Royal Society, science for the next hundred and fifty years played a very minor role. Significant as were the discoveries of Bradley in astronomy and Sibthorp in botany, in mathematical learning the reputation of Cambridge overshadowed that of Oxford. John Wilkins's brief term as master of Trinity, Cambridge, led to the appointment in 1663 of Isaac Barrow as the first Lucasian professor of mathematics. Though critical of Cartesian philosophy, Barrow was well read in advanced mathematical and philosophical writings and had a fertile and original mind; he has been credited with virtually inventing the differential calculus. He was succeeded as Lucasian professor in 1669 by his most brilliant pupil, Sir Isaac Newton. Newton had already formulated the theory of gravity before his election to a fellowship at Trinity. As professor he did his most impressive work in gravitation and optics, publishing his classic *Principia Mathematica* in 1687. Newton long continued to be the inspiration of Cambridge mathematicians and of his own pupils, Richard Laughton of Clare, much esteemed as a tutor, William Whiston, deprived of the Lucasian chair in 1710 for heresy, and Roger Cotes, the first Plumian professor of astronomy and reviser of the *Principia*, for whom the formidable Richard Bentley, Master of Trinity, had an observatory installed over the great gate of Trinity.

This interest in mathematics was only one aspect of the continued interest in scientific studies. Chemistry had made some progress under the direction of John Francis Vigani, 'a very learned chemist ... but a drunken fellow' as de la Pryme described him, who was made professor in 1703. The most interesting work was, however, probably done in the biological sciences, especially in botany and physiology. The greater part of John Ray's work in botany, ornithology and zoology was done away from Cambridge, though his important book *The Wisdom of God manifested in the works of Creation,* published in 1691, consisted of commonplaces which he had delivered in Trinity College chapel thirty years previously. His work cannot, however, be detached from his previous academic training or from the circle of friends in which he moved. Stephen Hales, a fellow of Corpus in 1703, and his friend, William Stukeley of the same college, gathered material for a new edition of Ray's catalogue of the plants of the Cambridgeshire region. Stukeley, more of a chemist than Hales, studied under Vigani and undertook chemical experiments in his rooms at Corpus. Hales was equally distinguished as a botanist and as an animal physiologist.

The impetus generated by Newton and his immediate successors was hardly sustained at the same level in the later years of the eighteenth century, though there were individual scholars of reputation and ability. The general level of achievement, in the sciences as in the arts, was pedestrian. When Richard Watson was made professor of chemistry, he confessed that he knew nothing about the subject, but he applied himself to it with great assiduity and reached a fair level of competence. Isaac Milner's tenure of the chair of natural and experimental philosophy was distinguished by industry and interest as well as by genuine inventive skill in experimentation.

Although much of the scholarship seemed amateurish and superficial, Newtonian philosophy still exerted a powerful spell over Cambridge, on which the new century was soon to capitalize. It had taken some time for advances in mathematical analysis already appreciated on the Continent to reach Cambridge; though in 1803 and 1809 Robert Woodhouse, a fellow of Caius, published his *Principles of Analytical Calculation* and *Elements of Trigonometry*, and his ideas were spread by his pupils, George Peacock, who introduced the new notation into the Senate House Examination in 1817, John Herschel and Charles Babbage. There were other indications of a slowly dawning awareness of the part that science was to play in the life of the community. The regius professor of physic at Cambridge, though the chair had been founded in the sixteenth century, had never delivered any courses of lectures, but the medical schools, for so long moribund, gradually awakened from their lethargy, aroused perhaps by the growing reputation of those which had been founded outside Oxford and Cambridge. 'His theatre,' wrote a Trinity undergraduate who matriculated in 1815 of the professor of anatomy,

was in the anatomical schools, opposite Queens' College. Here presided between the hours of twelve and one, another professor ... describing and exhibiting dried specimens of the different parts and organs of the human body, and once or twice, like the Edinburghians, cutting and carving the corpses sent down by the resurrection men of the metropolis.

John Haviland began lectures on pathology and a more effective system of examinations was introduced for the medical man. At Oxford the Earl of Lichfield bequeathed money for the reading of clinical lectures in the Radcliffe Infirmary to the students in medicine. In 1798 chairs were established through the beneficence of George Aldrich in anatomy, the practice of medicine and chemistry. John Sibthorp left money to establish a chair of rural economy. In 1813 and 1818 the Prince Regent sponsored the foundation of chairs for mineralogy and geology. At Cambridge under Adam Sedgwick's enthusiastic guidance geological studies made rapid progress, and the Cambridge Philosophical Society which did much to foster scientific interest among the senior members of the university was established in 1819.

Yet as the royal commissioners were soon to realize scientific studies laboured under many serious disadvantages. There was a suspicion of science deeply ingrained in the clerical and celibate dons of the unreformed universities which the emergence of Darwinian and associated ideas did little to diminish. 'Science,' Dr Opimian declared in Peacock's *Gryll Grange*, published in 1861,

is one thing, and wisdom is another. Science is an edged tool, with which men play like children, and cut their own fingers. If you look at the results which science had brought in its train, you will find them to consist almost wholly in elements of mischief. See how much belongs to the word Explosion alone.

If Peacock's words are now seen to be unhealthily prophetic, yet even in 1861 many at Oxford and Cambridge would have applauded his sentiments. 'Science,' in W. E. Gladstone's opinion, 'is but a small part of the business of education.' Samuel Wilberforce's unfortunate attack on Darwin's theory of evolution at the meeting of the British Association at Oxford in 1860 seemed to many to suggest that scientific studies represented a threat to orthodoxy and to the inviolable supremacy of a classical education.

It followed that while fellowships were available for mathematicians, for mathematics was an eminently respectable subject, it was rare for a scientist to become a fellow of a college. Professors were poorly paid and had to teach in ill-equipped rooms. The professor of chemistry at Oxford in 1817 was allocated the lower room of the Ashmolean Museum and when he asked for more accommodation was offered a share of the Keeper's kitchen with the use of the common pump. He rejected this generous offer as 'too humiliating to science'. Even when additional rooms were made available, Dr Daubeny had to equip them in part at his own expense. His counterpart at Cambridge declared that he had

one room with folding doors ... which is used both as a laboratory and lecture room; but there is neither museum nor apparatus attached to it. ... There is no residence, museum, library, collection or apparatus attached to the Professorship. ... Hitherto the study of chemistry has not only been neglected but discouraged in the University, as diverting the attention of pupils from what have been considered their proper academical studies.

For some time the apparatus in the engineering laboratory was the personal property of the professor, until it was purchased by the university after a somewhat sordid haggle.

It was not within the capacity of the colleges to cope with the rising demand for scientific education by themselves, though they set aside rooms for laboratories and established intercollegiate lectures. Trinity, which agreed in 1868 to appoint to a science fellowship every third year, St John's and Sidney Sussex arranged inter-collegiate lectures in 1873. The cost of building, developing and equipping science laboratories, though small by present standards, was something which the universities rather than the colleges had to bear. This identification of

scientific interests with those of the university, of whose
authority and policies the colleges were suspicious, had an unfortunate sequel, the results of which are still felt today at Oxford and Cambridge; it created an antithesis between the
humanities and the sciences which made the colleges for long
reluctant to absorb more than a comparatively small proportion of the scientific lecturers and demonstrators into their corporate life.

*

Yet many as were the difficulties obstructing scientific development at Oxford and Cambridge, the situation slowly improved.
At Cambridge a syndicate set up by the Senate in 1848 reported
that while its members admitted the 'superiority of the study
of Mathematics and Classics over all others as the basis of
General Education', the members were 'nonetheless of opinion
that much good would result from affording greater encouragement to the pursuit of various other branches of Science and
Learning which are daily acquiring more importance and a
higher estimation in the world.' Dr Philpott, the Master of
Catherine Hall, speaking in support of the resolution to establish a Natural Sciences Tripos, warned his listeners that

it would be a great calamity to the University, and to the nation
at large if an opinion should gain ground among the higher orders
of society that the studies of the University are not calculated to
prepare its Students for the active business and intercourse of life,
and if that opinion should prevail to the extent of making them
either forbear to send their sons to it altogether, or become indifferent about it.

Dr Whewell drew up the draft scheme for teaching and
examination; the subjects included human and comparative
anatomy, physiology, botany, geology, mineralogy and
chemistry. Gradually the increasing range of knowledge made
it necessary for the university to enable undergraduates to
specialize in rather fewer scientific subjects. The election of a
scientist to a fellowship at Downing in 1867 was the first of
many that followed in somewhat sporadic succession.

The interest in scientific education had been growing since

the middle decades of the century. Many observers had been greatly impressed by the system of education in the German universities, more especially their concern with *Wissenschaft*, pure research. This had been initiated in the eighteenth century through the application of objective criticism to textual studies, literary and biblical. In the early nineteenth century, influenced by the experimental science which already flourished in France, an objective and critical approach to science became a feature of the German universities, illustrated by the work of von Liebig (who had studied under the French scientist, Gay-Lussac, at Paris) at Giessen, of Bunsen at Marburg and of Wöhler at Göttingen. English visitors were attracted by the original interest in chemical research and by the deep-felt desire to advance the frontiers of knowledge, which compared so favourably with the somewhat haphazard and ill-supported British efforts in this direction. Liebig's research won the attention of the Prince Consort and led to the foundation of the Royal College of Chemistry in London in 1845, but the college had insufficient public support to flourish. What finally convinced the government of the need for promoting scientific study and research was the realization that British industry was falling behind its competitors, and so weakening the country's economic potential. The contrast between the success of British manufacturers at the Great Exhibition of 1851, where they won a great many awards, and at the Industrial Exhibition held in Paris in 1867, where they won very few, was a general alarm signal. Lyon Playfair credited it to the fact that 'France, Prussia, Austria, Belgium, and Switzerland possess good systems of industrial education for the masters and managers of factories and workshops, and that England possesses none'. A select committee was set up by the government to 'inquire into the Provisions for giving Instruction in Theoretical and Applied Science to the Industrial Classes'. It recommended that better facilities should be provided, and that degree courses and fellowships at Oxford and Cambridge should be instituted with this in view. It was the real beginning, if a small one, of the state's acceptance of some sort of responsibility for financing scientific and technical education.

The report of the commissioners compared the British universities unfavourably with their German counterparts, stressing the inadequacy of the facilities for higher research, but this was soon to be remedied. At Oxford the Science Museum, connected with the very active professor of medicine, Sir Henry Acland, designed by Sir Thomas Deane and Benjamin Woodward and so highly praised by Ruskin, arose in the Parks in 1860. At Cambridge a separate home for natural science was found at last in the New Museums building finished in 1864–5, but as this did not provide for the study of experimental physics, the university accepted gratefully the offer of its Chancellor, the Duke of Devonshire, to build and equip a laboratory. The famous Cavendish laboratory, with Clerk-Maxwell as the first Cavendish professor of experimental physics, started its distinguished career in 1873 and was soon fertilizing the scientific departments of other universities. William Garnett who was appointed principal of the Durham College of Science at Newcastle in 1884 and Arthur Schuster of Manchester were students of the Cavendish. To foster the same progress in the biological sciences a new building was constructed for the study of physiology and zoology in 1876–9.

Yet the General Board of Studies, reporting on the situation at Cambridge in 1883, still found it disquieting. They recommended that lectures and laboratory work should be henceforth a responsibility of the university and that college lectures in natural science should work within the university structure. As a result a professorship of pathology was instituted, some readerships and a number of lectureships, mostly worth £50 a year, such was the penury of the university. Finance was still the crux of the matter, for while the gap between revenue and expenditure could be met temporarily by contributions from the reluctant colleges, it was soon apparent at both universities that scientific expansion could only be subsidized effectively by grants from the state.

A remarkable amount was achieved in spite of these disadvantages. At Cambridge the commission had reported on the need for a new chemistry laboratory in 1883; six years later it was completed. The new anatomy and physiology buildings, hampered by lack of funds, were generously assisted by Henry Sidgwick, one of the most active and progressive sponsors of scientific research. An engineering laboratory, paid for by subscription, was opened in 1894 and expanded in 1900. The Downing site was expanded by the construction of a new geological museum bearing the name of Adam Sedgwick, and of a new medical school; accommodation in the same area was provided for botany, agriculture (admitted as a new subject with a professorship in agriculture dating from 1899 and in agricultural botany from 1908 endowed by the Drapers' Company), physiology (chairs of biology, genetics and biochemistry – though without stipend – were set up between 1906 and 1914), forestry and for a museum of archaeology and ethnology. After some dispute the Mechanical Sciences Tripos was established in 1892. 'The growth of science at Cambridge since the era of the Royal Commissioners,' another Commission report commented in 1919, 'has been perhaps the greatest fact in the history of the University since its foundation.'

The most spectacular work had been achieved in the Cavendish laboratory, further expanded in 1895 and 1907, under the direction of Lord Rayleigh and his successor J. J. Thomson.* Not only had an impetus been given to undergraduate studies in physics, but pioneer research work had been undertaken in electrical measurement and atomic physics. Thomson's major discovery of electrons was announced in 1897. The award of Nobel prizes to Rayleigh (1904) and to Thomson (1906) and to his pupil and later successor, Rutherford, indicated the high standing of the Cambridge school. It was maintained by such scholars as the nuclear physicist Sir John Cockcroft who became in 1960 the first Master of Churchill College which, like St Catherine's,† at Oxford, had a scientific bias. William Bateson's controversial studies in genetics threw a new light on

*Though in fairness it must be said that Clerk-Maxwell's work on electromagnetism was done at King's College, London, and Rutherford established the nuclear nature of the atom at Manchester.

† The college originated as the Delegacy of Non-Collegiate Students in 1868, was subsequently styled (in 1930) St Catherine's Society, and was granted a charter of incorporation as a full college in 1963.

Mendelianism and laid the foundations of a virtually new approach to genetic science. The studies in symbolic logic undertaken by A. N. Whitehead and Bertrand Russell, both fellows of Trinity, represented by Russell's epochal *Principia Mathematica* published in 1912–13, were of major importance in the development of mathematical theory. Hampered as Cambridge science may have been by inadequate funds, yet its record even before the ending of the First World War was respectable.

Oxford made slower headway than its younger sister. Its interests long continued to be predominantly classical, philosophical and historical rather than scientific. As a result of the first royal commission of 1853, chairs in chemistry (the Waynflete) and physiology (the Linacre) were founded. In 1861 the Rev. F. W. Hope gave his entomological collection to the university with an endowment for the professorship of zoology. The Clarendon Laboratory, which was to house the department of geology and mineralogy, was constructed in 1868. Seven years later Charles Barry designed the University Observatory. The inorganic chemistry laboratory, originally located in a building modelled on that of the Abbot's kitchen at Glastonbury, built near the Museum in 1860, was moved to new buildings in 1878. The physiology laboratory was built in 1884 and was expanded in 1907 and 1920. The department of human anatomy was re-housed in 1898–9 while the ethnological and archaeological collections given to the university by Lieutenant-General Lane Fox Pitt Rivers were housed in an extension on the east side of the Museum in 1882–5. The Radcliffe Science Library, designed by T. G. Jackson and paid for by the Drapers' Company, was built close to the Museum in 1901. Other buildings, for pathology (1901, which became the department of pharmacology after the completion of the Sir William Dunn laboratory in 1926–7), for forestry (1907–8), for electrical studies (1908–10) and for engineering (1914), the precursor of the magnificent laboratory completed in 1964, came into existence before the start of the First World War. The munificence of Dyson Perrins made possible the construction of another chemical laboratory, designed by Waterhouse, which was finished in 1916. A professorship of Engineering Science had been established in 1907. This tale of buildings testifies to steady progress and a growing reputation. Some scientific departments under scholars of distinction soon achieved world-wide fame, yet the great expansion of the science area had to wait effectively until the ending of the Second World War.

*

From the earliest days of their foundation the newer universities had shown an interest in developing medical and scientific departments nor did they labour under the constraint which for many years dogged the older universities. Indeed they had in some sense come into existence to supply the professional training in medicine, science and engineering which Oxford and Cambridge failed to provide. At a meeting of the Newcastle Literary and Philosophical Society in 1831 Dr Greenhow suggested the establishment of 'an academical institution of the nature of a college or university for the promotion of literature and science', which materialized as the Newcastle Medical School and opened on 1 October 1834. Its intake long remained comparatively small (an average of thirty-four a year between 1834 and 1844, twenty-two between 1844 and 1850) and its staff (among them J. C. Eno, the future patentee of the fruit salt) was ill-paid, in fact no salary at all was forthcoming between 1852 and 1863. In 1870 its ties with Durham University were strengthened, and its future assured, by its becoming the university faculty of medicine. Similar proposals for establishing colleges for the study of medicine were made between 1835 and 1840 at Birmingham, Liverpool and Manchester. At Manchester the Royal Medical School was joined with Owens College in 1866 in spite of the objection by a professor that the introduction of medical students who were naturally less sensitive and morally coarser than their non-medical colleagues might foster immorality in the college.

Much to the indignation of existing medical schools, London established a medical department at the very start, its ob-

THE UNIVERSITIES AND SCIENCE

ject being to provide an education more scientific in character than the empirical and mainly clinical training of practising surgeons and physicians. Although the organization of the medical school gave rise to considerable debate and some bitterness, it marked a great advance in medical education. Better facilities for clinical instruction were provided by the building in 1833–4 of University College Hospital. By the 1840s and 1850s the reputation of the medical school had waned, partly because of continuous friction among the professors, but the eclipse was only temporary. Although King's College had been founded under such different auspices, its curriculum was very similar to that of University College. It too made special provision for medical students; after many initial troubles the appointment of R. B. Todd as professor of physiology in 1836 inaugurated a happier era which was marked by the foundation of King's College Hospital in 1840.

The milieu in which the newer universities came to maturity was largely responsible for the stress on scientific studies and on their practical application to industry. 'Unless,' it was stated, 'we set up a more profound and intimate connexion between Science and Practice, our continental rivals who practise with knowledge must in the long run out-bid our own manufacturers who practise by rule of thumb.' At first much of the scientific work attempted was of an elementary standard. The students of the dyeing department at Leeds were said to be chiefly engaged in watching 'little bits of fabric boiling in little pots' and the professors' main job was to act as industrial consultants. But the relation between industrial needs and scientific research later developed on an impressive scale. Extra-mural courses in glass-making centres such as Mexborough led in 1915 to the establishment of a department of glass technology at Leeds which was consulted on optical problems by the Ministry of Munitions. By 1951–2 the department was supported by some ninety glass-manufacturing firms. Manchester engineering firms made possible the foundation of a chair of engineering in 1868. Durham had actually been the first university to offer courses in engineering, as early as 1838, being followed within five years by Glasgow and Trinity College, Dublin. Manchester had the good fortune to enjoy the services of H. E. Roscoe, to whom most of the credit for experimental science becoming a significant factor in university studies is due.

The new universities also did much to cater for more general science. At London, Professor Collie has written,* 'The Department of Chemistry has from the foundation played a prominent part in the development of the science of Chemistry. The laboratory was one of the first ... open to students for practical work.' In the 1860s, exercising the powers which it had received under its new charter, University College made much progress in experimental science, more especially in the departments of engineering, physics, mathematics and physiology. The physiologist Michael Foster carried the revival to Cambridge while his successor Burdon Sanderson went on from London to found the modern school of biology at Oxford. W. K. Clifford, the professor of applied mathematics at London from 1871 to 1879, was a near genius who died prematurely at thirty-three. The first professor of chemistry at King's College, London, was J. F. Daniell, who invented the hygrometer, and the chair of physics was held by Charles Wheatstone. 'Last night,' Bishop Copleston recorded in his diary for 2 February 1840,

I was hardly able to sleep from the strong impressions made on my mind by the stupendous discoveries and results of experiments by Mr Whetstone in electricity and his most ingenious mechanical apparatus for an electric telegraph. Gas and steam have done much, but this agent is destined to do much more, and to work an incalculable change in human affairs. It far exceeds even the feats of pretended magic, and the wildest fictions of the east ...

Victorian science had an optimism and a self-confidence which carried it through its difficulties. The university departments, small and highly specialized, sometimes closely attached to regional industries, housed in grim buildings, in grey surroundings, were the pioneers of the post-war scientific age.

It is impossible to sum up what British universities have

* J. N. Collie, *A Century of Chemistry at University College*, London, 1927, p. 5.

achieved in scientific research since the ending of the First World War, partly because of the universities' increasingly close association with industrial and government research. Nor is it possible to determine any order of precedence among different universities, for if Oxford and Cambridge have continued to house departments of great distinction, many others, Manchester, London and Bristol in particular, have won very considerable reputations.* Since 1918 nearly forty scientists connected with British universities have won the Nobel prize, including ten in physics, ten in chemistry and thirteen in medicine and physiology. It would be invidious to pick out single achievements, but one of the distinctions of university science in more recent years has been the breaking of really new ground. The advances made in the field of nuclear physics have been acknowledged by the Nobel prize awarded to Sir John Cockroft in 1951, and in pathology Lord Florey, who became Provost of Queen's College, Oxford, and Sir Alexander Fleming were awarded Nobel prizes for their work on the discovery of penicillin in 1945. Far-reaching discoveries in the study of genetics have resulted from the work done in the laboratory of molecular biology at Cambridge; a professorship of molecular biophysics was created at Oxford in 1966.

Still lagging behind America and possibly Russia in applied science, especially in the much-vaunted and expensive field of space research, yet British universities have a record in scientific achievement which draws research students from all over the world; it is in fact restoring the universities to the international position that they had occupied in the medieval world. But the exchanges are on a grander scale. A common scientific language has fostered intellectual unity. The migration of British scientists to the United States, much deplored by individual universities and patriotic publicists (though the movement is not entirely one-way), underlines the internationalism of science. Scientific research has perhaps done more than the study of any other single subject to weld together the uni-

* The civic universities were responsible in 1934-5 for the education of 41 per cent of all students in English universities in scientific faculties, in 1948-9, of 53 per cent.

versities of the world and to make of education (much as the outmoded but still powerful concern with national prestige may work against this development) something which transcends national boundaries.

Yet a query remains. The degree of specialization which has increased in the sciences even more quickly than in the arts has made communication between the scientist and non-scientist difficult, the more so as the scientist's loyalty must often be to his department rather than to his college or university. There are in fact more scientists teaching in the universities than arts dons,* but in recent years there has been a pronounced shift among school leavers from science towards the arts, † which has in some respects frustrated the government's intention of strengthening scientific and mathematical departments. Whether this shift is a temporary phenomenon or not, it suggests that too prolonged and narrow a specialization in a scientific subject can be culturally self-defeating. On the other hand the arts man is often more glaringly ignorant of science than the scientist is of the humanities. The mutual aversion and the dissatisfaction resulting from the traditional antithesis can perhaps best be overcome by combining scientific and arts subjects in a wide-ranging syllabus that will effectively blend the two into a coherent intellectual medium. The efforts already made in this direction promise success, and surely it is now the special task of the universities to continue their pioneering work in this new field of integrating science and humanities into a single culture.

---

*In 1963–4 arts teachers made up 25 per cent of the whole, pure scientists, 28 per cent. Since that date the incorporation of colleges of technology has shifted the balance even more heavily in favour of the scientist.

†The number of sixth-formers reading advanced level courses increased from 90,000 in 1963 to 111,000 in 1966, but the numbers reading only science and mathematics dropped from 40 per cent to 33 per cent, while those reading arts increased from 50 to 52 per cent. There was a small but significant increase in the numbers of those reading a course combining both an arts and a scientific subject.

CHAPTER TWELVE

The Universities and Politics

THROUGHOUT history the universities have been more or less closely connected with politics. Even in the Middle Ages a fair number of men who were later politically important were educated at the universities. E. F. Jacob has discovered from the rolls of petitions for benefices sent to Rome in the last quarter of the fourteenth century, when a clerical living was virtually a prerequisite for an aspiring student, that 'no less than fourteen young nobles are to be traced, including names like Grey, Despenser, FitzHugh, Bardolf, Zouche, and de la Pole'. In the Tudor period university-educated politicians became much more common. Sir John Neale has calculated that in 1563, as far as it can be ascertained, 49 Members of Parliament had been educated at Cambridge, 18 at Oxford. In 1584 Cambridge men in the House of Commons numbered 62 to Oxford's 83. In the Long Parliament 280 out of 552 M.P.s were university men.* This only means of course that the university was considered a suitable training ground for public life, and though it inevitably shaped the attitudes and development of those educated there during their impressionable years, for most of them it was in later life servant rather than master.

It was in the Tudor period that the universities first responded more actively to government pressure; headships and fellowships, leases and nomination to places were often placed at the disposal of the government. There were many precedents for James II's intervention in college elections, but they were generally more successful. The appointment of the chancellor of the university was important as a place both of

---

* It must be stressed that these numbers are only approximate since the records of those who matriculated would not include the many members of the upper class who resided in colleges without gaining a degree.

245

influence and patronage. In 1604 Parliament passed an Act
giving Oxford and Cambridge the right to send two representatives each to the House of Commons, a privilege they possessed until 1948, and which was extended to London in 1871
and to the remaining universities in 1918; Trinity College,
Dublin, acquired representation in 1613, and the Scottish universities later sent three members to Westminster.

The nineteenth-century historian of the university of Cambridge, Bass Mullinger, suggested that the first parliamentary
representation reflected the wish of the young Puritan dons to
establish contact with a pro-Puritan group in the House of
Commons and so to forward the Puritan cause, but this seems
an unlikely hypothesis. The Protestant Reformation had forced
the universities into dependence upon the Crown; there was no
higher court of appeal. While the infusion of new blood created
by the entry of young men of birth and substance brought in
benefactions and added to their wealth it reinforced their identification with the established order in church and state which
had already begun to arouse criticism; the townsmen of Oxford and Cambridge had for a long time been particularly hostile. Parliamentary representation enabled the dons to defend
their privileges and to reply to their critics in the national
assembly. In 1571 or 1572 Cambridge told its chancellor, Lord
Burleigh:

We also desire that the University may have two burgesses in
Parliament which Mr Speaker and others think requisite, as they
will not always have such as your lordship to assist them; not having any burgess in the House who can so aptly answer objections
against the Universities as they that remain in them, and best know
their present state.

It is, so runs a further petition of 1587, 'for the necessary
defence of the liberties of the University, lest anything through
... ignorance of some things might be enacted or pretermitted
to the hindrance of the University'.

The responsibility for sponsoring the universities' claim to be
represented probably rested with the lawyer Sir Edward Coke.
As Attorney-General Coke had to deal with questions relating

to disputes between the town and university of Cambridge. He was a loyal son of the latter, 'our most worthy Athens, the splendour of our kingdom, the very eyes and soul of our kingdom'. The decision to exclude the clergy from acting as burgesses (the Clerical Disabilities Act which prevented the clergy from sitting in the Commons dated only from 1642) may represent his professional suspicion of the clerical body, for surely given the clerical character of the voting body it would have seemed natural to have allowed clerical M.P.s.

The universities may have seen parliamentary representation as a means of defending their particular privileges and special interests, but in the first instance this seems to have been the view neither of the Crown nor of the universities' representatives. The comparatively flexible control exercised by the Crown in Elizabeth's reign became more rigid in the reigns of James I and Charles I, until the universities were definitely aligned with the Crown. The Duke of Buckingham was appointed chancellor of Cambridge, Archbishop Laud of Oxford. The Crown came therefore to regard the university seats as perquisites for its own spokesmen. Although there were notable exceptions like Dr Eden, the Master of Trinity Hall, the majority of the burgesses in this period were, as Miss Rex has demonstrated,* non-resident graduates employed in public service. Between 1621 and 1640 seven of the fifteen burgesses were Privy Councillors and five of these held the office of Secretary of State. Their distinction may have reflected glory on their universities – Sir Francis Bacon had been elected for Cambridge at an earlier date – as they were certainly intelligent and cultured men. Sir Francis Steward, the King's cousin but an opponent of Buckingham, was a friend of Ralegh and of Jonson who dedicated to him his play, *The Silent Woman*. Sir Isaac Wake was a good linguist who drew up the address to James I when he visited Oxford in 1605 – if he were not a King, the learned Scot declared he would like to be a 'university-man' – and from it Shakespeare is said to have

---

* M. B. Rex, *University Representation in England 1604–90*, Allen & Unwin, 1954, *passim*.

dredged some of the ideas for *Macbeth*. Sir Thomas Edmondes translated Caesar's commentaries. Such men as these were not primarily interested in university affairs or in defending the universities' interests and privileges.

From the very start many in the universities resented attempted dictation by the heads of the colleges and by the Crown. In 1614 a decree was issued at Cambridge saying that the method of electing M.P.s was to be the same as that used for the election of a vice-chancellor. This would have given the heads the practical nomination of the M.P.s; but the dons wanted to select their own members and to be able to nominate as well as to elect them. Though the heads of houses sought to dominate the election, the residents would not admit defeat; the Puritan minority were obviously opposed to dictation by the Crown, and the independents, stoutly Arminian and unreservedly loyal, were equally determined to have their say. The resultant collision of opinion probably gave rise to the tradition that if one of the representatives was a non-resident the other should be a resident or gremial.

In the Long Parliament most of the university burgesses were loyalists, though some were supporters of Parliament. None of them were extremists and, apart from the diplomat Sir Thomas Roe, seemed to represent the university's own interests much more directly. In 1643 Dr Eden of Trinity Hall, a civil lawyer, subscribed to the Solemn League and Covenant recognizing the necessity for a Presbyterian settlement of religion. Henry Lucas, who was later to found the professorship of mathematics which still bears his name, secretary to the chancellor of Oxford, the Earl of Holland, was a moderate Parliamentarian, but active in the university cause: in later years Isaac Barrow commemorating his life spoke of the strenuous exertions which he had made to defend the universities against their critics when a 'covetous Barbarity gaped after the Profits of the University, imposing Burthens upon all, and everywhere exacting the most unreasonable taxes'. Under the critical gaze of many Puritan members it was necessary to defend the universities' interests. Fortunately the fourth burgess, John Selden, was an exemplary representative, highly trusted, moderate

and scholarly. Although opposed to the use of the prerogative power in church and state, Selden was a man of superb common-sense. He had been made a member of the committee which prepared Strafford's impeachment, but resigned when he saw how tenuous the evidence was. He opposed Parliament's decision to remove John Cosin from the vice-chancellorship of Cambridge by a vote of the House. He prevented the decision to suspend the Laudian chair of Arabic at Oxford after Laud's execution in 1645 and secured the continuance of the eminent orientalist, Pococke, in possession of it. When Archbishop Bancroft's library was seized, Selden suggested to Cambridge that it should petition the House of Lords to win possession of it. 'It must be imputed to your extraordinary providence,' Dr Gerald Langbaine told Selden in 1648, 'that we have stood thus long – by your good acts and prudent manage our six months have been spun into two years.'*

*

The fall of the monarchy in 1649 and the early years of the Commonwealth spelt danger for the universities and even for their representation. Selden had once told the parliamentary commissioners that they seemed intent on destroying rather than reforming 'one of the most famous and learned companies of men that ever was visible in the Christian world'. In fact more moderate counsels prevailed. Oliver Cromwell favoured the universities as the potential depositories of true scholarship and pure religion. His personal physician Jonathan Goddard, his commissioner of the Great Seal Nathaniel Fiennes, his former Judge Advocate of the army Dr John Mills, his favourite preacher John Owen, the Dean of Christ Church (though the election was held to be invalid as he was in orders), his Secretary of State John Thurloe and his two sons Henry and Richard represented the universities at one time or another during the Commonwealth period.

But if Cromwell cherished Oxford and Cambridge, he never

*Langbaine was referring to Selden's part in winning time for the university against the intervention in its life of the Parliamentary Visitors and the Parliamentary Committee. (Quoted Rex, *op. cit.*, p. 173.)

won their affection. When the Long Parliament was returned in 1659, Oxford and Cambridge both hoped that General Monck could be persuaded to represent them but he, perhaps wisely, preferred to sit for Devon. In the main they elected loyalists, preferring an ejected fellow of King's, Cambridge, to the Puritan chancellor of the University and Lord Chief Justice, Oliver St John. Monck had pressed the Oxford dons to elect the Speaker, William Lenthall, but although he had the support of the aged Rector of Lincoln and the university presbyterians and entertained his supporters with roast beef and ale at the Mitre, the residents preferred to re-elect Dr Mills and the professor of medicine, Thomas Clayton, whom Wood described bitingly as an 'impudent and rude fellow – the very lolpoop of the university'.

In fact this election set the tone of what was to happen at the Restoration, when the universities outdid themselves in their eagerness to prove their loyalty to Crown and Church. It was not therefore a matter for surprise that their representatives were in the main men of strong Cavalier connexions. Sir Richard Fanshawe, envoy to Portugal and Spain and translator into English of the *Lusiad*, who was elected for Cambridge, 'had the fortune', as his wife put it, 'to be the first chosen and the first returned Member of the Commons House of Parliament in England after the King came home, and this cost him no more than a letter of thanks and two braces of bucks and twenty broad pieces of gold to buy them wine'. Another of the Members, Heneage Finch, later Lord Chancellor and Earl of Nottingham, was to be the chief spokesman of the Crown in the Cavalier Parliament; Oxford bestowed an honorary degree on him in 1665 when Parliament met in the city for his support of the Five Mile Act. His successor, Thomas Thynne, defeated Sir Christopher Wren in a by-election. In Wood's opinion, 'the pot-men slighted [Wren] and preferred Mr Thynne ... because he kept ... an open table for the masters for a week or ten days and went to the coffee houses to court stinking breaths'. The chancellor, Lord Clarendon's son, Lawrence Hyde, then 'young and ignorant' but to become the 'smoothest man in the court' was another burgess. To all intents and purposes the alliance between the Crown and universities had been effectively and thoroughly restored and cemented.

But it is fair to observe there was an undercurrent of dissatisfaction. 'Though willing to gratify the chancellor in the choice of his son,' Daniel Escott wrote, 'many think they should have been left free to choose the other burgess.' Yet when the first university Whig, James Vernon, was proposed to the Cambridge graduates they accepted him with reluctance, since he was associated with the party that was critical of the prerogative, and only at the express request of their chancellor, the Duke of Monmouth, whose secretary Vernon was. Later Cambridge accepted Charles II's virtual nomination of Sir William Temple, but Temple was a good Protestant and a worthy man. The new chancellor of Cambridge, the Duke of Albemarle, sought to secure the election of his cousin, Colonel Fairwell – 'When my Honour is concerned, I am in too high a Sphear to recede' – but the residents cared not a fig for their chancellor's honour and re-elected Sir Thomas Exton and Sir Thomas Brady. Strong as was the universities' devotion to the Crown there were, as James II was shortly to discover, limits to it. In 1688 the universities' 'devotion to the prerogative and to the doctrine of non-resistance', Miss Rex * has written, 'found itself in conflict with their Anglicanism, and it was Anglicanism that in the end triumphed'. Once the crisis had passed and the Non-Jurors had settled their consciences, the universities settled down to enjoy the St Martin's summer of the later Stuart rule.

At least it was a St Martin's summer for Oxford. We have already alluded to some of the effects which the separation between the university and the Whig government entailed for Oxford after 1714. 'Sir,' said a character in Thomas Baker's play, *An Act at Oxford* (1704), 'I have no opinion of Oxford Education, it breeds nothing but Rakes and rank Tories'; and this seems to have been the government's opinion in 1714. It seems doubtful whether Jacobitism was a really dangerous threat at Oxford, though the government's anxieties were understand-

* Rex, *op. cit.*, p. 327.

able at the time. No sooner had the Jacobite Duke of Ormonde vacated the chancellorship through his treasonable departure to the Continent than Convocation elected his brother, the Earl of Arran, and rejected the court nominee, Lord Pembroke, who secured only three votes; under Arran's auspices – and he died in 1758 aged eighty-eight – no Whig head of house at Oxford would be nominated vice-chancellor. Believing 'there were several thousands lying in and about Oxford ready to rise' the government despatched troops in 1717 to garrison the town, but the provocative behaviour of the officers gave rise to a series of scuffles. 'If,' as Archbishop Wake told the Warden of All Souls, 'there be no disaffection in ye Universityes to the present government ... I may truly say you are very unfortunate in the reports which everywhere spread abroad.'

Jacobitism was ventilated not in arms or conspiracies but in innuendos in sermons and speeches, in disloyal toasts and in drunken undergraduate indiscretions. Thomas Warton, the professor of Poetry, preaching on Restoration Day, 29 May 1719, 'forced all the events and circumstances of King George's Reign ... into a description of the miserable state of the nation during the usurpation of Cromwell'. Charity, he told his listeners, 'hopeth all things, *restoreth* all things'. Nearly thirty years later two undergraduates, celebrating the birthday of the Pretender's youngest son, uttered treasonable sentiments under the influence of liquor. 'I am the man,' said Dawes of St Mary's Hall, 'that dare say God bless King James the 3rd and tell you my name is Dawes of St Mary Hall. I am a man of independent fortune and therefore am afraid of no one or no man.' The university authorities took no action, but an officious master of arts reported the matter to the ministry which, in spite of contrary advice by the attorney-general, instituted proceedings against the vice-chancellor as well as against the two undergraduates. The vice-chancellor's trial was postponed *sine die* but the two unfortunate young men (who had not helped their cause by engaging a band to create further trouble outside Balliol) were sentenced to two years' imprisonment.

Oxford! I grieve at heart your hapless lot;
Your virtue, steady Loyalty forgot!
In this a strange absurdity there seems:
G(eorg)e cant be angry, that you turn'd out J(ame)s.*

Yet at the opening of the Radcliffe Camera in 1749 the sturdy Dr King, the Principal of St Mary's Hall, used the opportunity to lament the days of Queen Anne 'when no Briton need blush for our national honour; when our senate was uncorrupt'.

In fact, this angry innuendo represented less a defiant attitude to the government than an assertion of Oxford's political independence. It made no open show of resistance to the accession of George I; only a few dons refused to take the oath of allegiance. It had, however, been alienated from the ministry and so from the Crown by the treatment which it had received at its hands, the suspicion of Jacobitism, the threat of a visitation, the blocking of patronage and preferment. Nor in spite of a series of complex and unsavoury elections in the colleges was the ministry able to enlarge its influence much beyond those societies where the Whigs were already dominant or shortly to become so, Christ Church, Merton, Jesus, Exeter and Wadham.

The two representatives of Oxford in Parliament were long aligned with the independent interest. When Sir William Whitelock died in 1717, he was succeeded by George Clarke, a fellow of All Souls, a man of genuine and wide culture, who had served as secretary to Prince George of Denmark and was friendly with Queen Anne and the leading Tories then in exile. When his colleague, William Bromley, who had held the seat since 1701, died in 1732, he was followed unopposed by twenty-one-year-old Lord Cornbury, a Hyde, and popular in Tory literary circles. The Whigs could not allow the election to be undisputed for ever. On Clarke's death in 1736, they put up Robert Trevor, a fellow of All Souls who was closely connected with the Walpoles, but who as a son of Harley's friend was not entirely out of sympathy with moderate Tory opinion; he was, however, defeated by a substantial majority.

*Quoted in W. R. Ward, *Georgian Oxford*, Oxford, Clarendon Press, 1958, p. 175.

In 1750 Cornbury, whose Toryism was thought by many to have gradually cooled to lukewarm, was rewarded with a peerage. The 'old interest' selected Sir Roger Newdigate, a wealthy Warwickshire baronet who had become prosperous through the development of canals, turnpikes and coal-mines. He was an independent in politics for which, indeed, he had an increasing aversion. There were two other candidates, an Oxfordshire baronet and freeman of the city, Sir Edward Turner, backed by the Whigs, and Robert Harley, the second son of the third Earl of Oxford, who represented the church interest; but Newdigate was returned with a good majority. Although the 'new interest' was growing in strength, the Oxford Tories were strong enough to procure the election of Lord Westmorland as High Steward in succession to the Earl of Clarendon.

The death of the aged chancellor, Lord Arran, in December 1758, gave a new stimulus to political conflict, for if the Court party could secure the election of their candidate, Richard Trevor, Bishop of Durham, it would be a substantial triumph. Trevor was confronted by the High Steward, Westmorland, and Lord Lichfield, both *bon viveurs* attached to the old interest. There seemed a danger that the vote would be so evenly divided that Trevor might limp home. On the eve of poll Lichfield withdrew, reaping the reward of his action three years later when he became chancellor on Westmorland's death.

The accession of George III in 1760 was, however, a happy augury. 'The good things of this world,' Newdigate was told, 'are coming amongst us.' George Horne of Magdalen, a future bishop, called from St Mary's pulpit for the 'utmost endeavours to eradicate out of the minds of men those diabolical principles of *resistance to government in church and state*'. Oxford found it easier than Cambridge to applaud the peace of Paris, and the Sheldonian Theatre was redecorated for an expected royal visit which was not in fact to materialize for another two decades. Independence did not mean subservience, but the election of Lord North as chancellor, a 'compliment to me' as the King delightedly said, marked the restoration of Oxford to government favour. 'The main difference,' Dr Ward writes, was that the confessing 'Whigs' who under George II had been the apostles of party purity against a majority alleged to be Jacobites now besought the University to end 'that attachment to party names which their enemies charged them with ... those distinctions were worn out everywhere else, and are in fact found to be only nominal ... we were called upon to follow that example which his Majesty had so graciously set us'.*

Ironically Oxford's gain was, for the time being, Cambridge's loss, or at least a loss for its chancellor, the Duke of Newcastle. Cambridge had basked in Whig favour. It came as no surprise that when Lord Anglesey died in 1737, the Duke of Newcastle, moved both by a genuine love of his university and by the wish for further scope for power and intrigue, put forward his candidature for the office of High Steward. He was no doubt also aware that the chancellor, the Duke of Somerset, was in his seventy-fifth year. In fact Somerset lived another ten years and Newcastle was made profoundly uneasy by rumours that approaches were being made to the Prince of Wales to succeed him. George II, however, scotched this attempt to make capital out of the reversionary interest, letting it be known that he strongly disapproved of the projected invitation to his son. The importance of Newcastle's victory, when he was elected to the chancellorship at the end of 1748, was dramatized by the galaxy of guests and the splendour of the installation ceremony. 'Everyone, while it lasted,' Gray wrote to Wharton, 'was very gay and very busy in the morning, and very owlish and very tipsy at night.' No chancellor made as much use of his power and influence as Newcastle nor was so dismayed at its gradual decline once he himself had fallen from power.

In his remaining years of life the intriguing duke commented sadly on the prevalence of human ingratitude; but he did not easily give in. The death in 1764 of his friend, the High Steward, Lord Hardwicke, gave his opponents a chance to soften what remained of his political influence. The Court candidate was the notorious 'Jemmy Twitcher', John Montagu, Earl of Sandwich, whose family seat was at Hinchingbrooke

*Ward, *op. cit.*, p. 226.

only a few miles from Cambridge. He could hardly be said, as the poet Gray made clear in well-known verses on the contest, to add lustre to morality or learning. 'The lads, I hear,' the Master of Magdalene commented, 'assembled about King's Lodge on Thursday night last, made a riot, and cried aloud "Bring out your daughters, Jemmy Twitcher is come".' Newcastle's candidate was Hardwicke's son, Lord Royston, a respectable scholar but a languid politician. It was soon apparent that the contest would be hard and the outcome uncertain. Newcastle treated the election as if the government of the country was at stake, writing indefatigably to every conceivable voter; but he no longer had a cornucopia of preferment at his disposal. 'I am sorry to say,' he confessed, 'that some of the oldest and, I thought, most virtuous part of the university say that my Lord Sandwich might make a very good High Steward, though he would make a very bad bishop'; the last part of his statement at least was incontrovertible. After a singularly mismanaged election Newcastle's candidate was successful, but it was virtually his last victory, and on his death Cambridge reverted to its alliance with the Court by electing the Duke of Grafton as its chancellor; while the younger Pitt represented the university from 1784 to his death in 1806.

*

At the beginning of the nineteenth century both universities were therefore closely associated with the Tory establishment. Although there were minority groups, the bias was towards the maintenance of the *status quo* in the country as in the university. Political and university reform seemed, with some justification, closely allied causes. Both universities constantly dispatched petitions to Parliament against Roman Catholic Emancipation, political reform, the desecration of the Sabbath, and similar issues. The disputes that arose out of the passing of the Roman Catholic Emancipation Act in 1829 clearly demonstrated what was at stake. Oxford had no more loyal son than Sir Robert Peel who had been chosen to represent the university in succession to the Speaker, Charles Abbot, in 1817. Peel had been selected in preference to George Canning who was thought to be untrustworthy in character and by some to be possibly unsound on Roman Catholic Emancipation, whereas Peel was the more acceptable because of his known 'attachment to the Tory principles and the true interest of the Church of England'. 'We are all, Sir, greatly indebted to you,' the vicar of Bengeworth wrote, 'for that weight of argument by which when the House of Commons was in a state of portentous equipoise, you inclined it in behalf of "Protestant Ascendancy".' Yet his old tutor and supporter, Charles Lloyd, whose appointment to the see of Oxford Peel was soon to procure, was the more prescient when he warned Peel on his election that

Oxford will never vary from the Principles of Mr Pitt. ... So far then I think certain that any person who is a strenuous defender of those principles will hold his seat for ever. Now I would simply ask, whether any man of 29 years old, can say positively if he is left entirely to his own single opinion, this never can happen during the space of 40 years, which is (you see) the time I allow you to sit as our representative.

Within eleven years Peel had veered in favour of Roman Catholic Emancipation; it was a desertion that the majority of his constituents could not countenance. With the students of his own college, Christ Church, divided in their attitude towards him, his chance of success was limited and Sir Robert Inglis, his opponent, triumphed by 146 votes. The election, as Inglis commented, proved conclusively that the voters wanted the constitution of England 'to be preserved fundamentally and exclusively Protestant'.

The Tory High Churchmen had little confidence in the Whig ministry of the 1830s, for they feared that a readiness to reform the legislature and even to touch the sacred property of the Church augured ill for the universities. The most unpopular opponent of the Reform Bill, the Member for Bristol, Sir Charles Wetherell, was himself the son of a former Master of University College, Oxford. Young W. E. Gladstone of Christ Church spoke at the Union debate to the effect that the Reform Bill threatened to change the character of the British constitu-

tion and to break up the frame of society; when it came to voting against the Bill 'the decision was favourable beyond anything we had hoped – ninety-four to thirty-eight'. Oxford's
representative, Sir Robert Inglis, a high-minded Evangelical in a kindly, cheerful way, continued to uphold the Tory
line, voting against every liberal measure from the Reform Act
and the Irish Church Bill to the relief of the Jews, the Maynooth grant and the abolition of the Corn Laws. The election
of the Duke of Wellington as chancellor of Oxford in 1834 –
though his 'liberalism' at the time of the passing of the Roman
Catholic Emancipation Act had made him momentarily suspect, and Newman commented that some people were 'vexed'
at the choice – was a reflection of the university's deep-seated
Toryism. At Encaenia, the Oxford ceremony at which honorary degrees are conferred on distinguished persons, the new
chancellor played the bluff soldier, plentifully sprinkled his
Latin with false quantities and placed his tasselled cap back to
front, listening perhaps a little wryly to an ode written by John
Keble recalling the chancellorship of the Duke of Ormonde
and that 'sainted monarchy' whom he had served, but huzza'd
by the undergraduates and by the Tory aristocrats who had
deserted Ascot for the occasion.

The die-hard Tories at both universities had cause to be
anxious, especially as there were many signs of a readiness to
compromise with the new situation. When the Duke of Nor-
thumberland, who had been chancellor of Cambridge, died in
1847, a number of Cambridge seniors headed by Dr Whewell,
the brusque, influential Master of Trinity, suggested the choice
of the Prince Consort as his successor. Although the Prince
was an intellectually gifted man, he was not a graduate of a
British university; but his candidature was seen by Whewell
and those who supported him as raising the chancellorship
above the political arena. The alignment between the university and the Tory party, both equally opposed to university
reform, was thought by more liberal-minded residents to be
potentially disastrous. In the Prince they saw a neutral who
would certainly take his responsibilities seriously and would
not be simply the mouthpiece of a party. (It is possible that

similar motives led in 1960 to the nomination of Lord Franks against the successful candidate, Harold Macmillan, who was then the head of the Tory party.)

The Prince, much attracted by the invitation, was, however, very eager that it should be unanimous. This was not to be, for St John's, resentful as ever of anything that smelt too strongly of its neighbour, Trinity, had already put forward the name of Lord Powis, described by one of his critics as a 'deaf old woman whose only distinction is a close connexion with Puseyism',* the latter a disadvantage but one which he had overcome by his known opposition to any kind of change in church or state. 'Your election', Whewell wrote in a letter to Powis which he ultimately decided not to send, 'will mark the resolution of the University and the Church to assume an attitude of suspicion and hostility towards the state.' The contest was closely fought and as with so many university elections it was marked by the riotous behaviour of the non-voters, the undergraduates who blew horns and pelted the voters with peas, shot and halfpence. The Prince won the day by a narrow margin and Whewell could rest assured that in the difficult days ahead the chancellor would stand as a neutral arbiter, withdrawn from party politics.

At Oxford, too, the situation had changed enough to allow W. E. Gladstone to be put forward as a candidate in 1847 in succession to the doubtless estimable but unnoteworthy Bucknall Estcourt. Gladstone's known sympathy with Tractarianism – he had failed to vote for the degradation of W. G. Ward, who had been deprived of his degree for heresy in 1845 – aroused fears among the older conservatives and Evangelical clergy. His intellectual interests some people found vaguely disquieting but his supporters stressed his opposition to the admission of Dissenters to the university and his attachment to the Church of England, demonstrated by his interest in the work of missions overseas. As it was his followers had the good fortune to discover that his opponent, Round, had certainly voted

* After Newman's defection to the Church of Rome, E. B. Pusey became the leader of the Oxford Tractarians; hence the word 'Puseyism' was sometimes used to describe the Oxford movement.

for Peel in 1829 and had been known to attend Dissenting chapels. Of the three candidates there was no question that the High Tory Sir Robert Inglis would be top of the poll, but Gladstone with the support of the younger men was placed above the conservatives' candidate, Round. Gladstone had been opposed by 16 heads of colleges, but he was supported by 157 men who had taken a first class in the final examinations to Round's 46. The election, Northcote told him, 'has brought together the younger men without distinction of party. ... The victory is not looked upon as a "Puseyite"; it is a victory of the masters over the Hebdomadal Board. ... It is not as a May-noothian * that you are dreaded here ... but as a possible reformer and a man who thinks.'

These words were prophetic. As Gladstone was gradually converted to the cause of university reform, a nucleus of opponents was created, including some like Pusey who had hitherto voted for him. At first he had withstood the commission of inquiry but gradually he came to see how necessary it was for the university. The Tories began to remember the ominous signs in his earlier career, of how he had supported relief for the Jews and how he had voted against the anti-papal legislation, in both instances expressly going against the will of Oxford's Convocation. In an open letter to Bishop Skinner of Aberdeen he had reaffirmed his belief in complete religious freedom in words which the aged Dr Routh of Magdalen thought made it plain that he should not represent the university. At the next election a number of the heads of houses supported by Evangelicals and die-hards urged the Warden of Merton, Dr Marsham, to contest the seat. He declared himself in no uncertain terms:

At a time when the stability of the Protestant succession, the authority of a Protestant Queen, and even the Christianity of the national character, have been rudely assailed by Rome on the one side and on the other by democratic associations directed against the union of the Christian church with the British constitution – at such a time, it becomes a protestant university from which ema-

* Gladstone had supported the proposal to give a subsidy to the Roman Catholic college at Maynooth in Ireland.

nates a continuous stream of instruction on all ecclesiastical and Christian questions over the whole empire, to manifest the importance which it attaches to protestant truth, by the selection of a *Protestant representative*.

But although Sir Robert Inglis was again easily top of the poll, Gladstone polled 250 votes more than his opponent, and the die-hards had to be content with the election of the Tory leader, Lord Derby, as their chancellor. By 1853 Gladstone had been won over to the cause of university reform and was actually drafting the bill which was to bring it about. 'Gladstone's connexion with Oxford,' Sir George Lewis wrote in March 1853,

is now exercising a singular influence on the politics of the university. Much of his high-church supporters stick to him, and (insomuch as it is difficult to struggle against the current) he is liberalizing them, instead of their terrifying him. He is giving them a push forwards instead of their giving him a pull backwards.

Although Gladstone's defection alarmed many in his party, he was returned unopposed in 1857; but the Tories were rallying and Gladstone was losing the goodwill of some of his younger supporters. Two years later they nominated Lord Chandos, the son of the Duke of Buckingham. Gladstone was 'angry, harassed, sour', but he was still returned with a majority of a hundred over his opponent. 'Win or lose,' Goldwin Smith had sought to reassure him, 'you will have the vote of everyone of heart and brain in the university and really connected with it. Young Oxford is all with you. Every year more men obtain the reward of their industry through your legislation. But old Oxford takes a long time in dying.' So it turned out. Gladstone himself, devoted as he was to his university, began to wonder whether 'in the estimate of mere pleasure and pain, the representation of the university is not worth my having'. Thus, when in 1865 he was defeated by Gathorne Hardy, after the introduction of the postal vote which effectively enfranchised the clerical backwoodsmen, he took leave of his constituency with sorrow but not without relief. 'A dear dream is dispelled,' he wrote in his diary, 'God's will be done.'

Gladstone's defeat may be taken as the end of a period of political history in the university. In Dr W. R. Ward's judgement, 'Oxford no longer manned the political and ecclesiastical ramparts of society, nor cast its weight into the struggles of church and party. Like the East India Company, the Civil Service and the church, it had been reformed by being taken out of the field of strife.'* In the years that followed the electorate was much changed and enlarged. The Members for Oxford and Cambridge were joined in 1871 by representatives for London and in 1918 for the remaining universities. They preserved their in-bred Conservatism, and something of their independence of spirit, which together with the plural vote proved disconcerting to more progressive politicians. In 1948 the university seats were abolished.

Leading politicians continued, of course, to be educated at a university. Out of 34 Prime Ministers between 1800 and 1966, 28 were university men and 26 had been at Oxford or Cambridge; Lord John Russell, who initiated the major reform of Oxford and Cambridge, studied at Edinburgh and Neville Chamberlain at Birmingham university. The non-university Prime Ministers were Wellington, Disraeli, Lloyd George, Bonar Law (though he attended lectures at Glasgow), Ramsay Macdonald and Winston Churchill. In the British Parliament of 1966, 349 out of 630 M.P.s had been educated at a university, 225 at Oxford or Cambridge and 124 at other British universities. Out of 364 Labour M.P.s (including the Speaker) 178 were university educated, 80 at Oxford or Cambridge (excluding those who had studied at Ruskin College, Oxford, not a constituent college of the university) and 98, among them a number of dons, at other universities. Out of 253 Tory M.P.s 139 had been at Oxford or Cambridge, 22 at other universities. Of the 12 Liberal M.P.s 6 had been at Oxford or Cambridge and 4 at other universities. In fact in the 1960s it could be argued that the connexion between the universities and politics is closer than it has ever been; Harold Wilson, who became Prime Minister in 1964, had been a don, and numbered among his Cabinet other dons, former university lecturers and fellows

* W. R. Ward, *Victorian Oxford*, Frank Cass, 1965, p. xiv.

of colleges, and among his close advisers university economists, notably Thomas Balogh of Balliol and Nicholas Kaldor of King's College, Cambridge. It seems inconceivable that while the universities remain independent seats of higher education their political importance, though changed in context and content, is ever likely to fall below what it has been in a long and at times stormy history.

CHAPTER THIRTEEN

The Universities and Religion

ALTHOUGH the modern universities, excepting King's College, London, and Durham, were secular in their foundation and more or less so in their outlook, Oxford and Cambridge, as must by now be apparent, were for the greater part of their history essentially religious societies. In practice they were clerical seminaries preparing men for ordination, and if their instruction was not exclusively theological, scholastic discipline was interpreted in a theological context. For at least seven centuries of their existence there would have been few to contradict Pusey's statement to the university commissioners in 1853 that

all things must speak of God, refer to God, or they are atheistic. History, without God, is a chaos without design, or end, or aim. ... Physics, without God, would be but a dull enquiry into certain meaningless phenomena: Ethics, without God, would be a varying rule, without principle, or substance, or centre, or regulating hand; Metaphysics, without God, would make man his own temporary god, to be resolved, after his brief hour here, into the nothingness out of which he proceeded.

Theology as an academic discipline was the special province of those who took the higher degrees of bachelor and doctor of divinity. The Theology Honour School at Oxford and the Theological Tripos at Cambridge came into operation in 1870–71 after it was realized that the standard of theological teaching at both universities was low and that there was no real provision for educating in theology the undergraduate or young graduate who wished to take holy orders. Though the actual theological teaching underwent the same depression as most other subjects in the later eighteenth century the theological professors did play a prominent part in university affairs; the doctorate of theology or divinity was, and still is, the most senior degree of each university. Furthermore, although there were minor exceptions, more frequent at Cambridge than at Oxford, until the reforms of the mid-nineteenth century only those already in orders of the Church of England or intending to take them were allowed to hold a fellowship. College statutes often required that their fellows should proceed within a certain time to the B.D., and their heads to the D.D. The majority of dons were therefore already in holy orders, and most of their pupils were intending to take them. The two ancient universities were most closely related to the Church of England; from them came many of the town and country clergy as well as all the higher dignitaries of the church. As far as the latter are concerned, this is still largely true.

If the ecclesiastical character of Oxford and Cambridge is accepted, and until the 1850s it was their determining feature, it will come as no surprise that their daily life was enacted within a distinctive religious framework. Every college had its chapel, some of them of great architectural merit and beauty, where from their foundation mass, and after the Reformation daily prayers, were said. The Sunday sermons at the university church, St Mary's at Oxford, Great St Mary's at Cambridge, were part of the established ritual, attended in large numbers by senior and junior members alike. Indeed it was Dr Tatham's fanciful belief that St Mary's at Oxford should be pulled down and replaced by a building more modern in style, more appropriate in dignity to the university and large enough to house the numbers who wished to attend the preaching. Universities' ceremonies, like the degree ceremony, had a religious texture. Attendance at service in the college chapel was for long a matter of obligation. 'If I were asked to name one thing,' said Mr Thorp, a Trinity tutor at Cambridge in 1841,

which you would be bound to grant me on condition that I should ask no more, it would be a promise that you would every morning of your life be in your proper place in the college chapel. . . . It is your duty. . . . At your time of life, coming here to be trained, agreeably to certain settled rules, to the formation of a sound judgment and wholesome habits of thought, it can never be for your profit to have your mind continually distracted by a captious spirit of doubt and cavil and crude questioning of the laws framed for your direction by the concentrated wisdom of many bygone generations.*

By 1841 Mr Thorp was already on the defensive, for the wisdom as well as the reverence of compulsory attendance at chapel was being questioned; but for centuries the chapel had been an unchallenged feature of college life, and religion an inseparable part of everyday discussion, not as meat for criticism but as the bone of intellectual argument. It was impossible for an undergraduate to remain unaffected by this atmosphere. Disputations in theology were a regular feature of college life. 'We decree then,' so the statutes of two Cambridge colleges, Emmanuel and Sidney Sussex, 'that the fellows of the aforesaid college hold a theological disputation every week, in which each one will answer in his turn.' Undergraduates were obliged to attend and take notes of sermons; all the current theological issues were discussed in the determinations for degrees. If the young men tired occasionally of the interminable conversations about the nature of free-will and grace, and sighed for more lusty and sensual pleasures, a tankard of ale, sweet music or a pretty girl, their elders lived in a theologically minded world and were deeply involved in spiritual concerns.

In the late fourteenth century the halls buzzed with talk of Wyclif and the Lollards. 'When I was reading the *Sentences* concurrently with him at Oxford,' William Woodford recalled,

speaking of transubstantiation he asserted and long held that it was a mathematical replacement of the Body that was present, in an equivalent of the Body which ceases to be ... and I have his words in his own hand before me now. For it was his custom to write his replies to the arguments which I made to him in a note book which I sent him with my points.

By the 1530s they were talking, sometimes secretly and in whispers, for there was wisdom in discretion and danger in lack of it, of Luther's writings, of grace and justifying faith, of the King's Great Matter, of the authority of the Scriptures, of the falsity of the Church of Rome. And so it continued. Intermin-

*Thomas Thorp, *A Few Words to Freshmen*, 1841.

ably, learnedly, with what must seem to a modern reader ponderous rhetoric and prolix tedium, the Puritans and their critics debated the great questions of assurance and faith; nor was it until the Oxford Movement began to fade before the onset of secularization that religion ceased to be a matter of such abounding and relevant interest. Even in the twentieth century few subjects are discussed with such relish by undergraduates and dons alike.

The close association between Oxford and Cambridge and the church meant that for a long time the history of one was virtually the history of the other. It was after all at Oxford that Wyclif, a former Master of Balliol, launched the Lollard movement, the first major essay in nonconformity. We need not concern ourselves with the details of his teaching; but it is worth recalling that the extreme conclusions he came to, his denial of the doctrine of transubstantiation, his criticism of the church's sacramental teaching, his stress on the theory of predestination, his absolute reliance on the authority of the literal words of the Scripture – whether or not he was brought to them by his disappointment at not winning the preferment which he thought he deserved – can be traced to the ideas he formulated while he was, philosophically speaking, a conservative Augustinian at Oxford. He won an early following among dons and graduates attracted by the intellectual cogency of his teaching, but when Lollardy had aroused the ardent – the word is used purposely – disapproval of the authorities in church and state these men tended to retract their opinions and return in orthodox fashion to the bosom of Mother Church. The smear of Lollardy at Oxford persisted long after Wyclif died at Lutterworth in 1384; it made Archbishop Arundel regard the university of Oxford with grave suspicion and it may have led many parents, perturbed by the dangerous and scandalous teaching said to be circulating there, to send their children to Cambridge.

*

If the first Oxford movement was in many respects a failure, few can doubt that the first Cambridge movement was an outstanding success. The initial phases of the English Reformation stemmed from Cambridge, for the leaders of the Reformed church were Cambridge men, many of them dons and heads of houses, and the theology which they disseminated, heavily tinctured as it may have been by continental writers, was a product of the Cambridge schools. Although Oxford made an important contribution to the Puritan movement, it was at Cambridge that Puritanism, fertilized by the wealth and favour of the sturdy East Anglian merchants and farmers, started to become a significant force in English religious life.

The rise of Puritanism represented a dynamic revival in the face of the characteristic university religion, which tended to be formal and fossilized. On the one side there existed a conventional routine, on the other an intellectualized concept of religion, both seeming in the eye of the spiritual beholder to deprive religion of its necessary sacrificial ardour. The Puritans of the sixteenth century complained bitterly of the pastoral neglect of the Cambridge dons 'who tarry in their Colleges, and lead the lives of loitering losels'. 'Spots and blots' of the university, they did not only 'go very disorderly in Cambridge', wearing the latest fashions 'too fine for scholars' and scandalous for clerics, but even went to London in similar guise: 'A great sort of godly men,' so it was said in 1571, '. . . are greatly offended, to see such unseemly going of scholars, and especially of proctors and ministers.' While the universities remained clerical societies these attacks were launched against them with monotonous regularity, sometimes with good reason, sometimes from malice aforethought.

Puritanism stood not merely for sombre apparel and a sober life but also for scrupulous attention to morality, which contrasted with the indulgent negligence of conventional university religion. Puritan teaching may seem unattractive in its pursuit of narrow virtue. It encouraged spiritual introspection, witness the contemporary Puritan diaries like that written by Samuel Ward, the future Master of Sidney Sussex, when he was a fellow of Emmanuel College. They are pervaded by an earnest desire to subdue the flesh and to follow the good, and were written to stimulate the writer to greater effort by noting his aberrations from virtue and by stressing the need for a high standard of moral conduct. Ward grieved over many faults, neglect of study, over-indulgence in food and sleep, pride, anger, roving fantasies, too much laughter, concern with worldly profit, and insufficient concentration in prayer and worship; phrases that were to recur in the diaries and journals of John Wesley, the Evangelicals and the Tractarians during their university days. 'Thy dulness in the morning in prayer,' he wrote on 11 May 1595, 'Thy little affection in hearing Mr Chatterton [Chaderton]'s good sermon. . . . Thy adulterous thoughts that day.' 'My desire of preferment over much' on 13 May. 'My late rising in the morning to sanctify the Sabaoth,' he noted on 1 June, 'My negligence all that day, and idleness in performing the dewtyes of the Sabaoth.' He was troubled by his neglect in preparing for the reception of the sacrament, his drowsiness in time of service, his idle talk and immoderate consumption of cheese and fruit, his 'over-much mirth at bowling after supper' and his 'anger at Mr Newhouse [another fellow] after dinner for singing so long a psalm'.

Cambridge Puritanism did not stand merely for high and narrow ethical standards. It represented a concern for divine things, a firm belief in the justifying faith in Christ and an assurance of grace. Not all the Puritans were cantankerous pedants. Many seem to have been men of genuine holiness, like William Perkins, the fellow of Christ's, who was so much esteemed by his Puritan contemporaries; 'this holy man' who attracted large congregations of senior and junior members of the university to hear him preach at St Andrews 'did spend himself like a candle, to give light unto others'. 'An excellent gift he had,' said another, 'to define properly, divide exactly, dispute subtly, answer directly, speak pithily and write judicially.' '*He was one peaceable in Israel*,' Thomas Fuller wrote of another Puritan, Henry Smith, a Cambridge graduate who emigrated to Oxford and later held a London living:

he could unite with them in *Affections* from whom he dissented in *Judgement* : He disdained Railing and Invective, (the symptom of a sick wit;) ... He was commonly called the silver-tongued Preacher, and that was but one metall below St Chrysostome himself. His

Church was so crowded with Auditours, that Persons of good quality brought their own Pews with them I mean the legs, and stand therefore in the alleys. Their ears did attend to his lips, their hearts to their ears, that he held the Rudder of their Affections in his hand, so that he could steer them whether he was pleased; and he was pleased to steer them onely to God's glory and their own good.

Sir Walter Mildmay when he founded Emmanuel, which with Christ's became the chief Puritan college in Cambridge, expressed the hope that it 'would render as many as possible fit for the administration of the Divine Word and Sacraments; and that from this seed ground the English Church might have those she can summon to instruct the people and undertake the office of pastors, which is a thing necessary above all others.'

No doubt the 'comfortable certainty of the faith' which Puritanism provided fitted in well with rising mercantile ambitions and some donnish intellectualism. The merchant was sustained by a conviction that material success was a sign of virtue and profit the reward of thrift. The don, attracted to Puritanism, found in a personal devotion based on the Bible, the rejection of the miraculous incorporated into the Catholic faith and the dependence on the guidance of his conscience an encouragement to introduce into his studies a more experimental and scientific note. A mind that questioned religious orthodoxy could also question modes of academic thought no less hallowed by tradition. It is in this sense that there was a connexion between the rise of scientific studies and radical Protestant thinking, which found a momentary outlet at the universities in the middle of the seventeenth century.

The Commonwealth saw some of the old evils reappear. Once Puritanism was established it was in danger of falling victim to the same deficiencies which it had attacked in others. The regulations imposed by the university authorities at the behest of the government in London, insisting on attendance at sermons and various other religious observances, tended to force religion into a strait-jacket. 'Come not drooping in to College chapel,' a Cambridge tutor told his pupils, 'after the uncouth and ungodly manner of some, when almost all is done.

Doe not gaze or stare or look about you.' 'Come duely to prayers in your Tutor's Chamber at Night, and that as soon as the Bell hath tolde.' Undergraduates were ordered to attend St Mary's on Sundays 'forenoone & afternoones' and to take notes of the sermon. 'If you be in company on the Lord's day, let your discourse be of the sermon or some other point of Religion.'

*

By the early eighteenth century, in reaction to the stringent Puritanism of the Commonwealth, religion had once more become formal and conventional, a series of attendances at university sermons and college chapels, the infrequent celebration of the Holy Communion; as early as 1636 it was reported that at Trinity, Cambridge, 'some fellows are there who scarce see the inside of ye Chappell thrice in a yeare'. This was still true of Oxford and Cambridge when John Wesley became an undergraduate at Christ Church in 1720. Theology had reacted, too, to the formidable Calvinism of the earlier period, loosening the tight reins which the doctrines of human depravity, predestination and election exerted upon life and living. The Cambridge Platonist Henry More, like so many of his colleagues a product of the Puritan environment of Christ's, could not accept the 'bleak doctrine of Absolute Reprobation' nor 'swallow down that hard Doctrine concerning *Fate*'. One of his colleagues, Ralph Cudworth, later master of his college, said later that he had himself rejected Calvinism because of its arbitrary doctrine of predestination, damning men, women and children without regard for lives lived piously and well.

Sharp on the heels of the Cambridge Platonists came the Latitudinarians who were sometimes charged with depriving Christianity of its doctrinal content and with stressing merely the need for beneficent living in agreement with the teaching of right reason. The accusation was unjust but understandable. 'Nor is there any point in Divinity,' said Simon Patrick, a fellow of Queens', Cambridge, who later became Bishop of Ely,

where that which is most ancient doth not prove the most rational, and the most rational the ancientest: for there is an eternal consanguinity between all verity; and nothing is true in Divinity, which is false in Philosophy, or on the contrary. ... I shall always think him most conscientious who leads the most unblameable life, though he be not greatly scrupulous about the externals of Religion.

While reason was invoked as the chief guide to the truths of revelation on the one hand, and on the other the institutional character of the church was less and less regarded, there appeared the religious philosophy of Deism which sought to stress the rational truths of Christianity and to eliminate its more supernatural aspects, in fact, in the words of a leading Deist book, to make *Christianity Not Mysterious*. Deism was not, could hardly be a university movement, though one of its initiators had been Matthew Tindal, a fellow of All Souls, but it had some near-sympathizers in senior common rooms and a growing attraction for some of the undergraduates. Even Oxford, loyal in the main to its High Church tradition, became so alarmed by the spread of Deism that the vice-chancellor requested colleges to call the attention of undergraduates to its dangerous manifestations by posting up a notice to that effect in the halls of colleges.

It would appear to have been the Dean of Christ Church's refusal to cooperate with the vice-chancellor that first awakened young Charles Wesley, an undergraduate at Christ Church, to the sorry state of university religion. With a few others of his college he formed a society to foster more regular and frequent attendance at the Holy Communion, to engage in prayer and Bible-reading and to abstain from the vicious living which sometimes characterized the young bloods of his college. The society might have had a short life had not its inauguration more or less coincided with the return to Oxford of Charles's elder brother John, who had been elected to a fellowship at Lincoln in 1725, and came to take up his tutorial duties. An earnest, genteel, very widely read young man, conscientious and serious, he had been brought up in the devout atmosphere of Epworth Rectory in Lincolnshire where High Church Toryism, to which his father, Samuel, adhered, combined with the theology of Dissent in which his mother had

been educated, to create a sense of high endeavour, hard but
joyous living and genuine piety. John's sense of vocation was
fostered by his return to Epworth to act as his father's curate
to difficult and sometimes hostile parishioners; but in 1729 he
was recalled to Lincoln College. In his hands the religious
society which his brother had founded became a significant
protest against laxity and unbelief, the tendencies which
seemed to the two brothers to have acquired so strong a hold
over contemporary Oxford.

John Wesley was a natural leader, self-confident, dominating
and attractive, and what might have been a small and ephemeral society became the foundation of a great religious movement. This was not foreseen at the time, but it spread slowly,
gaining friends especially in their own college, Christ Church,
and attracting some young dons and a few undergraduates in
other colleges. The Holy Club was never large, but it became
an active influence in Oxford's religious life. Its members met
together to engage in devotional exercises, praying, reading the
Bible and singing hymns. They made a point of taking the
Holy Communion regularly and frequently, a practice which
made some accuse them of spiritual exhibitionism and gave
them the nickname of the Sacramentarians, while others called
them the Bible-Moths or the Methodists. They sought also to
find opportunities for putting their religious beliefs to the test.
They began to visit the Oxford prisons, the Castle and the
Bocardo, praying, holding services and distributing religious
literature, but they did not confine their attention to purely
religious activities. They helped the prisoners with legal
advice, gave them fuel, money and clothing, taught them and
their children to read. They also began to visit and assist the
inmates of the workhouses. These works of charity and compassion, unusual in the university, aroused interest, brought in
some of the townspeople to the Holy Club and even attracted
the patronage of the Bishop of Oxford and subscriptions from
well-wishers among the dons.

But the Holy Club also evoked criticism and even hostility.
The undergraduates, averse to what may have seemed to many
of them the priggish behaviour and attitude of their fellows,

mocked the members and sought to dissuade them from their pious practices. 'I am as much laughed at and despised by the whole town as any of them,' Richard Morgan told his father, 'and always shall be so while I am his pupil. The whole College makes a jest of me. ...' Some of the seniors began to be perturbed as they observed the possible dangerous implications of an unregulated enthusiasm. The death of one of the original members of the Holy Club, Richard's brother, William Morgan of Christ Church, from the effects of a nervous breakdown which some credited to the austerities of the Holy Club precipitated a crisis in its affairs. 'You cannot conceive what a noise that ridiculous society in which you are engaged has made here,' his father, an Irish lawyer, had written to William before his death, in March 1732.

Besides the particulars of the great follies of it at Oxford (which to my great concern I have often heard repeated), it gave me sensible trouble to hear that you were noted for going into the villages about Holt; calling their children together, and teaching their prayers and catechism. ... I could not but advise with a wise, pious and learned clergyman. He told me that he has known the worst consequences follow from such blind zeal; and plainly satisfied me that it was a thorough mistake of true piety and religion.

John Wesley replied vehemently and persuasively to such criticisms in a long letter to Morgan's father; and William Law defended the Methodists against a hostile newspaper article.

The atmosphere could never be quite the same again. The Rector of Lincoln, Dr Euseby Isham, very friendly to Wesley personally, was perturbed by rumours that Wesley was indoctrinating his pupils at Lincoln. Wesley denied that this was so, but his faith was too indomitable to be lived in a vacuum. He did not intend to force his pupils into the Holy Club, but he could not forbear from communicating something of the faith which sustained him. They came to drink tea and they stayed to pray; they came to pray and they visited the prisoners. It was hard to withstand the pressure and personal attraction which the older man exerted; and they found it difficult once they discovered that the activities of the Holy Club were not to their liking to withdraw without embarrassing emotional scenes. Without doubt the Holy Club was for good or ill a disturbing factor in the religious life of the university. This was certainly the view of the complacent clerical dons who did not wish their own unhurried leisure and more worldly standards of vocation to be shown up by the contrasting lives of John Wesley and his colleagues. But shown up they were, and the religious conscience of Oxford was awakened to the need for the outward expression of the Christian faith in works of charity and compassion and to the fact that religious experience was a necessary concomitant to sincere belief.

In 1735 John Wesley left Oxford to go to Georgia as a chaplain in the service of the Society for the Propagation of the Gospel. For some time he had been increasingly dissatisfied with his life in Oxford, with the supposed sophistication and worldliness of his surroundings, which he doubtless exaggerated, and with his own inability to find complete spiritual satisfaction in the work which he was doing. He had besides experienced the failure of a series of romantic attachments. He had refused the opportunity on what seem to have been rather specious grounds of following his father at Epworth; and he now decided to test his vocation in missionary work in America. The mission had apparently little success, though its importance in Wesley's own life was to be immense. Through his contact with the Moravian Brethren, and Peter Böhler in particular, and as a result of his own spiritual depression, the way was paved for the conversion he experienced on 24 May 1738, the climacteric of his career.

Wesley remained a fellow of Lincoln until his disastrous marriage in 1751, but his visits to Oxford became less and less frequent. His last university sermon in 1744, the last because he was purposely not asked to preach again, was a scathing denunciation of the university, more especially of its religious life.

Is this city a Christian city? Is Christianity, scriptural Christianity, found here? ... Are you lively portraitures of Him whom ye are appointed to represent among men? ... Is this the general character of Fellows of Colleges? I fear it is not. Rather have not pride and haughtiness of Spirit, impatience and peevishness, sloth and indolence, gluttony and sensuality, and even a proverbial uselessness, been objected to us, perhaps not always by our enemies, not wholly without ground. . . . May it not be one of the consequences of this, that so many of you are a generation of triflers; triflers with God, triflers with one another, and with your own souls?

Methodism continued to attract a small following among like-minded senior and junior members in the university, but as far as Oxford was concerned it had become a lost cause. Yet from its beginnings at Oxford, for which John Wesley had an unyielding love, the Methodist revival was destined to revitalize the religious life of the Church of England.

The exact connexion between the Methodist movement and the Evangelical revival is not easy to establish. In its early stages it seems likely that the Evangelicals, who soon had followers at Oxford and Cambridge, may well have reached their conclusions independently of the Methodists, influenced, however, by the same factors which had brought that movement into being. Yet the Evangelicals were in close and friendly contact with the Methodist leaders, especially at Cambridge, for Berridge's rectory at Everton and Venn's rectory at Yelling, to which pious undergraduates resorted, were held in high esteem by Wesley. Moreover the Evangelicals aimed at much the same ends as Wesley, the religion of personal experience, the revival of genuine Protestant Christianity, the confidence provided by salvation through justification by faith and the assurance of sanctification. There were, however, differences, arising in part from the more Calvinist theology of the Evangelicals (who had in this instance more in common with George Whitefield than with John Wesley) whilst the Methodists remained convinced Anglican churchmen. A slender thread bound the Oxford Methodists of Wesley's day and the Evangelicals who became so prominent at St Edmund Hall, to those of a century later when St Aldate's under Canon Christopher and St Ebbe's became the chief centres of evangelical religion at Oxford.

At Cambridge Berridge of Everton, formerly a fellow of Clare, stood a somewhat solitary figure until a group of seniors in Magdalene, Samuel Hey, William Farish and Henry Jowett, formed an Evangelical circle and attracted like-minded under-graduates, some of them sponsored by the Yorkshire society of Evangelical clergy known as the Elland Society. Magdalene thus became 'the general resort of young men seriously impressed with a sense of religion', and the 'sober Maudlins' were ridiculed by the more worldly men in the university as a tea-drinking set of pietists, a tradition which was still strong in 1828 when the first Magdalene boat was known as the tea-kettle. Soon the Evangelicals had a more powerful supporter in the learned, scientifically minded, formidable Isaac Milner, the President of Queens' and, through the favour of Wilber-force, Dean of Carlisle. Milner, a forceful personality, made sure that the Queens' senior common room was an Evangelical preserve, but Milner was too senior, too much the university administrator, vice-chancellor and professor, too aloof, to win much of a following among the majority of pious under-graduates. They looked elsewhere and found a guide, pastor and friend in Charles Simeon, a fellow of King's who was in 1782 given the cure of Holy Trinity where he remained until he died in 1836.

Simeon was an utterly devout man, full of scriptural holiness, who exerted an unparalleled influence over the more religious young men of Cambridge. 'If you knew what his authority and influence were, and how they extended from Cambridge to the most remote corners of England,' Macaulay wrote eight years after his death, 'you would allow his real sway in the Church was far greater than that of any primate.' To a modern generation Simeon may seem too genteel and even smug – and even in his own day the 'Sims' were held by many of their contemporaries to be near-hypocritical – but what he tried to do was to foster a genuine personal religion, to create the conditions for a life of prayer and missionary service by regular Bible reading and decent living. The missionaries, Henry Martyn of St. John's, Thomas Thomason, a fellow of Queens', Daniel Corrie, who became the first Bishop of Madras, and Claudius Buchanan all served under Simeon. Much esteemed, he was also much criticized: 'the novelty of an evening service in a parish church in Cambridge,' it was noted, 'conveyed at once the impression that it must be established for the advancement of true religion or what the world would call Methodism'. But the 'old Apostle' as he came to be called was a loyal and devoted Anglican.

The Evangelical movement was a reaction against the aridity of contemporary university religion; it is instructive that Simeon rarely attended services in his college chapel, even when he was Dean. Religion in the colleges had become desiccated and formal. The chapel services were hurried and irreverent; there was no sense of genuine devotion or real worship. 'As things go now,' a Trinity man who had matriculated in 1815 wrote, 'there is not one man who goes to pray. ... In the morning they muster, with all the reluctance of a man going to be hanged; and in the evening, although now awake, and enlivened with the convivialities of the bottle, there is the same feeling.' Attendance at chapel was upheld by sanctions; three or four markers went up and down the chapel with lists of names in their hands, running a pin through the names of those present. Failure to attend might lead to a man being 'put out of Sizings and Commons' or of getting impositions such as learning by heart a satire of Juvenal, a book of Homer or being obliged to give an analysis of Butler's *Analogy*. 'Spiritual influences,' wrote W. E. Heitland who went up to St John's in 1867, 'needed to be very powerful if they were to retain their virtue in the tainted atmosphere of a tariff.' The more pious preferred to make their devotions elsewhere, attending Holy Trinity or listening to the popular Harvey Goodwin at St Edward's; or at Oxford making their way to St Aldate's or one of the other city churches. But although the defects of university and college religion continued to be much publicized the clerical dons of Oxford and Cambridge, who were still for the most part resisting the entry of non-Anglicans into the university, were convinced that the abolition of compulsory attendance at chapel, together with some of the other privileges enjoyed by the established Church, would mean the end of the university as a religious institution.

At Oxford, the laxity of contemporary religious practice together with the threat to the Church which political and religious liberalism seemed to imply brought into being the Tractarian movement, which was in its own way to be as great a force as the Evangelical and Methodist societies in reawakening the Church of England. Its foster-father was a fellow of Oriel, John Keble, whose attack on the government bill dealing with the Irish bishoprics in 1833 has been held to have sounded the first real trumpet call in an attempt to reassert the Catholic and sacramental character of the English Church. Some of the foundations however had been laid in Caroline theology of the seventeenth century, in the patristic writings of an earlier age and even in the so-called high and dry school of Oxford theology. Keble and his younger friends at Oriel, Hurrell Froude, J. H. Newman, Marriott, and the scholarly professor of Hebrew, Pusey, tried to bring home to Englishmen the supernatural and spiritual character of the Church and its authority, and to create through the medium of tracts and other writings a theological synthesis which should assert what was basic to the Church's being, above all its continuity with the past (in spite of the Reformation) and its apostolic authority.

Tractarianism was as unwelcome to the moderate clericals of Oxford in the 1830s and 1840s as Methodism (with which indeed it had much in common) had been a hundred years earlier. It too was a reminder of ascetic renunciation, none too popular a theme in Oxford common rooms, with its seemingly antiquarian revival of feasts and fasts, with Newman's monkish community at Littlemore and its concern with vocation, so often smothered in the daily routine of Oxford life. It savoured for some of sacerdotalism; a tutor, in the view of its adherents, had a primary responsibility for his pupil's spiritual well-being. 'You consider tuition a species of pastoral care, do you not,' Coleridge asked Keble. 'Otherwise it might seem questionable whether a clergyman ought to leave a care of souls for it.' The Tractarians' resentment at the subordination of the church to the state alarmed others, among them Thomas Arnold, headmaster of Rugby and a former fellow of Oriel, who wrote a harshly critical article in the *Edinburgh Review* entitled 'The Oxford Malignants'.

The main cause of the opposition was theological. Its opponents thought that it was a Romanist movement in disguise, that its doctrines were only dubiously Protestant, that its liking for ceremonial was but the thin end of a large wedge; the bishops were anxious and the Evangelicals very much perturbed by what seemed a threat to the Reformed faith itself. If the Tractarians awakened in Oxford, and even more so in the parishes where the young men absorbed into the movement later worked, a renewed understanding of holiness and gave to worship and to faith a lustre which had seemed lost in the formalities of the early nineteenth-century churches, yet the suspicion of their papalist inclinations grew rather than diminished. The eager, sensitive Hurrell Froude in his posthumously published *Remains* dismissed the Reformation with disapproval. Pusey's sermon at Christ Church on the Eucharist, wholly orthodox in its teaching as it undoubtedly was, led to his unjust suspension from preaching. Newman's famous Tract No. 90 suggested that the teaching of the Tridentine articles was not so very different from the Thirty-nine Articles. Its publication in 1841 created a furore which led to its condemnation and eventually to his resignation of the vicariate of St Mary's church, from which he had wielded so much influence over his undergraduate congregations, and to his reception in 1845 into the Roman Church. Ward of Balliol, whose *Idea of a Christian Church* appeared even more offensive, followed him after the university had deprived him of his degrees in 1845 for his heretical opinions. But the university and the church were left to deal with the aftermath.

In spite of all this, and in spite too of its ultra-conservatism, Tractarianism infiltrated into the Church of England, helping to make it a more vital and dynamic body; nor were its theological tenets lost. In the neo-Tractarian writings of Gore and his contemporaries, of which neither Pusey nor Liddon would have approved, Anglican Catholic theology sought to come to terms with the prevailing Hegelian and Idealist philosophy.

By the middle of the nineteenth century the universities were entering the liberal age, and this meant that everywhere the rigid control which the established church had exerted was on the wane. In many of the newer universities there was no place for religious activities or even for theological study. The impossibility of securing any measure of agreement between the Anglicans and Dissenters lay behind the establishment of the 'godless society' in Gower Street. King's College had been founded on a deliberate religious basis; all regular students were at first expected to attend chapel on Sundays. In 1853 the Bishop of London told the principal, R. W. Jelf, that he would decline to recognize the certificates issued by the college as long as F. D. Maurice taught divinity there, on the grounds of his heterodox teaching; Maurice, who was actually a poor teacher, was dismissed, raising an outcry from his sympathizers. Tennyson wrote scathingly that all liberal-minded men and women would continue to support him.

> Should eighty-thousand college-councils
> Thunder 'Anathema'.

At Durham too there was a degree of religious compulsion until the Dean and Chapter in 1865 exempted non-Anglicans from attendance at cathedral or chapel; nor do the compulsory services seem to have been conducted with a greater sense of decorum than those at Oxford and Cambridge college chapels. Religion of the old and dry variety was too deeply entrenched to be overthrown at the first attack.

It is, however, difficult to gainsay that the liberalization of the universities in the first instance was all to the advantage of true religion. The schools of theology at the older universities became much more lively and learned under the guidance of Lightfoot, Hort, Westcott and Swete at Cambridge and Gore, Moberly and Sanday at Oxford. The foundation of Nonconformist and Roman Catholic halls introduced new and valuable scholarship as well as fertile spirituality. In the later nineteenth and early twentieth centuries religious life was in many ways more vigorous and fresh than it had ever been. The undergraduate religious societies, of which the Christian Union and its foster child the Student Christian Movement were the most important, attracted a wide following and in the post-war

years penetrated the other universities, some of which if a
trifle reluctantly decided to create theological chairs and
faculties. Perhaps too narrowly pious, doctrinally imperative
and scripturally literal, but influential and full of good works
and missionary zeal, the Christian Unions sponsored missions
and stimulated the religious life of the universities. The ending
of compulsory chapel attendance, occurring over several years
but much accelerated by the generation that survived the First
World War, meant, especially at Cambridge, that, apart from a
quondam revival in the 1950s, they were relegated to a peripheral position in college life. Even though the religious societies in the 1960s have lost some of their following, religious
activity has been very extensive in all universities, finding
expression in church reunion, in social causes, in support for
Oxfam, in running Borstal camps and in innumerable practical
activities; but except among the narrowly earnest conservative
evangelicals it has been less directly Christian and biblical in
inspiration.

The religious life of the other universities differed from that
of Oxford and Cambridge. Except for Durham, which in this
respect had been modelled on Oxford, the nineteenth-century
universities were secular institutions. Their founders were
partly motivated by the desire to provide an education that
was free of the religious tests and they were strongly supported
by Free Churchmen and humanists. King's College, London,
on the other hand, had been founded by those who were
alarmed at this tendency and, although in some respects it was
freer than the colleges of Oxford and Cambridge, its teaching
and religious life were rooted in Anglicanism. At first it followed the policy of the 'half-open' door, making no inquisition
as to creed on entry but expecting its students to conform to
the established religious usages of the college. Religious tests
at King's were abolished in 1903 and compulsory attendance at
chapel and divinity lectures ceased except for members of
the theology faculty. Other universities long displayed a
marked unwillingness to permit any official alignment with
the established Church, or even to sponsor departments of
theology, which were only gradually admitted. This was not

because they were anti-religious – men of strong religious convictions were among their teachers and administrators – but because they wished to stand aside from the sectarian hostilities all too common in the later nineteenth century. The founders of London university would have been ready to sponsor the teaching of theology if the pitch had not been queered by fierce denominational rivalry. Although John Owens laid it down in his will that the students and teachers 'shall not be required to make any declarations as to, or submit to any test whatsoever of their religious opinions',* the founders of Manchester University were not secularists. The first principal, A. J. Scott, was a devout Presbyterian. Although a faculty of theology was not established until 1903, they were eager to provide religious instruction, but they were determined to avoid sectarian exclusiveness or teaching which was offensive.

This meant that religious life was sponsored by unofficial bodies inside and outside the universities. At London a hall of residence was established in 1848 to commemorate the 'passing of the Dissenters' Chapels Act in 1844 ... that statute being the first recognition by the legislature of the principle of unlimited religious liberty' and to provide in addition to residence non-denominational instruction in religious subjects. Gradually denominational hostels were founded which were ultimately absorbed into the residential system of the universities.† For long, however, religious activity centred around the student societies, more especially the Christian Unions and the Student Christian Movement. At London a Student Christian Association was founded in 1861.

Denominational rivalry and hostility abated in the early years of the twentieth century, opening the way for an extension

---

*Quoted in B. W. Clapp, *John Owens, Manchester Merchant*, Manchester University Press, 1965, p. 73.

† An Anglican hall of residence was set up at Manchester in Plymouth Grove but failed for lack of funds. The Quakers established Dalton Hall in 1876, the Anglicans, Hulme Hall in 1887, Langdale Hall and St Anselm's Hall in 1903 (though the latter, a college for ordinands, was not officially recognized as a hostel until 1920).

of religious activity at the new universities. Theological colleges, Free Church as well as Anglican, were affiliated to the universities in their vicinity.* Theological faculties were established. At Leeds, one of the more aggressively secularist foundations, Miss Fawcett bequeathed £20,000 in 1931 to found a chair of theology. The authorities compromised by establishing a professorship of the philosophy and history of religion, but a faculty of theology was set up in 1934–5. In the post-war years a new stimulus was provided not merely by the work of the religious societies but also in some instances by the provision of chapels and the appointment, sometimes under the aegis of the university and sometimes directly by the churches concerned, of university chaplains to care for the pastoral needs of the students. At the new university of Kent denominational chaplains, Anglican, Roman Catholic and Free Church, were appointed, while Sussex had a distinguished Free Churchman, Daniel Jenkins, as its first chaplain. It has been the more necessary to provide for this side of the students' lives as more of them now live away from their home town. The problems confronting the new universities are doubtless much the same as those which affect the religious life of Oxford and Cambridge, though there religion may not be associated in the mind of the undergraduate, as it still is at the older universities, with an established order which many of them have

* At Leeds, the College of the Resurrection at Mirfield, and Rawdon College (Baptist); London, New College (Congregational) and Richmond College (Methodist); Manchester, the Baptist College, Hartley Victoria College (Methodist), Moravian College, Northern Congregational College and Unitarian College; Bristol, the Baptist College, Clifton Theological College and Tyndale Hall (Anglican), Didsbury College (Methodist) and Western College (Congregational). In Wales associated theological colleges include the United Theological College, Aberystwyth (Calvinistic Methodist), the Bangor School of Theology (interdenominational), Memorial College, Brecon (Congregational), the Cardiff School of Theology (interdenominational) and the Presbyterian College, Carmarthen (Free Church). St David's College, Lampeter, an Anglican foundation, was long denied full recognition (though entitled by charter to award the B.A. and B.D. degrees), but it has since widened the scope of its entry and courses and has at long last become entitled to a grant from the U.G.C.

grown to distrust. It cannot, however, be pretended that it is more than a minority interest.

In all ways the secular impulse which the liberation of the ancient universities from their tutelage to the Church of England had helped to release, has continued strong. The universities are not now in any specific sense religious institutions nor does religion in the 1960s play a very significant part in their life. A generation has grown up which is more critical of received views on doctrine and morality and far less ready than previous generations to accept the orthodox conception of what the church practises and teaches. It might be assumed from the cycle of past history that the current dissatisfaction with the existing state of affairs could pave the way for a new movement of protest and spiritual revival, on the pattern of Lollardy, early Protestantism, Puritanism, Methodism, Evangelicalism and Tractarianism. But this now seems unlikely; there are intimations that the process of secularization may go very much further. There are, however, odd straws in the wind, such as the tracts of the Bishop of Woolwich, a former fellow of Clare College, Cambridge,* and some of the notions put forward by the Cambridge theologians, which indicate a revival of interest. A large congregation listened Sunday by Sunday to the carefully argued Bampton lectures given by David Jenkins of Queen's College, Oxford, in St Mary's Church in 1966. There are signs of a deeper and basically fresh, if orthodox, rethinking in the theological faculties which may ultimately make an impact on religious thought. These are in any case portents that although the shape of things must be very different from what it has been during the long history of the older universities, religion is not yet either an entirely negligible or even an outmoded force.

* Appointed in 1969 Dean and fellow of Trinity College, Cambridge.

CHAPTER FOURTEEN

Dons and Undergraduates

I T is practically impossible to make accurate generalizations about dons and undergraduates when they cover a span of eight hundred years. In the race of professors and lecturers, generically called dons since the middle of the seventeenth century,* there have certainly been great changes, especially over the last hundred years. For six centuries most dons were in holy orders. Religion and religious observance played a necessary part in their daily life, as doubtless in their reading and conversation. Yet it has to be remembered that in many cases ordination was simply the conventional portal to the academic profession and did not necessarily carry with it a deep sense of vocation. There was not that distinction between the clerical and lay professions which the sacerdotal revival of the nineteenth century tended to stress. The clerical order has always been as various in character as that of the laity, and if it has not ordinarily included so many of the self-seeking and the would-be criminal type, yet it has never been drably uniform. Character, being the product of things over which men have very little control, is rarely fully shaped by vocation. That the dons of an earlier period were usually ordained clergymen does not therefore imply that they were all alike.

Is it possible to deduce anything about their social status and standing? As members of the clerical profession they ranked with the beneficed clergy but had the additional claim to respect which learning has evoked in most civilized societies; their academic robes which for long constituted their ordinary walking-out costume signified their calling. Yet if they were treated with more respect than the schoolmaster, their place in the social hierarchy remained a moderately sub-

*The word is derived from the Latin *dominus*, a title by courtesy attached to members of the clerical and academic professions in the Middle Ages and later.

ordinate one. They knew where they belonged and if not always sycophantic they recognized both the worth and importance of their betters. They had an eye to the world, and were not averse to patronage. A rich living or a canonry paid better than a college fellowship and made possible marriage and a family. Mr Pretyman's fortune was made when the younger Pitt came to Pembroke College, Cambridge, as his pupil; the see of Lincoln was his reward. Paley, commenting on the way in which clerical dons fawned on the young Pitt, adapted the words of Scripture: 'There is a lad here, who hath five barley loaves and two small fishes, but what are *they* among so many?' If in the republic of letters scholarship won esteem, it was sometimes a disadvantage in the great world which has always been somewhat suspicious of mere cleverness. Dons had not very often the advantages of good birth or inherited wealth; had they possessed these blessings they would seldom have become dons. There have been exceptions to this rule; the younger sons of the aristocracy or members of the landed gentry, a Sir John Thorold, a Lord David Cecil or a Lord Rothschild, have made their way into academic society; but this was unusual either in the thirteenth or in the twentieth century.

The social hue of the universities was predominantly middle-class, with a significant shot even in earlier times of proletarian blood.* As a result senior common rooms were sometimes lacking in social grace and elegant behaviour. Even in the twentieth century dons occasionally appear brusque and socially ill at ease and some remain downright uncouth. In the nineteenth century the distinguished classical scholar Dean Gaisford of Christ Church was known to his contemporaries

---

* An evident distinction must be made between the older English universities, the civic universities and the Scottish universities. It has been observed that '61·3 per cent of Glasgow students were from tenant farming, business and artisan families, while 66·5 per cent of Cambridge students were from church, noble and landed families' (W. M. Mathew, 'The origins and occupations of Glasgow students' in *Past and Present*, 33, April 1966, pp. 74–94). cf. Hester Jenkins and D. Caradog Jones, 'Social class of Cantab. alumni of the 18th and 19th centuries', *British Journal of Sociology*, i, 1950, pp. 93–116.

as the 'Athenian Blacksmith' while the historian E. A. Freeman was described in a toast at the Architectural Society's dinner as one who was 'singularly familiar with the manners of our rude ancestors'. But there were far worse things than brusquerie. The senior common rooms in the seventeenth and eighteenth centuries, though clerical assemblies, must have had at times the atmosphere almost of a bar parlour, characterized by heavy drinking, wagers and card-playing, suffused by the mingled smell of wine, tobacco-smoke and linen that was not always clean. Such societies because of their in-bred and celibate character were often quarrelsome, and in earlier days acts of violence were not unknown. Dr Bentley's running fight with the fellows of Trinity, an epic battle lasting more or less from 1700 to 1738, was only an extreme example of behaviour all too familiar in other colleges which suffered what Lord Carteret, defending Bentley, called 'the distempered frenzies of cloistered zealots'.

Drunkenness was for long endemic in their life. 'Several of our fellows,' wrote Parson Woodforde in 1763, when he was a fellow of New College, Oxford, 'went at four o'clock in the morning for Stow; and all drunk; some in a phaeton, some in a buggy, and some on horseback.' The future Lord Campbell describing a fellowship dinner at Christ's, Cambridge, said that

as soon as the cloth was removed, we all returned to what is called the Combination Room, where there was such a drinking bout as I have seldom witnessed. Alma Mater lay dissolved in port. Each man must have had about two bottles. ... By some means I got safe home to my inn, but several of the Fellows continued reeling through the streets for a great part of the night.

'Poor Greenwood,' said Romilly in 1834 of a fellow of Trinity, Cambridge, 'was sadly overcome: whether he had drunk wine on an empty stomach, or had ventured on a glass of spirits in the morning, he was not able to walk after Hall.' In such an atmosphere it is hardly surprising that dons often became unduly sensitive about their rights and privileges, and suspected discourtesy where none was necessarily intended. 'Not long ago in Hall,' the contentious Mr Metcalfe of Lincoln College complained to the Rector, Mark Pattison, 'the Bursar, in the presence of a non-Fellow, said to me, "May I take some salt, I suppose I may not do that even without asking your permission?" I made no reply whatever.' The fellows, often bereft of social grace, speaking, as did their social betters, the dialect of the region from which they came, seemed members of an essentially provincial society.

This is, however, only one side of the picture. There was never a time when the senior common or combination rooms were confined to one social group, for their membership fluctuated constantly. They were the recruiting grounds for bishops and prebendaries as they were later to be the chief sources of headmasters and civil servants. Politicians, as we have seen, bullied and flattered them. Individual fellows were often in company or correspondence with leading figures in literary and intellectual life. Thomas Gray, although an ineffective professor of history at Cambridge, residing at Peterhouse and Pembroke (whence he had removed after an embarrassing practical joke), enriched English literature more than the majority of historians. Dr Johnson never forgot the other Pembroke at Oxford and ever held his university in high esteem. Provincial Oxford and Cambridge may have long been, but their tentacles reached far into cathedral closes, government offices and the literary circles of the metropolis.

Such contacts as these were made easier after the great changes of the 1850s and 1860s, for a new type of don then made his appearance, the politician and the public figure, mixing without difficulty in high society, familiar with civil servants, bankers and administrators, a development which led to the fusion between the worlds of academic learning and practical business, so characteristic of a twentieth century which has seen in Lord Franks, the Provost of Worcester, Oxford, a don who has been British ambassador to Washington and the chairman of Lloyds Bank. The coming of the railway to Oxford and Cambridge, regarded at first with acid disfavour by the university authorities, fostered social mobility, making an evening in London at a meeting or dinner party or on the other hand a dinner at a college high table much more feasible than they had been in earlier days. Although there were boorish members of senior common rooms, colleges were also in some sense polite societies, often enriched by contacts with the metropolis.

Dons have had many opportunities to live and work in the outside world. In the twentieth century it is a commonplace for dons to move, temporarily or permanently, into the civil service or to be seconded to work outside their own university; they travel widely and often study and teach at non-British universities. In earlier periods, they travelled on the Continent, sometimes accompanying their richer pupils as private tutors, enjoying a wider social experience than the common room and country rectory could provide. Patronage led to their becoming chaplains in noble houses and to the gift of livings which opened the doors of the aristocracy; skill in amateur theatricals brought a future professor of history at Oxford, Edward Nares of Merton, to the notice of the household of Blenheim whence he more or less eloped with a ducal daughter. Furthermore the system of fellow-commoners, which allowed a rich young man following an undergraduate course to share in the privileges and dining rights of the senior common room in return for financial contributions to his college must have diluted their academic and clerical atmosphere, for if fellow- or gentlemen-commoners often lacked scholarship, they contributed something in the way of polish, social grace and conviviality.

Thus the senior common and combination rooms of Oxford and Cambridge colleges were never simply unfashionable backwaters; nor were they, as is often supposed, companies of old men. In fact the average age was low, for fellows were generally elected shortly after graduation, and did not ordinarily hold their office for very long. There were generally a few seniors who had found all that they wanted in college life, and who were vowed to celibacy and port, but the company consisted predominantly of young men. They were usually well-read, educated men, not scholars of great note but interested in contemporary intellectual developments. Their conversation was often good and if gossip played its part this has ever been, and still is, true of any community. The books they possessed and the additions to their college libraries which they sponsored are an index to their interest in learning. To a greater or lesser extent dons have been educated, civilized, serious men, interested in scholarship, not free from the temptation to idle the time pleasantly away, but deserving well of their colleges and universities.

It is true that university life has provided a niche for the genuine eccentric, the scholarly recluse, the man who might find it difficult to secure congenial employment outside the cloistered courts. Doubtless some were tempted to become drones, secure in their possession of a fellowship; even in the twentieth century the virtual security of tenure which a fellowship provides and the natural unreadiness of any polite society to dismiss cursorily one of its members may make possible either a steady decay of the faculties or a life of agreeable indolence. In such surroundings native eccentricities, vagaries of dress and behaviour, have flourished. Some have been harmless madmen, such as William Pugh, a fellow of Trinity whose dismissal from the work of cataloguing the university library, sufficiently explained by his insistence that he could not properly catalogue a book without reading it through, so preyed on his mind that he took to smashing the Cambridge lampposts saying, as he did so, 'Death to the villain Marat! destruction to Robespierre', or the nineteenth-century cleric, Cuthbert Shields of Corpus Christi, whose final gesture of coming to dine at high table stark naked even his colleagues could hardly overlook. These were the kind of men whom Wordsworth recalled in the *Prelude*:

> Nor wanted we rich pastime of this kind
> Found everywhere, but chiefly in the ring
> Of the grave elders, men unscoured, grotesque
> In character, tricked out like aged trees,
> Which through the lapse of their infirmity
> Give ready place to any random seed
> That chooses to be reared upon their trunks.

On the other hand there were the more genuine scholars in whose life a mild degree of imbalance gave colour to their personality; the mineralogist Buckland of Christ Church, of whom Keble wrote, 'Buckland is come with a diploma from the Geological Society at Petersburg, a bottle of red snow in his pocket and a fixed opinion that there is no N.W. passage', and whose son turned the canon's lodgings into a veritable menagerie, or F. W. Bussell of Brasenose, whose hobby was the collection of extinct livings eroded by the North Sea, and who dressed, as Compton Mackenzie remembered him, in a costume unusual for a nineteenth-century Anglican clergyman, 'a black frogged riding-coat buttoned by the top button over a black silk waistcoat, above which was a white bow tie and a bowler hat'. The classical scholar, Robinson Ellis, Gilbert Murray recollected as being

very tall, rather shabby, with a long overcoat and with one boot – or sometimes both – slashed open to give his toes more room. The toes were rather a mystery. There was nothing to see, and they did not exactly hurt. He sometimes got the landlady at our lodging to look at them. The landladies were generally shy and could only remark that there was not much to see. 'That,' he would say, 'is what makes me uneasy.'*

'An ancient wizened rake,' the unhappy E. H. W. Meyerstein recalled, 'if a fire was burning, he would sit by it, requiring a newspaper to shade his profile from the heat.'† Canon Claude Jenkins, professor of ecclesiastical history at Oxford, who died in 1959, lived in a tatterdemalion house filled with books where the gas and the water-pipes had ceased to function, a scholar of immense learning with a 'ragbag of a mind', a devout churchman, yet sublimely shabby and unkempt, even dirty, surreptitiously taking the toast from dinner at high table to provide the provender for his breakfast. The English don at Cambridge, M. D. Forbes, imaginative and superb in society, indulged his artistic taste by 'painting on the inside of the servants' bath a full-length of a Grenadier Guardsman in ceremonial uniform, to keep them happy'.

* Gilbert Murray, *An Unfinished Autobiography*, Allen & Unwin, 1960, pp. 89–90.

† E. H. W. Meyerstein, *Of My Early Life, 1889–1918*, ed. Rowland, Watson, Spearman, 1957, p. 68.

The natural eccentric is no monopoly of Oxford and Cambridge, though he may be happier in their peaceful courts. The first professor of natural philosophy at London, the Rev. Dr Dionysius Lardner, was idiosyncratic, and was satirized in Thackeray's *The Yellow-plush Papers*. After he had resigned his chair in 1831, he eloped with the wife of a cavalry officer (and had to pay £3,000 damages for seduction) and proved an extremely successful lecturer in the United States and Cuba. Cardinal Newman's brother, Frank, the professor of classics at London, was another picturesque figure:

his complexion dark, his hair very black and long – a Jonathan beard – a soft-felt hat with a broad brim, a high Gladstone collar, a black and white shepherd's plaid scarf wound around his neck, trousers of which the lower six or eight inches were of black leather, and an outer garment consisting of a rug with a hole in the middle through which he puts his head.

It is surely one of the saving graces of academic society that it has proved tolerant of individuality and ready to permit a mild and colourful exhibitionism. The twentieth-century don is perhaps too much the efficient civil servant, tending to work set hours and turning out a standardized end product; but it is safe to say that innocent eccentricity still plays its part in university life.

It would, however, give an entirely incorrect impression to suggest that the eccentric scholars were ever more than a mere handful in the community. The principal changes in the don's life were a result of the admission of the layman and the married man to the common room. As a result of the latter the college ceased to be a home, except for a few bachelors, and became more and more a dining and a lunching club. If marriage had the effect of humanizing the dons and removing some of their sexual frustrations, it may have diminished their interest in the life of the community and their contacts with undergraduates, introducing a somewhat flat domesticity into social relations.

The female don was a new phenomenon; at first a suspect minority, the women dons advanced in status until now there are no positions in the university world from which they are debarred. The early female dons were women of considerable personality, learned and rather masculine, not unlike the suffragettes, more given than their male colleagues to high thinking and austere standards of living; academic women indeed have tended to be dowdy in appearance, intense and rather serious, though generally more conscientious than academic men. Equally there have been some endowed with conspicuous charm and ability, who would be ornaments to any society. The common rooms of the newer universities were mostly from the beginning mixed communities but at Oxford and Cambridge, loath as dons may be to admit it, a degree of what must still be to many welcome segregation persists; though the signs are that in the egalitarian society of the twentieth century all such barriers, for good or ill, will eventually be removed.

The degree of liberty which the twentieth century don enjoys still provides for a measure of individuality in behaviour and appearance and for the opportunity to undertake research work in his subject. The don can be notoriously unbusinesslike, irritatingly pedantic, shabby in appearance and often unworldly in attitude. He is in outlook generally far removed from the so-called world of the common man even when he prides himself on being the opposite. His common-room conversation will range very widely and embody a great many topics, covering a large field of culture, scientific as well as humanistic, and embracing art, music and behaviour. He will often talk about religion but rarely accept its credentials. More often than not he will be a product of a grammar school education; the belief that dons are mainly recruited from the preserves of the older public schools is woefully misleading. The senior common rooms of many universities remain the most classless and republican societies in the kingdom; within the common room itself, at least at Oxford and Cambridge, heads of colleges rank as little more than very limited monarchs and senior professors, if recently elected, no higher than the recently graduated junior fellow. It has not always been so. The redoubtable Dr Whewell, Master of Trinity, Cambridge, disapproved of fellows having private keys to the college and sought to bring to an end the privilege by which smoking was allowed in the senior combination room on various stated days; 'Smoking,' he declared, 'cannot be allowed publicly. If it was, the college would soon be ... degraded in manners.'

The modern don may find himself involved in the propaganda machinery of the twentieth-century world, contributing to the Sunday newspapers, acting as a television personality and summoned to give counsel in Whitehall. Such functions which are no doubt serviceable to society may diminish his potential contribution to scholarship. Yet the don is by and large a responsible and hard-working teacher, lecturer and research worker. He is adequately if not lucratively paid, perhaps less adequately housed and if until recently rated by the Registrar General below the doctor and the bank manager in the social grading, he enjoys an enviable status in society. The foundation of new universities has increased greatly the numbers of his tribe, not without some diminution in academic quality.

If the nature of dons has changed with the passing of time, reflecting the evolution of society itself, this is no less true of the junior members of the universities from whom the dons are necessarily recruited. Yet the social and even the academic relationship between dons and undergraduates has always been, and still remains, limited. 'The dons,' Bertrand Russell admitted, 'contributed little to my enjoyment of Cambridge'* when he was an undergraduate. 'As for the dons, they might just as well have been at Cambridge,' Louis MacNeice wrote of his time at Merton College, Oxford, in 1926. 'Few of them were interested in teaching. They lived in a parlour up a winding stair and caught little facts like flies in webs of generalization. ... Some of them had never been adult, their second childhood having come too early. Some of them had never been male, walked around in their gowns like blowsy widows or wizened spinsters. They had charm without warmth and knowledge without understanding.'† Such a comment provides an unfair picture but may underline the lack of contact which exists even

---

* Bertrand Russell, *Autobiography*, Allen & Unwin, 1967, p. 66.
† Louis MacNeice, *The Strings are False*, Faber, 1965, p. 105.

in the collegiate universities between dons and undergraduates, and which is the more noticeable in the other universities. Although apparently united by a similar interest in learning, don and undergraduate seem often to live in two different worlds.

We have seen already how the history of the universities has been effectually altered both by the type and social genesis of the contemporary undergraduate and by the changing character of his studies. The age of the undergraduate has shifted through the centuries, age of entry falling sometimes as low as fourteen or even lower, and rising as a result of national service in the post-war period to twenty and beyond, though the average was for long seventeen. The comparative youthfulness of the undergraduate in the Tudor and Stuart period – though boys then matured at an earlier age – explains the seeming harshness of the discipline, including corporal punishment and the setting of lines more reminiscent of a Victorian boarding school, which were imposed by the authorities for misdemeanours. 'Dr Potter,' says Aubrey, 'while Tutor of Trinity College (Oxford), *whipt* his pupil *with his sword by his side* when he came to take his leave of him to go to the inns of court.' The list of undergraduate misdemeanours is perennial; though rudeness and impertinence to their seniors are faults one would normally associate with only a very small minority of modern undergraduates, however casual an attitude they may seem to adopt towards their elders. Violence is another element in undergraduate life which has more or less disappeared, though in the 1960s there have been an increasing number of acts of student hooliganism which suggest that the gap between some undergraduates and contemporary 'mods' and 'rockers' is a very narrow one. In 1608 a Cambridge undergraduate, Raphael Edwards, was fined ten shillings for attacking a freshman 'laying violent hands on him, punching him and turning him out of his bed-room'. In 1675 John Dennis, who later achieved some reputation as a dramatic critic, was fined, deprived of his scholarship and recommended to leave the college for drawing his sword and wounding one of his fellow students. The wearing of swords was forbidden by the university regulations, but students probably carried knives, presumably clasp knives for use at meals, which could serve the same purpose as the modern flick-knife. Some Cambridge undergraduates, Gunning recalled, were 'scarcely less ferocious than the members of the "Mohock and Sweating Clubs" '. 'When they walk together in *bodies*,' it was said of eighteenth-century undergraduates at Oxford, 'how impregnable are their *foreheads*? They point at every soul they meet, laugh very loud, and whisper as they laugh, *Demme* Jack, there goes a prig! *Let us blow the puppy up* – upon which, they all stare him full in the face, turn him from the wall as he passes by, and set up an *horse-laugh*.' Even in March 1834 two Trinity undergraduates were expelled for assaulting their landlady and holding a razor to her throat at three in the morning.

Heavy drinking, for long the familiar vice of seniors and juniors alike, is not as prevalent as it seems once to have been; the occasional orgy or boat-club dinner may promote exhibitions of uncouth behaviour but the general consumption of alcohol is more modest. The poet, William Shenstone, during his time at Pembroke College, Oxford, in the 1730s fell in with a 'set of jolly, sprightly young fellows, most of them west-country lads; who drank ale, smoked tobacco, punned, and sung bacchanalian catches the whole evening'. 'Baker and Croucher, both of Merton Coll.,' Parson Woodforde noted in his diary for 11 March 1761; 'spent their evening in the B.C.R. [Bachelors' Common Room]. Croucher was devilish drunk indeed, and made a great noise there, but we carried him away to Peckham's Bed in Triumph.'

A community of full-blooded adolescents inevitably created the opportunity for sexual play; a celibate society (for if the married don is a comparatively recent invention, the married undergraduate, still a rare phenomenon, was hardly known before the ending of the Second World War) affords an obvious temptation to homosexual or irregular heterosexual relationships. Lack of evidence makes it impossible to assess the measure of homosexuality then as now; but the occasional scandal, such as that created by the flight of Warden Thistlethwaite of Wadham in 1739,* testifies to its continued and natural existence. 'This evening I hear,' Thomas Wilson wrote on 20 November 1732, 'that Mr Pointer Chaplain of Merton 40 years standing was called before the Warden and Fellows upon a complaint made by one of the Commoners of the House whom he had got into his chamber, and after urging him to drink, would have offered some very indecent things.' The Romantic movement and its corollary, the revived interest in classical learning and customs, may have fostered homosexual inclinations; John Addington Symonds, the historian of the Renaissance, was deprived of his research fellowship at Magdalen, Oxford, because of his indiscretions. In early twentieth-century Cambridge homosexual conduct appealed to some of the intellectual and fashionable as well as athletic undergraduates, stemming from King's College and numbering among its devotees the economist Maynard Keynes and the author Lytton Strachey.

The presence of a moderate number of prostitutes at Oxford and Cambridge (whom the university authorities had the power to expel and detain) indicates that there was a certain demand. 'Oh the greivous sinnes in Trinity Colledge,' a Puritan fellow commented in February 1596, 'which had a woman which was carried from chamber to chamber on the night tyme', and he characteristically condemned himself for 'My adulterous dream that night'. 'Chum, Chum,' a scholar whispered to his companion in chapel in 1700, 'tho' I have the Word of God in my mouth to tell thee the Truth on't I have a Lyn Devil in my Breeches', King's Lynn having apparently at that time 'so fair a Reputation for the foul practise of venery'. 'Bawdy-Barnwel' at Cambridge was so called 'from the Numerous Brothel-Houses it contains for the Health, Ease and Pleasure of the Learned Vicinity'. 'The three great temptations of the place,' Mark Pattison wrote of Oxford in the 1860s, were 'fornication, wine and betting'. 'We are here,' the vice-chancellor of Cambridge told Charles Yorke in January

*Described in the pamphlet *A faithful Narrative of the Proceedings in a late affair between the Rev. John Swinton and Mr George Baker both of Wadham College, Oxford*, London, 1739.

1770, 'as much pestered with lewd women who swarm as much in our streets as they do in Fleet Street or Ludgate Hill.' The American C. A. Bristed, in general appreciative of his English university, commented in the 1840s: *

> There is a careless and undisguised way of talking about gross vice, which shows that public sentiment does not strongly condemn it; it is habitually talked of, and considered as a thing from which a man may abstain through extraordinary frigidity of temperament or high religious scruple, or merely as a bit of training with reference to the physical consequences alone; but which is on the whole natural, excusable, and perhaps to most men necessary.

The older universities had the right to arrest and detain prostitutes. At Oxford a zealous nineteenth-century proctor was said to have chased one such woman as far as Witney. At Cambridge the university was involved twice in law suits as a result of its attempt to deal with this problem, in 1860 and in 1893.

The twentieth century has seen a change in this respect too. Not that the modern undergraduate is necessarily more moral, but the shift in public morality has made the dividing line between what is and what is not moral very much less clear than it was in the last century or in the early years of this. The female undergraduate has arrived on the scene, in the minority at Oxford and Cambridge but at least in equal ratio and sometimes in the majority at the other universities. There is a widespread latitude in social relationships, often greater in the Oxford and Cambridge colleges than in the halls of many other universities, and unthinkable to an earlier generation, which permits the much-desired female companionship, and rules relating to the hours at which women are permitted in college have been greatly relaxed. Then too the moral sanctions of a religious faith have lost much of their force thus permitting a greater degree of casual sexual relationships, though possibly not to the extent that the more advanced humanists would claim or desire. It is probably true to say that male undergraduates make far less use of the services of the profes-

* C. A. Bristed, *Five Years in an English University*, 2nd edn, 1852, pp. 341–2.

sional prostitute than in the past but may engage very much more often in casual sexual relationships, sometimes leading, even from necessity, to conventional marriage with girls of their own status. An increasing number of men and women become engaged during their undergraduate course, and statistical evidence would suggest that married and engaged undergraduates may perform more satisfactorily in their final examinations than men and women who have no such relationship. Certainly modern undergraduates mix with each other more freely and naturally than they did in the past; and it is doubtful, though the evidence is necessarily hard to come by, whether promiscuity is anything like as widespread as some of the more sensational newspapers sometimes suggest, or even as some undergraduates would have the public believe.

There has been simultaneously a relaxation of discipline on the part of the university authorities. In the past it was not unknown to use corporal punishment – 'my little pity,' Samuel Ward notes in his diary in 1595, 'of the boy who was whipt in the hall'; but fines, impositions, rustication and expulsion were the principal sanctions employed. 'The subwarden,' wrote Woodforde on 30 January 1760, 'set me Part of the 1st Lesson for this morning service to translate into the Sapphic Metre, for not being at Prayers this morning.' On the other hand it is probable that only in more recent times have faulty work and indolence aroused such marked disapproval.

For many years the university authorities insisted on proper attire as well as orderly behaviour. The wearing of academic dress on stated occasions is still enforced at the older universities, but the attempt to impose a sober dress on juniors and seniors alike has been given up and seems to have been a pretty vain effort from the very start. As early as the fourteenth century

great complaint was made against the clergy and the students in the Universities on account of their extravagance in dress, hair either hanging down on their shoulders in an effeminate manner, or curled and powdered ... attired in cloaks with furred edges, long hanging sleeves not covering their elbows, shoes chequered with red and green, and tippets of an unusual length.

'All that are undergraduates,' Dr John Cosin wrote to Archbishop Laud in 1636,

> wear ye new fashioned gowns of any colour whatsoever, blew or
> green, or red, or mixt, without any Uniformity but in handing
> Sleeves. And their other garments are light & gay, Some with
> bootes and Spurs, others with Stockings of diverse Colours re-
> versed one upon another ... in all places, among Graduates and
> Priests also, as well as the younger Students, we have fair Roses
> upon the Shoe, long frizled haire upon ye head, broad spred Bands
> upon the Shoulders, and long large Merchant Ruffs about ye neck,
> with fayre feminine Cuffs at ye wrist.

In the early eighteenth century Amhurst spoke of young men
who 'having been kept short of money at school' at the university 'cut a daring figure in silk gowns, and bosh it about town
in lace ruffles and flaxen tye wigs'. In 1788 the dress of undergraduates was condemned as 'indecent, expensive and
effeminate'. In the 1840s normal undergraduate dress consisted of a 'not too new black coat (frock or cutaway), trousers
of some substantial stuff, grey or plaid, and a stout waistcoat,
frequently of the same pattern as the trousers ... The only
showy part of the attire is the cravat, which is apt to be blue
or some other decided colour, and fastened in front with a
large gold-headed pin'.

The self-conscious sloven was not unknown in earlier days,
the man who

> greas'd his cloathes on purpose, tore his gown to make it ragged,
> broke the board of his cap. ... He seldom allow'd his hair to be
> combed, or his shoes to be japann'd. He would put his shirt on at
> bed time, because he was ashamed to be caught in a clean one. ...
> He was hail fellow well met with all the townsmen in general,
> would swig ale in a penny pot-house with the lowest of the mob.

'These hobbledehoys,' a contemporary wrote of Durham undergraduates in the 1870s, 'are to be seen in our streets in the
crudest of trousers and coats, with a ragged gown and a dilapi-
dated cap, reminding us of 'Arry of Whitechapel trying to
imitate a Piccadilly swell.' Tight jeans, leather jackets and

long hair had their equivalents in previous centuries, even if the attitude of university authorities to casual costume is now so much more sympathetic. As late as 1857 a Cambridge under-graduate was told by the senior dean to remove his moustache. The dean's verdict was upheld by the master, who told Mr Tennent that he 'agreed with the officer of the college in think-ing a moustache unsuited to the character of a student of the college, particularly when conspicuous, as it appears that Mr Tennent's' is but this as Victorian photographs make abun-dantly clear must also have been a failing cause.

The non-resident universities of the nineteenth century found such a complex of rules unnecessary. At London it was hoped that it would be enough to remind the students of 'that propriety of demeanour and delicacy of feeling which are always conspicuous in young men of liberal education', a misconceived statement if ever there was one then or now, but it cannot be said that either were much in evidence and the professors were often hard put to it to maintain order in their rowdy classes. 'We think,' *Punch* commented in 1846, referring to the frequent appearance of the university medical students before the magistrates, '[that] as far as vulgarity goes, the concern in Gower Street may vie with the older establishments of the Cam and the Isis.' Durham as a residen-tial university took over many of the rules of the older in-stitutions. Students had to be present at breakfast and dinner in hall, at chapel prayers and cathedral service, to attend such lectures as directed and to be in the college before the gates closed. They were always to wear academic costume in public, except on the river where they might wear an academical cap or boating cap but not a hat in the boat itself. Dice, cards, betting and all forms of gambling were forbidden. As late as 1919 the discipline committee of Sheffield University com-plained of a 'prolonged epidemic of dancing ... even in the cor-ridors' which it thought to be 'irregular and highly undesirable'.

*

The character of undergraduate study has changed with the different demands of the degree syllabus. The basic pattern at the older universities has remained the same; the lecture, at one time mostly given in college, and the individual periods with the tutor. The lecture system, once somewhat haphazard, is now arranged by the faculty boards so as to cover the majority of the topics in the course. At all the universities lectures have always been of widely varying value; even where the material has been well arranged, the manner of presentation has been sometimes execrable. At Oxford and Cambridge, where lectures are not obligatory, attendance has greatly fluctuated, though it is only infrequently that a lecturer finds that his numbers increase after the initial lecture. Since the sixteenth century the tutorial system has been the foundation of teaching. At best the weekly tutorial can be an exciting intellectual debate between the tutor and the pupil and at worst a dull, tedious, repetitive routine which leaves tutor and pupil mentally exhausted. In many cases the relationship is something more than a pure intellectual exercise; it is a personal exchange which may involve a friendship that outlasts the years. Inevitably there have always been some who have found the tutorial relationship frustrating and unrewarding. The youthful Gibbon spoke contemptuously of his tutors at Magdalen; but it would be equally interesting to discover what his tutors thought of their unusual pupil. How far undergraduates have been fully engaged or personally involved in the work that they have been doing is a matter of opinion; but at least measured indolence is far less conspicuous now than it was in previous centuries.

Study has never been a full-time occupation. The nature of undergraduate recreation has changed, though its centre has shifted only from the tavern of the college buttery to the college or Union bar. The characteristic 'wine' of the eighteenth and nineteenth centuries – 'thirty lads,' Thackeray recalled, 'round a table covered with bad sweetmeats, drinking bad wines, telling bad stories, singing bad songs over and over again' – has been replaced by the crowded sherry or cocktail party; expense normally prohibits the luncheons and dinners that were an enviable feature of earlier days. There was a time when it was common for dons to invite pupils to breakfast and even for undergraduates to invite each other; an undergraduate noted in 1815 that he breakfasted after chapel with a friend, consuming toast, muffins, crumpets, eggs, two inches each of butter, ham, cold chicken, beef steaks, audit-ale, tea and coffee, honey, marmalade and anchovies. The disappearance of compulsory chapel attendance (and of its alternative, roll call) and changing social custom have made breakfast an optional meal.

The coffee house, first appearing in the seventeenth century, provided a social centre for dons and undergraduates. 'It is become a custom, after chapel, to repair to one or other of the coffee-houses,' wrote Roger North, 'where hours are spent in talking; and less profitable reading of newspapers, of which swarms are continually supplied from London. And the scholars are so greedy after news (which is none of their business), that they neglect all for it.' 'In order to prevent Intemperance,' a notice relating to the Emmanuel coffee house which opened at Cambridge in 1763 read, 'no Spirituous Liquor will be admitted, unless meliorated and duly authorized according to law; but harmless Tea, Lacedemonian Broth, and invigorating Chocolate, comforting Cakes, with cooking Tarts and Jellies.' A library of books was available 'and for the entertainment of such Gentlemen who are musically inclined, Instruments will shortly be provided'. The authorities regarded the coffee houses with distaste and in 1750 had forbidden undergraduates to frequent such places between nine and twelve in the morning.

Dinner in hall is no longer so formal a social occasion as it once was. In the early eighteenth century it was served at noon, by 1799 at half past two and steadily later as the nineteenth century progressed. The food supplied does not seem to have been particularly exciting; 'abundance of plain joints, and vegetables and beer and ale ad libitum, besides which soup, pastry and cheese can be "sized for", i.e. brought in portions to individuals at an extra charge', an undergraduate commented in the 1840s. The service was often rough and ready. Both dons and undergraduates dressed for dinner; John Wright who entered Trinity College, Cambridge, in 1815 recalls that he was rebuked by the master of his college for appearing in hall in trousers, breeches and gaiters or stockings being the required garb. In all these ways time has brought change. The coffee house has disappeared and been replaced, though less completely at Oxford and Cambridge than at other universities, by the rather more sordid coffee bar. Dinner still remains something of a function, but in many colleges even the dons, and certainly the undergraduates, wear casual clothing.

*

Perhaps the greatest changes in undergraduate life have been brought out by the development of organized games and the multiplication of undergraduate societies. The former were practically unknown until the nineteenth century, though Woodforde noted on 29 April 1760 that he 'went and play'd Crikett, being the first time of our Clubb's playing'. The clubs were mainly of a convivial nature though some aspired to literary conversation and debate. The rich rode and hunted. An order of 1750 forbade riding on horseback to Cambridge undergraduates without special leave. Ten years later the writer of *Advice to a young man of quality upon his coming to the university* suggested that he would be better advised to travel in the neighbourhood of the university rather than to waste his time hunting; he should spend the vacation in towns in Britain, visiting manufactures, interesting buildings and antiquities. The poor walked, often great distances. Such 'constitutionalizing', as this came to be called, might entail a jaunt of eight miles – twelve or fifteen on Sundays – in less than two hours, varied by the jumping of hedges, ditches and gates; young men took to wearing low-heeled shoes instead of boots to accomplish these feats the more easily.

There had always been more violent sports. In the sixteenth century some of the richer men went hawking or indulged in falconry; an edict of 1606 was directed against those 'who kept grey hounds and some of them hunting horses, for coursing and hunting'. Bull- and bear-baiting were also popular at this time. Dr Perne of Peterhouse was told how a 'great multitude of younge schollers' went to the bear-baiting at Chesterton 'in the sermon time between one and two of the clocke' on a Sunday afternoon in April 1581. The proctor who was despatched to deal with the students was mocked and jeered and his bedel was 'thrust ... upon the beare, in sort that he could hardly keepe himself from hurt'. Football of a kind was also indulged in. It occasionally ended in riotous behaviour, since for many years it was an excuse for a free fight between the Trinity men and the Johnians; it was, thought James Duport in 1650, 'a rude, boistrous exercise, and fitter for Clownes than for Schollars'. Duport recommended bowls, shooting or pitching the bar, or 'such like gentle and handsome and harmless exercises'. He was, he confessed, no great friend 'to going down the water because I observe sometimes it hath occasioned the going downe of the wind too much, and some under colour of going a fishing, drop into a blind house and there drink like fishes'. A decree of 1571 forbade bathing under penalty for a first offence of a beating and for a second of expulsion; nor did boating become common until the eighteenth century and then mainly in sailing boats. Horse-racing, and the proximity of Newmarket to Cambridge fostered the interest, attracted some of the 'fast' men.

Some are off to Newmarket-a-la-tandem; others are barouching to Bury, Huntingdon, or Colchester, to kick up a row at the ball; a third party have trundled away to Chesterton to learn the science of billiards; a fourth gone 'boating' to Cherry Hinton, Fen Ditton or Grantchester, there to 'swing on a gate all day and eat fat brawn' with the clodpoles, until, kissing the pretty rustic maidens, their sweethearts go near to skewer them with the pitch forks, and actually break their knowledge-boxes; and ... a fifth cricketing on Parker's Piece, or racketing away in the Tennis Court.

Such was a contemporary account of undergraduate recreation in the year of Waterloo.

All this was changed in the nineteenth century, partly by the institution of organized exercises in the schools from which the colleges recruited most of their undergraduates. Rowing became the acknowledged athletic status symbol of the two older universities, finding expression in the curious national popularity of that annual venture, the University Boat Race. In every college a boat club was founded and the inter-college races, known variously as the Mays or the Eights, combined the virtues of a gladiatorial show, an entertainment and a fashion parade. The Trinity Boat Club dated from 1825; but only one of the Trinity Boats, the Second Trinity, admitted poor scholars or sizars to membership. At St John's the Lady Margaret Boat Club, claiming to be select, for a time chose its members by ballot. The dominance of rowing, if from time to time questioned by those who resented its expense and its prestige and by dons for its demands on students' time, was such that other universities, conveniently close to a river, followed suit.* Every other form of athletic activity soon had its clubs and devotees, so that whether *mens* was *sana* or not it was at least housed in *corpore sano*.

At the older universities sporting activities, though engaged in on a university level, were centred in colleges, each of which had its own clubs and sports grounds. At the newer universities, such activities were directed at a university level by clubs which formed one of the many components of the university union. At Oxford and Cambridge the Unions were in the first instance debating societies, founded in 1823 and in 1814–15 respectively, though their facilities were expanded later. Here many undergraduates who were to become politicians and prominent men had their earliest experience of public speaking. In other universities the union became the social centre of undergraduate life, combining the functions of the older university unions and college common rooms and being the focal point of all the multifarious university clubs and societies; the responsibilities of the union president are so onerous that he is sometimes released from his academic obligations during his term of office. The great growth in the number of societies, cultural, musical, artistic, political, religious and theatrical, represents the most positive change in undergraduate society in the past century.

The performance of plays had been at one time a regular

* Even the Mancunians for a time rowed on the dreary Irwell, though only until 1874.

part of university life; in 1590 the tragedy *Roxana* was acted in the hall of Trinity, Cambridge, with such passion that a gentlewoman 'fell distracted and never recovered her senses'. But drama became associated with immorality and the vice-chancellors of Oxford and Cambridge exercised a strict censorship over theatricals in their cities as they were by law entitled to do. In the mid nineteenth century twenty-three Oxford dons petitioned the vice-chancellor against the performance of 'plays by amateurs in Oxford ... having in mind the serious detriment to the morality, industry, and economy of the younger members of the University by the prevalence of Amateur Theatrical amusements'. In the 1960s the Playhouse at Oxford became a university theatre, and elsewhere, as for instance at Bristol, dramatic art became a serious subject for study. The extent and range of all such activities may fairly suggest that the twentieth-century undergraduate is in all probability more genuinely concerned with culture than his ancestors were.

*

It is difficult to make generalizations about the social life of the newer universities, since it is changing rapidly as more and more undergraduates live away from home and reside in hostels or lodgings. For some time students at modern universities attended their colleges much as they had attended their schools, spending a 9 a.m. to 4 p.m. day there and then returning to their homes in the suburbs or the outskirts of the city. 'College finishes for me,' one student observed, 'when I leave at mid-day on Saturday. They are two separate existences.' The growth in the number of undergraduates living near the university has widened the scope of their social activities, allowing societies to hold meetings in the evening which would otherwise have not taken place.

In these universities the students' extra-curricular activities are largely sponsored by a guild of undergraduates or a students' representative council. The students elect their own officers and manage the affairs of the guild which are centred on the union, a building which is usually owned by the univer-

sity but controlled by its junior members. The gradual establishment of the university unions provides an index of the development of their activities and of a growing sense of social
homogeneity. A union was set up at Owens College, Manchester, in the first year of its existence. It collapsed in 1857,
but was revived four years later. Once a fortnight after coffee
a paper was read and followed by a discussion; it was said
that the authorities vetoed an Egyptian student's proposal
for debating the motion that a man should be allowed more
than one wife. At Leeds a union was formed in 1886 and
an athletics union was founded in 1889 to coordinate the
sporting activities of the students. The different associations
were merged in 1904 and reconstituted in 1922 to make it more
representative of the students' interests. The London university
union took shape in 1893 and one for women was set up in
1897. From small beginnings the student unions came to be all-
embracing institutions, though possibly never involving more
than a minority of the students in their activities. (Because
of this the new university of York has not created a central
union of this sort, believing that decentralization may provide
a richer social life.) The unions provide dining-rooms and
cafeterias, halls for debating and dancing, gymnasia, lounges,
libraries, television rooms and quiet rooms. All the major
societies, intellectual and social, debates and athletic clubs,
are organized as part of the union's functions, and most
student societies meet within its walls. The importance
which the union occupies in social life and the prestige which
its officers enjoy demonstrates one of the major differences
between the social life of Oxford and Cambridge, which is
still largely centred on the colleges, and that of the other
universities.

It may be possible to detect differences in social *mores*,
though because of the similarity of social groupings from
which all universities now draw their undergraduates this is
more difficult than it would have been in the past. Oxford and
Cambridge still attract students who have greater home advantages and are more predominantly middle-class. Undergraduates at the other universities more often come from homes

with lower cultural standards.* Social contacts between dons and undergraduates, though fostered at the newest universities, seem to be few and far between at the 'redbrick' societies. It is probable that intellectual interests only engage the attention of a minority outside 'working hours'. This phrase represents an attitude to life which may have crept in from industrial society, a division of the day into work and leisure. 'How many hours a day shall I be supposed to work?', one prospective undergraduate asked a college tutor, 'and shall I have the week-end free?' Many students spend a fair part of their leisure drinking at the union bar or the local pub, in taking a girl to the Saturday dance, in jazz or beat sessions, in visits to the local cinema and in various athletic activities, in other words enjoying the pastimes which engross the majority of their contemporaries. The higher proportion of girls to men at these universities makes for a greater degree of mixed companionship than there is at Oxford and Cambridge, possibly diminishing sexual frustration but almost certainly limiting intellectual discussion. In general life at a university outside Oxford and Cambridge may tend to be somewhat less sophisticated socially and intellectually.

Social change at all universities has created new problems. In the past life at the older universities mirrored the social gradations of the outside world. The student's gown reflected a social differentiation. A fellow or gentleman-commoner was arrayed in a gown ornamented with gold or silver lace and wore a velvet cap with a metallic tassel. The second sons of peers, that is, those who were entitled to be called the honour-

---

*Inquiries show that in general no more than 20 to 25 per cent of students have working-class backgrounds. In a recent analysis (*The British Journal of Sociology*, 1965, XVI, pp. 206–20), Miss Joan Abbott provides the following information about the social origins of students at Edinburgh, Durham and Newcastle.

	Edinburgh	Durham	Newcastle
Upper class	·6%	0%	0%
Upper middle	39%	29%	32%
Lower middle	44%	46%	44%
Working	15%	21%	20%
No occupation	2%	4%	4%

able, wore a hat instead of a velvet cap. Noblemen and the eldest sons of peers wore a plain black silk gown and the hat of an M.A. Lowest on the social scale were the poor scholars or sizars, who were educated more cheaply and had to give certain services in return; in the late seventeenth century they sat down at the fellows' table after they had finished their dinner and ate what was left. The author of a poem entitled *The Servitor* (1709) showed how some undergraduates viewed their humbler brethren:

> An o'er grown Looby, with Armes dangling,
> And Pendant Noddle like a changling;
> With Cap in form of Cow-Turd stinking
>
> I took him for some Natural,
> Or Idiot, from an Hospital
> Rather than a Schollar – Why! he's none,
> Says he, although he wears a gown
>
> A Clever Servitour's a Fiction,
> The Words imply a Contradiction.

Feeling on the other side was as strong: 'I, Sir,' said Chum in Thomas Baker's play *Hampstead Heath* (1706), 'was a Gentleman-Serviter at BrazenNose-College, my Business was to wait upon Gentlemen Commoners, to dress 'em, pimp for 'em, clean their Shoes, and make their Exercises; and the differences, Sir, between us Serviters and Gentlemen-Commoners is this, we are Men of Wit and no Fortune, and they are Men of Fortune and no Wit.' All this has disappeared. At least outwardly the universities are democratic societies, drawing their students and dons from all social classes without distinction or differentiation.

Yet social problems still exist. While class divisions have become blurred, social tensions find articulation in contrasts of clothes, accents and behaviour. For the majority of British undergraduates life away from home is itself a novel experience, creating its own questions. While some students prize their independence, to such an extent that their parents may feel that they have alienated themselves from their home background, for others independence is not so easy to accept. Leaving home means a break with friends and the social activities of the neighbourhood in which they may have been involved. They have to create for themselves a new pattern of relationships. They may find it difficult to achieve integration into a group. They are faced with the problem of finding a satisfactory relationship with members of the other sex. They are confronted, especially if they are shy or reserved, with the possibility of apparent isolation, experiencing the annihilating burden of loneliness. 'If there was not such a very good Union,' a Newcastle student observed, 'half the value of the university would be lost. Talking over a cup of something is of irreplaceable value.' But there are students who do not find it easy to confide their problems. Some are tempted to create for themselves an artificial existence, seeking to establish, perhaps by mannerisms, by the wearing of unusual or outlandish clothing, or by generating a reputation for sexual or alcoholic prowess, an image which serves temporarily to conceal the inner anxieties and frustrations of their existence. A university is inevitably rather an artificial society, and there is among its members greater prevalence of *Angst* than there once was. 'Sometimes,' C. A. Bristed wrote in 1849, the undergraduate 'has a nervous attack from over-work just before, or over-excitement at an examination.' But in the post-war world, so marked by confusion and anxiety, there have been more perturbing indications of mental and neurotic instability* among the young, caused less by work than by problems of a personal nature and by the competitive character of modern society.

The modern undergraduate is thus often unsure of himself. The man from the middle-class home and the boarding school may give a first impression of self-confidence and social maturity. He is much more likely than the boy from the grammar or comprehensive school to feel at ease with his seniors. The man from the working-class background may be less aware of

---

*There is evidence of a certain amount of drugs, soft rather than hard, being taken by a small minority of undergraduates, often for the sake of experiment.

social conventions. Unlike his contemporary from a boarding school who is used to being economically dependent on his parents, he may resent his economic dependence, aware that his parents were, and that some of his friends are, earning their own living at seventeen or eighteen, as they may occasionally remind him. He tends to think of the university as a means to a good job, and he looks forward to a settled married life. While undergraduates appear more physically mature than their Victorian predecessors (and in consequence more concerned with sexual security), the comparatively early age at which they enter the university, their lack of experience of life and the inadequacy or total lack of guidance from their parents and schools can cause acute unhappiness. There is much to be said for an interval between school and university. Moreover many students are probably no more prepared morally for university and college life than the juvenile delinquent who may have attended the same school. They have not merely to work out for themselves worthwhile social relationships but to establish standards for living and to investigate the nature of value itself. It is hardly surprising that there should be a degree of social and moral confusion which may occasionally end in tragedy.

Yet when all is said and done, great as have been the changes which have invested the universities through the centuries, a thread of continuity links the student of medieval Oxford with his successor in modern York or Sussex.

Studens Vulgaris, or common British undergraduate, Variety *Cantabrigiensis*. A hardy triennial. *Habitat*: abundant in meadows and by rivers, in winter and spring: has been found also in chapels and lecture rooms. Flowers profusely in May and June. Seeds occasionally later on. Use in the Pharmacopoeia: has been recommended as an irritant in obstinate cases of anchylosis, or tutor's stiff jaw.

The definition is doubtless as accurate now as it ever was. The universities remain in W. J. Cory's words 'the highland reservoirs of spring waters gathered, the springs of youth'. Yet what ultimately constitutes the *bene esse* of the ancient and modern societies may be less the transient lives of dons and under-graduates than the atmosphere created, as David Knowles has finely put it, by the 'beauty of stone and leaf and flower, the *genius loci*, the innumerable harvests of mind and heart, the nursery of poets many and great'.

CHAPTER FIFTEEN

The Problem of the Modern University

THE intellectual and social revolution which has occurred since the end of the Second World War and is still in process has not merely brought about a reorientation of university life but has had repercussions on British education at all levels. Its most spectacular result has been the great increase in the number of universities and the corresponding multiplication of students and graduates. Since 1945 ten new universities have been created, bringing the total in 1968 to forty-four, and other colleges have been raised to full university status. University status has been granted to the ten colleges of advanced technology which were so constituted in 1956.* More universities are contemplated to meet the needs of an increasing population; colleges of technology and other institutions connected with further education may well be brought under the university umbrella. There are plans to establish a University of the Air in 1970. The number of undergraduates has doubled since 1939 and is likely to be in the neighbourhood of 220,000 to 225,000 by 1971–2.

The rise in the number of universities and the subsequent

* In 1962 the Royal College of Science and Technology, Glasgow, was authorized to prepare a charter and in 1964, as the University of Strathclyde, became the first British technological university. Following the Robbins report in 1963, which recommended that colleges of Advanced Technology and the Heriot-Watt College, Edinburgh, should be given university status, nine new autonomous universities of the technological type were founded. These are Battersea, Brunel, Northampton (in London), Birmingham, Bradford, Bristol, Loughborough and Salford, and Heriot-Watt, Edinburgh, with an intake of 10,300 students in 1962–3 and probably of 21,000 in 1970. Brunel, moving to Uxbridge, became Brunel University, Bristol, the University of Bath, the city to which it has moved, Battersea, transferred to Guildford, became the University of Surrey, Bradford, the University of Bradford, Salford, the University of Salford, Birmingham, the University of Aston, and Northampton College, London, after some dispute, the City University.

315

output of graduates would not have occurred unless the outside world had wanted to utilize their services. The source of the demand has shifted, and the traditional employers of university graduates – administration, teaching, the church, the law and medicine – are beginning to be replaced by business and industry.* The requirements of these professions which are likely to absorb more and more graduates are already tending to modify the universities' courses, if indirectly, and the eagerness of industrialists to sponsor scientific research in directions in which they are particularly interested might, if it were allowed to do so, diminish the university's freedom to choose its curriculum. The number of scientists engaged in research, both post-graduate and post-doctoral, has greatly increased. There is a growing demand, doubtless influenced by the high reputation of American institutions like the school of business management at Harvard, to provide courses which are specifically designed to train the future leaders of business and industry. Many of the new universities have now rejected the stricter academic training of single-subject honours courses in favour of multi-subject courses which try to avoid the divisions inherent in traditional learning patterns and may be more stimulating and more useful to the student who does not want to be confined to a single academic discipline but hopes to gain from university a training that will be of benefit in whatever career he or she may choose from the wide range of occupations now open to both sexes.

The expansion of the universities and the changes in curriculum made or contemplated have not gone unquestioned. The very rapidity of the expansion, it is argued, has inevitably meant some lowering of academic standards, both on the part of

*The nature of the change is indicated in the figures provided by the report of the Oxford Committee for Appointments in 1964–5: 'A total of 11,829 vacancies for men was recorded, of which 8,252 called for graduates with scientific qualifications. Of 2,196 non-technical vacancies in industry and commerce, 2,165 were for arts men going down into first posts.' Yet at the moment graduates do not play a conspicuous part in modern business. In 1966 of 2,400 members of the Institute of Directors only 18 per cent had a university degree.

those who teach and those who learn. Clearly there is a short-age of first-class scholars, especially in certain departments of learning, and inevitably some of second-class calibre have been selected for university teaching posts. No doubt in terms of measurable productivity, in the form of articles in learned journals and books involving research, the present generation of university dons, though their work may be sometimes more pedantic than stimulating both in content and presentation, are an advance on their immediate predecessors, but it is doubt-ful whether there has been any real increase in actual scholar-ship and intelligence. Others have questioned whether there are enough university students of sufficient intellectual calibre to benefit from the interesting and intellectually demanding courses which the new universities have devised. The changes made in the courses of study have been under fire from two sides. Wide-ranging courses challenging specialization, it is claimed, foster intellectual superficiality. The traditionalists have also deplored the extent to which the emphasis placed on technology threatens to upset the balance of studies, while others, conscious of Britain's economic needs, have argued that as the culture of the modern world is pre-eminently scientific, science should be more solidly defined as the univer-sities' main business.

Others have seen in the present state of affairs yet another danger. The expansion of the universities and their continued maintenance has only been made possible by the very large amounts of money provided by the British taxpayer. Financial dependence has necessarily raised the question of accounta-bility which could in its turn have important implications for the universities' cherished autonomy and freedom. The scale of government expenditure on the universities is indeed unpre-cedented and likely to increase, and its possible repercussions must be closely examined.

Perhaps the most far-reaching change of all is that the univer-sities are coming to occupy a position in British society wholly different from that which they have had in the past. Until the Second World War the universities were primarily training grounds for a comparatively small segment of the country's population, its intellectual and social élite, the sons of the aristocracy and gentry and those who were likely to enter the church, teaching, the law, government service, medicine. Though they always included a minority drawn from the lower middle and working classes, they were in fact devoted to the further education of the established and professional classes. The recent increase in the number of university places with the availability of public funds to subsidize university education has led to a social revolution, if not as great a one as some progressive educationalists might desire. The social milieu from which so many undergraduates now come has made integration into the university environment, designed for another era, something of a problem. More significantly the university has become the obvious and natural apex of the educational pyramid, though still a narrow apex on a very broad base, and is the natural goal towards which the boy or girl of moderate intelligence moves from school. This in itself raises a host of problems, but it also serves to establish the university to a greater degree than ever before as the arbiter of school courses. The demands of the university establish the criteria at least for sixth-form studies. If, on the one hand, the universities' influence is likely to penetrate more and more into every channel of British life, more especially into the world of business and industry, on the other hand it already increasingly pervades the whole fabric of British education. Indeed never in history have the universities been so well placed to shape the quality and direction of the nation's life.

*

The claims and criticisms and far-reaching changes arising out of this unprecedented expansion cannot be assessed *in vacuo* or without considering the primary question of what a university should do and be. Past history would suggest that the universities thought it their task first to inculcate a set of values of an essentially religious and Christian character, secondly to foster scholarship (but hardly research in the modern meaning of the word) and thirdly to prepare their graduates for the service of church and state. With some qualifications they performed these tasks more or less effectively. The very motto of Oxford university, *Dominus illuminatio mea*, demonstrates that such values were rooted in the Christian tradition. Universities were to be places of 'sound religion and true learning', and the object of the latter was to serve the former. They aimed to produce not merely good citizens but good Christians. Their scholarship was by and large less concerned with opening new veins of knowledge than with preserving the culture of the past and handing it down in a comprehensible form. 'Universities,' Dr Whewell, the Victorian Master of Trinity, Cambridge, declared, 'so far as they are schools of *general* cultivation, represent the permanent, not the fluctuating elements of human knowledge. . . . They have to transmit the civilization of past generations to future ones, not to share and shew forth all the changing fashions of intellectual caprice and subtlety.' More recently Bonamy Dobrée asserted that the universities' main object should be the 'creation, generation by generation, in a continuous flow, of a body of men and women who share a sense of civilized values, who feel responsible for maintaining and developing them, who are unified by this culture and who by simple pressure of their existence and outlook will form and be enlightened popular opinion.'

But universities have always existed also for purely utilitarian and functional purposes. The medieval universities provided a technical training for a clerical ruling class. The Tudor and Stuart universities continued to do this, enlarging their task by paying more attention to the laity of the established orders. 'I know,' said the sixteenth-century scholar, Roger Ascham, that 'universities be instituted only that the realm may be served with preachers, lawyers and physicians.' The eighteenth-century universities failed to fulfil this objective and fell by the wayside because they failed to understand the new needs created by the changing order of society. That there has been some change in interpretation of the university's role is obvious. For one thing, while the vestigial remains of Christian belief are still with us, the universities do not accept and cannot reasonably be expected to accept a set of essentially Christian values. 'The older universities,' Sir Walter Moberly wrote in

1949 in *The Crisis in the University*, 'grew up in a world very unlike our own. Their traditional assumptions are, to some extent, out-dated and, in practice, discarded.' But, he added cogently enough, 'there is no agreed answer to the question how far this process should go and what alternative assumptions should take the place of the old'.

Modern expositions of the university's role tend to disregard this literally conservative function, less certain perhaps of what ought to be conserved, and to concentrate on a utilitarian interpretation tempered by social idealism. So the authors of the Robbins report, rightly eschewing any attempt to describe the purposes of higher education in terms of any single end, adumbrated four objectives. In the first place, higher education is designed to provide training and instruction in 'skills suitable to play a part in the general division of labour'. 'We deceive ourselves if we claim that more than a small fraction of students in institutes of higher education would be where they are if there were no significance for their future careers in what they hear and read; and it is a mistake to suppose that there is anything discreditable in this.' Yet 'what is taught should be taught in such a way as to promote the general powers of the mind'. Universities should be concerned to produce 'cultivated men and women'. They should be concerned with the advancement of learning and the search for truth. Finally the Robbins report envisaged the university as the channel for 'the transmission of a common culture and common standards of citizenship'. It is, the authors commented, 'a proper function of higher education as of education in schools, to provide in partnership with the family that background of culture and social habit upon which a healthy society depends'. The traditional functions reappear, though with a different priority. Utilitarian attitudes, however, are not allowed the last word, and more recently Lord Robbins himself has observed that he would not regard the 'maximization of growth of the gross national product' as necessarily the final criterion of policy.

The report of the Franks commission of 1966, primarily concerned with making university administration more efficient, naturally underlined the utilitarian interpretation. It stressed teaching and research as the obvious function of a university without inquiring into the reasons which make this so; the expansion of post-graduate study was accepted as a development made necessary by history. Perhaps its most obvious defect was its neglect of the personal function in university education, even if this did not come directly within its brief, its failure to pay much attention to many real undergraduate problems, such as housing and health, and to cover the pastoral side of life in a collegiate university. In many ways remarkably well-balanced, only discreetly radical, sagely aware of the interests of the colleges (though ready to delimit peripheral college benefits and to override vested interests), it only occasionally suggested that the velvet glove clothed an iron hand.

No exception can be taken to the realistic notions underlying the Robbins and Franks reports; but it is possible to add to them. The university, as I see it, has a twofold function. In the first place it is an association of scholars, engaged in teaching and research, the latter being a necessary concomitant of the former. Such teaching and research, though in some sense performed for its own sake, is necessarily related to the needs of contemporary society. But although a university's primary task may be intellectual, it can never be purely that. Concern with scholarship and true research cannot be separated from postulates of a moral and spiritual nature: a genuine sense of inquiry, a real concern for discovering the truth, the conviction that things of the mind are worth pursuing, a concern with exactness and precision, an ability to weigh evidence, and above all else intellectual integrity. Some of these, as has been well said, are 'presuppositions inherent in the undoubted task of the university, some postulates without which it cannot proceed'. Cumulatively they form a sense of value which is essential to the well-being of a civilization. It was lack of these that made the German universities, in other ways the most distinguished homes of scholarship and research of their time, susceptible to becoming the compliant tools of National Socialism. The university cannot be simply concerned with the accumulation of knowledge; it must pursue the cultivation of truth, goodness and beauty, of social equality and freedom. It must see as its primary task the formation, cultivation and transmission of a sense of value. It is, or ought to be, as much a school of morals as a community of scholars and teachers.

*

If we accept that one purpose of the modern university is to stimulate intellectual achievement relevant to contemporary society and that the other is to provide society with a sense of values – and there is likely to be less agreement about the second than about the first – then we must ask how the universities measure up to these criteria. It is not very plain that modern universities hold any very precisely articulated values. For lack of confidence in any larger role, they seem to cling for the most part to a rather superficial utilitarianism, and often appear not as schools for the development of the whole man, but as workshops in which a particular craft can be taught or the elements of a subject acquired. The absence of any real sense of community in most universities outside Oxford and Cambridge, though some of the newer universities are evidently anxious to establish one, and the attitude to members of the teaching staff who are often treated as employees with little or no say in the formation of business or the conduct of affairs, are symptoms of the malaise. This failure to admit or transmit any real sense of value is deeply embedded in the contemporary situation. The universities are not, of course, alone in being unsure of their values, though one might look to them to make the moral and intellectual effort necessary to discover or recreate them. The need is less obvious in the sciences than the arts, which long rested on the cultural heritage, shared at least by the established classes, of humanistic studies embracing the classics, theology, history, literature, and mathematics. But the confidence of the humanists in their capacity both to lead and to instruct, shaken by the stress on science and social change, is far less than it was even half a century ago.* It becomes plain that teachers of the

* See the articles in *Crisis in the Humanities*, ed. J. H. Plumb, Penguin Books, 1964.

humanities have to think out their subjects anew, to work out new evaluations and interpretations and to recast them so that they may be relevant to the educational and social needs of the modern world.

If there is a considerable degree of confusion as to the purpose of a university among dons and university administrators, it is hardly surprising that there should be signs of frustration and apathy among university students. The expansion of the universities has led to the creation of an intellectual proletariat – their junior members – many of whom share no real involvement in their university, either as a home of scholarship or as a community. In Britain this crisis is not yet as severe as elsewhere. There is nothing quite comparable to what is being said about many contemporary American universities, what, for instance, Professor Baly in his book *Academic Illusion* * describes as the 'developing break-down in classroom relations between the student and the professor, each feeling frustrated and betrayed because he is unable to get what he thinks is his due', a disintegration of community 'evident in the desperate loneliness of so many students, the emotional disturbances, the poor work, the irresponsibility, the excessive drinking, the wild parties, and the constant apathy'.

Yet the 1960s have witnessed a relatively new phenomenon in university life, that of student militancy, the significance of which it is as yet difficult to assess. In Britain it led to troublesome scenes of protest in 1967–8 at some universities, notably Essex, Leicester and the London School of Economics. Basically it appeared to be a reaction against the accepted values of existing society, more especially at the American way of life and the war in which the Americans were involved in Vietnam. In so far as it has a positive philosophy (and in content its leaders' affirmations seem more negative than positive), it draws its inspiration from the writings of Marx, Trotsky and the American philosopher Herbert Marcuse, and it has made Mao Tse-tung, Ho Chi Minh and the guerilla fighter Che Guevara its folk heroes. Although it is mainly a protest, sometimes violent in form, against the established political

* Denis Baly, *Academic Illusion*, S.P.C.K., 1961, pp. 50–51.

and economic order, its most extreme spokesmen aim to secure student control over the government and curriculum of the universities. 'As far as the universities are concerned,' an Oxford undergraduate observed in 1968, 'we want them run on a completely democratic basis. We want them run on the assumption that every member of a university is an adult and capable of participating in its affairs.'

The more extreme radical students and their fellow-sympathizers among the junior lecturers believe that the British universities as they are now constituted are a sinister expression of the established order in society, whether they act as parasites or exploiters, and that they condition their students by an outmoded and archaic syllabus, an arbitrary examination system and an authoritarian method of government, all designed in the interests of the governing class. The radicals' critique thus stems from their repudiation of the values of the bourgeois society in which, and by which, they live, which they find morally and spiritually bankrupt, and which they claim the universities exist to maintain and foster. If the universities could be taken over by the students, or rather by the self-appointed minority of revolutionaries, they could form a spearhead for changing society itself, acting as ' "red bases" ' of revolutionary agitation and preparation 'to guide the working class to final victory', or, alternatively, by transforming the universities, the students could frustrate the objects of the capitalistic society which increasingly depends for its effective control on the production of skilled graduates, 'a crucial mechanism in the maintenance of the capitalist relations of production'. Their demands are plain enough, for 'the power of students to determine the structure and content of their education',* that is, to gain control over the administration of the universites (in which professors and lecturers, together with laboratory assistants, cleaners and cooks, will apparently have parity of esteem with their pupils), of their curricula (which will be revised according to the suppositious philosophy, neo-Marxist in character, by

* Alexander Cockburn in *Student Power*, Penguin Books, 1969, p. 14, from which the other quotations in this and the following paragraph are taken.

which, the revolutionaries seek to interpret all learning), and of their examinations, where this old-fashioned practice is allowed to continue; and finally, 'to capture the structure of British culture'. While the student radicals profess to be anti-authoritarian, their movement is far from anarchistic. It is basically totalitarian, anti-democratic and illiberal, even in its outward manifestation neo-fascist; it is difficult to believe that many of Britain's university teachers would remain long in office once the student radicals achieved their aims unless they assented to the essential radical dogmas, or that moderate opinion among the students themselves would be tolerated for very long. Many of the student leaders are dedicated, highly intelligent men but so obsessed with semi-millennarian concepts that they are quite willing to impose minority rule over the apathetic majority, 'to inflict, if necessary, sanctions of sufficient economic, social, or political magnitude to force its opinions to be heeded', and are not only intolerant of those with whom they disagree but readily employ every device, including slander and false rumour, intimidation and force, to achieve their ends.

Their analysis of the corruptions of society and even of the universities is often penetrating. University syllabuses have been too inelastic, discipline too paternalistic, administration too top-heavy, the purpose of higher education too closely aligned 'to train the flood of technicians and manipulators which neo-capitalism ... demands'. But the remedy which the radicals offer, as far as the pattern of the university is concerned, appears more repellent than the disease. To those who still believe that universities and colleges can be communities of teachers and scholars (a notion which the revolutionaries seem explicitly to disavow, 'as illusory as the philosophy of the guild system in the first stages of the industrial revolution' since students and teachers must be in 'inherent and permanent conflict'), who hold that dialogue and discussion with people of differing views are a necessary element in any worthwhile civilization, who regard any form of authoritarianism, even if popular in origin, as a contravention of true freedom, the radical concept of a university must seem profoundly depressing. That it bears little resemblance to traditional British universities can hardly be a matter of regret to the revolutionary student, but for scholars who still believe in the evolution of society rather than in revolution, there can be no compromise with those who seek to destroy rather than to reform the existing universities. Universities, by historic necessity reflections of the contemporary social spectrum, have always numbered radical idealists among their dons and these men, sometimes after prolonged struggles, have generally triumphed over ingrained conservatism. It seems probable that if the political and economic situation remains relatively stable, reformers are more likely than the revolutionaries to change the universities' structure in future years, for if the final objectives of the radicals are clear enough, their programme seems festooned with nihilistic confusion. No one can predict, however, what changes the next few decades may have in store or how far the revolutionary movement may profit from the moral and intellectual vacuum which engulfs so many students. Even in the British universities where the problems seem fundamentally different from those in their massive American, Asiatic and continental counterparts, student radicalism is certainly a meaningful and significant force which cannot be lightly dismissed. At least it has had the merit of making universities look more critically at their traditions and purpose.

In Britain student militancy has a voluble but numerically small following. Sympathetic and impressionable undergraduates are, however, easily engineered or manipulated by left-wing pressure groups into giving their support to confrontations with the university authorities; this was notably the case at the London School of Economics which was closed for several weeks in 1969 as a result of agitation among the students. Student radicalism has almost certainly contributed to the division already existing between the university world and the mass of the citizens who tend to regard the students as a privileged élite supported by taxes paid by the community. Yet it would be wrong to dismiss the movement simply as an eccentric and ephemeral demonstration of the wide-spread frustration felt by contemporary youth. Its international solidarity, if largely negative, has shown that the cult extends into the eastern as well as the western world. The demand for full student power, the claim to control or to participate with the senior members on equal terms, would seem arrogant and unreasonable. The senior members who spend their whole lives in the service of the university, who are men of greater experience and maturity, have more claims to determine the university's life than a transient generation of students, only a minority of whom are effectively interested in what goes on. Yet, having said this, there may well be good grounds for seeking to ensure a greater element of student participation in university affairs, for securing more facilities for consultation and joint discussion about those questions which directly involve undergraduates. The university authorities will never be able to meet the demands of the extreme radicals, who have as yet only a very small following.* But they well may find it expedient to conciliate those students who may later be persuaded to take a more extremist line. The greater the degree of integration between the senior and junior members of the university, the happier and more purposeful the society itself is likely to be.

If British universities are relatively free from the more disquieting features of some American and continental universities, this is in part because a measure of integration has been achieved but in part because of the apathy which seems often to characterize them. 'Most of the young people I met at universities,' Maurice Punch, a member of the Research Centre in Education located at King's College, Cambridge, wrote in *New Society* in 1968,

were ordinary, dull, mundane, inarticulate, pedestrian, apolitical, ill-informed philistine sheep who no doubt faithfully reflected their background and who seemed so 'unintelligent' as to raise grave doubts as to the efficacy of current selection procedures. But then this could be said of most of the staff too – and in mitigation I must

---

*In 1967 two students at Sussex, one an American, threw red paint at a visiting speaker from the U.S. Embassy. Subsequently the vice-chancellor rusticated the two men. An attempt was made to initiate a strike of students in protest at this action. Of the 3,000 students in the university 1,200 attended a meeting but 1,100 of them approved the action taken by the university authorities.

add that nearly all these young people were conscientious, hard-working, God-fearing, conventional, bourgeois men and women with a healthy respect for love, marriage, domesticity, a stable career.

Moreover if we use the words 'intellectual apathy' to characterize the modern university, it must be clearly understood that there was almost certainly less interest in learning, less good work done, among the student population before the Second World War than there is now. Against this it may be urged that although the undergraduate was sometimes more of a playboy, more indifferent to scholarship and often of very meagre academic attainments, yet in some degree he had inherited a cultural background and a sense of value, even though he made little use of them. But it is not suggested that earlier generations were better suited to university life than their successors; past history would suggest that the reverse is true. It is simply that the great expansion of the university population, the social change which this represents, the larger changes in modes and morals, and an atmosphere of political uncertainty, make it particularly difficult for the modern student to find his bearings.

Through no fault of its own the present generation of university students, although probably more mature physically than its predecessors, is inadequately prepared for the strains and stresses of university life. This is partly because most schools have not yet adjusted themselves, except on the strictly academic plane, to the generally accepted fact that the university is the natural sequel to school life for their more intelligent pupils, and do not encourage them to think why they are going there or what its object is. 'They come,' a young Balliol tutor has written recently,* 'without intellectual interest or moral sense of direction because it is the done thing to do. ... The New Student is able, but lacking in any interest or drive, both in scholastic work and in the conduct of life.' This judgement is supported by substantial evidence, though this is harder to find at the older universities (and possibly at the

* R. M. Ogilvie in *The Expanding University*, ed. W. R. Niblett, Faber, 1962, p. 86.

newest). Many students drift into the universities simply because they want to secure a degree which will enable them to get a job that can act as a passport into the professional middle class; they come to the university, as many students have come in every age, to gain social and material advantages in later life. There can be no objection to this motive in itself, but as a result many undergraduates do a modicum of work without any real involvement or enthusiasm. Their contact with senior members is often slight or non-existent, and a meeting when it occurs may be fraught with embarrassment and superficiality on both sides. The university, Professor Butterfield has said,* should be 'the arena in which there is to occur the electric contact between teacher and pupil', but there is too often a prolonged power-cut. As a result of the tepid character of their intellectual interests, undergraduates' conversation may be ill-informed and philistine, and their way of life is still sometimes unduly boorish and juvenile. Some of the activities of the so-called rag weeks indicate an absence both of taste and of a sense of public responsibility, and help to invalidate the occasional demands made by junior members for participation in university government. The exceedingly poor quality of much university journalism betrays a latent and continuing immaturity of outlook, the more sinister because it appears sometimes equally characteristic of the national newspapers on which the graduates find employment. Many, though this is said in no censorious way, have a defective moral perception, and little sense of community. Even at Oxford and Cambridge the character of college life is imperceptibly changing, for a minority of undergraduates dislike the institutional atmosphere and would prefer to live a private life rather than to converse in hall while they take their common meals. This trend may appear the more perturbing as the new universities were founded with the deliberate intention of encouraging residence. In 1938 41·7 per cent of all students lived at home whereas in 1961 no more than 21·9 per cent did so. For good or ill it is doubtful whether colleges will

*H. Butterfield, *The Universities and Education Today*, Routledge & Kegan Paul, 1962, p. 8.

ever again create the loyalties, the almost romantic pull that they exerted in the past over their old members; few will re-echo Newman's sentiment that a college constituted a 'second home, not so tender, but more noble and majestic and authoritative'. At many universities the union constitutes a monolithic structure, absorbing far too much of the energy of a few students but rarely creating a genuine sense of community.

No moral judgement is intended by these statements, most of which apply to a sizeable minority rather than to the majority of undergraduates. Yet a state of affairs in which the university is treated (and perhaps because of its approach to its students is deservedly treated) as a kind of second-class workshop, from which a student, however intelligent he may be, can emerge without much understanding of the function of a university is salutary neither for the university nor for the community. Many students have been provided with a kind of package deal and have never been confronted with the challenge offered by scholarship or even by existence itself. There is a real danger that the universities can become, in the words of a recent report, 'factories for the processing of human material'. They may embrace certain values, but for the most part these have been obscured from view. All universities have long had to live with problems of this sort and they will continue to have to do so; but this is no excuse for pretending that they do not exist.

These problems demonstrate how necessary it is for the universities to think out more clearly and to proclaim more explicitly their true function. If their primary job must be to teach and to further research, they have also a social and moral responsibility. 'What the student needs from his university,' the first vice-chancellor of Sussex has said, is not merely a

refining and furthering of his intellectual competence and skill in his chosen field; he does not go there only to become a master of his subject. ... If he sets about his task in the right way, decisively important qualities of character and personality will be added to his intellectual development; in addition to becoming master of his subject he will also become master of himself, learn to think independently and resourcefully; and come to maturity in a society which, through its own characteristic way of life, will enrich him in proportion as he enriches it.

This is fine, but there is a gap between the ideal and the reality. The university can no longer be the arbiter of student morals or impose a rigid moral code, yet it cannot merely condemn or ignore those things which it regards as socially and morally dangerous. It has some responsibility for assisting the students to work out a moral code or even a philosophy of existence for themselves. It cannot or should not be altogether indifferent to sexual promiscuity, drug-taking or alcoholism any more than it can disregard infectious diseases or mental ill-health or ignore intellectual dishonesty. It may well have no right to impose regulations, since many dons will disagree among themselves about, for instance, standards of sexual morality, but it has a responsibility to foster discussion, to promote understanding, to provide for physical and mental health services, to show concern in those matters which affect the development of the whole man. It is not its job to teach morals or to mould character, but to provide the means by which both may be more clearly understood and those who study there may be the better able to work out a purposeful solution for themselves. Justifiably the modern student resents any form of dictation and even direction, but many would welcome greater opportunity for consultation and counsel. Just as greater attention to working out syllabuses which are likely to arouse the interest of the undergraduate might do something to alleviate his intellectual apathy, so some concern to cultivate a sense of values would do something to make the university more than a mere teaching and examining institution. If students and teachers are to be involved in the society and scholarship which a university represents, they should be affected by the integrity of outlook which ought to be its outstanding feature.

If these general criticisms of modern universities may be allowed to contain a grain of truth, what of some of the particular questions which are closely associated with them? What, for instance, of the courses which the universities provide for the first degree? The specialized degree course offered by some universities, *par excellence* by Oxford, stands comparison with any others in the world as the training of the mind. Clearly the first degree courses of most British universities compare very favourably with the series of grades and tests offered by the majority of American universities. For a future lecturer or professor, research worker or teacher, few better courses could be devised and there is undoubtedly still much truth in the saying that 'a young man destined for a career in public life … is best prepared by a rigorous apprenticeship to scholarship shared with those who will be the scholars of their generation'. Here alone, it may well be said, will he be trained intensively and in depth. The subject that he studies matters little so long as his mind has been fully stretched and enriched. What the future business executive gains in his three years of university life (which incidentally may do much to deprive him of his facility for early rising, promptness in the despatch of business, tidiness of appearance and an aptitude for the regular and consistent work which his future job will require of him), is a training of the mind which will make him the better able to use his intelligence. No one will deny that there is much in this argument, and it would be the greatest pity if all such courses were discarded.

But the student who like most of his kind has no intention of entering on an academic career and who has no great interest in intellectual activity *per se* may be forgiven for asking in what way the knowledge of English medieval history fits a man for employment by the Metal Box Company or an acquaintance with sixteenth-century French drama prepares him for life as an oil salesman or some understanding of eighteenth-century English literature equips him to be a good advertising executive. The specialized one-subject course may not be the best training for such a student, and some of the intellectual apathy that is so depressing a feature of his life may be traced to the seeming irrelevance of much of the work which he has to do. Too much of the work for the degree course is performed without genuine interest, and becomes rather a recitation of facts culled from an elementary text book than a judicious and thoughtful assessment of evidence. University examinations are really geared to the making of dons; the man with the first class degree, the potential professor and fellow of the Royal Society, is the university's pride and joy. This is appropriate to the university's primary role of training an intellectual élite, the future scholars and scientists as essential for the well-being of a civilized and prosperous society as the farmers who till the soil and the men who make and run the machines. But it cannot be said to cater adequately for the non-academic students, now so numerous, who are attending the university because this is the means by which they are going to get a better job in later life. In their case the traditional methods do not fulfil the prime task of training the mind, let alone the second, of cultivating a sense of value; and for them more multi-subject courses and a greater degree of professional training should perhaps be made available.

It is fair to say that many of the recently founded universities have tried to make good these deficiencies. With some exceptions at York, single-subject honour courses have been rejected in favour of multi-subject courses modelled on new patterns. The university of Sussex has created schools of studies rather than separate departments. Students are able to opt for English and American studies, European studies, African and Asian studies, physical studies, social studies, biological sciences or engineering sciences. The preliminary course requires three papers, one in the field of study which the undergraduate intends to take as his main degree course, one in general history and one on language and values which will involve a thorough study of the nature and justification of value judgements, especially of moral judgements and judgements about society and policy. 'The type of curriculum offered,' the first vice-chancellor of the University, Dr J. S. Fulton, has said, 'matches the mood and, one hopes, the needs also, of many school-leavers of high ability.' A similar pattern is being followed at East Anglia where the first degree provides for a progressively more specialized course of studies, the intention being to give a broad introduction which will enable the student eventually to study an individual subject in depth in one or other of the seven schools of English, European and social studies, fine arts, chemical sciences, mathematics and physics, and biological sciences. Essex insists on a compulsory science paper in the first year. More and more universities may have to provide courses of a purely vocational character: the new university of Warwick has instituted a course in business management and an Institute of Business Management has been set up at Oxford, partly under the aegis of the university. Many of the older universities in fact are well aware of the problem and are seeking to adjust their courses to contemporary needs. Oxford has established an honour school of economics and engineering that provides a course of study obviously relevant to the world of business and industry. The Kneale committee has made important proposals for modifying the Oxford one-subject honour courses,* and, in addition to recommending that the undergraduates may have an opportunity for taking two examinations of medium size, it has asked that provision should be made for combinations of subjects. But if the traditional curriculum of the British university, less than a century old even at Oxford and Cambridge, does not necessarily meet the requirements of students of the expanding universities and some of the professions which they intend to enter, it is nonetheless vital that the older disciplines, tried by time, should not be flung overboard. What is needed is a situation in which both kinds of programme are made available.

If this is the state of affairs in university teaching, what of the research which is its concomitant and the supplier of some at least of the source material? How relevant is it to contemporary society? Teaching is necessarily fertilized by research, which the authors of the Robbins report define as a 'convenient portmanteau word to cover the wide range of intellectual activities that serve to increase man's power to understand, evaluate and modify his world and his experience'. At every university there has been a great increase in the number of research students. At Oxford the proportion of research students rose from a tenth of the total in 1939 to a

* An honour school of history and modern languages was instituted in 1967; and other proposals for combined courses have been accepted and more are under consideration.

fifth in 1960, and the Franks report envisages a further increase
in number and the more satisfactory assimilation of the research
students in the college set-up. In science research has become
almost a *sine qua non* for the man of average capacity. The
point and importance of scientific research, quite often directly
connected with (and sometimes patronized by) industry, needs
no labouring. Moreover the scientific research worker is normally a member of a team, engaged in a project which can be
integrated into the programme of his laboratory.

His arts colleague is differently placed. He is often doing
research on an individual topic which he may only be able to
discuss with his supervisor whom he sees at infrequent in-
tervals, and the efficacity of many research projects in the arts
is questionable. Whether a man of second-class ability, without
genuine academic ambition, benefits himself or the community
by spending two or three years grubbing up all the material he
can find on an obscure topic the elucidation of which adds
only minimally to the sum of human knowledge and not at all
to human happiness is doubtful. There are grounds for thinking
that research in arts subjects at most British universities could
be more effectively organized. Many of them still leave their
research students in arts severely on their own and American
graduate courses are in this respect often very much better.
The Oxford B. Phil. degree designed a few years ago to provide
a course of an intermediary character, combining some of the
essentials of a written examination with a degree thesis, is a
more respectable academic exercise than some doctoral theses.
Peter Laslett has suggested that Oxford and Cambridge should
gradually become post-graduate institutions, a view that might
possibly have attracted Mark Pattison a century ago. The two
older universities with their libraries, laboratories and specialized teaching are far better equipped to provide a favourable
environment for research than many other universities. While
there can be little doubt that more of their students than in the
past will be doing research, yet, quite apart from the loss to the
other universities which the concentration of post-graduate
research would necessarily entail, something would surely be
lost, from the standpoint of both the older and the younger

man, if the two were not blended together into the community.

It is only with reference to the purposes of the university in the twentieth century that the rise of other institutions to university status can be considered. Here again the critics have urged that a move of this kind must inevitably result in a debasement of the university, both by narrowing its intellectual foundation and by lowering its standards. In any case the colleges of advanced technology, as we have noted, are already destined to become full universities, and they are beginning to fulfil this role. Most of these colleges provide a four-year course, alternating six months in college with six months in industry. They also try to provide the elements of an education in liberal subjects, which is more than most of the scientific and engineering departments of the older universities seek to do. The Heriot-Watt university at Edinburgh, for instance, has three faculties, science, engineering and humanities, twelve professors and over a thousand students. Better American colleges of this type such as the famous Massachusetts Institute of Technology, founded in 1865, have demonstrated their capacity to engender a liberal culture as well as to help bridge the gap which exists between pure and applied science.

It is doubtful whether the as yet amorphous 'University of the Air' will deserve its grandiose title, for while it will transmit lectures by men of outstanding reputation, and meet an occupational need on the part of those who cannot attend full university courses, it must lack that personal contact between teacher and student which should be an intrinsic feature of a British university. It has been suggested that colleges of education should be brought within the framework of the universities; already some seventeen or eighteen, Oxford among them, have agreed to award the degree of bachelor of education to their members.* These colleges are to date one of the worst affected legatees of university expansion. Like the schools they have lost potential staff to the new universities.

* At Oxford where three colleges are involved – Westminster, Culham and Wheatley – it is anticipated that the candidates will in the first instance form 7½ per cent of the total, rising to about 15 per cent in 1970 and 20 per cent in 1975.

Inevitably their standards, which have never been high, have been lowered, at least for entrance. One sympathizes with their wish to be associated with the universities, but they can only claim in a very indirect sense to be sponsoring advanced teaching and research. If therefore there is much to be said for bringing them into closer association with the universities, it is important to ensure that the standard of the degrees awarded to their members should be fully maintained. There is, and has long been, a considerable variation between the academic reputations of the different universities, as of faculties within them, and it would be a mistake to let this become too great, or to follow the American example and increase the number of universities by admitting institutions, admirable in themselves, which are yet below what is ordinarily demanded of a university in the form of advanced teaching and research.

These then are some of the features, good and bad, of the twentieth-century university. What should its role be in the future? It will not differ essentially from that of any other educational institution except in so far as it must be in a real sense a centre of scholarship and research, and more than any other school or college it must never lose sight of its concern to prepare the students for life in the world, to be a school of values, established not through a system of indoctrination or inculcation but by common discussion, research, experience and true education. Because the university will be dealing with intelligent adolescents its methods will differ appreciably from those of the normal school, even though it may pursue a similar objective. The courses which the universities offer will form both an intellectual discipline, a first-class mental training and a preparation for a vocation or a professional career. However, the great, overriding aim of the university is the pure pursuit of knowledge, free from social, political and dogmatic limitations. 'I have never done anything "useful",' commented the eminent Cambridge mathematician, G. H. Hardy. 'No discovery of mine has made or is likely to make, directly or indirectly, for good or ill, the least difference to the amenity of the world.' It is as well to recall so forthright a tribute to genuine scholarship in the utilitarian atmosphere of twentieth-century education. It is in the light of this twofold purpose, as a centre both for intellectual and for moral training, that the university must be seen as the desirable and natural apex of the educational pyramid, the final rung on the ladder of educational achievement, and school courses must be logically interlocked with its requirements for entrance.

If this is so it may well be argued that universities ought to open their doors to all who seek admission or possess the minimal requirements for entry. For centuries the university made few demands on its aspiring students; entrance examinations and matriculation requirements were mostly an invention of the nineteenth century. Many American and continental universities make only minimal demands on their entrants. To confine university entrance to a supposed intellectual élite might seem a contravention of the principles of democracy. It has been argued that, as is the practice in the United States where a third of the relevant age group secure entry to some form of higher education, everyone ought to have the right to avail himself or herself of a university course. 'I do not see,' Peter Marris writes,* 'on what principle of justice a university education can be denied to anyone who genuinely wants it, and believes he can gain from it, whatever occupation his abilities suit him to. We shall never reconcile the inconsistency of our democratic ideals until we can adapt the aims of universities to different levels of intellectual skills.'

This may be an honourable aim, but given the present situation any attempt to implement it would have catastrophic results. To begin with, it must be remembered that the American state does not pay for its undergraduates to the same extent as the British, and for the British state to provide university education on an American scale is, bluntly, out of the question on economic grounds for the foreseeable future. Secondly, unlimited entry would involve a prodigious degree of wastage, since students who do not make the grade at the end of their first year could clearly not be allowed to continue. This wastage is already large enough in some universities to be

* *The Experience of Higher Education*, Routledge & Kegan Paul, 1964, p. 184.

THE PROBLEM OF THE MODERN UNIVERSITY

disturbing.* The results of wastage include, as well as the drain on the country's money, a great loss of teaching time and an incalculable degree of personal frustration. Thirdly, and independently of any economic argument, cluttering the university's precincts with even more young men and women with no genuine intellectual interests would further dilute the intensity of such intellectual activity as exists. Finally a university's freedom (and at collegiate universities a college's freedom) to select its own students constitutes an academic privilege which ought not to be easily surrendered. In the present circumstances it is more expedient that higher education should be regarded as a restricted luxury (and people generally, it may be said without cynicism, value more what is not freely available) for the very large minority who can properly enjoy it rather than as a kind of British restaurant for the many who neither have the capacity nor the powers of appreciation to make good use of it. Whatever may be said in favour of a doctrinaire equality of entry, economic, social and academic reasons suggest strongly that minimal academic requirements should not by themselves be enough to open the door of the university to every aspiring student.

Inevitably any such expansion of university intake would require the academic standards for entry to be lowered. Already the reliability and the level of these are a cause of some concern. The minimal academic requirements in England and Wales are generally taken to be two passes at A level in the General Certificate of Education,† though it is held that these do not in themselves give adequate evidence of the intellectual capacity to benefit from a university course; particular qualifications are demanded for entry to the different courses. Much has been done to secure uniformity of entry through the Universities' Central Council on Admissions established in

* At British universities, apart from Oxford and Cambridge, where the failure rate is about 5 per cent, about 14 per cent fail to complete their course.

† In 1956, 27,000 candidates obtained 2 or more A levels; there were 21,000 university places. In 1966 75,000 obtained 2 or more A levels; there were 43,000 university entrants.

1961, but certain problems remain which affect both schools and universities. Some of these arise from unrecognized differences in the standards adopted by the various examining boards, so that an A grade of one board would not be judged an A grade by another. Some injustice may very well result at this level. Moreover though the examining is carried on in the main conscientiously and under the ultimate supervision of an experienced examiner, it is occasionally wildly wide of the mark, for the work of examining is hard, often monotonous and confined to a limited space of time so that boards have grave difficulties in recruiting examiners.*

In general the entry system represents a rough justice, but even within its own terms there are still doubts as to its validity for deciding entry to the university. This is one reason why the colleges of Oxford and Cambridge, except for one group of colleges at the latter, only consider A level results in special cases, relying for the most part on their own entrance examination on which they award entrance scholarships and exhibitions. This system, as the report of the Franks commission has suggested, is badly in need of reform since it can no longer be claimed that a scholarship is awarded to a poor boy to enable him to come to a university; there is every reason to believe that the number will in future be severely cut, and eventually abolished.† The Franks commission has intimated that there should be a national university entrance examination, but whether such an examination is necessary would seem to depend upon the extent to which the existing G.C.E. examination can be reformed. The multiplicity of boards and syllabuses, the different standards by which they seem to oper-

---

* But the suggestion that the examining should be done by the schools themselves must perpetrate even greater injustice.

† In 1964–5 the Oxford men's colleges made 695 open and 73 closed awards (by comparison with 501 made by the Cambridge colleges); in one Oxford college, Queen's, award-holders accounted for 72 per cent of places. The Franks commission recommended the abolition of all closed awards and the reduction of all other awards to approximately 10 per cent of the college intake. Colleges have recently reduced the number of their awards, and contemporary opinion is veering slowly in favour of their abolition, at least as a means of entry to the universities.

ate, would appear to make this desirable. Furthermore the examinations have been criticized, but not with complete justice, as promoting 'gratuitous competitive pressures, premature specialization, and narrowing of curriculum'.

Although the most obvious impact of the universities on society is through their output of graduates, they exercise an equally important indirect influence, through their entrance requirements and the training of future teachers, on the curricula of schools. And not only through their entrance requirements: what the schools teach in their upper forms, shaped as it is by the A level or separate entrance exam, is related ultimately to the needs of the degree courses. The A level syllabus, except for those subjects which the students start afresh at the university such as law, often amounts to a preparatory university course. Although the university entrance examiners may disclaim any wish to deal with this sort of material and argue that what they are looking for is promise rather than performance – often, it must be feared, a pretty illusory objective – they are almost necessarily influenced by the fact that many of the better candidates will already have covered a part of the degree syllabus and that, for instance in history, they will be acquainted with recent historical controversies and with the more important articles in the learned journals. In other words many able pupils are virtually covering a university course in their sixth-form year, to the detriment of their interest in the work they may eventually do in the university as well as of their general education. While the specialized honour course at a British university remains one of the finest academic trainings in the world, it is doubtful whether the degree of specialization it encourages in many school sixth forms is in the true interests either of the schools or of the universities to which many of their pupils will go. With the advent of more wide-ranging courses at the universities it would be wise to overhaul the existing system of university entry and consequently what dictates the pattern of teaching in the sixth form; in many ways there is more to be said for modifying or reorientating the General Certificate of Education than for initiating a new university entrance examination.

At the moment the General Certificate of Education lies betwixt a general leaving certificate and a university entrance examination. In time as an increasing number of boys and girls from the sixth form enter the university it must surely become more and more the latter. What its components should be is not a matter which can be discussed here, but sooner or later schools and universities must work together to adapt it more effectively to their needs.

All this activity, or at least the greatest part of it, is made possible by money supplied by the British taxpayer. Hence the universities are accountable to the nation, or more precisely to the Treasury. What, it must be asked, ought to be the boundaries to government control? It could be claimed that he who pays the piper has the right to call the tune, to the extent of re-organizing university courses, governing the right of entry, making and confirming appointments, as well as exerting a direct control over expenditure. It may seem ludicrous in present circumstances to suggest that any government would go so far in its contravention of academic freedom. There are, however, disquieting hints that paternalistic statism, smothering its critics by the seeming benevolence of its intentions, could promote a silent revolution. So far the Treasury grants have been administered by the apparently independent body, the University Grants Committee; but there are indications that the U.G.C. has been placed on the defensive by the Treasury. Without consulting the universities the government decided in 1967 to raise the fees of overseas students. Grants to universities were made conditional from 1968 on the Comptroller and Auditor-General being given access to the books and records of the U.G.C. and the universities. The U.G.C. itself for the first time in 1967 issued a memorandum on 'general guidance' which amounted in effect to a national strategy which universities would be well advised to follow. Although the universities still enjoy the discretion to expend the block grants they receive from the government as they wish, there are undoubtedly hints of more rigid supervision and control to come. Some people argue that the U.G.C. has outlived its usefulness and that the universities should be brought, like the schools, fairly and squarely under the authority of the Ministry of Science and Education, ultimately answerable to the *diktat* of a minister and under the control of the Civil Service. Although the universities strongly criticized the proposal to place them under the supervision of a department of the Ministry, no notice was paid to their protest, and the measure came into effect in April 1964.

The implications of full government control must not be underestimated. In the long run it could lead not merely to examining catering accounts and vetting the purchase of electric light bulbs, but to the appointment of committees at the discretion of the minister to apportion stipends (which in a sense is already being done), to review and revise syllabuses, to inspect teaching, to demand proof of productivity before promotion, indeed to run rather than to exercise a remote-control supervision over the universities. There is already a tendency to treat the don like the civil servant and the factory manager, measuring his effectiveness in his profession in terms of his output and research. No one would deny that occasional drones exist, but the carrying of some passengers is a risk that the state must accept in the interests of the whole.

In fact every move which permits more direct government control is tantamount to a loss of independence. As Professor Brook has cogently observed, 'Vortigern invited the intervention of Hengist and Horsa but found that withdrawal was not part of their plan.' All this may seem an unlikely prospect, an academic 1984, but it is not completely out of the question. 'Nothing,' Lord Radcliffe told a group of vice-chancellors, 'is more important at this stage of our social development than that academic freedom should be preserved. What then do I see as involved in academic freedom? I mean diversity instead of uniformity, liberty to swim against the tide. What I fear is the benevolent application of principles exactly the reverse, appropriate enough to the organization of a factory, inculcated by men who do not understand that in the pursuit of knowledge, the cultivation of the intellect, the art of teaching, the only certainly false doctrine is a belief in certainty. He who

pays the piper calls the tune and generally experience has shown
that he had much better not.'

> Afar will Democracy chase it,
> That gang of impenitent dons,
> Who drowned the soft murmur of *Placet*
> By bawling their truculent *Nons*.

'Academic freedom,' R. M. Hutchins, a distinguished American scholar, rightly commented, 'is simply a way of saying we
get the best results in education and research if we leave their
management to people who know something about them.' The
preservation of liberty, as always, demands constant vigilance.

Whether the universities are particularly well-placed to take
a lead in this matter may be doubted. No one can be entirely
complacent: the system is imperfect and could be bettered. The
continuance of abuses offers an irresistible temptation to would-
be reformers and angry young men.* The universities do not
present a homogeneous front. Many of the modern universities are suspicious and resentful of the seemingly privileged
position of Oxford and Cambridge; nor can the latter by
reason of their particular administrative and collegiate set-up
(which some radicals would ruthlessly destroy) fit easily into
the uniform framework beloved of bureaucrats. There is a
body available for negotiation, the so-called Committee of
Principals and Vice-Chancellors, a caucus of high-powered
administrators in which the vice-chancellors of Oxford and
Cambridge are apt to appear as impermanent amateurs; but it
is doubtful whether this really represents university opinion.
The University Grants Committee conducts impartial and

---

*The point is illustrated by a recent controversy. The graduate college
at Oxford, All Souls, has been thought to have been unduly slow in
implementing proposals made by the Royal Commission in 1922 and in
making good use of its considerable financial resources. This led to an
explosive article in *Encounter* (March 1966) by a former fellow, David
Caute, who apparently had no qualms of conscience in releasing information which had been confidential to him as a fellow. Later the Franks
Report severely castigated the college, though it had by that time made
arrangements to deploy some of its funds by instituting a system of
visiting fellowships.

sympathetic investigation into the universities' financial needs by a system of visitations, but it is under constant fire from the Treasury and the Committee of Estimates. Sooner or later some other body, unofficial in character (there already exists a kind of university trades union, the Association of University Teachers, which has done some good work in safeguarding salaries), may have to be established to ensure that if the universities play their part, their freedom to determine their own destinies within the limits bounded by legitimate government interference will be fully respected.

Much of this chapter has been critical and may well provoke disagreement. But, all things considered, it would be wrong to close on a sombre note. Great changes cannot take place without incidental growing pains. Inevitably wrong decisions are made, inevitably an element of confusion and obscurity persists. If an English schoolboy has less chance of attending a university than his contemporaries in some other countries (but it would not be too complacent to add what universities some of these are!) at least once he gets there he will be better instructed and almost certainly receive more personal attention. The ratio of staff to students in British universities is higher than elsewhere: 1 to 8 as against 1 to 12 in the U.S.S.R., 1 to 13 in the U.S.A. and 1 to 30 in France. Although the actual cost of British universities to the state is far less than it is in many other countries, proportionately to the number of students, the student's grant, though often the cause of complaint, is likely to be on a more generous scale. In the Scandinavian and West German universities the students are financed by a combination of outright grants and loans. In Sweden the student may enjoy a maximum grant of £638 but of this £140 will be a direct grant and the remainder will be repayable by small instalments spread over 15–25 years. If the British undergraduate's grant is only marginally adequate he or she is at least free from the obligation entailed in the loan system, and the investigation which, as in Denmark, this involves into the student's academic capacity and financial standing. Moreover the British universities enjoy at present a degree of academic freedom which most of their contemporaries both lack and envy. They are comparatively free from interference by non-academic trustees, professional administrators, business interests and government ministers. Through the vicissitudes of their long history they have never completely lost sight of their *raison d'être*, and today, equipped with a surer perception of their function and a grasp of social realities, they have an even greater potential for influencing the life of the community. Nor have they yet become impersonal. A British university is still, in Newman's words, 'an Alma Mater, knowing her children one by one, not a foundry, or a mint, or treadmill'; it is surely desirable that it should remain so.

LIST OF BOOKS FOR FURTHER READING

Part One

THIS list includes books that are, in general, easily accessible and readable. The medieval history of the universities is described admirably in Hastings Rashdall, *The Universities of Europe in the Middle Ages*, ed. A. B. Emden and F. M. Powicke, 3 vols., Oxford University Press, 1936. Vol. II, pp. 301–4, includes a review of the medieval Scottish universities by R. K. Hannay. Vol. III includes full histories of Oxford and Cambridge. See also Gordon Leff, *Paris and Oxford Universities in the Thirteenth and Fourteenth Centuries*, Wiley, 1968. Sir Charles Mallet, *A History of Oxford*, 3 vols., Methuen, 1924–7, provides a scholarly and competent narrative. There is no equivalent for Cambridge, but G. M. Trevelyan, *Trinity College*, Cambridge University Press, 1943, is a short, entertaining account of a college's history. Of the number of books which describe the life, history and architecture of Oxford and Cambridge several may be mentioned: John Masterman, *To Teach the Senators Wisdom or an Oxford Guide Book*, Hodder & Stoughton, 1952; Dacre Balsdon, *Oxford Life*, Eyre & Spottiswoode, new edn, 1962; William Gaunt, *Oxford*, Batsford, 1965; Felix Markham, *Oxford*, Weidenfeld & Nicholson, 1967; James Morris, *Oxford*, Faber, 1965; R. J. White, *Cambridge Life*, Eyre & Spottiswoode, 1960; Michael Grant, *Cambridge*, Weidenfeld & Nicholson, 1966. See also S. C. Roberts, *Introduction to Cambridge*, Cambridge University Press, 1934. There is an interesting but not wholly accurate critical account of Oxford and Cambridge in Jasper Rose and John Ziman, *Camford Observed*, Gollancz, 1964.

The history of the other universities has evoked some scholarly and painstaking studies but little that is enthralling or illuminating. An excellent survey is W. H. G. Armytage, *Civic Universities*, Benn, 1955; a succinct account is Sir James Mountford, *British Universities*, Oxford University Press, 1966.

Some of the problems relating to the modern university are discussed in Sir Walter Moberly, *The Crisis in the University*, S.C.M. Press, 1949; Bruce Truscott (Allison Peers), *Redbrick University*, Faber, 1942 (revised edn. Penguin Books, 1951); *The Expanding University*, ed. W. R. Niblett, Faber, 1962; H. Butterfield, *The University and Education To-day*, Routledge & Kegan Paul, 1962;

LIST OF BOOKS FOR FURTHER READING

F. Zweig, *The Student in the Age of Anxiety*, Heinemann, 1963; Sir Eric Ashby, *Community of Universities*, Cambridge University Press, 1963. P. Marris, *The Experience of Higher Education*, Routledge & Kegan Paul, 1964; *Theology and the University*, ed. J. Coulson, Dalton Longman & Todd, 1964; G. L. Brook, *The Modern University*, André Deutsch, 1965; Lord Robbins, *The University in the Modern World*, Macmillan, 1966; *The New University*, ed. John Lawlor, Routledge & Kegan Paul, 1968; Michael Beloff, *The Plateglass Universities*, Secker & Warburg, 1968; A. H. Halsey and M. Trow, *The British Academics*, Faber, forthcoming. Although the essays are somewhat uneven – the best essays are the introduction by Alexander Cockburn, 'The Meaning of the Student Revolt' by Gareth Stedman Jones and 'Components of the National Culture' by Perry Anderson – *Student Power*, ed. A. Cockburn and Robin Blackburn (Penguin Books, 1969), provides a useful account of the radical point of view. Better-informed and more authoritative is another collection of essays, *Anarchy and Culture, The Problem of the Contemporary University*, ed. David Martin, Routledge & Kegan Paul, 1969.

A useful introduction for the student considering the different claims of university courses is *University Choice*, ed. Klaus Boehm, Penguin Books, 1966.

Some interesting biographical material is contained in H. R. Harrod's two books, *J. M. Keynes*, Macmillan, 1951 (Papermac, 1963) and *The Prof., a personal memoir of Lord Cherwell*, Macmillan, 1959; G. Faber, *The Oxford Apostles*, Faber, 1936 (Penguin Books, 1954); G. Faber, *Benjamin Jowett*, Faber, 1957; R. J. White, *Dr Bentley*, Eyre & Spottiswoode, 1965; Evelyn Waugh, *A Little Learning*, Chapman & Hall, 1964; A. L. Rowse, *A Cornishman at Oxford*, Jonathan Cape, 1965; C. M. Bowra, *Memories*, Weidenfeld & Nicholson, 1966; Basil Willey's two volumes, *Spots of Time, 1897–1920* and *Cambridge and Other Memories, 1920–1953*, Chatto & Windus, 1965 and 1968; Arnold Toynbee, *Acquaintances*, Oxford University Press, 1967. A detailed account of a small but important segment of Cambridge society has been given by Michael Holroyd in the first volume of his biography of *Lytton Strachey*, Heinemann, 1967.

Part Two

This list provides a brief bibliography to supplement the books noted above.

OXFORD AND CAMBRIDGE 1

It is impossible to list all sources, but attention may be drawn to the following: for Cambridge, J. Lamb's *A Collection of Letters, Statutes, &c.*, 1838, deals with the Reformation period; there is abundant information in C. H. Cooper, *Annals of Cambridge*, 5 vols. 1842–1908, and *Memorials of Cambridge*, 3 vols. 1860–66. See also *The Original Statutes of Cambridge University*, ed. M. B. Hackett, Cambridge University Press, 1969; G. Dyer, *The Privileges of the University of Cambridge*, 2 vols., 1824; T. Fuller, *History of the University of Cambridge to 1634* (1655), edited M. Prickett and T. Wright, 1840; J. Heywood and T. Wright, *Cambridge University Transactions during the Puritan Controversies of the 16th and 17th centuries*, 2 vols., 1854. *Two Elizabethan Diaries*, ed. M. M. Knappen, Peter Smith, 1933, throws light on Elizabethan Puritanism at Cambridge; Henry Gunning, *Reminiscences of Cambridge*, 2 vols., 1854, gossipy in character, is a relatively entertaining account of late eighteenth- and early nineteenth-century Cambridge; J. M. Wright, *Alma Mater or Seven Years at the University of Cambridge*, 2 vols., 1827, informative reminiscences of a Trinity undergraduate; C. A. Bristed, an American's account of *Five Years at an English University*, 2nd edn, 1852. J. P. T. Bury has edited Romilly's *Cambridge Diary 1832–1842*, Cambridge University Press, 1967.

For Oxford, the publications of the *Oxford Historical Society*, printed by the Clarendon Press, Oxford and listed in *Texts and Calendars*, E. L. C. Mullins, 1958, pp. 412–25, are invaluable. They include *Remarks and Collections of Thomas Hearne*, 10 vols., ed. H. E. Salter &c., 1885–1915; *The Life and Times of Anthony Wood*, ed. A. Clark, 5 vols., 1891–1900; *Medieval Archives*, ed. H. E. Salter, 1920–21; *Registrum Cancellarii Oxon.*, ed. H. E. Salter, 1932; *Canterbury College*, ed. W. A. Pantin, 3 vols., 1947–50; *The Early Rolls of Merton College, Oxford*, ed. J. R. L. Highfield, 1964. An interesting account of early seventeenth-century Oxford will be found in *The Diary of Thomas Crosfield*, ed. F. S. Boas, Oxford University Press, 1935. N. Amhurst, *Terrae Filius*, 3rd edn, 1754, is a critical account of eighteenth-century Oxford; see also R.

Newton, *University Education*, 1726, and Vicesimus Knox, *Essays Moral and Literary*, 1782. The nineteenth century is described in W. Tuckwell's entertaining but not wholly accurate *Reminiscences of Oxford*, 1901, and G. V. Cox, *Recollections of Oxford*, 1870. Mark Pattison's *Memoirs*, Macmillan, 1885, is a minor classic.

There is a tremendous amount of information in the *Biographical Register of Oxford* (to 1500), 3 vols., Oxford, Clarendon Press, 1957–9, and that of *Cambridge* (to 1500), Cambridge University Press, 1961, both meticulously edited by A. B. Emden. For the later period see J. Venn, *Alumni Cantabrigienses*, Cambridge University Press, 1922 *et seq.*, and J. A. Foster, *Alumni Oxonienses*, 4 vols., 1887–91, some of the entries in which now require much emendation.

Finally reference should be made to the published reports of the various commissions on the universities, 1852–4, 1873 and 1922; and to the volumes of the *Robbins Report on Higher Education*, H.M.S.O. Cmnd 2154, 1963 and the *Franks Report on Oxford University*, 2 vols., Oxford University Press, 1966. Authoritative reports have been published every five years by the University Grants Committee under the title *University Development*. Its annual *Returns from Universities* is statistical; its *Annual Survey* deals with matters relating to policy. The annual *Yearbook* published by the Association of Commonwealth Universities contains much useful information.

OXFORD AND CAMBRIDGE 2

J. Bass Mullinger's three volumes, *The University of Cambridge from earliest times to the decline of the Platonist Movement*, 1873–1911, are scholarly but old-fashioned. J. P. C. Roach's sketch of Cambridge in the *Victoria County History of Cambridge*, vol. III, Oxford University Press, 1959, pp. 150–311, is excellent and more satisfactory than Strickland Gibson's treatment of Oxford in the *Victoria County History of Oxford*, Oxford, Clarendon Press, 1954, pp. 1–39.

Some useful studies on different aspects of the universities' history include: C. R. Thompson, *Universities in Tudor England*, Washington, 1959; M. H. Curtis, *Oxford and Cambridge in Transition, 1558–1642*, Oxford, Clarendon Press, 1939, a brilliant book, some of the conclusions of which have been questioned (e.g. by Christopher Hill, *Intellectual Origins of the English Revolution*, Oxford, Clarendon Press, 1965, pp. 301–14); J. Simon, *Education and Society in Tudor England*, Cambridge University Press, 1966, is more concerned with schools but has some useful material. The political aspects of universities are studied in M. B. Rex, *University Representation, 1604–1690*, Allen & Unwin, 1954, and W. R. Ward's two learned volumes, *Georgian Oxford*, Oxford, Clarendon Press, 1958, and *Victorian Oxford*, Frank Cass, 1965. An interesting but unconvincing attempt to rehabilitate English education in the eighteenth century is N. A. Hans, *New Trends in Education in the Eighteenth Century*, Routledge & Kegan Paul, 1951. For Cambridge, D. A. Winstanley's works, *The University of Cambridge in the Eighteenth Century*, Cambridge University Press, 1922, *Unreformed Cambridge*, Cambridge University Press, 1935, *Early Victorian Cambridge*, Cambridge University Press, 1940, and *Late Victorian Cambridge*, Cambridge University Press, 1947, are essential reading, though the author was happier in dealing with eighteenth- than with nineteenth-century Cambridge. An important scholarly work on Cambridge in the last half of the nineteenth century has been written by Sheldon Rothblatt, *The Revolution of the Dons*, Faber, 1968. Eighteenth-century Oxford is treated in J. R. Green, *Oxford during the 18th century*, ed. Mrs J. R. Green and K. Norgate, Macmillan, 1901, and A. D. Godley, *Oxford in the Eighteenth Century*, Methuen, 1908. V. H. H. Green, *Oxford Common Room, a study of Mark Pattison and Lincoln College*, Edward Arnold, 1957, is a study of nineteenth-century Oxford; see also the elegant essay by John Sparrow, *Mark Pattison and the Idea of a University*, Cambridge University Press, 1967; A. L. Tillyard, *A History of University Reform*, Heffer, Cambridge, 1913, is self-explanatory.

The close connexion between the two older universities and religious movements is discussed in a general survey, V. H. H. Green, *Religion at Oxford and Cambridge, c. 1160–1960*, S. C. M. Press, 1964. There are a number of monographs, among them W. Gumbley, *The Cambridge Dominicans*, Blackfriars, Oxford, 1938; A. G. Little, *The Grey Friars at Oxford*, 1892; A. G. Little and F. Pelster, *Oxford Theology and Theologians*, Oxford, Clarendon Press, 1934; D. E. Sharp, *Franciscan Philosophy at Oxford in the 13th Century*, Oxford, Clarendon Press, 1930; J. R. H. Moorman, *The Grey Friars in Cambridge, 1225–1538*, Cambridge University Press, 1952; J. A. Robson, *Wyclif and the Oxford School*, Cambridge University Press, 1961; H. C. Porter *Reformation and Reaction at Tudor Cambridge*, Cambridge University Press, 1958; L. Tyerman, *The Oxford Methodists*, Hodder & Stoughton, 1873, and V. H. H. Green, *The Young Mr Wesley*, Edward Arnold, London, 1961 (Wyvern Books paperback, 1963). Later religious history is treated in J. S. Reynolds, *The Evangelicals at Oxford 1735–1871*, Blackwell, Oxford, 1953, rather too much of a catalogue; the same author's biography of the Evangelical rector of St Aldate's, Oxford, *Canon Christopher 1820–1913*, The Abbey Press, Abingdon, 1967; C. H. Smyth's excellent *Simeon and Church Order*, Cambridge University Press; and J. C. Pollock's account of Evangelicalism, *A Cambridge Movement*, John Murray, 1953. Among many studies of the Oxford Movement attention should be drawn to R. W. Church, *The Oxford Movement*, Macmillan, 1891; W. Ward, *W. G. Ward and the Catholic Revival*, 1889, repr. Longmans, 1912; T. Mozley, *Reminiscences*, 2 vols., Longmans, 1882; W. Ward, *Life and Letters of Cardinal Newman*, 2 vols., Longmans, 1912, and among more recent books, Y. Brilioth, *The Anglican Revival*, Longmans, 1925; Maisie Ward, *The Young Mr Newman*, Sheed & Ward, 1948, and G. Battiscombe, *John Keble*, Constable, 1963. See also J. Davis McCaughy, *Christian Obedience in the University, Studies in the life of the Student Christian Movement, 1930–1950*, S. C. M. Press, 1958.

Biographical and autobiographical studies contain useful material: J. H. Monk's *Life of Richard Bentley*, 1830; Mrs Douglas, *W. Whewell*, 1881; J. W. Clark and T. McK. Hughes, *Life and Letters of Adam Sedgwick*, 2 vols., 1890; W. Liddon and J. O. Johnston, *E. B. Pusey*, 4 vols., 1893–7; E. Abbott and L. Campbell, *Life and Letters of Benjamin Jowett*, 2 vols., 1897; Lord Annan's *Leslie Stephen*, Macgibbon & Kee, 1951, may be studied in conjunction with F. W. Maitland, *Life and Letters of Leslie Stephen*, Duckworth, 1906. Other memoirs worth noting include: J. R. M. Butler, *H. M. Butler*, Longmans, 1925; G. L. Prestige, *Charles Gore*, Heinemann, 1935; R. St John Parry, *Henry Jackson*, Cambridge University Press, 1926; W. Austen Leigh, *Augustus Austen Leigh*, Smith, Elder & Co., London, 1906; H. E. Wortham, *Victorian Eton and Cambridge, being the life and times of Oscar Browning*, London, A. Barker, 1956; G. Lowes Dickinson, *J. E. McTaggart*, Cambridge University Press, 1931; F. L. Cross, *Darwell Stone*, Dacre Press, London, 1943; P. E. Matheson, *Hastings Rashdall*, Oxford University Press, 1928; A. E. Shipley, *John W. Clark*, Smith, Elder & Co., London, 1913; R. D. Middleton, *Dr Routh*, Oxford University Press, 1938; N. Wymer, *Thomas Arnold*, R. Hale, London, 1953; T. W. Bamford, *Thomas Arnold*, Cresset Press, 1960; F. Brittain, *B. L. Manning*, Heffer, Cambridge,

1942; E. W. Kemp, *N. P. Williams*, S.P.C.K., 1954; E. Waugh, *Ronald Knox,* Chapman & Hall, 1959 (Fontana paperback, 1962).

There is interesting autobiographical material in T. G. Bonney, *Memories of a Long Life*, Cambridge, Metcalfe, 1921; T. F. Higham, *Dr Blakiston recalled*, Blackwell, Oxford, 1967; J. J. Thomson, *Recollections and Reflections*, Bell, London, 1936; W. E. Heitland, *After Many Years*, Cambridge University Press, 1926; J. W. Clark, *Old Memories at Cambridge and Elsewhere*, Macmillan, 1900; M. R. James, *Eton and King's*, Williams & Norgate, London, 1926; T. Thornley, *Cambridge Memories*, Hamish Hamilton, 1936; T. R. Glover, *Cambridge Retrospect*, Cambridge University Press, 3rd edn, 1942 (and H. G. Wood's memoir of *Glover*, Cambridge University Press, 1953); Charles Oman, *Memories of Victorian Oxford*, Methuen, 1941; Ernest Barker, *Father of the Man*, The National Council of Social Service, 1948; E. L. Woodward, *Short Journey*, Faber, 1942; G. G. Coulton, *Fourscore Years*, Cambridge University Press, 1944; Bertrand Russell, *Autobiography*, vol. I, 1872–1914; vol II, 1914–44, Allen & Unwin, 1967 and 1968.

Histories of all the Oxford and Cambridge colleges were written at the end of the nineteenth and beginning of the twentieth century, but vary widely in value and interest. Attention may be called to J. R. Magrath, *The Queen's College, Oxford,* 2 vols., Oxford, Clarendon Press, 1921; A. B. Emden, *An Oxford Hall in Medieval Times*, Oxford, Clarendon Press, 1927; H. W. C. Davis, *Balliol College*, Oxford, Blackwell, revised edn, 1963; A. H. Smith, *New College*, Oxford University Press, 1952; W. C. Costin, *St John's College, Oxford, 1598–1860*, Oxford, Clarendon Press, 1958. Among more recent Cambridge histories may be mentioned M. D. Forbes, *Clare College*, 2 vols., Cambridge University Press, 1928; Patrick Bury, *Corpus Christi College (1882–1952)*, Cambridge, Heffer, 1952; H. E. Howard, *An Account of the Finances of St John's College, Cambridge, 1511–1925*, Cambridge University Press, 1935; E. Miller, *St John's College,* Cambridge University Press, 1961; Alan B. Cobban, *The King's Hall*, Cambridge University Press, 1969; A. Gardner, *A Short History of Newnham College*, Bowes & Bowes, Cambridge, 1921; B. Stephen, *Emily Davies and Girton College*, Constable, 1927; M. A. Hamilton, *Newnham*, Faber, 1936; M. C. Bradbrook, *That Infidel Place: A Short History of Girton College*, Chatto & Windus, 1969.

OTHER BRITISH UNIVERSITIES

The best introduction is W. H. G. Armytage, *Civic Universities*, Benn, London, 1955, mentioned above. See also Brian Simon, *Studies in the History of Education, 1780–1870*, Lawrence & Wishart, London, 1960; J. F. C. Harrison, *Learning and Living, 1790–1960, A Study of the History of English Adult Education Movement*, Routledge & Kegan Paul, 1961; R. O. Berdahl, *British Universities and the State*, University of California Press and Cambridge University Press, 1959; W. H. Draper, *University Extension, 1873–1923*, Cambridge University Press, 1923; Thomas Kelly, *Outside the Walls, Sixty Years of University Extension at Manchester, 1888–1946*, Manchester University Press, 1960; N. Jepson, 'Staffing Problems during the early years of the Oxford University Extension Movement', *Rewley House Papers*, Vol. III, no. 3 (1954–5), pp. 20–33; 'Leeds and the Beginning of University Adult Education', *Proceedings of the Leeds Philosophical Society*, XIII, Pt iii (1957), pp. 216–231. On the Dissenting academies: I. Parker, *Dissenting Academies in England*, 1917; H. McLachlan, *English Education under the Test Acts*, Manchester University Press, 1931; H. McLachlan, *Warrington Academy*, Chetham Society, New Series, vol. 107, 1943.

There are a number of individual histories, some of rather a pedestrian character. There is no modern study of Gresham College, but see J. Ward, *Lives of the Professors of Gresham College*, London, 1740 and F. R. Johnson, 'Gresham College: Precursor of the Royal Society' in the *Journal of History of Ideas*, I, 1940, pp. 413–28. On London, there is a short account by D. W. Logan, *The University of London*, Athlone Press, 1962; Consult also H. H. Bellot's informative *University College, London, 1826–1926*, University of London Press, 1929; T. L. H. Humberstone, *University Reform in London*, Allen & Unwin, 1926; P. Dunsheath and M. Miller, *Convocation in the University of London*, University of London, Athlone Press, 1958; C. D. Burns, *Birkbeck College*, University of London Press, 1924; F. J. C. Hearnshaw, *The Centenary History of King's College*, Harrap, 1929. C. E. Whiting has written an exhaustive *The University of Durham, 1832–1932*, Sheldon Press, London, 1932. The most recent history of Manchester is H. B. Charlton, *Portrait of a University, 1851–1951*, Manchester University Press, 1951, but reference may also be made to J. Thompson's *The History of the Owens College*, Cornish, 1886; E. Fiddes, *Chapters in the History of Owens College and Manchester University*, Manchester University Press, 1937, and a recent study of the founder by B. W. Clapp, *John Owens*, Manchester University Press, 1965. On the foundation of Keele see W. B. Gallie, *A New University, A. D. Lindsay and the Keele Experiment*, Chatto & Windus, 1960. On other universities see A. W. Chapman, *The Story of a Modern University*, (Sheffield) Oxford University Press, 1955; A. N. Shimmin, *The University of Leeds*, Cambridge University Press, 1954; E. W. Vincent and P. Hinton, *The University of Birmingham*, Cornish, 1947; A. C. Wood, *A History of the University College* (Nottingham), Oxford, Blackwell, 1953; W. M. Childs, *Making a University* (Reading), Dent, 1933; B. Cottle and J. W. Sherborne, *The Life of a University* (Bristol), Bristol, Arrowsmith, 1951; J. Simmons, *New University* (Leicester), 1958.

On Wales see T. I. Ellis, *The Development of the Higher Education in Wales*, Wrexham, Hughes, 1935; W. C. Davies and W. L. Jones, *The University of Wales*, F. E. Robinson, 1905; W. Emrys, *The University of Wales*, University of Wales Press, 1953. On Queen's University, Belfast, there is a very thorough account by T. W. Moody and J. C. Beckett, *Queen's University, Belfast, 1845–1949*, 2 vols., Faber, 1959.

On recently founded universities see *The Idea of a University* (Sussex), ed. David Daiches, André Deutsch, 1964; A. E. Sloman, *A University in the Making* (Essex), Reith Lectures, 1963, B.B.C., 1964; *New Universities in the Modern World*, ed. Murray G. Ross, Macmillan, 1966 (on Sussex, J. S. Fulton, on York, Lord James, on East Anglia, F. Thistlethwaite).

On women and the universities see M. J. Tuke, *History of Bedford College* (1849–1937), Oxford University Press, 1939, and M. Tylecote, *The Education of Women at Manchester University, 1883–1933*, Manchester University Press, 1941. For an examination of some aspects of university selection see W. D. Furneaux, *The Chosen Few*, Oxford University Press, 1961.

SCOTTISH UNIVERSITIES

R. G. Cant, *The University of St Andrews*, Edinburgh, Oliver & Boyd, 1946, is scholarly and interesting, J. D. Mackie's *The University of Glasgow*, Glasgow, Jackson & Co., 1954, thorough and exhaustive. See also J. Coutts, *A History of the University of Glasgow*, Glasgow, Maclehose, 1909. There are three histories of Edinburgh, Sir Alexander Grant, *The University of Edinburgh*, 2 vols., 1883; *A History of the University of Edinburgh, 1883–1933*, ed. A.

Logan Turner, Edinburgh, Oliver & Boyd, 1933; D. B. Horn, *A Short History of the University of Edinburgh, 1556–1889*, Edinburgh University Press, 1967. J. M. Bullock, *A History of the University of Aberdeen, 1495–1895*, 1895; *The Fusion of 1960, a Record of the Centenary Celebrations, a History of the United University of Aberdeen, 1860–1960*, ed. Douglas Simpson, Edinburgh, Oliver & Boyd, 1963, a somewhat pedestrian account. See also G. E. Davie, *The Democratic Intellect, Scotland and her Universities in the Nineteenth Century*, Edinburgh, 1961.

TRINITY COLLEGE, DUBLIN

J. P. Mahaffy, *An Epoch in Irish History, Trinity College, Dublin*, 1903, a scholarly account of its foundation and early history. A shorter survey in *The Book of Trinity College, Dublin, 1591–1891*, J. P. Mahaffy and others, 1892; see also *A History of Trinity College, Dublin*, vol. I, 1591–1892, Constantia Maxwell, Dublin University Press, 1946: vol. II 1892–1945 Kenneth C. Bailey, Dublin University Press, 1946–7; H. L. Murphy, *Trinity College, Dublin*, Dublin, Hodges, Figgis, 1951.

CURRICULA

Specific studies include R. Weiss, *Humanism in England during the 15th century*, 2nd edn, Oxford, Blackwell, 1957, which studies the rise of humanism at Oxford and Cambridge; *Erasmus and Cambridge*, trans. P. S. Thompson, ed. H. C. Porter, Toronto University Press, 1964; W. J. Costello, *The Scholastic Curriculum at Early Sixteenth Century Cambridge*, Harvard University Press, 1958, a very informative book; C. Wordsworth, *Scholae Academicae. Some Account of the Studies and the English Universities in the 18th Century*, 1877, a scholarly but old-fashioned work; B. R. Schneider, *Wordsworth's Cambridge Education*, Cambridge University Press, 1957, interesting and important; M. L. Clarke, *Greek Studies in England, 1700–1830*, Cambridge University Press, 1945; M. L. Clarke, *Classical Education in Britain, 1500–1900*, Cambridge University Press, 1959; R. M. Ogilvie, *Latin and Greek, a history of the influence of the classics on English life from 1600 to 1918*, Routledge & Kegan Paul, 1964; Foster Watson, *The Beginnings of the Teaching of Modern Subjects in England*, Pitman, 1909; C. H. Firth, *Modern Languages at Oxford, 1724–1929*, Oxford University Press, 1929; E. M. W. Tillyard, *The Muse Un-*

chained. An Intimate Account of the Revolution in English Studies at Cambridge, Cambridge, Bowes & Bowes, 1958; D. J. Palmer, *The Rise of English Studies*, Hull University Press, 1965; H. G. Hanbury, *The Vinerian Chair and Legal Education*, Oxford, Blackwell, 1958; F. H. Lawson, *The Oxford Law School, 1850–1965*, Oxford University Press, 1968. J. McLachlan has discussed 'The Origin and Early Development of the Cambridge Historical Tripos' in the *Cambridge Historical Journal*, I, 1947, pp. 78–105. See also W. H. G. Armytage, *The German Influence on English Education*, Routledge & Kegan Paul, 1969; Will G. Moore, *The Tutorial System and its Future*, Oxford, Pergamon Press, 1968.

MATHEMATICAL AND SCIENTIFIC EDUCATION

On mathematics: E. G. R. Taylor's two books on *The Mathematical Practitioners of Tudor and Stuart England*, Cambridge University Press, 1954, and *of Hanoverian England*, 1966; D. E. Smith, *A History of Mathematics*, Harrap, 1923; W. Rouse Ball, *A History of the Study of Mathematics at Cambridge*, 1889.

Among books dealing with science in general see R. T. Gunther's *Early Science in Cambridge*, 1937, *Early Science in Oxford*, 1923, and *Oxford and the History of Science*, 1934, all by the Clarendon Press at Oxford; S. F. Mason, *A History of the Sciences*, Routledge & Kegan Paul, 1953; T. J. N. Hilken, *Engineering at Cambridge University, 1783–1965*, Cambridge University Press, 1967. See also Phyllis Allen, 'Scientific Studies in the English universities of the seventeenth century', *Journal of the History of Ideas*, 1949, X, pp. 219–53. A stimulating essay is Sir Eric Ashby's *Technology and the Academics, An Essay on Universities and the Scientific Revolution*, Macmillan, 1958.

Medical studies are discussed in W. Langdon Brown, *Some Chapters in Cambridge Medical History*, Cambridge University Press, 1946; Humphrey Rolleston, *The Cambridge Medical School*, Cambridge University Press, 1932; T. M. Bickerton, *A Medical History of Liverpool to 1920*, Murray, 1936. Biographical material is contained in J. J. Thomson and others, *James Clerk-Maxwell*, Cambridge University Press, 1931; C. B. Bateson, *William Bateson, Naturalist*, Cambridge University Press, 1928; A. S. Eve, *Rutherford*, Cambridge University Press, 1939; A. E. Eve and C. H. Creasey, *John Tyndall*, Macmillan, 1945; Lord Rayleigh, *J. J. Thomson*, Cambridge University Press, 1942.

SOCIAL LIFE

R. S. Rait, *Life in the Medieval University*, Cambridge University Press, 1912; J. Venn, *Early Collegiate Life*, London, Heffer, 1913; C. Wordsworth, *Social Life at the English Universities in the 18th Century*, 1874, a vast amount of material badly organized; abridged in R. Brimley Johnson, *The Undergraduate*, London, S. Paul, 1928. For the Unions at Oxford and Cambridge see P. Cradock and others, *Recollections of the Cambridge Union, 1815-1939*, Cambridge, Bowes & Bowes, 1953; C. Hollis, *The Oxford Union*, London, Evans Bros., 1965. Sporting events are chronicled in H. M. Abrahams and J. Bruce-Kerr, *Oxford versus Cambridge, 1827-1930*, Faber, 1931.

University etiquette and procedure are described in *Oxford University Ceremonies*, ed. L. H. Dudley Buxton and Strickland Gibson, Oxford, Clarendon Press, 1935. On Scotland see A. Morgan, *Scottish University Studies*, Oxford University Press, 1933.

Some articles which throw light on the social composition of the universities include: Hester Jenkins and D. Caradog Jones, 'Social Class of Cambridge Alumni', *The British Journal of Sociology*, vol. 1, 1950, pp. 93-116; Joan Simon,'The Social Origins of Cambridge Students, 1603-1640', *Past and Present*, 26, 1962, pp. 59-67; L. Stone, 'The Educational Revolution in England 1560-1640', *Past and Present*, 28, 1964, pp. 41-80; Joan Abbott, 'Students' Social Class in Three Northern Universities', *The British Journal of Sociology*, vol. XVI, 1965, pp. 206-20; W. M. Mathew, 'The Origins and Occupations of Glasgow Students', *Past and Present*, 33, 1966, pp. 74-94.